The Changing Face of the

World's Navies

1945 to the Present

The Changing Face of the
World's Navies
1945 to the Present

BRUCE W. WATSON

ARMS AND
ARMOUR

Arms and Armour Press
A Cassell Imprint
Villiers House, 41–47 Strand, London WC2N 5JE.

Distributed in the USA by Sterling Publishing Co. Inc.,
387 Park Avenue South, New York, NY 10016-8810.

Distributed in Australia by Capricorn Link (Australia) Pty.
Ltd,
P.O. Box 665, Lane Cove, New South Wales 2066.

British Library Cataloguing in Publication Data
Watson, Bruce W.
The changing face of the world's navies: 1945 to the present.
1. Navies, history
I. Title
359.00944
ISBN 1-85409-017-8

Designed and edited by DAG Publications Ltd. Designed by
David Gibbons; edited by Michael Boxall; typeset by Ronset
Typesetters, Darwen, Lancashire; camerawork by M&E
Reproductions, North Fambridge, Essex; printed and bound
in Great Britain by Butler & Tanner Ltd, Frome, Somerset.

The information in this book is based on the research of the
author and does not represent the positions or policies of any
agency or department of the United States Government. The
information was derived from unclassified publications and
sources and is intended neither to confirm nor deny, officially
or unofficially, the views of the United States Government.

Contents

Tables

Note: Unless otherwise stated, the principal sources for the figures in the tables are *Combat Fleets of the World*; *Conway's All the World's Fighting Ships, 1947–1982, Part I: The Western Powers* and *Part II: The Warsaw Pact and Non-Aligned Nations*; *Jane's Fighting Ships*; and *The Military Balance* (various editions).

To
Lieutenant Commander Frank Colonna
US Navy (Retired)
(16 August 1916 – 5 May 1979)

and

Senior Chief Hospitalman Louis Colonna
US Navy (Retired)

My uncles, for a lifetime of guidance and support,
and for convincing me that the Navy was
the only way to go.

Acknowledgements

The scope of this project has required calling on 25 years of personal experience in naval operations, naval intelligence, and academic research. Over that time, I have met many people who affected the perceptions expressed in this book and deserve to be acknowledged. First among them all is my wife, Susan, for her love, support, counsel, help and criticism over the years. This and so many of my other works have benefited from her point of view.

This book is dedicated to Lieutenant Commander Frank Colonna, US Navy (Ret.), and Senior Chief Hospitalman Louis Colonna, US Navy (Ret.), my uncles, who began it all by telling me of life in the Navy. Frank served on the USS *Mineappolis*, was at Pearl Harbor on 7 December, 1941, and related its horrors to me. Later Frank served in the Navy throughout the war in the Pacific. Louis served in the Mediterranean during the war, took part in the invasion of Sicily, and later saw action off Wonsan in the Korean War. Together, they began my lifelong love and pride in the US Navy. My gratitude also goes to Vice Admiral and Mrs. John T. Parker, US Navy (Ret.), who as the executive officer and XO's wife on the USS *Sellers* (DG-11) in the 1960s, showed me what the Navy could be and should be, setting an example that I and many others have emulated. In respect of academic inquiry, I am forever grateful to Joseph Schiebel and Patricia Schiebel Howard, who set standards of academic excellence and devotion to their students that I have tried to carry on, and to Paul Holman, whose guidance and counsel were so valuable in my early studies of the Soviet Navy. I should also like to thank John Cardinal O'Connor and Father Cornelius O'Brien for their intellectual and spiritual support over the years. Additionally, I should like to thank many associates – Bruce George, M.P., James George of the Center of Naval Analyses, Professor Raimondo Luraghi of the University of Genoa, Dr. Ingemar Dorfer of Upsala University, Frank Uhlig, editor of the *Naval War College Review*, Colonel C. Douglas Lovejoy, US Army, Colonel Peter M. Dunn, US Air Force (Ret.), Robert De Gross, Provost, Defense Intelligence College, and to all the others – for their support and advice over the years. Maurice Kramer, Ted and Evelyn Michon, Thomas Kramer, Margaret Huggins, Elizabeth Colonna, Elizabeth and John Bligh, Lillian Smith, Peter and Sue Becque, and Merle and Margaret Stromberg are among the many people who have encouraged my efforts over the years, and I am forever grateful for their help. Finally, I should like to thank my son, Bruce, for his hours of research assistance. It is to be hoped that this effort will help him progress toward writing his first book.

In closing, my thanks go out to my daughters, Susan, for her editorial help, Jennifer for her help and assistance, and Ella, whose occasional visits and commentaries made the production of this book more enjoyable.

As always, any errors or weaknesses in this book are attributable to me alone, and I take sole responsibility for them.

Bruce W. Watson, Sr.
Fairfax, Virginia
February 1991

Glossary

AA	Anti-air
AAW	Anti-air Warfare
ASW	Anti-submarine Warfare
CIWS	Close-In Weapon System
C³	Command, Control, and Communications
ECM	Electronic Countermeasures
JCS	Joint Chiefs of Staff
SLBM	Submarine Launched Ballistic Missile
SS	Diesel-powered Attack Submarine
SSB	Diesel-powered Ballistic Missile-equipped Submarine
SSBN	Nuclear-powered Ballistic Missile-equipped Submarine
SSG	Diesel-powered Guided Missile-equipped Submarine
SSGN	Nuclear-powered Guided Missile-equipped Submarine
SSN	Nuclear-powered Attack Submarine

Introduction

THE INFLUENCING FACTORS

The era from 1945 to 1990 was one of intense, directed naval competition, as the world became polarized into Soviet and US coalitions and each often developed its naval power in reaction to the maritime advances of its opponent. It began with the world settling into this bi-polar superpower relationship and ended with the hope that this rivalry had reached a peaceful conclusion. As such, the period might become a self-contained era in the history of world naval development, one in which naval progress had been influenced significantly by a symbiotic Soviet–American relationship in which each developed its naval power in reaction to the threat that it perceived from the other through very expensive naval programs that eventually left all other naval powers behind. If the era had ended or was nearing an end in 1990, and there were many indicators that implied that it had, it might be replaced in the 1990s by one in which future naval progress would be made by several nations that relied on the seas for their welfare rather than just the United States and the Soviet Union.

If this study has a bias, it is for the cause of diversified naval development, that centuries-long force that has enabled man to make ever greater use of the seas for his defense. In this context, the following pages examine the relevant post-Second World War maritime events in an attempt to determine why the nations of the world developed the navies and naval systems of today. To begin, five factors – political events, technological progress, naval affairs, the importance of the seas and sea power, and the continued influence of valid traditional theories of maritime power, had a great effect on the world's navies. We shall see that during this period, while there was a great deal of innovative naval development, it was very directed as the leading nations made maximum use of available technology to build systems that responded to threats from their competitors.

Political Events

The political environment exerts such a significant influence on naval development that the latter cannot be considered fully outside its political context. From 1945 to 1990, political events and upheavals had a most dramatic effect on naval developments. In the five years after the war, there was stagnation, as the Western Allies trimmed down their bloated wartime navies to forces that were adequate to meet perceived peacetime needs and defined their post-war foreign policy goals. But the world quickly became polarized into the eastern and western blocks, prompting naval development on both sides. Then in 1950, the Korean War showed the continued need for a good sea projection capability and the threats posed by both sides determined the types of naval development that occurred. In his secret speech at the Soviet Union's 20th Communist Party Congress in 1956, Premier Nikita Khrushchev announced the beginning of the policy of peaceful coexistence, stating that the USSR would play a greater role in the Third World. This and the appointment of a brilliant, relatively young naval officer, Sergei Gorshkov, to command the navy, not only prompted the beginning of an ambitious naval construction program, but also encouraged developing specific types of Western naval power to counter it. Further conflict, including the Suez Crisis of 1956, the Lebanon Crisis of 1958, the Vietnam War, the Arab–Israeli Wars of 1967 and 1973, and several major wars and crises in Asia, the Mediterranean and Indian Ocean also were significant catalysts for further naval development. In the aftermath of Vietnam, however, an introspective United States forgot its maritime tradition and heritage and neglected its Navy. Indeed, the early 1970s were a nadir and it was not until the Reagan years that the Navy managed a significant comeback. Yet, other nations sustained naval development into the 1980s. More recently, the Falklands War, US operations in Grenada and against Libya, continued strife in the Middle East, Iranian and, in 1990, Iraqi activities in the Persian Gulf, all included naval reactions and prompted further naval development.

This trend was influenced from 1987 onward by Secretary Mikhail Gorbachev's perestroika, a policy that opened the door to great changes. In the Soviet Union, greater freedom, changes in the Soviet ruling hierarchy, an intense program that was meant to show that the Soviet Union had reconsidered its policies and no longer intended to pose a threat to the West, widespread unrest in Kazakhstan, Armenia, and Turkestan, nationalistic rumblings in Georgia, Lithuania, Estonia, and the Ukraine, economic problems, the promise of reduced defence spending, and food and energy shortages were among the more significant results. In eastern Europe, the changes were even more profound. One after another, in the almost classic situation of dominoes, the eastern European regimes fell to the forces of freedom after they were advised by Moscow to reform. The results were profound and promised to affect sea power's future development. In 1989, as Western intelligence continued to report that there had been no substantial reduction in the Soviet military machine, it also reported that the political changes in eastern Europe had reduced the Warsaw Pact Ground Forces threat. It appeared certain that the Soviet Union would curtail its military spending in order to shift sorely needed funds to research and development. It also seemed certain that, in a nation that had relied on its Army for its national security for centuries, if these cuts were significant – and all indications in 1990 were that the cuts would be deep – then the Army, the force that had provided for national security for centuries, and the Rocket Forces and the Navy's SSBN fleet that provided strategic security, would be emphasized in the resulting force. This implied that other types of naval development – specifically general purpose naval forces – might be curtailed significantly. Although there were other needs for US naval power – against terrorism, drug trafficking, and Third World insurgency – the absence of the Soviet naval threat would impede justification for continuing US naval development at its previous pace. The US Navy looked toward an uncertain future in the 1990s.

Technological Progress

Technological progress was influenced by political factors to the extent that both sides developed those programs and systems that promised to influence the power balance most favorably. In this context, in naval matters, the most important – nuclear propulsion and weapons, jet propulsion, missiles, and advances in electronics and communications – revolutionized naval affairs. The submarine and the aircraft carrier, two systems that had already achieved prominence during the Second World War, remained as the pre-eminent naval systems of the post-war era. Both had their strengths *and* their weaknesses.

The aircraft carrier evolved into the US nuclear-powered aircraft carrier of today. Here it is important to note the distinction that John Jordan makes between the European and the US carrier traditions.[1] In Europe, the carrier was developed in a land-based air environment and was meant to extend air cover farther outward from a nation's shores. In this milieu, she was heavily armoured and was given significant armament. When attacked by enemy aircraft, she would secure her aircraft, engage enemy aircraft with her weapons and rely on support from friendly land-based aircraft. In contrast, the US carrier was developed for operations in the broad expanses of the Pacific Ocean. Here land-based air cover was not available and the carrier was meant to be a floating air base, rather than an extension of land-based air power. As such, her operating range was crucial, which meant that the lighter the ship, the farther she could travel and the more effective she could be. Thus, weight was a premium and she was designed without the heavy armour of her European counterpart. Likewise, she was lightly armed, relying instead on her escorts, those heavily armed components of the task force that would protect her. Also owing to her missions, she was larger so that she could carry more aircraft, which were superior to the European sea-based aircraft that had been designed to operate in an environment that was dominated by superior land-based air power.

The result was that she was fast, versatile, and capable – the epitome of power projection. And yet there were many who, noting her expense, size, and vulnerability, questioned the wisdom of building such a ship, suggesting instead that large numbers of smaller ships or even alternative forms of air power projection might have been wiser.

Likewise, the submarine progressed from the diesel-powered boat of the Second World War. It is true that, in operating in that hostile environment beneath the waves, it continued to be very vulnerable to destruction *if* detected. But following the war, technological advances produced much quieter submarines, thereby improving their chances of eluding detection.

Meanwhile, applying nuclear power to their propulsion systems and missiles made them potent strategic systems. Soviet Admiral Sergei G. Gorshkov was correct when he argued that his nuclear-powered ballistic missile-equipped submarine fleet had advanced the Navy to the forefront of the five branches of the Soviet military. We shall see that two iron-willed, dictatorial naval admirals – Sergei Gorshkov of the Soviet Union and Hyman Rickover of the United States – blessed with the resolve, foresight, and other qualities that few others had, were able to create the strategic submarine fleets that their nations have today.

Jet propulsion was fully developed after the war, and more capable high-performance aircraft that posed a constantly more serious air threat to surface combatants were built. Conversely, they vastly increased the potency of carrier task groups, since sea-based jet aircraft, armed with conventional or nuclear weapons, could make strategic strikes deep into enemy territory. Indeed, the mating of such weapons, jet aircraft, and the carrier's nuclear propulsion created a vastly more powerful sea projection system – one that would be deadly in wartime and a first rate peace-time political instrument.

The missile was also a major technological innovation. Fast, light, accurate, and with devastating destructive capability, it prompted changes in contemporary naval doctrine and tactics and challenged the conventional wisdom concerning the direct relationship between a ship's size and its fire power.

Finally, a plethora of other technological breakthroughs and advances in electronics, communications, propulsion, metallurgy, fire control, command and control, and in a host of other fields down to such factors as food processing and crew habitability, all contributed to the modern navies of today.

Naval Affairs
In naval affairs, naval development, the diffusion of naval power, the continued need for amphibious forces, and re-emergence of the battleship were the four most significant factors.

Naval development was dynamic to the extent that both sides sustained research and development efforts that produced significant naval advances and inhibited to the extent that the Second World War had reduced a world of many centers of power to two – the US and Soviet camps which would restrict the creativity of their naval development by focusing it exclusively on the threat posed by the other. By the end of the Second World War, naval advancements had occurred in a variety of nations. Some, such as Great Britain, France, and the United States, had world-wide obligations and concentrated on developing force projection. Others, such as Italy, while they built large combatants, also built small ones that were appropriate to warfare in the Mediterranean and other more restricted areas. Still others saw the importance of defensive forces, such as mine warfare ships. Now these divergent inputs were gone, because the expense of contemporary research and political considerations had replaced the inputs of many with the perceptions of two, the Soviet Union and America. Thus, future naval development would be influenced greatly by the geographic and political perceptions of these two centers and by the threat that each perceived from the other. For the United States this meant sea projection, but it also meant great attention to the sea line of communication that ran from America to Europe. A major theme would be the protection of this sea bridge against Soviet threats and defending it against the Soviet submarine force. For the Soviet Union, initially it meant protecting the nation's four sea approaches – northward through the Norwegian Sea and then eastward north of North Cape and into Northern Fleet waters; eastward through the Baltic to Baltic Fleet waters; through the Turkish Straits and onward to Soviet Black Sea ports; and in the Pacific, through the Sea of Japan to Soviet ports. After 1956, it would mean projecting power out on to the world's oceans to compete with the US Navy and protecting the ballistic missile submarine sanctuaries in the Arctic. Again, antisubmarine warfare (ASW) would be stressed, but for very different reasons than those that spawned Western ASW research.

While the Soviet–American theme would come to dominate naval development, it did not happen immediately. Rather, after the Second World War there was a diffusion of naval power among many of the world's nations. Following the Axis defeat only America, Great Britain, France, and the Soviet Union had significant navies. This began to change almost at once as the Japanese and German fleets were taken as prizes to be distributed by the victors, while the United States and Great Britain began selling off portions of their fleets in order to tailor their navies to anticipated peace-time operations. The result was a diffusion of naval power as other nations bought ships and built up their navies. In subsequent decades, this trend continued as the world's major naval powers, participating in a continuous rivalry that required newer and newer ships and systems, would sell their older ships to less affluent nations, often at bargain prices and without restrictions on their use. This was particularly important in respect of the development of naval missiles and the provision of missile-equipped boats to less affluent nations created danger for the major maritime powers. The combat power of a ship had depended traditionally on her size and newness. Now small, fast, cheap missile patrol boats challenged the validity of both standards, Egypts's sinking of the Israeli destroyer *Eilat* by missiles from two Soviet-supplied missile boats in October 1967 caused a great reaction – 'the missile fever' of the latter 1960s. Now the world's developing nations could buy such boats that, in certain situations, could threaten the much larger, more expensive ships of the world's leading navies. Indeed, the world's seas were a dangerous place in the 1960s and 1970s, which prompted the development of systems to combat these boats. The trend of selling off older units continued, creating a further diffusion of naval power.

Concerning amphibious warfare, the advent of the nuclear age prompted predictions that Marines and naval infantry forces were now so vulnerable that they had become obsolete in today's 'push-button war'. The fallacy of this premature epitaph was vividly demonstrated during the Korean War, when one of history's greatest amphibious operations was conducted at Inchon. A continued need, coupled with equipment modernization and tactical and doctrinal innovations, assured the future of amphibious forces. And they have certainly proven their value – as part of Soviet naval forces stationed in Guinea, Angola, Somalia, and Vietnam, and in naval operations in Suez in 1956, Lebanon in 1958, in Africa and the Caribbean, in the Vietnam War in the 1960s and 1970s, the Falklands War of 1982, the US operations on Grenada in 1983 and Lebanon in the 1980s, and in a host of other operations. Indeed, over the years, the need for such forces has increased rather than diminished.

Likewise, the immediate post-war conventional wisdom questioned the future need for large, gun-armed combatants, the epitome of which was the battleship. The tremendous destruction of battleships at Pearl Harbor in 1941, the emergence of the aircraft carrier and the submarine as the key naval combatant systems of the Second World War, and the appearance of jet aircraft and missiles after the war were all factors that indicated that the battleship had seen its day. Thus, in spite of their impressive operations in the Korean War, as the missile age progressed, they and other large gun-armed combatants were retired from many of the world's naval forces. And yet the need for these ships persisted. The US Navy recommissioned the *New Jersey* during the Vietnam War, only to retire her after the US withdrawal. Then in the 1980s, as the world's powers realized the sustained need for large gun-armed ships, the United States recommissioned four battleships, and the Soviet Union built *Kirov* and *Slava* cruisers. Indeed, by the mid 1980s, it was obvious that while the missile was important to naval warfare, it had not replaced the huge naval guns in delivering sustained, massively destructive, fire power. This point was demonstrated again as the US battleships conducted shore bombardment operations in the Persian Gulf in 1991.

The Sea's Importance

While the first three factors – technological, political, and naval development – had a significant effect on naval affairs over the short term, the last two factors were more significant over the long term, thereby assuring the continued importance of maritime power well into the 21st century.

The first of these was the continued importance of the seas and sea power. On the one hand, naval power managed to thwart effectively the challenge from developing air power in that, in the early 1990s, it remained the best means of projecting massive military power world-wide and sustaining it for extended periods in order to fulfill a nation's defense and foreign policy needs. Meanwhile, the seas became vastly more important as sources of energy, food, and minerals for a world facing shortages. Indeed, it was continually demonstrated in the British–Icelandic Cod War, the UN conferences on law of the seas, and dozens of incidents involving a littoral nation's exclusive rights to its coastal waters, that the seas were becoming more important, and that this theme was certain to remain operative well into the 21st century.

Mahan versus Mackinder

While geopolitics has fallen into disrepute in the eyes of many political scientists and historians, primarily because it was abused by Haushoffer and later by the Nazis, one cannot ignore geography's influence. In naval development, Alfred Mahan's and Halford Mackinder's views have great relevance to naval affairs in the Atlantic and Europe, and Mahan's views are also important to our understanding of events in the Pacific.

Twice in this century, a great maritime coalition had fought and defeated a great European land coalition. Then, similar coalitions were created in the post-war era as a NATO maritime coalition spearheaded by British and US naval power opposed a Eurasian land coalition under Soviet leadership. Now many will take exception to this view, claiming that it ignores the great European land battles of both wars and does not do justice to the tremendous power of contemporary Soviet Ground Forces. On a superficial level, this criticism appears valid, but when one examines the particulars in all three cases, the center of gravity, as Carl von Clausewitz would say, lies in the Atlantic; for it is here, in the bridge between the tremendous power of the new world and the battlegrounds of the old that the deciding power has passed and must continue to pass if the Western coalition is to prevail. German Admiral Friedrich Ruge and Soviet Admiral Gorshkov both espoused this theme. Ruge prefaced his remarks by noting that he had played the land side in the land–sea war at the end of the Second World War. He then stressed NATO's maritime import over its relevance as a European land coalition because the center of gravity in any sea-land confrontation over Europe was found at sea. Likewise, Gorshkov, when he addressed NATO, viewed it as essentially a maritime coalition of which the US Navy was the key force.[2] Thus, two strategic theorists, Alfred Mahan, the sea power advocate, and Sir Halford Mackinder, the geopolitican often judged *passé* by many contemporary political scientists, were reconsidered as Mackinder's heartland again faced Mahan's seas in the NATO–Warsaw Pact rivalry.

Certainly many of Mackinder's views, particularly those dealing with the invulnerability of the Eurasian heartland, were dated in the age of long-range nuclear missiles. And yet his views concerning the tremendous potential inherent in that region appeared valid. Since 1917, the region had been controlled by a Soviet system which, despite its grossly inefficient economy, had managed to achieve world superpower status. Did this feat reflect the area's inherent power and value? And to what heights could the region's nations rise if they rejected inefficient communism; adopting instead capitalist systems? Also, Mackinder had implied that the region's rulers could reduce the threat posed by an opposing maritime coalition by creating powerful navies of their own. The Soviet Union has done just that.

And what of Mahan, the great sea power advocate who wrote during that period of US expansionist imperialism? Certainly many of his views were also dated, but the truth of his beliefs concerning the world's choke points, sea lines of communication, sea power projection, and other maritime matters was confirmed by events in the post-war era. Indeed, it seemed that the US Navy had managed to avert the upheaval that the US Army and Air Force experienced after Vietnam because it had remained faithful to Mahan and Mahan had remained valid. Conversely, Great Britain might have found the Falklands War a far less costly enterprise if she had not ignored Mahan's views on preserving one's naval power. In fact, if she had heeded Mahan, there was a good chance that Argentina would not have dared to start the war at all.

In sum, the NATO–Warsaw Pact rivalry, the ascension of both the United States and the Soviet Union to superpower status, and the conflict inherent in their opposing democratic capitalist and totalitarian communist systems assured the continuation of the animosity between them into 1989. Then the possible dissolution of the Warsaw Pact, as the Eastern European nations made rapid strides toward democracy, implied that the Soviet-led land coalition was coming apart, creating an uncertain future. Still the land coalition versus sea power had been valid in three situations, accounting for much of 20th-century history. Indeed, it seemed that, regardless of whether the Soviet land coalition remained intact, the conflict of land versus sea for influence remained valid as one of several possible futures for Europe, although the constitution of the coalitions might change again. We will return to this theme in the final chapter. The reader should note, however, as the following pages are read, how great an effect the two coalitions have had on sea power.

Turning to the Pacific, Mahan's views were most important. Contrasting a British colonial system that placed great emphasis on land-based colonial administrations protected by British sea power as the key to British influence over regional affairs, the US approach emphasized sea power. Mahan stressed the Panama Canal's importance, saying that the way to protect it was to possess territories in its approaches. In the Pacific, this meant projecting power westward to Hawaii and the Philippines and then to bases along the Asian coast. The bitter results of America's Vietnam experience seemed not only to justify Mahan's views, but to influence subsequent US policy. US military influence would not be land-based on the Asian mainland. Rather it would be projected from a string of sea and air bases along the Pacific coast. Through such an arrangement, US regional political and economic interests could be protected.

The variable in this calculus was Japan. Her military imperialism and aggressive economic policies had brought her into direct conflict with expanding US influence, and the two had fought a very devastating Pacific War. This ended with Hiroshima and Nagasaki, prompting a Japanese renunciation of war and an intention to progress peacefully in the future. The result was bizarre as Japan proceeded to capture market after market from her old enemy, America, while relying on the same nation to provide for its defense. Indeed, it was unprecedented historically for a nation that relied so heavily on the seas for her prosperity to pay so little attention to her navy. At a minimum, it would have been prudent for Japan to have been able to guarantee the security of her sea lanes at least as far as the Straits of Malacca. Yet her naval strength was far less than what was needed to assure this, as she relied on the United States. The answer to this apparent enigma was Japan's fear of her militarists. She placed a ceiling of 1 per cent of her GNP on her defense expenditures, believing that this would control her militaristic elements. Additionally, the defensive orientation of her military forces was reflected in their names, such as the Japanese Self-Defense Force. This situation continued into 1990, often creating friction between Washington and Tokyo. We will also return to this problem in the final chapter, as it may play a role in future naval development.

Summary

The following chapters relate the naval development that occurred from 1945 to 1991. In them, not only are facts and figures given concerning the types and numbers of ships that were produced, but the influence of circumstances and political changes also are examined in order to provide insights into the political motives and the reasons why nations did or did not develop their navies. The reader will note that each chapter attempts to be international in scope, mentioning briefly important changes that occurred in the lesser navies as well. However, this is a period in which significant naval advancements were made by only a few nations and were used by the rest of the world, and the book's emphasis is definitely weighted toward those innovating nations. It is now time to examine the post-war naval scene to see how the interaction of the five factors – theory, the importance of the seas, technology, and political and naval developments – produced the navies of today.

NOTES

1. John Jordan, 'Aircraft Carriers', in *The Soviet Naval Threat to Europe: Military and Political Dimensions*, edited by Bruce W. Watson and Susan M. Watson (Boulder, CO: Westview Press, 1989).
2. Tubingen, West Germany. Author's interview with Friedrich Ruge, July 1984; and Sergei G. Gorshkov, *Sea Power of the State* (Moscow: Voyenizdat, 1976). One might also mention General Sir John Hackett and his colleagues, who, in *The Third World War*, noted that the Soviet Union lost the conflict because Gorshkov had died, his successors had not followed his precepts concerning adequately defending Soviet submarines operating in the Atlantic, and the Allies were able to destroy enough of these to keep the sea lanes open. This allowed them to send US troops and supplies to France, which in turn allowed the French to move their forces into Germany to reinforce Allied forces there. This was enough to stem the Warsaw Pact offensive and when it stalled, it set in motion forces that resulted in the Soviet Union's loss of the war.

1
The Early Post-War Years, 1945–50

In the years immediately following the Second World War, political and strategic factors and technological advances significantly influenced the development of sea power. The political factors pertained to the fact that, in the early post-war years, the Soviet Union perceived herself to be weaker than the West, particularly the United States, and successfully concealed this by projecting an inflated military threat. She did this because she believed that Western military operations against her, up to and including an invasion, were a real possiblity. She could find support for this belief in recent history, when in 1918 the West had landed forces at Archangel and the United States and Japan had landed forces in the Soviet Far East, at a time when the new communist regime was still weak and embroiled in a civil war. Her projection of an inflated threat, waged largely through concealing accurate information about the weakness of her defenses and through propaganda, was convincing and prompted fears of growing Soviet military power.

The influence of technology, while significant, did not produce new combatant systems. These would come later, as initial post-war naval construction often involved building combatants based on designs that had been prepared during the war. This five-year period also would witness the assimilation of captured German technology, adapting navies to the atomic era, and conducting research and development that involved both assimilating the new technologies developed during the war and combating the threats to naval forces that this technology had produced. Here, proving that navies could operate in a nuclear environment, that aircraft carriers were capable of launching and recovering jet aircraft, and that navies could be protected from the jet aircraft threat, were among the major accomplishments.

POLITICAL AND STRATEGIC FACTORS

To understand accurately the influence of politics on post-war sea power development, one must go back to the foreign policy views of V. I. Lenin, because his observations reflected accurately twentieth-century's political forces and greatly influenced Soviet policies which, in turn, both *prompted* and *determined the type of* Soviet and Western naval development that would occur in the post-war period. Specifically, one should consider the speech that Lenin delivered to the leaders of the Bolshevik cadres on 6 December 1920. In it, he noted that Soviet policy should be based firmly on the manipulation of five long-range adversary situations – international problems that were difficult if not impossible, to resolve and would, therefore, dominate the century's international relations. These were: *Germany versus Europe*, owing to the unfairness of the Treaty of Versailles and the Allies' failure to integrate Germany into the European community; *the United States versus Europe*, because of the different views of the two concerning the world order; and *the United States versus Japan*, because of conflicting economic interests in the Pacific basin. Lenin continued by actually predicting the Second World War in both Europe and the Pacific, noting that both of the future conflicts should be used to advance Soviet interests if at all possible. The final two conflicts were not discussed as fully, but were, none the less, identified. These were *the conflict between the emerging nations of the third world and the European colonial nations*, and the *systemic conflict between capitalism and communism*. In the former, the Soviet Union was to support the aspirations of the emerging nations in their disputes with the European mother nations – progressive nationalism against 'imperialism'. The latter conflict, Lenin implied, would be played out between the Soviet Union, the bastion of communism, and the United States, which he felt was the epitome of 'imperialism'. However, this last conflict should be de-emphasized, Lenin warned, until the Soviet Union was strong enough for a frontal assault on imperialism. In the interim, the de-emphasis should be effected by emphasizing the first four animosities. By keeping the Western powers preoccupied among themselves, Lenin believed that the Soviet Union could buy the time necessary to develop her strength for the final assault.[1]

In this context, the Second World War was truly a watershed in that it temporarily resolved the first three conflicts and accentuated the latter two. Concerning the former, Germany was destroyed and, henceforth, serious attempts would be made to integrate West Germany into the European community. Likewise, Europe lay in rubble and the regional differences with the United States would be sublimated to an alliance. Finally, Japan was decisively defeated in the Pacific and US power now prevailed. The same war unleashed forces which brought the last two animosities into vivid relief and the problems of the emerging Third World and the US–Soviet superpower rivalry would dominate international politics for more than four decades. Both of these themes would encourage naval development on the one hand and would stifle the creativity of this development on the other. As such, their importance cannot be overstated.

However, we are getting ahead of ourselves in that the importance of these themes was not immediately realized at war's end. Rather, there was a transition from 1945 to 1953, as the world moved from the Second World War to the Cold War. From the Soviet perspective, it was a time filled with both opportunities and fears. On the plus side, eastern Europe had been occupied, thereby providing a buffer zone that insulated her from possible Western aggression. Additionally, western Europe lay in rubble, making further advances possible. On the negative side, the Soviet Union was weak militarily and Moscow believed that if this weakness were known, the West might take advantage. The Soviet response was multifaceted: it moved quickly to strengthen its defenses; through propaganda, it magnified the threat it posed against the West, in the hope that this would deter aggression; and it encouraged efforts such as the Chinese Revolution, which deflected US attention away from Europe. The result was that the regional animosities, those in the Balkan States and elsewhere that had been put on hold as the world divided itself into the Axis and Allied powers and fought the Second World War, remained suspended as the world now became divided into the Cold War's eastern and western camps. In the Pacific, there were similar results. The Japanese–American animosity that had spawned the Second World War was suspended as the Soviet Union seized the northern Japanese islands in the closing days of the war and defense against the Soviet threat was perceived to be of paramount importance.

This political context exerted influence on the naval scene, which was a subset of the larger political picture. In naval affairs, the situation was as follows. By 1945, this century had witnessed the world's two most devastating wars. In both, a European land-based alliance had been defeated by an Atlantic maritime coalition. And, as German Admiral Friedrich Ruge and Soviet Admiral Sergei Gorshkov noted, the events from 1945 to 1950 resulted in the creation of yet another land-sea rivalry, involving a Soviet-led land-based coalition against an Atlantic maritime alliance. However, the world was unable immediately to perceive this strategic relationship. Instead, such perceptions gradually emerged over the subsequent decade so that sides were determined in Europe and the superpower rivalry was realized from 1945 to 1950. The importance of sea power in this dispute was then realized from 1950 to 1955. The four primary players in this period – the United States, Great Britain, France, and the Soviet Union – each faced issues that deterred the development of their navies.

In the United States, the problems were two-fold. The first concerned the nation's difficulty in accepting its world power status. In the past, it had often deferred to British policy, participated in conflicts, but extricated itself as quickly as possible thereafter, in order to return to a traditional isolationist stance. In 1945, America hungered for peace and was not ready to accept its responsibilities and the concomitant defense expenditures required of a world power. Such an acceptance would not occur until the outbreak of the Korean War in 1950. The second difficulty was America's refusal to recognize that it was becoming the greatest sea power in history (to the extent that it would use its sea power most consistently and most effectively), to be challenged only by the British use of sea power in centuries past.[2] Rather, in the vicious inter-service rivalry that would prevail during the period, first the Air Force and then the Army would be emphasized. The result was that, while sea power was vitally important to America's future, this would not be perceived by those outside the Navy, and US actions would involve decreasing the size of its bloated wartime fleet, without adequately providing for the Navy of the future.

No such illusions existed in London, where British leaders had a firm understanding that their's was a maritime nation and that the Royal Navy was crucial to their security. Here, however, the problem was a financial one, in which the limited resources of a nation recovering from war were stretched to meet the post-war needs of an empire.

If the situation in London were difficult, conditions in Paris were virtually impossible. Ravished by the war, France had far too few resources to provide an adequate defense, and while she had an accurate perception of the need of a post-war navy and tried to develop one, the war in Indo-China, the lack of a maritime infrastructure that had been destroyed in the war, and financial difficulties thwarted the achievement of this goal.

Finally, in the Soviet Union, the period witnessed the Soviet realization of the Soviet–American superpower rivalry, but Moscow's attention remained focused on Europe and north-east Asia where Soviet Ground Forces provided the relevant military power. Additionally, Stalin's views of maritime power would prevail over the Navy's and this meant an incorrect conclusion as to the type of navy that was needed in the post-war period.

In sum, all these political and strategic factors would make this a period of transition for naval power – one in which the powers divested themselves of obsolete systems, but would limit the resources devoted to developing new ones.

TECHNOLOGICAL FACTORS

Technology was a major factor that interacted with political and strategic perceptions. The Second World War had shown that the carrier and submarine were the naval systems of the future, but this perception was masked by four other factors resulting from the war. The first was nuclear energy. While it would play a significant role in subsequent naval development, contemporary discussions focused on its destructive power, and those who believed that a future conflict would be a 'push button war' saw little use for naval power. The second was jet propulsion. Opponents argued that jet aircraft made navies obsolete because they could overwhelm naval anti-air defenses, while they could not be carried on naval ships. The third factor, guided missiles, posed a similar threat to naval forces. Finally, technology had so improved the range and accuracy of weapon systems that the concept of theater warfare was considered obsolete, to be replaced by combined arms warfare. From 1945 to 1950, these technological issues dominated discussions on naval development, as the more profound political and strategic issues were perceived more gradually. The four major contributors to naval development in the immediate post-war years were, in order of naval strength, the United States, Great Britain, France, and the Soviet Union. Each was preoccupied with technological issues in the years immediately following the war and each responded differently, according to its national perceptions.

SOVIET UNION

Although the Soviet Union had the fourth strongest navy, during this period, it helps to address her first because she had such a dramatic effect on Western naval development. In order to understand this relationship, it is best to start by examining Soviet policy. It is simplistic to think that, 26 years later, Soviet foreign policy-makers slavishly obeyed the above-described tenets that Lenin had established in December 1920. Rather, his views were more like a prism through which Soviet policy-makers viewed the international arena. Lenin's postulations concerning the United States, Germany, and Japan had proven to be correct, and no new themes had appeared on the international scene to challenge these traditional animosities that he had identified.

From the end of the war until 1953, the USSR remained preoccupied with her defense and attempted to manipulate the Leninist themes for her benefit. The first of these was Europe, where at war's end, the chances seemed good for additional Soviet gains. Europe lay in rubble and Austria sat naked, vulnerable to Soviet advances. The French and Italian communist parties were powerful and might succeed in influencing their governments. Soviet pressure on Greece and Turkey reflected Moscow's belief that opportunities existed there as well. Finally, Germany was partitioned and Berlin was surrounded by East German territory.

Likewise, it was prudent for the Soviet Union to expect the United States to abandon Europe. Previous US actions had been traditionally myopic, in that the United States would garner its forces, defeat the foe in combat, and then insist on 'bringing the boys home' as soon as possible. Continued US involvement in Europe simply was not in the cards, if one used past US actions to predict an operating pattern. None the less, in vivid contrast to its traditional policy, the United States made a sustained commitment to post-war Europe, one that would still provide US forces to its defense into the 1990s. Additionally, it provided the Marshall Plan, which assured the rebirth of a Europe that was independent of Soviet control. The result was that, while the Soviet Union remained preoccupied with and continued to exert pressure on western Europe, it made no additional gains. As this theme was played out in the late 1940s, Soviet attention was also focused on the ongoing Chinese revolution that resulted in a communist victory in 1949 and the Korean War that was waged from 1950 to 1953.

While these themes pertained to opportunities for furthering Soviet influence, there was an additional theme operative – capitalism versus communism, specifically the United States versus the Soviet Union – that presented a danger. In 1945, the Soviet Union was weaker than the United States and, while it had made gains in eastern Europe and hoped to make further gains in western Europe, it also feared possible American action. Hence, the Soviets deliberately encouraged those Western perceptions that inflated existing Soviet military power with the goal of deterring American aggression.

These themes all had one thing in common – they concerned Soviet or Soviet-controlled borders. This and the fact that Stalin remained in power meant several things. First, his views on maritime power prevailed over the opposing views of the Navy, including the Navy's Young School of the 1920s and 1930s. Second, since these events concerned nations on Soviet or Soviet-controlled borders, the Soviet Army remained the politically relevant form of military power. *It* had forced the revolutions in eastern Europe by occupying countries and guaranteeing the success of Soviet-supported political factions. *It* sustained pressure on Western Europe in the years immediately following the Second World War. And while it was not actively involved in either China or Korea, *it* remained a force, a factor which anti-communist forces had to consider because of the possibility that the Soviet Union might opt to become involved.

It is curious that, just as with the US Navy, the Soviet Navy would be attacked by the civilian hierarchy and the other military services. However, the battle here was even more brutal, owing to Stalin's viciousness and to the fact that the Navy did not enjoy the proud centuries-long tradition of its counterpart and it had not conducted significant independent operations during the Second World War. Thus, one cannot exaggerate the stifling effect that Stalin, who had his own ideas of what the Navy should look like (ideas that were not at all appropriate to the Soviet Union's actual post-war naval needs), the ignorant civilian hierarchy, and the Ground Forces' domination had on naval development. The West found it strange that of all the military leaders that Stalin decorated at war's end, he could find only one naval leader, Sergei G. Gorshkov, to decorate. Likewise, in the changes occurring after Stalin's death, it was the same Gorshkov who ascended to lead the Navy in 1956. However, the full dimensions of the oppression were not revealed for 42 years. Finally, in 1989, Sergei Zonin, writing in *Morskoy Sbornik*, provided some of the details concerning the brutal psychological terror.[3] The crisis began with Stalin's post-war naval construction program:

> The 'Law of the Five-Year Plan for the Restoration and Development of the USSR National Economy for 1946–1950' stated: 'Increase shipbuilding in 1950 twofold in comparison with 1940.' It called for the construction of nine battleships, each of 75,000 tons displacement, twelve heavy and 60 light cruisers, fifteen aircraft carriers, and more than 500 submarines.[4]

While this program might seem appropriate for the time, it ignored the technological advances that had been made in aircraft carriers during the Second World War. In fact, Admiral Nikolai G. Kuznetsov, Commander-in-Chief of the Soviet Navy from 1939 to 1947, and Admiral L. M. Galler, Deputy People's Commissar for Shipbuilding and Armament from 1940 to 1947, both believed that the aircraft carrier had become 'the basic element of the fleet'.[5] They also felt that the construction of all the classes and types of ships should include advances resulting from the knowledge gleaned from the military-technological progress of the fleets during the war, and it was here, in the sophistication and expense of the new major combatants that the problem existed.

A major factor in the crisis was civilian domination of the military. The 'apparatchik' Nikolai G. Bulganin, who became Minister of the Armed Forces in March 1946, criticized the high cost of the new combatants.[6] The same problem that the US Navy had in selling its post-war fleet – that ships were now much more expensive and naval appropriations would have to be increased considerably if the country were to be defended adequately – confronted the Soviet naval leadership. In the Soviet case, the opposition was overwhelming. Not only did Stalin have his rigid, preconceived views of what the post-war navy should look like, but the civilian- and Ground Forces-dominated decision-making apparatus was incapable of conceiving of the new complexities in naval warfare resulting from the advances of the war. In commenting on Kuznetsov's and Galler's position, Zonin stated:

> This trend did not receive the support of the shipbuilding leadership headed by I. I. Nosenko, who preferred not to push the construction of aircraft carriers; battleships, cruisers, and destroyers were to be built in accordance with modified pre-war projects. Kuznetsov and Galler objected sharply, stating that under such a technical policy in shipbuilding the country would waste billions, but the level of ships would be inferior to that of the ships of the US and British navies.[7]

While this was the issue of contention between Stalin and the naval hierarchy, however, the immediate causes of the rupture pertained to naval affairs – Kuznetsov's opposition to Stalin's wish to divide the Baltic Fleet. When Kuznetsov's position was narrowly accepted by the Main Military Council, it 'evoked the Generalissimo's wrath'. In February 1946, the Baltic was divided into the Fourth and Eighth Naval Fleets and the People's Commissariat of the Navy was abolished. Kuznetsov was clearly in official disfavor and further friction may have occurred when he opposed a similar division of the Pacific Fleet.[8]

During the following years, Kuznetsov, Galler, and other naval leaders were accused of divulging important knowledge concerning weapon systems to the Western Allies during the war. Zonin vividly, accurately, and closely documented the subsequent proceedings. All leaders were subjected to the most psychologically brutal investigations, and in the deliberations – sham show trials reminiscent of the purges of the 1930s and dominated by hand-picked civilians and Ground Forces officers – the leaders were expected to denigrate and dishonor themselves. Zonin noted proudly that the naval leaders, while doing what was expected by debasing themselves did so with honor, refusing to implicate others falsely in the fabricated web of lies.

This meant that, while captured German ships and naval construction personnel would influence early Soviet post-war naval development, the oppression of Stalin's traditionalist views, the civilian and ground forces opposition, the gross ignorance of the true nature of naval forces, and the playing out of European and north-east Asian land-based themes would prevail, preventing innovation in Soviet naval construction. As a result, such construction centered on building large, gun-armed naval combatants, that would be less capable than Western ships and submarines.

Contemporary Western Perceptions of the Soviet Navy
A significant consequence of Soviet naval construction was the perceptions that it prompted in the West, because it was on these that Western naval construction policies, particularly those dealing with nuclear propulsion in submarines, and anti-air, anti-submarine, and mine warfare were predicated.

In one sense, the creation of the Russian and then the Soviet empire from its earliest days in ninth-century Muscovy resulted from the Russian movement on to and assimilation of weaker nations and peoples from a stronger power base, and Soviet actions in eastern Europe continued this theme. Contemporary analysts, in a quest to discern future Soviet moves, while finding it difficult to define Soviet post-war policy in eastern Europe, were alarmed by the Soviet occupation. Leon B. Blair described it as a continuation of Tsarist expansion under the guise of a 'quest for security'. He maintained that the United States had either to check this expansion or abandon Europe to the Soviet Union. A second assessment was provided by J. V. Davidson-Houston, who believed that there were three motives behind Soviet political strategy: security, economics, and imperialism. From this it followed that there were several danger areas, places where the Soviets could be expected to assert themselves. Here he identified Manchuria (the Rivers Amur and Usuri), Korea, Turkey, Afghanistan and Iran – all areas that would play prominently in subsequent Soviet policies.[9]

From this speculation, it was even more difficult, given Soviet security, to predict the type of navy that the USSR would develop. R. F. Corvile stated that the history of Russian foreign policy revealed that they would probably opt for limited endurance surface ships with anti-surface and anti-air armament, plus a large submarine force. Richard Hilton made a similar prediction, postulating that the Soviets would not build an oceanic battle fleet. Rather it would be based on submarines and air power to block the ocean routes. An astute analysis by John Erickson identified the motives of this policy. Since, in the war the Soviet Navy had been an extension of the Army, the post-war policy was to build a big ship navy but to tie it to the coasts and the Army. Other observers provided additional insight. P. W. Rairden, Jr., noted that during the war the Soviet Navy had fought defensively and in close cooperation with the Army and Air Force, and believed that this relationship would continue. J. Burke Wilkenson, concurring with Hilton's and parts of Rairden's analyses, said that the Russians had traditionally fought successfully in coastal waters and narrow seas, but that they could boast of only a few great battles on the high seas, and the humiliation inflicted by Japan at Tsushima Strait in 1905 only reinforced this trend. Alternatively, a strong Russian tradition in submarines dated back to 1914–17, and since 4,000 German submarine experts and two high-ranking German admirals had been captured by Soviets, Soviet naval interest would be chiefly in the submarine. Noting that they had the fourth strongest navy, he believed that, because of British austerity and French uncertainty, the Soviets were assured of rising to second place in the near future. With such a navy, they could dominate the Baltic to its Straits, would not be able to secure the Turkish Straits, but with the recent island acquisitions from Japan, could close the Sea of Okhotsk. The purpose of this navy was to prevent British and US maritime intervention while they absorbed key countries in the heart of the old world.[10]

Taken collectively, the Western assessments predicted fairly accurately Stalin's post-war naval policy. It would be defensive, would rely heavily on submarines and large gun-armed combatants, and would place greatest importance on defending the Baltic approaches which led to the Soviet Union's vital industrial centers that were situated in the Baltic region.

Contrary to these measured assessments, the dominant, more public, reaction was more emotional. It viewed reported Soviet military advances with a fear that at times bordered on hysteria, and this, coupled with a purposeful Soviet policy which magnified the threat by deliberately minimizing the information available because it feared Western aggression if Soviet military weakness were revealed, could not help but affect Western estimates, which often exaggerated Soviet military power. The result was a rather unhealthy symbiotic relationship, in which a Western defense response – manifested in research and development programs and the creation of new systems – prompted a Soviet military response which produced new systems that encouraged further Western development, and so on. The end result amounted to an arms race, in which both Western and Soviet naval technology was advanced, spawning creativity on the one hand, as the nations' resources were focused on developing newer systems. On the other hand it was inhibiting because each reacted to the threat it perceived from the other, directing and focusing its research accordingly.

Determining the Post-War Construction Program
One thing was certain: the Soviets intended to pursue a post-war naval construction program of some import. Very soon after war's end, Stalin stated:

> The Soviet people wish to see their fleet grow still stronger and more powerful. Our people are constructing new battleships and bases for the fleet.
> The tasks of the fleet are: unceasing preparation; improvement of naval personnel; mastery of the fighting experience of the Patriotic War; the raising of naval culture, discipline, and organization to a still higher level in its ranks.[11]

Given the Soviet submarine tradition, it seemed likely to the West that emphasis would be placed on submarine development and post-war acquisitions from Germany made this even more likely. Vice-Admiral Sir Arthur Hezlet stated that 'the Russians ended the war with between one and two hundred submarines and in the post-war years built up their number steadily until by 1950 they had about three hundred and fifty.[12] Several German XXI boats had been turned over, so the Soviet program had full knowledge of German developments. Drew Middleton's figures were more precise. He said that the Soviets had about 190 submarines, including three boats transferred to them in 1944. They received seventeen German and two Italian boats as war booty, and confiscated large amounts of equipment, hundreds of scientists and engineers, and took over and completed six Type XXI boats from Schichau yard in Danzig.[13] He believed that the function of the fleet was to defend the homeland or possibly to attack US Army communications in Europe. He astutely noted that, although many of their submarines were coastal types and were divided among four fleet areas, this expansion provided an impetus to the policy of allotting an ASW role to British and American subs. Thus, while the Soviet policy of projecting a maximum threat to the West was meant to hide her weaknesses, it prompted a Western reaction which only exacerbated that threat. The Western response often exaggerated the Soviet submarine force's size, with some sources predicting an eventual force of more than 1,000 modern submarines.

Because of Soviet secrecy and because its Navy rarely operated on the high seas, Western analysts had great difficulty in determining the Soviet naval order of battle in the immediate post-war years. *La Revue Maritime* estimated the following force level in 1947. In the Baltic, there were a battleship, three cruisers, ten destroyers, and 30 submarines. The Black Sea Fleet had a battleship, three cruisers, ten destroyers, and fifteen submarines. The Northern Fleet had a battleship, a cruiser, six destroyers, and some submarines, and in the Pacific Fleet, there were one or two cruisers, ten destroyers, and a large number of submarines.[14] In 1948, US Naval Intelligence estimated that the Soviets had 250 submarines, but the US Naval Institute took issue with this estimate, stating that it was probably too high. It believed that the Soviets had an unknown number of the 1400-ton K-class, nine completed ex-German Type XXI-class, and 50 to 100 unassembled Type XXI submarines. Besides submarines, the Institute estimated the Soviet naval order of battle to be; three obsolete battleships, eight or nine cruisers, more than 60 destroyers, and more than 30 destroyer escorts. In May 1949, the Royal United Services Institute estimated a slightly higher order of battle: three battleships, an armored ship, an incomplete and damaged aircraft carrier, two ex-German cruisers (one damaged), eight Russian-built light cruisers, and 50 fairly modern destroyers, plus six building.[15] The figures in Table 1.1, while even they are speculative, offer a reasonably accurate compilation of the exaggerated contemporary Western perceptions of the Soviet fleet.

In a hurried attempt to bolster the defence against possible Western aggression, Soviet naval construction from 1945 to 1950 was directed toward restoring a naval shipbuilding capability, completing ships that had been begun before the war, building ships based on designs drawn up either before or during the war, and designing new ships and submarines. The initial focus was on surface combatant construction. German occupation of Nikolaev and advances on Leningrad had retarded Soviet shipbuilding during the Second World War, so that at war's end, she was far behind the United States and Great Britain.[16] Stalin's plan was ambitious. Not only were the Baltic and Black Sea facilities to be restored, but facilities were to be developed at Severodvinsk in the Northern Fleet and Komsomolsk-on-Amur in the Pacific,

Table 1.1
Selected Force Levels – Soviet Navy, 1946–50[a]

	Year				
	46	*47*	*48*	*49*	*50*
Submarines	130	100	123	360	360
Battleships	3	3	4	3	3
Cruisers	7	8	13	11	11
Destroyers	68	62	51	91[b]	62
Minesweepers	68	75	83	85	86

[a]This Table is an attempt to determine the Soviet naval order of battle from 1946 to 1950 and considers other relevant sources as well as the *Jane's* data. It and many of the tables that follow are limited to those types of ships that could present a combat threat and omits auxiliaries, coastal and patrol craft, and other types. Thus, the actual naval orders of battle far exceed the figures often presented.

[b]Many of these ships and submarines were ex-German, -Italian, or -Japanese units.

and a submarine factory was to be built at Gorki. Concerning construction, some existing destroyers were refitted, and Italian and German ships that had been captured or awarded as prizes provided a stopgap until new ships were operational. The Soviets began the 3,181-ton *Skoryy* destroyer program. Based on a pre-war design, it was considered highly successful by the Soviets, and became a work horse that would support their naval operations for more than 25 years. Seventy-two were built from 1950 to 1953, several were modified from 1958 to 1960, and twelve were still active in 1983. *Skoryy* was armed with anti-surface and anti-air guns, torpedo tubes, depth-charge throwers, and about 50 mines. Western observers questioned the effectiveness of the anti-air guns, since they could not elevate above 45°, and since there were radar stabilization and discrimination problems, they concluded that the weapons were intended for directed surface fire, with only a limited anti-air capability. She was a shift from the Italian influence seen in earlier Soviet ships, to a German influence, seen in the fire control systems and the unique stern design.[17]

The Soviet cruiser construction program involved several classes of ships. The remaining ships of the five-unit *Chapaev* class were completed. *Zheleznya-kov* and *Komosomolets* (ex-*Chkalov*) would remain in the naval inventory until 1976 and 1980, while *Kuibishev*, *Frunze*, and *Chapaev* were stricken or broken up in the 1960s. These 15,000-ton ships were heavily armed with 6in surface, 3.9in dual-purpose, and 37mm anti-air guns. Reflecting Stalin's big ship policy, they offered little innovation. Meanwhile, the pre-war designs for the *Sverdlov* cruiser were refined, and construction began, while plans for a new *Stalingrad*-class were probably drawn up.[18]

In submarines, Western estimates greatly exaggerated the Soviet program. Construction was completed on the remaining Shch-, S-, M-V-, and K-class hulls by 1947, but, with a limited range, they offered only a stop-gap until newer boats could be built. Design work had been done on the *Whiskey*-, and *Zulu*-classes during the war, but, unlike the surface combatant program, the Soviets modified the wartime design plans considerably in order to incorporate German technology. The *Whiskey* was probably intended to protect the nation's sea approaches, while the *Zulu* was intended as a long-range submarine. The program progressed more slowly than the West estimated; the first *Whiskey* did not appear until 1950, and *Zulu* even later.[19]

To summarize, the Stalinist post-war naval construction program aimed at producing a fleet of heavy, gun-armed surface combatants and a force of submarines that would defend the Soviet sea approaches and coasts from expected Western aggression. It is ironic that so much Soviet effort was spent on a fleet so unsuited to the post-war scene. Years later, Soviet theoreticians would criticize this Stalinist program. Apparently ignoring the fact that one of the missions of the US Navy was to project power ashore, they would demean it, cynically characterizing it as being predicated on the naive belief that the West would foolishly allow their fleets to be drawn into Soviet coastal waters where they could be attacked and, presumably, destroyed. It is also relevant that this ill-directed policy would have the effect that it did in the West, one that would focus post-war construction on anti-submarine (ASW) and anti-air warfare (AAW) and on submarine development. Working from admittedly incomplete information on Soviet naval affairs and in an emotional atmosphere, Western defense policy-makers reacted as best they could and directed the sparse defense funds available into these systems, thereby de-emphasizing or even ignoring other possible trends in naval development.

THE UNITED STATES

> With victory, a stampede for demobilization swept over the country. The rush
> to disarm, premature and unwise though it turned out to be, was the natural
> reaction of a nation that detests war and wants only a just, honorable, and
> enduring peace.[20]

Thus spoke Secretary of Defense James Forrestal in his first annual report in 1948. And a stampede it was; Table 1.2 shows that demobilization was continuous and significant. At war's end, the Navy had 3 million men, 6,626 ships, including 99 aircraft carriers, dozens of cruisers, and hundreds of destroyers. In the rush to demobilize, some planners even talked of reducing the fleet to 400 ships. As to bases, the Navy announced in late 1946 that Guam was to be a second Pearl Harbor, but to economize, more than 53 other overseas bases would be closed.[21] Some believed that the Navy was taking an unfair share of the cutbacks and one critic stated that 'after proving itself beyond all doubt in this war, the amateur strategists are commencing again to proclaim the Navy is obsolete and no longer necessary,' while others observed that 'immediately after World War Two, first the new Air Force then the Army was the main element of the national security policy mix. . . . Indeed, it took the Korean War to convince Congress that the demonstrated efficacy of naval air power deserved a new generation of aircraft carriers.'[22] In such an atmosphere, which would lead to the revolt of the Admirals, the Navy found it difficult to acquire the needed resources to provide for its future needs.

Winston Churchill's characterization of Russia as an enigma could have been applied equally to US policy. In the post-war period, this was confused by: the nation's failure to realize that it had become a maritime power of the first order and that national security and destiny were linked to the sea; incomplete and erroneous perceptions of Soviet military power; the influence of disarmament forces and isolationist sentiment; tangible threats to naval power such as the atomic bomb, jet aircraft, and submarines; civilizing and unifying the defense department; the influence of bureaucrats over strategists;

Table 1.2
Order of Battle – US Navy, 1945–50[a]

	Year					
	45	46	47	48	49	50
Submarines	232	85	80	74	79	72
Fleet Aircraft Carriers	28	15	14	13	11	11
Escort Aircraft Carriers	71	10	8	7	7	4
Battleships	23	10	4	2	1	1
Cruisers	72	36	32	32	18	13

Destroyers	377	145	138	134	143	137
Destroyer Escorts	361	35	24	12	12	10
Mine Warfare Ships	586	112	55	54	52	56
Patrol Vessels	1204	119	74	50	50	33
Amphibious Vessels	2116	275	107	86	60	79
Auxiliaries	1556	406	306	273	257	218
Totals[b]	6626	1248	842	737	690	634

[a]US Department of the Navy, *US Navy Ship Force Levels, 1917–1989* (Washington, DC: Ships History Branch, Naval Historical Center, Department of the Navy, 1989), p. 4; US Department of the Navy, *Annual Report of the Secretary of the Navy for the Fiscal Year 1948* (Washington, DC: GPO, 1949), p. 7; and US Department of Defense, *Second Report of the Secretary of Defense and the Annual Reports of the Secretary of the Army, Secretary of the Navy, and Secretary of the Air Force for the Fiscal Year 1949* (Washington, DC: GPO, 1950), p. 218. The figures reflect the force level on 30 June of that year.
[b]In this book's Tables, totals (and complete orders of battle) are only provided in the US Navy Tables, because such totals tend to be misleading. Therefore, they have been omitted for all other navies and only relevant force projection forces are listed. In the US Navy's case, so much has been made of the '600 ship Navy' that totals are provided for comparison.

and bitter fighting among the military branches. At a minimum, there was a significant failure by the defense hierarchy to develop a coherent policy from existing strategic formulations. The result was that these disparate forces came together to form an ill-defined and confusing policy. Indeed, one can almost sympathize with the Soviet analyst of the period, tied as he was to a firmly defined Stalinist policy and confronted with an imprecisely defined enemy strategy. One Soviet commentator stated that the difficulty in understanding the Americans was that so few of them truly understood their own strategy and even fewer of them felt obliged to conform to it.

It is incorrect to say that the Navy has been blessed with too few Secretaries of the Navy of the stature of James Forrestal or John Lehman, too few Chiefs of Naval Operations with the depth of Raymond Spruance, Chester Nimitz, Arleigh Burke, or Elmo Zumwalt, or too few admirals with the intelligence and depth of conviction of Hyman Rickover. In fact, all these men served during the post-war period. Rather, the problem was systemic and involved the bureaucratic structure created at war's end to unify US military forces. In it, the Navy began the post-war period with certain assumptions concerning naval power, tried to defend these beliefs in order to preserve its power, and concluded the period without convincing the national leadership that what it believed was correct.

The Evolution of Naval Policy and the Navy's Building Programs The defeat of the Axis powers prompted a drastic revision of US naval policy. The result, the work of Secretary of the Navy James Forrestal and Admiral Ernest J. King, noted four post-war naval missions: supporting the US peacekeeping commitment to the United Nations; maintaining a Navy stronger than the Soviet fleet; protecting US interests abroad and preventing an attack on the United States; and supporting the Army and Air Force in joint combat operations.[23] Hezlet noted that this meant that:

The American post-war navy was based on the aircraft carrier whose aircraft were armed with the atomic bomb. They conceived the new strategy of commanding the sea by a massive nuclear attack on the enemy air and naval bases, and the function of all other units of the fleet was to protect the carriers whilst they launched their strikes. Two altogether new types of submarines were converted from the fleet type to co-operate in this general strategy.[24]

Thus the post-war navy would conform to Alfred Mahan's precepts concerning force projection. The major weapon systems would be the aircraft carrier, which could project power overseas and then ashore, and the submarine, which initially was to assist in the protection of carrier task groups, but later became one of the Navy's major anti-submarine systems, anti-surface ship systems, and its strategic weapons platform. Anti-shore forces would be provided by the Marine Corps, which would perfect and modernize its amphibious operations. Thus, the Navy's focus would be on the aircraft carrier, the submarine, and systems that would further the security of the carrier task groups.

The US Navy's Assumptions

The Aircraft Carrier and the Submarine The first assumption was that the aircraft carrier and submarine had emerged as the major post-war naval systems.[25] Concerning the aircraft carrier's advantage, one can do no better than to quote the views of Fletcher Pratt:

> The effect of the plane is not to localize sea power but to overcome what localization previously existed; not to extend the influence of the air arm for 300 miles out to sea, but to enable naval power to reach 300 miles inland and almost completely to neutralize the value of fortified bases. The individual superiority of the land plane, about which so much talking was done early in the war, has proved of little consequence beside the fact that the enormous strategic mobility of the ship enables this quality to be conferred upon the planes it carries and permits a concentration of so many seaborne aircraft at the point of attack that the defense is overwhelmed.[26]

A second observer, Paul B. Ryan, stated that carrier task forces were ideal for establishing a naval presence in cold war crises and that they were the core elements of the Sixth and Seventh Fleets. Carriers and their support ships could project power anywhere on the oceans and from them, aircraft could strike countless inland targets, except those deep in Asia. With such a capability there would be no need for access to foreign bases that were dependent on the political whims of host nations.[27]

The Atomic Bomb The second assumption, that the atomic bomb did not signify the end of naval power, was difficult to support, given the controversy after the bomb was dropped on Japan. Proponents of the 'push button war theory' reasoned that navies had become superfluous because atomic bombs could easily sink ships, and therefore sea power could be largely discounted as a factor in future wars. Calmer minds attempted to assess the effect that the bomb would have on sea power, concluded that it would be only slightly greater than that of the explosive shell. They argued that exclusive reliance on the atom bomb would jeopardize the nation's security, was morally untenable, and had dubious chances of success politically and militarily. The answer, they averred, was a defense composed of nuclear and conventional weapons.[28]

As the controversy continued, trials, known as the Bikini Tests, were held on 1 and 25 July 1946, to determine more accurately the effects of nuclear weapons on seaborne forces. These confirmed the Navy's contention that 'the atomic bomb is not at present, nor will it be for some time to come, a practical weapon for use against a fleet at sea'.[29] In its subsequent analysis, the Navy came to believe that atomic weapons would require dispersing existing naval bases and having smaller ones.[30] Admiral Hezlet provided the most accurate conclusions concerning the controversy, stating that atomic bombs could exert great effect because they could be used to destroy ports and ship-building facilities. At sea, however, it was different because if fleets were dispersed, the bomb's effect could be limited.[31]

Guided Missiles and Jet Propulsion US naval analysis of captured German systems proved that the Allies were eight to ten years behind Germany, but since German technology and personnel had been divided among the Allies, the Soviets did not enjoy an undue advantage. Thus, analysis was confined to considering the effects of German and Allied technological advances on naval warfare. Concerning missiles, the conclusion was that while there would be more guided missiles than atomic bombs, their destructive effect would be far less and so the measures taken to counter nuclear weapons would also counter missiles.[32] The jet propulsion problem was also considered solvable, as the Navy considered how to adapt its carriers so that they could launch and recover jet aircraft, while it began the work needed to produce anti-air systems that could defeat the enemy jet aircraft threat.

Specialization in Combatants The War had shown that some types of combatants were obsolete. In 1949 Frank Uhlig summarized the argument that the battle cruiser had been ineffective in the war, that it could do little that a battleship could not do, and that it had no place in post-war naval warfare.[33] The Navy concluded that the battleship had seen its day as well and gradually retired these ships, although they would return to play an important role in the Korean War. It was accepted that the war had introduced a different type of specialization, one that involved entire navies and required that they be designed not to conduct any type of naval operation in a particular ocean, but to conduct only one kind of operation in any ocean. Such specialization was extended from individual ships to entire naval forces, and meant that many of the world's navies were no longer equatable with one another quantitatively, because they were composed of ships and planes with widely varying strategic and tactical characteristics.[34] Years later, in one of the most profound discussions on naval warfare to appear in the post-war period, Admiral Gorshkov made a similar argument. Since the Navy would build the most versatile combatants possible by providing them with complex, expensive systems, when these ships were brought together they would provide the most versatile forces possible. This, coupled with technological advances that made equipage so much more complex, meant that the ships of the future would be vastly more expensive than those of the Second World War.

Qualitative vs. Quantitative After testing captured German naval equipment, the US Navy concluded that, while German technology was years ahead of the Allies', Germany had made a tactical mistake by placing quantity over quality as the top priority in submarine production. US naval planners concluded that future naval superiority would be based in part on superior-quality naval ships.[35] Pursuing this view would only add to the expense of future ships.

Force Projection Comtemporary naval forces were now more self-sustaining, allowing for a more complete fulfillment of Alfred Mahan's views concerning force projection. The war had demonstrated that sea power was 'ubiquitous'. Admiral Raymond Spruance, for example, conducted operations for weeks off Okinawa, 1,500 miles from the nearest base, without supply. With logistical support, a force now could stay on station indefinitely. Naval strategists were not long in realizing the strategic implications and the fact that such projection mated nicely with existing research and development programs and the existing Soviet threat. In discussing the wisdom of using naval forces rather than troops to respond to a situation, Admiral Ernest M. Eller stated that with a naval task force moving on the free sea, the strategic and tactical problems were far less complicated in that the danger of precipitating an incident was reduced and the power that was brought to bear was greater and more prolonged.[36]

Unified Warfare and Amphibious Warfare Concerning armed forces unification, the Navy was in a unique position because of the nature of its Marine Corps. Whereas other nations' corps were small, highly trained, limited-endurance forces that were shock troops on enemy beaches, the US Marine Corps had developed uniquely, conforming to Mahan's postulations. Large and highly trained, it was capable of sustained operations worldwide. This and the fact that its performance in combat situations was often superior to the Army's rankled and made it a target of the Army, which wanted to see its demise. And the fact that it had its own air arm brought it into direct conflict with the Air Force after the latter's creation in 1948. The Navy's position was that, while 'the twilight zone along the beaches where the functions formerly sharply separated between army and navy are now combined,' the optimal '. . . land and naval strategies, while mutually supporting, do not need an integration of one with the other for success'.[37] This position brought it into conflict with the other services and the civilian defense hierarchy.

Operations and Events
US naval operations in the late 1940s, while they were often intense, provided less than complete justification for the funds that the Navy was requesting for its further development. In March 1946, in response to Soviet pressure on

Greece, Turkey, and Iran, the USS *Missouri* was dispatched to the Mediterranean, and steamed through the Bosphorus in April. This incident placed the Navy in the role of providing relevant US military power to uphold US interests against Soviet aggression. The Navy was called upon again in August 1946 to react to conflict in Greece, and the nucleus of a permanent Mediterranean Fleet was formed in September. In 1947, it continued operations because communists were strong and active in Italy. In the autumn, Admiral Bieri, then commander of the Mediterranean Fleet, stated that the fleet would remain in the Mediterranean indefinitely and that it would probably be based at Naples and Palermo. It was then composed of an aircraft carrier, five cruisers, seven destroyers, and twelve auxiliaries. As operations were continued into 1948, the force averaged one carrier, three light cruisers, and ten destroyers, and was supplied by the Atlantic Fleet. The Navy said that its purposes were to evacuate US occupation forces from Germany and Trieste and from the missions in Greece and Turkey, if necessary, and to act as a show of force. Elsewhere in April 1949, the North Atlantic Treaty was signed and, on 8 June, the United States announced that it would soon complete its withdrawal from the Republic of Korea, while it reaffirmed its commitment to the freedom of South Korea. In January 1950, Mao Tse-tung announced his intention of 'liberating' Formosa in 1950, and, in June 1950, US naval forces began a six-month reaction to events in Lebanon.[38]

These operations and occurrences, while they were quite significant and often involved opposing communism, caused several problems for the Navy. First, with the defeat of Japan, the Navy faced no substantial opponent.[39] There was much talk of Soviet naval expansion and this had great influence on US naval planning, but the Soviet fleet simply was not out on the high seas confronting US forces. Thus the Navy was in the more difficult position of espousing the abstract argument that additional naval appropriations would continue the benefits to be accrued from such naval superiority. This argument was much more difficult to convey than one that could identify a clear and present danger, particularly to a nation tired of war and sensitive to accusations of imperialism. Thus, while the Navy accomplished a great deal and performed its missions expertly, it had found that it was difficult to use this to support its requests in the bureaucratic battles it waged in Washington.

Second, since the operations that the Navy conducted and such events as the creation of NATO were largely in reaction to Soviet-supported, communist-inspired aggression, US policy-makers and naval proponents viewed the international arena as a bi-polar world, often judging events and policies solely in terms of their contribution to containing communism. This focused naval planning on the Soviet threat and de-emphasized other problems, such as Third World crises, that could be influenced by naval power. The result of all this was that it directed the naval development that occurred, and focused the types of naval operations that were accomplished. To a nation such as Great Britain which had a centuries-long seafaring tradition, saw herself as a maritime power, and viewed shipbuilding and naval power rather like national industries on which the nation's security and prosperity depended, this dilemma could not have occurred. However, in a United States that refused to see itself as a maritime nation that sorely depended on its naval power for its prosperity and refused to admit the fact that it used its power in its own interests, lest it be accused of imperialism or selfishness, this was a dilemma.

The Navy's Self-Perceptions

Additional insight into US naval development can be gained from examining the Secretary of the Navy's official reports. While it is true that these addressed only the most pressing issues, they reflected the Navy's perceptions of its most significant achievements and greatest problems. Beginning in 1948, these were attached to the Secretary of Defense's reports, and comparing the two often gives insight into how successfully the Navy had presented its position.

In the 1946 report, submitted by James Forrestal to cover the period from 1 July 1945 to 30 June 1946, emphasis was placed on the surrender of Japan and rapid demobilization. In aviation, there were massive decommissionings of carrier air groups, marine aircraft Wings, and squadrons. In deployments and operations of the Atlantic Fleet, the significant cruises were to Europe, involving the constant stationing of four cruisers and eight destroyers, and the part-time presence of a carrier. In the Pacific, US Forces Japan had a cruiser, four destroyers, two minecraft, and requisite support, while the Seventh Fleet had two carriers, six cruisers, three destroyer squadrons, some amphibious ships, and support ships.[40]

In 1947, affairs associated with the Unified Command Plan that had been approved by the President on 14 December 1946 dominated the report submitted by Secretary of the Navy John Sullivan. US naval operations in the Atlantic and Pacific were again mentioned, but no problems were identified. However, the strong naval supplement by the British, who maintained a naval presence at Trieste and carried out routine patrols, was noted. Whether this was a tip of the hat to London or reflected that the Navy was having difficulty meeting its responsibilities in the Mediterranean was not stated. The report emphasized research in guided missiles, noting that it was sharing development programs with the Army, an obvious attempt to reflect its willingness to accept unification and its cost-savings consciousness. The Marine Corps received particular emphasis, probably a defense from the criticism it had received from the Army, Air Force, and the Department of Defense. It was noted that the Corps' missions were to: provide Fleet Marine Forces of combined arms, together with supporting air components, for seizing advanced naval bases, and for such land operations as were necessary in naval campaigns; develop and perfect amphibious operations; provide detachments to naval ships, naval stations and bases; and be prepared for mobilization.[41]

The 1948 report, also submitted by Sullivan to Forrestal, noted that a lack of funds was the Navy's greatest problem, and emphasized that newer ships and modern weapons and equipment were vastly more expensive.[42] The report attacked the concept of a push-button war as too restrictive, and stressed the application of atomic energy, development of guided missiles, and the Soviet submarine threat. Mention was made of ASW, including developing special ASW aircraft. In construction, submarines and ASW ships of a new design were mentioned. Planning for a large, flush-deck carrier had begun and jet aircraft had operated from ships for the first time. The primary problems were identified as combating fast submarines, high-speed aircraft, and guided missiles.[43]

The greatest significance of the 1949 Secretary of Defense report, submitted by Louis Johnson, and the attached report by the Secretary of the Navy, was the bureaucratic crisis over the aircraft carrier USS *United States*, which is discussed below. The report also mentioned designing a newer, faster destroyer, converting the first guided-missile ship; *Norton Sound*, and developing new amphibious techniques by the Marines. It emphasized that jet aircraft had been used in Marine exercise operations for the first time. It noted that the evaluation of German submarines had been completed, that US Second World War submarines had been modernized with snorkels, creating 'Guppies', and that these would be replaced by a new class of 'high submerged speed' submarines that were being built. Three new ASW ships were being built, and mine warfare, which had been neglected, was improved during the year, but mine countermeasures remained a problem.[44]

Naval Construction, 1945–8

Submarines At war's end, the Navy scrapped many older submarines and cancelled many boats then being built, leaving it with a force of 78 boats in 1948. In response to Soviet naval operating patterns, the Navy's themes switched from command of the sea and destroying the enemy's surface fleet, operative during the Second World War, to ASW and attacking coastal and inland land targets. The submarine would play an important role in both themes. After testing the German Type XXI submarine, the Navy produced the Guppy conversion, and then built the *Tang*, the American version of the Type XXI, that was equipped with a new homing torpedo based on the German acoustical torpedo. Submarines also were fitted with snorkels, but unlike the Royal Navy, the Navy did not experiment with hydrogen peroxide. Initial submarine research was tied to the carrier. It was realized that adequately to protect carrier task groups from the increased air threat as they advanced toward enemy shores, it was necessary to have radar pickets patrol farther out so that timely detection of incoming aircraft could be achieved. Since destroyers were vulnerable, submarines were to serve as pickets.[45]

The submarine, however, was to move beyond this supportive role, and here, one man, Hyman Rickover, would develop a nuclear propulsion program that crucially affected its future. In 1947, he convinced Admiral Nimitz that a nuclear-powered submarine was feasible, and was appointed to head the Bureau of Ships' Nuclear Power Branch and Atomic Energy Commission's Naval Reactor Branch. Working quietly within the Navy hierarchy while developing influential support on Capitol Hill, he would create an empire that would assure US submarine superiority for decades.

Even before his efforts were fully under way, converted diesel-powered submarines were armed with nuclear missiles. Similar to the German VI but equipped with a nuclear warhead, the Regulus missile was designed to hit shore targets several hundred miles inland. The original configuration was primitive by modern standards, as the submarine carried one missile in a hangar and had to surface to launch it. Still, its importance as a warship was greatly enhanced by this development, since in the past, the best that any submarine had been able to do was to sink ships. Now it could destroy land targets.[46]

Surface Combatants The Navy perceived that the major threat to the carrier was the air threat, specifically missile-equipped bombers that could attack at night or in bad weather. The aircraft carrier and the submarine claimed the lion's share of available Navy funds from 1945 to 1950, and in the carrier's case it was to protect against this threat. Here there were many problems to be resolved if the carrier were to continue as a key surface naval platform in the future. Flight decks had to be redesigned and strengthened in order to accommodate jet aircraft. Propulsion systems were needed to launch aircraft, while improved arresting systems were necessary to recover them. Radar systems and procedures were needed to permit flight operations at night or in times of reduced visibility. All-weather, missile-equipped aircraft and surface-to-air missile systems that could engage incoming bombers also were needed for protection. The Navy went about solving these problems with optimism, stating that high-speed aircraft would not change the carrier's being the essential feature of naval fleet and convoy operations. Commander John T. Haywood and Frederick L. Ashworth led a successful drive to show that heavy aircraft could carry and deliver atomic bombs from aircraft carriers. By the winter of 1946–7, the Navy had developed a radar-controlled landing approach system for aircraft carriers that solved the problems associated with landing at night or in poor visibility. The new method, the carrier control approach, was tested and 141 night landings were made. The research and testing that were continued throughout 1947 and into 1948 were so successful that the Navy believed that, although there were very significant operational problems still associated with carrier-based jet aircraft, they were the wave of the future and propeller-driven aircraft were becoming obsolete.[47] The significance of these advances cannot be exaggerated, because they reflected the overcoming of substantial handicaps in the carrier's evolution. Bureaucratic opposition, discussed below, was one thing, but tangible problems were quite another matter. By progressing towards the successful solving of the latter, the Navy insured that the carrier could be a key system of the future.

By 1948, the Navy was ready to begin further carrier construction. While $1 million was allotted for modernizing *Midway* to enable her to carry larger aircraft, the budget, submitted on 26 January, clearly was centered on the new carrier. Funds were requested for a new 'giant' 60–80,000-ton carrier, and for high-speed submarines, small submarines, and a special ASW ship somewhat larger than a destroyer. Additional requests permitted planning for missile submarine conversions and special ASW ships.[48] The planning was flexible enough to allow for independent ASW and submarine programs, but was directed sufficiently to allow for integrating them into a fleet that emphasized the force projection of its carrier task groups.

This program was continued and, on 4 June 1948, it was reported that the new carrier might be named *United States*. It would be of 82,349 tons and would carry more than twenty half-ton aircraft. It would be 1,088 feet long, 190 feet wide, would be capable of speeds up to 33 knots, would take 46 months to build, and would cost $189 million at the time of its completion. $6 million of this cost had been provided in the fiscal year 1949 budget. On 8 August the Navy announced that the carrier would be built at Newport News, on 3 February 1949 Truman approved the name *United States* and, in April the keel was laid.[49]

Appropriations on other surface combatants were restricted as the Navy steamed ahead on its carrier program. In 1947, work on the 45,000-ton battleship *Kentucky*, then 70 per cent complete, and the 27,000-ton battle cruiser *Hawaii*, then 85 per cent complete, was stopped. Additionally, the fourth of the *Des Moines*-class cruisers, laid down in 1945, was cancelled in late 1947. (One had been launched in 1946, and two in 1947. While the USS *Des Moines*, the first of its class, was commissioned on 16 November 1948 and two more were commissioned subsequently, nine others were cancelled.) In 1948 the Navy admitted that it was having budgetary problems, and said that it was meeting its operating requirements by extensive use of war-reserve stocks, which had become depleted sorely, and that it had been forced to defer maintenance. Further force shifts occurred and the Navy went to only one battleship, *Missouri*, when it deactivated *Iowa* on 1 September. ASW was to be emphasized in the new Navy, and nine smaller ships would be reactivated to compensate for *Iowa*'s loss. The Navy also firmed up its ASW tactics, and the combat missions of the fleet pertaining to enemy submarines were to: attack enemy submarine bases and yards; conduct offensives in areas through which enemy submarines must pass; conduct forward reconnaissance in areas where friendly forces and convoys must pass; and conduct countermeasures against enemy submarines. All these missions pertained to the perceived Soviet submarine threat.[50]

The Revolt of the Admirals
Restricted defense funds and service unification brought the services into direct conflict, and the fact that technology had advanced to the point where the post-war systems were vastly more expensive than earlier ones only exacerbated the situation. The civilian defense hierarchy's failure to develop a coherent strategy that identified specific services and systems to fulfill a national strategy, meant that the services vied with one another in order to prove that each was best suited to accomplish a mission. The situation deteriorated to the extent that it reached crisis proportions. One commentator noted, 'Instead of the military implementing directives *received from above*, they are attempting to reach a compromise solution based on three sets of ideas which represent the expression of service ambitions *generated from below*.'[51] The assault on the Navy was not long in coming, as the Army and nascent Air Force called upon its best to wage a vicious bureaucratic battle. The attack was focused on amphibious warfare forces and the sea-based air program.

The Army's attack on the Marines stressed the feasibility of conducting amphibious landings in the nuclear age. In April 1949, Secretary of Defense Johnson said that plans were under way to transfer Marine aviation to the Air Force and Army Secretary Kenneth Royall told a Senate panel that he favored making the Marine Corps part of the Army. However, the high point of its assault probably occurred in October, when General Omar Bradley appeared before Congressman Carl Vinson's committee and prophesied an end to amphibious landings.[52]

The Corps' response was impressive. Proceeding from the position that its mission was amphibious warfare, it noted that this was the chief mission assigned to it by the National Security Act of 1947, that the Navy and Marine Corps had accomplished more than 300 landings since 1776, and that a lack of a Marine Corps would restrict US options unsatisfactorily.[53] This theme was developed by Lieutenant Colonel Robert E. Cushman, who argued that air power alone was passive power, that naval power was essential to the national defense, and that it could and should be powerfully supplemented by air power operating from bases protected by naval power. Amphibious warfare was the means of seizing bases, and since the need for bases would increase in the future, the need for the Marines would increase as well. In response to the push-button war proponents, Cushman conceded that bases would make lucrative targets for atomic bombs, but argued that dispersing them into many smaller ones would make them much less attractive and therefore survivable.[54] This was a successful argument and although the Corps was grossly curtailed in the force reductions, it survived. This was very significant because it meant that due attention subsequently would be paid to developing amphibious ships and forces. The aircraft carrier program was less successful.

The USS United States The Air Force's mission brought it into direct conflict with the Navy over the issue of air power, and the point of contention centered on the relative value of long-range Air Force aircraft and carrier-based naval air power. In November 1945, even before the Air Force had been created, its proponents went on the offensive when General James Doolittle testified before the Senate that the carrier had passed its usefulness because it could be sunk. He called for the development of long-range bombers. The conflict was continued throughout 1948 and became a crisis in 1949. The Navy had identified the carrier as a major naval program, it had received Congressional support, and its name had been approved by the White House. When Secretary of Defense Forrestal, who had previously served as Secretary of the Navy, entered Bethesda Naval Hospital in March and subsequently died on 22 May, the Navy lost a great ally in its bureaucratic battle.[55] His successor, Louis Johnson, cancelled the carrier without notifying Secretary of the Navy, John L. Sullivan, an act that prompted Sullivan's resignation, and resulted in the culmination of the ongoing 'revolt of the Admirals'. In his 1949 report, Johnson felt compelled to address the issue. He stated:

> In the course of my administration this year I requested the JCS to consider the advisability of continuing work on the supercarrier, *United States*,

construction of which had previously been authorized and begun. The Joint Chiefs did not reach unanimous agreement but the majority favored abandonment of the project. After review and discussion with this President, I directed cancellation of plans for the $188,000,000 naval aircraft carrier.[56]

The Secretary of the Navy's report did not specifically address the crisis, but it did state that all the problems related to the carrier had been met, implying that technical problems (or any other problems for that matter) did not stand in the way of building a new carrier. It noted that 'conspicuous this year was the reverse of emphasis and reversal of *slight* naval expansion that had been authorized' (author's italics). Thus, what had amounted to the Navy's bloodiest, most devastating fight outside of actual combat was reflected in public reports at the highest levels of government. The Navy's efforts had no effect, however, and it was unable to resurrect its carrier program before the Korean War. What did occur was the revolt of the Admirals. In April 1949, Secretary Sullivan resigned and on 13 May, Francis P. Matthews was appointed as Secretary. On 27 October, the Chief of Naval Operations, Admiral Louis Denfield, was removed as CNO after he criticized the JCS in his Congressional testimony. On 19 December, Denfield, who had been replaced by Admiral Forrest Sherman, refused assignment as Commander, US Naval Forces in Europe. His '. . . refusal was based on the belief that other nations might not have the necessary confidence in him which a Commander in Europe should have'. Denfield retired on 1 March 1950, following Admiral William Blandy, CINCLANTFLT and commander of the Bikini tests, who retired on 1 February.[57]

Naval Construction, 1949–50

Surface Combatants Having lost its carrier battle in a bureaucratic battle of unprecedented viciousness, the Navy attempted to pick up the pieces in 1949 and 1950. While its hopes for the *United States* were dashed, it tried to continue its sea-based air program with existing resources. On 30 October 1949, several ships, including three carriers, were retired, and the force was to be reduced by 54,891 men by 1 July 1950. Some light carriers and other ships were recommissioned to offset the loss, and three carriers – *Franklin D. Roosevelt*, *Midway*, and *Coral Sea* – and the battleship *Missouri* were kept in commission. In January 1950, *Missouri* was placed in training status in order to allow the addition of a third *Essex* carrier, the *Philippine Sea*, to the Pacific Fleet. In the same month, the Navy began converting three *Essex* and two *Midway* carriers to enable them to carry jet bombers. The changes included strengthening decks and increasing catapult load and gasoline handling capacities. The conversions took two years, and other *Essex* carriers were converted subsequently. *Saipan*- and *Independence*-class carriers were converted for ASW duties, and two converted *Saipans* joined the fleet. In 1950, the Navy declared that naval aviation's most important mission was ASW, and that its other missions were air defense of fleets and convoys, air strikes against land and surface targets, and supporting land forces. All these could be considered to be measures against the perceived Soviet threat.[58] Clearly though, these were damage control measures, reflecting the fact that the Navy had lost its bid to advance significantly the field of sea-based aviation.

Submarines Largely through Admiral Rickover's efforts, the nuclear submarine program incurred less damage. A low-profile program, it progressed and significant advances were made. Meanwhile, on 18 June 1949, the Navy said it was developing a submarine with radio-controlled missiles. Although on 26 August, the USS *Cochino*, while on patrol in the Arctic, sank after suffering explosions, this had no permanent affect on the submarine programs. On 29 April 1950, the Navy requested and was subsequently granted authority to build four new submarines, including Rickover's $40 million nuclear-powered submarine. This meant that Rickover's group had completed all preliminary work, started a school to train naval engineers, finished plans for the first boat and power plant, won government approval, and convinced Westinghouse and General Electric to participate in the program.[59] Thus, as with the aircraft carrier, the period had begun with many tangible problems for the submarine, and the advances made were most significant because they represented the overcoming of many of the prohibitive problems that barred the submarine's becoming a key naval system of the future.

Communications and Electronics Command, control, and communications (C^3) and electronics would become major aspects of naval warfare. However, the period from 1945 to 1950 was one of research from which some results would appear in the early 1950s. An obvious priority was ASW, since German technology meant that future submarines would be faster, would be able to stay under water much longer, and would therefore be harder to detect. A new sonar which sent out a single signal simultaneously in all directions and displayed echoes on a display was a great advance in tracking high-speed submarines, while a high-frequency airborne radar was also developed to detect the snorkels of submerged submarines.[60]

Conclusions
It is hard to conclude that the US Navy was not in trouble in 1950. Its strategists and tacticians had correctly identified the aircraft and submarine as the naval systems of the future, and naval power as the key to America's security. But it had not convinced the civilian defense hierarchy and had lost its argument for a new carrier in an all-or-nothing gamble. After the cancellation of *United States* in 1949, the Navy attempted to continue its programs, but it was clear that it could not thrive unless something occurred that would change prevailing perceptions drastically. That something was the Korean War.

GREAT BRITAIN

Great Britain did not suffer from the same misperception of the value and utility of naval power. Having the benefit of centuries of colonial experience and having firmly identified herself as a maritime nation, she had no illusions concerning the pre-eminent importance of naval power to her national security. Rather, her problems were in adjusting the colonial empire to the post-war environment and a lack of funds.

Colonial issues, expensive ones, dominated as Great Britain recovered from the war. In 1946 one of the military's major tasks was to prevent illegal immigration into Palestine and, from May to November, fourteen ships, carrying from 400 to 2,500 immigrants, were intercepted. These and other colonial operations continued to deplete the Treasury in 1947 and 1948. In February and March 1948, Royal Navy ships landed troops to defend British Honduras against Guatemalan actions and, in an incident that foretold a major problem in 1982, Argentina took action against British rule of the Falkland Islands. On 16 February, the House of Commons noted that Argentine and Chilean naval forces were operating in Falklands waters and had set up military commands with the aim of enforcing claims to their sovereignty over the area. Steps were taken to support the Governor of the Falklands, and in March, the sloop HMS *Snipe* and the light cruiser HMS *Nigeria*, with the Governor embarked, toured the illegal bases.[61]

To many, it was already evident that the empire had to be radically transformed. The final results, the Commonwealth and the East of Suez policy, were years away, but the stage was set during this period. On 15 August 1947, India and Pakistan were created as Great Britain gave up control of India. However, while possession might be relinquished, London's perceptions of her responsibilities concerning her former colonies would linger until economic problems would bring home the reality that these were too costly for the nation to bear. In 1950, the Indian Ocean's approaches were composed of weak nations that relied on the sea for their communications and possessed ports that would make excellent bases, but were unable to confront nations with significant maritime power. A suggested solution was a British–Indian–Ceylonese–Pakistani defense pact.[62]

The war's end prompted radical reductions in British military strength. Ships were removed from active service, and were either retired, sold, or transferred to other nations. The Navy Estimates for 1947–8 amounted to a 23 per cent decrease from the previous year. Drastic manpower reductions by 31 December 1946 caused disruption and reductions in operational efficiency. In a very candid speech, the Prime Minister allowed that while Great Britain could no longer have the world's largest Navy, he hoped that it would have the best equipped. The rapid naval demobilization was continued and was not reversed until the outbreak of the Korean War.[63]

While these themes evolved, a second, the possiblity of confrontation with the Warsaw Pact, became more pronounced. In January 1946, the USSR demanded that Great Britain remove her troops from Greece, an act that also elicited a US response when the *Missouri* was sent to the Mediterranean in a show of force. The relevant point, however, was that Great Britain took a resolute stand, an indication that there might be other such confrontations in the future. Such resolve was also demonstrated as she maintained her station at Trieste. The consolidation of Soviet control in eastern Europe, pressure on Austria, Greece, Turkey, and Iran, and the Berlin blockade all reflected a hard-line policy which Prime Minister Winston Churchill termed an 'iron curtain'. A significant aspect of the British response was support for the North Atlantic Treaty, but many warned that this was not sufficient for national defense.[64]

British Naval Policy, 1945–50

Great Britain had much less difficulty adjusting to the atomic bomb than did America because many of the strategic issues concerning military power that the United States deliberated during this period had been decided decades if not centuries before when Great Britain first perceived herself to be a maritime nation. Her interests and security were bound to the sea and this was reflected in her military expenditures. Thus sea power remained a given and the atomic bomb was considered in terms of its influence on sea power, vice in terms of replacing sea power. In this context, in 1946, many were already predicting that the effect of atomic warfare on ship design and naval operations would be less than many observers had assumed. Rather, the Navy's missions would be to protect the sea lines of communication and to attack immediately if hostilities broke out. Many warned that the enemy could pose a serious threat with submarines and aircraft alone, and called for a highly mobile fleet of capital ships, aircraft carriers, and destroyers strategically based, and submarines for attacking enemy shipping.[65] In May 1950, this argument was expressed even more convincingly. Addressing the issues of the atomic bomb and joint service operations, P. D. H. R. Pelly averred that while the bomb was significant, it did not mean the end of traditional warfare. Rather, any future war must be fought by defending the sea lines of communication and, once this fact was accepted, it was then up to the services to determine the force mix that could best defend them.[66] And it was here, in the context of a severe shortage of funds and a clear perception of the Soviet threat, that the British policy was played out.

Submarines British submarine policy was based on the belief that the Soviet Union posed a significant submarine threat and that the submarine would play a major role in ASW. This approach was accepted also by those who saw that, with the tremendous power of nuclear weapons against ships, in the future the submarine would be able to compete better than anything else.[67]

At the end of the war the British scrapped 45 old or worn-out boats and cancelled another 50 under construction, leaving a fleet of just less than 100 submarines. Realizing that their technology was years behind the Germans, their first goal was to assimilate German technology. Several *T*- and *A*-class submarines were modernized along the lines of the Type XXI, with enlarged batteries and streamlined hulls. A Type XXI German U-boat, *U 2518*, was put into commission for experiments and, over the next few years, snorkels were fitted on all British submarines. After testing *U 2518*, British designers decided to lengthen a number of their *T*-class boats to get similar performance, and a new class based on XXI was laid down. Thus, British submarine design, while the construction methods were British, was influenced heavily by German designs.[68]

In submarine propulsion, *U 1407*, one of the smaller German Walter boats, was tested and two hydrogen peroxide boats, *Explorer* and *Excaliber*, were authorized for experimentation.[69] These were expensive, tying up valuable resources and expending sorely needed funds. Conversely, the knowledge gained from them would be applied to a new design, the *Porpoise*-class.[70] Table 1.3 presents selected Royal Navy force levels for 1946 to 1950. While the reduction from 1946 to 1947 reflects the continued disarmament then occurring, from 1948 onward, newer boats were put into service to replace those being removed, so that in 1949 there was a lean submarine force of 64 boats, 31 of which were in reserve.

Surface Ships The aircraft carrier was seen as the weapon system of the future. In contrast to the US carrier that had been born of the experience in the Pacific, however, the British carrier, influenced by the European land environment, was smaller, more heavily armored, and less capable.

The post-war reductions reflected the beliefs that the huge wartime fleet now amounted to excessive power and that many of these ships were either obsolete or worn out. Additionally, the fleet was so expensive that the nation simply could not afford to support it. Thus, some ships were scrapped, while others were either sold or given to other nations. The battleships were considered for conversion to missile-armed ships, but the expense involved, coupled with the fact that they would only provide a minor improvement to the fleet's capabilities, precluded this. Likewise, many of the carriers were not modernized because they simply were not big enough to carry the new post-war aircraft. Three of the *Centaur*-class, laid down during the war, were completed and then almost immediately modernized, so that they could carry modern aircraft. A fourth, *Hermes*, laid down in June 1944, was radically redesigned, was launched in 1953, and served in the Mediterranean and elsewhere. Her biggest problem was her size, which limited the number of aircraft that she could carry. *Victorious* was rebuilt almost entirely from 1950 to 1957 so that she could carry modern jet aircraft. *Eagle*, laid down in 1942, was completed and launched in 1946, while her sister, *Ark Royal*, was delayed so that many improvements could be incorporated and was launched by Queen Elizabeth at a christening in May 1950.[71]

The new ships, produced from designs developed late in the war, began to appear in 1949 and reflected the belief that Soviet submarines and aircraft posed great threats to surface ships operating in the North Atlantic and European waters. As a result, ASW and AAW were stressed. While battleships were no longer considered necessary, there was feeling for the continued need of cruisers, and three designs were developed in the late 1940s. None of these went on to construction. The decision to proceed with the *Tiger*-class, laid down during the war, would not be made until the early 1950s. In 1949, the first two of eight 3,580-ton *Daring*-class destroyers, *Daring* and *Decoy*, were launched. Designed during the war, the class was laid down from 1945 to 1949. Four succeeding units, *Diamond*, *Defender*, *Dainty*, and *Delight*, were launched in 1950; *Duchess* was launched in 1951, and the last ship, *Diana*, was launched in August 1952.[72]

Electronic Warfare and Command and Control As in the US experience, while the British accomplished significant research in command, control, and communications (C³), most of the results would not reach the fleet until the 1950s. A sonobuoy was produced, experiments were conducted with homing torpedoes, and significant effort was devoted to a new sonar set. It was a vast improvement over previous sonars and, when mated with weapon systems, would provide a capability against fast-moving, submerged submarines.[73]

Conclusions Thus from the end of the war to the beginning of the Korean War, while the Navy's size was decreased, significant investment was made to combat the perceived Soviet submarine and air threats. Although the fleet was reduced to thirteen aircraft carriers (five in active service) and a lean force of surface combatants and submarines, it was adequate to meet the Navy's SLOC mission and to respond to events in the colonial empire.

Table 1.3 Selected Force Levels – Royal Navy, 1946–50

	\ *Year*				
	46	*47*	*48*	*49*	*50*
Submarines	107	99	93	33	32
Fleet Aircraft Carriers	12	12	12	3	1
Light Aircraft Carriers	11	11	6	4	4
Escort Aircraft Carriers	2	1	1	0	0
Battleships	14	8	5	1	0
Cruisers	50	43	37	15	14
Destroyers	208	148	119	53	34
Frigates	83	88	174	43	27
Fleet Minesweepers	121	61	23	16	10

FRANCE

The situation in France was similar to that of Great Britain, although the severity of the factors was greater. If the war had wreaked damage on the British Isles and had disrupted the British economy, it had devastated France. Her fleet was in a shambles. Part of it had been scuttled at Toulon in 1942, while the rest had seen heavy action during the war. Further, she had neither the funds, the shipbuilding infrastructure, nor the popular support necessary to rearm properly. None the less, the demands of the empire and national defense required attention. She turned to her allies, who generously provided surplus ships from their own inventories, as well as German and Italian war prizes. The government's position was explained fully on 21 June 1949, when M. Ramadier, Minister of Defense, discussed its naval policy. He said the Navy's first task was to defend France's eastern frontier and this called for small riverine vessels. Its second mission was to maintain communications with North and Central Africa, and this called for a light fleet. He stressed the growing importance of submarines and suggested that if more than the two carriers were needed (as some suggested), they should be bought from the Allies.[74]

A brief survey of French naval events and an examination of Table 1.4 shines further light on this problem. In 1946, the Navy was placed under great budget constraints. No new ships were approved and those being built would be completed only if the cost were less than that of abandoning construction. Also, a 1.5 billion franc reconditioning of the battleship *Jean Bart* was slowed.

Table 1.4
Selected Force Levels – French Navy, 1946–50

	Year				
	46	*47*	*48*	*49*	*50*
Submarines	14	15	16	14	12
Aircraft Carriers	1	1	1	1	1
Escort Aircraft Carriers	1	1	1	1	1
Battleships	3	2	2	2	2
Cruisers	9	9	10	11	11
Destroyers	26	24	22	21	20
Sloops	4	4	4	4	4
Frigates	12	15	24	18	12

In response to what Great Britain perceived as a dangerously weak French naval force, in August the British lent France the carrier HMS *Colossus*, which was renamed *Arromaches*.

The situation appeared to improve slightly in August 1948, when France announced that reconditioning of *Jean Bart* was almost completed and, in November, France had received most of her share of Italian ships: three small cruisers, four destroyers, two torpedo-boats, six tugs, and two water-carriers, and announced her intention to build a new 16,700-ton carrier, *Clemenceau*. However, pessimism again set in when the budget was released on 21 June 1949. It included 250 million francs for building two submarines, three escorts, a river gunboat, and amphibious units, but no money for *Clemenceau*. Pessimism was alleviated slightly when, on 27 April 1950, the reconditioned *Jean Bart* left Brest on her first cruise. The severe financial problem was again reflected on 19 July, when France's response to the Korean War was to provide the sloop *La Grandière* as her sole contribution to the United Nations naval force. The result was that, while France took measures to provide for her defense, because of the ruin caused by the war and the demands of the empire, these were relatively meager when compared to those of the United States, Great Britain, and the Soviet Union. That the perception of a danger was realized in Paris was demonstrated in French actions in Indo-China and her participation in Allied naval exercises such as one in June and July 1949.[75] None the less, her problems limited her to making only a minor contribution to the advancement of naval technology during this period, and while she had the world's third strongest navy, many predicted that she would soon be overtaken by the Soviet Union.

OTHER NATIONS

While the United States and Great Britain led the field in naval technological innovation and the Soviet Union was busy building large combatants and

submarines, naval technology trickled downward as other nations strengthened their naval inventories when the Americans and British divested
themselves of excess naval ships by selling or transferring them.

Europe

In Europe, the major theme was the perceived Soviet threat. The primary
dangers had been identified as the submarine, air, and mining threats, and
ships were shifted among the western European nations to provide an
adequate NATO defense. In northern Europe, developments in Norway,
Denmark, and Sweden were noteworthy. The transfer of three British
submarines in September 1946 augmented the modest Norwegian ASW and
anti-mine warfare capability (see Table 1.5).[76] At war's end, the Danish Navy
had ceased to exist. Through transfers, however, she developed a small force
of ships that gave her a modest surface and submarine warfare capability,
and a mine warfare force that responded to a perceived Soviet mining threat.

Table 1.5
Selected Force Levels – Norwegian Navy, 1946–50

	Year				
	46	47	48	49	50
Submarines	5	5	5	5	5
Destroyers	6	7	7	8	8
Frigates	2	2	2	2	2
Corvettes	3	3	3	3	3
Mine Warfare	11	11	11	11	11

Table 1.6
Selected Force Levels – Royal Danish Navy, 1946–50

	Year				
	46	47	48	49	50
Submarines	7	7	7[a]	4	3
Frigates	2	2	2	2	2
Corvettes	0	1	1	1	1
Small Torpedo Craft	2	4	6	8	10
Minesweepers	24	24	24	32	40
Minelayers	1	2	3	2	1

[a]Includes three 600-ton British submarines on 3-year loan.

Neutral Sweden's fleet dominated the Baltic in the late 1940s. While it
curtailed its destroyer force from 1948 to 1950, it maintained a strong Navy
that included a number of minesweepers (see Table 1.7). The Netherlands
Navy had seen heavy service during the war and the Germans had destroyed
almost completely the nation's shipbuilding infrastructure and capability.
During the post-war years, the Dutch began building a modern navy, and
relied on transfers and purchases to provide a navy in the interim. It purchased
the British light carrier *Venerable* which was transferred on 28 May 1948, and

Table 1.7
Selected Force Levels – Swedish Navy, 1946–50

	Year				
	46	*47*	*48*	*49*	*50*
Submarines	27	28	29	27	24
Battleships	3	3	3	2	0
Cruisers	3	3	3	3	3
Coastal Defense Ships	5	5	5	5	5
Destroyers	23	23	23	16	10
Minesweepers	41	41	41	42	44

Table 1.8
Selected Force Levels – Dutch Navy, 1946–50

	Year				
	46	*47*	*48*	*49*	*50*
Submarines	7	7	8[a]	9	9
Escort Aircraft Carriers	1	1	1	1	1
Light Cruisers	2	2	3	3	4
Destroyers	6	6	6	6	6
Frigates	1	1	1[b]	1	1
PT Boats	19	19	19	19	19
Patrol Craft	0	0	1[c]	6	8
Gunboats	4	4	4	3	1
Squadron Minesweepers	8	8	8	8	8
Minelayers	3	3	3	3	2
Small Minesweepers	26	26	26	23	21
Tenders	1	1	1	2	2

[a]Obsolete submarines. [b]Ex-British frigate. [c]Ex-US patrol craft.

also received three British and two US destroyers which bolstered its naval capability. Table 1.8 shows that this fleet was expanded slightly during the period from 1946 to 1950. At war's end, Belgium had only two ships, neither of which was in good condition. However, things began to improve when, in response to the vulnerability of the huge Belgian ports to mine warfare, its Navy was bolstered with the delivery of six British *Algerine*-class minesweepers, the first two of which arrived on 29 November 1949 and 31 January 1950.[77]

In the Mediterranean, perhaps the biggest event was the distribution of the Italian fleet. It was divided as follows: Great Britain received a battleship, two submarines, eight motor torpedo-boats, three landing craft, and fourteen auxiliaries; America received a battleship, two submarines, eight motor torpedo-boats, three landing craft, and twelve auxiliaries; the Soviet Union received a battleship, a cruiser, three destroyers, three torpedo-boats, two submarines, ten motor torpedo-boats, three vedettes, three landing craft, and nineteen auxiliaries; France received three small cruisers, two submarines, a sloop, four destroyers, six motor torpedo-boats, three vedettes, five landing craft, and eighteen auxiliaries; Greece received a cruiser and an auxiliary; Yugoslavia received three torpedo-boats, seven minesweepers, two landing craft, and five auxiliaries; and Albania received a gunboat. The battleships and some smaller craft given to Great Britain and the United States were scrapped in Italy. The distribution of the fleet took a considerable amount of time because the Soviet Union was required to return a British battleship and eleven US ships – a cruiser, seven destroyers, and three submarines. Although these were to be scrapped, the Allies blocked the transfer of Italian ships until they were returned and arrangements were finally made for their transfer in the winter of 1948–9. For its part, Italy was allowed to retain an old battleship, two cruisers, and some destroyers, torpedo-boats, and corvettes, but no submarines. On 27 September 1949, Italy announced its intention to re-establish its naval power and developed its shipbuilding program for 1950–5. Costing about 20 million pounds, it included rebuilding two cruisers and building two light AAW ships, six destroyers adapted to AAW and ASW, a convoy escort, fast motor gunboats, and lagoon and coastal vessels for supporting an army on a sea front. Italy had to comply with the provisions of the peace treaty and therefore could neither lay down war vessels before 1 January 1950, nor exceed a total tonnage of 67,500 tons. In addition, she could not build aircraft carriers, submarines, motor torpedo-boats, or assault craft, which inhibited her contribution to evolving naval technology.[78]

In southern Europe, the threat of Soviet naval power was also perceived. Spain, which was ostracized after the war, modernized four cruisers, while Portugal received two British *River*-class frigates in May 1949. Greece and Turkey also refurbished their naval forces. The Greek Navy had been decimated by German occupation and the Civil War from 1944 to 1947. In 1947, it was composed almost completely of ships lent by Great Britain. The United States supported Athens with large quantities of arms, including ships, and its naval order of battle was increased accordingly (see Table 1.9). Even greater progress was made by Turkey. On the extreme south-eastern flank of NATO, it was vulnerable to Soviet pressure such as the Soviet actions of 1946. In 1948, four US *Balao* submarines and four auxiliaries were transferred. By April 1949, two US destroyers had been transferred, followed by two more in August.[79] This was a sizeable naval force that included a battle-cruiser and ten submarines (see Table 1.10). In essence, through transfers of British and

Table 1.9

Selected Force Levels – Greek Navy, 1946–50

	Year				
	46	*47*	*48*	*49*	*50*
Submarines	6	6	6	6	6
Cruisers	0	1	1	1	1
Destroyers	10	10	10	10	10
Corvettes	4	4	4	6	8
Fleet Minesweepers	22	22	22	22	22
Landing Ships	3	9	11	12	12

Table 1.10
Selected Force Levels – Turkish Navy, 1946–50

	Year				
	46	*47*	*48*	*49*	*50*
Submarines	6	6	10	10	10
Battlecruisers	1	1	1	1	1
Destroyers	8	8	10	12	12
Minesweepers	11	19	29	28	26

American ships, Europe's maritime defenses were strengthened against the perceived Soviet naval threat.

Canada
In 1945, the Royal Canadian Navy was the most sophisticated of the British Commonwealth Navies. Like the United States and Great Britain, it experienced force reductions, maintaining a smaller force, including an aircraft carrier and two cruisers (see Table 1.11). The high point was the acquisition of the aircraft carrier *Magnificent* on 21 May 1948.[80]

Table 1.11
Selected Force Levels – Royal Canadian Navy, 1946–50

	Year				
	46	*47*	*48*	*49*	*50*
Aircraft Carriers	2	1	1	1	1
Cruisers	2	2	2	2	2
Destroyers	13	12	11	11	11
Frigates	18	11	9	7	7
Minesweepers	11	11	11	10	9

Latin America
Many Latin American nations took advantage of the bargain prices for surplus ships in the immediate post-war years. Brazil's support for the Allies in the war resulted in a closer relationship and the transfer of ships under Lend-Lease, so that in the late 1940s, its Navy approached parity with Argentina. Chile, concerned about her relations with Argentina, because of disputed territories, and with Peru, improved her naval strength in 1946 when she acquired three frigates and three corvettes from Great Britain. In January 1947, Argentina announced its intention to acquire an aircraft carrier, three submarines, a cruiser, four destroyers, and ten patrol boats.[81]

The Indian Ocean
The development of naval power in the Indian Ocean was linked to the departure of India from the British empire on 15 August 1947, in that the British hoped to create a group of friendly powers that would assure the region's security. Attention was focused on India, Pakistan, and Ceylon, as London acted to create such an arrangement. Upon independence, the Royal Indian Navy was split between India and Pakistan. On 5 July 1948, less than a year after independence, India received the British cruiser *Achilles* which it had purchased, renamed it *Delhi*, and made it the flagship of the Indian fleet

Table 1.12

Selected Force Levels – Indian Navy, 1946–50

	Year				
	46	47	48	49	50
Cruisers	0	0	I	I	I
Destroyers	0	0	0	3	3
Frigates	5	2	3	3	4
Sloops	7	7	4	4	4
Corvettes	2	2	0	0	0
Minesweepers	16	16	12	6	6

(see Table 1.12). In September, London transferred three *R*-class destroyers, which were delivered in July 1949. A similar program was accomplished with Pakistan and, on 30 September and 30 November 1949, two British *O*-class destroyers were delivered, followed by a third in March 1951.[82]

The Pacific Ocean

Fears of Soviet expansion into the Pacific prompted a similar security policy in that region. In north-east Asia, the Chinese Navy was bolstered in 1947, when it was allocated 23 Japanese warships, including three destroyers. In 1948, the British cruiser *Aurora* and frigate *Mendip* were transferred as Great Britain and the United States tried to strengthen the Chinese Navy. However, this policy failed with the successful Chinese communist revolution, and no incident symbolized its failure more than when the crew of *Chung King*, the ex-*Aurora*, deserted the Nationalist cause with their ship on 1 March 1949. The *Chung King* was subsequently sunk by Nationalist forces.[83]

Farther southward, a *River*-class frigate was transferred to the Burmese Navy in 1947, and New Zealand purchased six *Loch*-class frigates from Great Britain, which were delivered in 1948 and 1949. New Zealand announced its intention to have a navy consisting of a cruiser, six *Loch* ASW frigates, and a surveying vessel. However, the most significant activity occurred in Australia, for it was on this subcontinent that London placed its hopes for regional stability. Australia had had the largest Commonwealth Navy before the war, but had lost right of place to Canada during the war. None the less, at war's end, it had a sizeable naval force, which it continued to develop in the early post-war years. On 16 December 1948, HMS *Terrible* was transferred to Australia and was renamed *Sydney*, while HMS *Majestic* was acquired in 1949

Table 1.13

Selected Force Levels – Royal Australian Navy, 1946–50

	Year				
	46	47	48	49	50
Light Aircraft Carriers	0	0	I	2	2
Cruisers	4	3	3	3	3
Destroyers	8	8	8	9	10
Frigates	12	12	12	12	12
Sloops	2	2	2	2	2
Corvettes	38	31	31	32	32

to become *Melbourne*. Australia also built the *Battle*-class destroyer *Anzac*, the second of two such ships, and announced that it was also building *Daring* destroyers. (One of these would be cancelled in 1954.) In March 1950, *Tobruk*, the first *Battle* destroyer, began her sea trials and, on 13 June, Australia announced that three *Q* destroyers on loan from the Royal Navy were to be permanently transferred at no expense (see Table 1.13). They would be converted to ASW frigates at a cost of A400,000 pounds each. On 14 August, Australia announced that the STAAG Mark II twin, stabilized 40mm AA gun, would be fitted in the destroyers *Tobruk* and *Anzac*. Power-operated and radar-controlled, it would carry the twin 40mm guns that would be the destroyers' secondary armament. Finally, on 20 September, Australia's naval policy was revealed when Prime Minister Menzies announced that Australia felt that there would be no major war with Second World War-type sea battles in the Pacific, because Japan had been destroyed and the communist powers did not have large navies; however, there was a threat from long-range submarines. In response, the Australian Navy would have two carriers, ten destroyers, and four large destroyers under construction in 1952, and would begin building six ASW frigates when the large destroyers were completed.[84]

CONCLUSIONS

In the forefront of naval development, the period from 1945 to 1950 saw the Soviet Union attempt to maximize the threat that the West perceived concerning its naval power in order to discourage any Western aggressive designs on a Soviet Union that was in reality weaker militarily. The effects of this on Western naval development were mixed. On the one hand, it perceived Soviet submarine and mining threats and technical advances were made to combat them. On the other, problems and preoccupations in the politics of the four major sea powers prevented more significant naval progress. In the United States, it was preoccupation with the Air Force and then the Army, as the push-button war received the lion's share of attention. The result was the cancellation of the *United States*, a critical setback for America's sea-based air program. Meanwhile, the US submarine program made steady progress. In Great Britain, the issue was money, as London realized that it could no longer field the world's strongest navy, but still intended to have the world's best equipped. Its contribution during this period was significant. In France, the Indo-China war, political uncertainty, a destroyed shipbuilding infra-structure, and a critical paucity of funds restricted French naval development, although proposed programs certainly reflected France's appreciation of naval power. Finally, Moscow remained preoccupied with the old themes lingering from the war, as Stalin began a program that would have produced a fleet tied to the shore and oddly out of place in the post-war environment of the 1950s. Thus, in January 1950, while many critical problems associated with aircraft carrier and submarine development either had been solved or were well on their way to resolution, the further development of sea power was uncertain, as the world's leading maritime contenders remained preoccupied with problems and issues that argued against significant development. All this was to change with two political events, the outbreak of hostilities in Korea in 1950 and Stalin's death in 1953.

On a lower level, the reduction of the bloated wartime British and US navies, the distribution of British and American naval ships among the Western European nations to provide a maritime defense against a perceived Soviet naval threat, and the transfer of many ships to nations outside Europe caused a diffusion of existing naval power. The German, Japanese, and Italian fleets were distributed among the victors. The iron curtain was drawn and the cold war set in, as the world became bipolar. Only a few far-sighted individuals realized that NATO was essentially a maritime coalition, as attention was centered on Europe.

NOTES

1. V. I. Lenin, Speech Delivered at a Meeting of the Moscow Organization of the RCP(B), 6 December 1920, in *Lenin Collected Works*, vol. 31 (Moscow: Progress Publishers, 1966), pp. 438–9, 442–50.
2. This fact was certainly realized by the British. Even a cursory perusal of 'Navy Notes' in the *Journal of the Royal United Services Institute For Strategic Studies* (hereinafter referred to as *RUSI*) reveals repeated reports on Parliamentary discussions on this issue. In most cases the British were uneasy, particularly with a comment by the Prime Minister which noted that the Royal Navy could no longer be the world's strongest naval force. Some comfort was found in the fact that it had lost this position to the United States, and that the traditional warm Anglo-American alliance would prevail.
3. Sergei Zonin, 'An Unjust Trial,' in *Morskoy Sbornik*, no. 2 (February 1989), pp. 78–84.
4. Ibid.
5. Ibid.
6. Ibid.
7. Ibid., pp. 78–9
8. Ibid.
9. Leon B. Blair, 'A Historical Examination of Soviet Foreign Policy,' in *US Naval Institute Proceedings* (hereinafter referred to as *Proceedings*), vol. 75, no. 9 (September 1949), pp. 979, 981; J. V. Davidson-Houston, 'The Political Strategy of Russia,' in *RUSI*, vol. xcii, no. 565 (February 1947), pp. 119–20, 122; Raymond L. Garthoff, 'Sea Power in Soviet Strategy,' in *Proceedings*, vol. 84, no. 27 (February 1958), pp. 85–93.
10. R. F. Corville, 'Russia's Foreign Policy: The Lessons of History,' in *RUSI*, vol. xcv, no. 579 (August 1950), p. 478; Richard Hilton, 'The Soviet Armed Forces,' in *RUSI*, vol. xciv, no. 576 (November 1949), p. 558; John Erickson, 'The Soviet Naval High Command,' in *Proceedings*, vol. 99, no. 5 (May 1973), p. 68; P. W. Rairden, Jr., 'Soviet Sea Power,' in *Proceedings*, vol. 74, no. 1 (January 1948), pp. 65–6, 67; J. Burke Wilkenson, 'The Big Bear Wets His Paws,' in *Proceedings*, vol. 74, no. 10 (October 1948), pp.

1224–7, 1230–32. Paul Martin agreed with this analysis and stated, '. . . the Russian Navy ranks fourth in world naval power, behind the United States, Britain, and France. At her present rate of construction, she will soon outstrip the latter country. Her fleet is a fairly well-balanced one, much of it modern.' See: Paul Martin, 'The Russian Navy – Past, Present, and Future,' in *Proceedings*, vol. 73, no. 6 (June 1947); p. 660.
11. Martin, p. 657; and Wilkenson, p. 1225.
12. Vice-Admiral Sir Arthur Hezlet, *The Submarine and Sea Power* (New York: Stein and Day, 1967), p. 244.
13. Drew Middleton, *Submarine: The Ultimate Naval Weapon – Its Past, Present and Future* (Chicago: Playboy Press, 1976), p. 146.
14. 'Navy Notes,' in *RUSI*, vol. xcii, no. 565 (February 1947), p. 140.
15. 'Professional Notes,' in *Proceedings*, vol. 74, no. 5 (May 48), pp. 652–3; 'Navy Notes,' in *RUSI* vol. xciv, no. 574 (May 1949), p. 301; and (November 1948), p. 662.
16. Wilhelm Hadeler, 'The Ships of the Soviet Navy,' in *The Soviet Navy*, ed. M. G. Saunders (New York: Frederick A. Praeger, 1958), pp. 141–2.
17. *Combat Fleets of the World, 1988–9*, eds. Jean Labayle Couhat and A. D. Baker III, with Bernard Prézelin (hereinafter referred to as Labayle Couhat), p. 616; *Conway's All The World's Fighting Ships, 1957–1982, Part II: The Warsaw Pact and Non-Aligned Nations*, ed R. Gardiner (hereinafter referred to as *Conway's, Part II*) (Annapolis, MD: Naval Institute Press, 1985), pp. 464–5, 486–7; Norman Polmar, *Soviet Naval Power, Challenge for the 1970s* (New York: National Strategy Information Center, 1972), pp. 25, 102–3; *Jane's Fighting Ships, 1971–1972* (New York: McGraw-Hill, 1971), p. 630; Siegfried Breyer, *Guide to the Soviet Navy* (Annapolis, MD: US Naval Institute, 1970), pp. 24–6, 67, 89, 90, 92, 96, 226; and Hadeler, pp. 40–1, 51, 86, 93–4, 145, 153.
18. Labayle Couhat, p. 606; *Conway's, Part II*, pp. 464–5, 476, 481; and *Jane's Fighting Ships 1971–2*, p. 614.
19. *Conway's, Part II*, pp. 467–8, 476–7, 492–3.

20. US National Military Establishment, *First Report of the Secretary of Defense, 1948* (Washington, DC: GPO, 1948), p. 59.

21. 'Navy Notes,' in *RUSI*, vol. xcii, no. 565 (February 1947) p. 141.

22. Paul B. Ryan, *First Line of Defense: The US Navy Since 1945* (Stanford, CA: Hoover Institution Press, 1981), p. 7; Russell H. Smith, 'Notes on Our Naval Future.' in *Proceedings*, vol. 72, no. 4 (April 1946), p. 489; Hezlet, *Submarine*, pp. 242–3; James A. Nathan and James K. Oliver, *The Future of United States Naval Power* (Bloomington: University of Indiana Press, 1979), pp. 1–2.

23. Ryan, p. 7

24. Hezlet, *Submarine*, p. 244.

25. Ernest M. Eller, 'Sea Power and Peace,' in *Proceedings*, vol. 73, no. 10 (October 1947), p. 1169.

26. Fletcher Pratt, 'World War II and the Changing Conception of Sea Power,' in *Proceedings*, vol. 72, no. 1 (January 1946), pp 9–10.

27. Ryan, p. 8

28. John Philips Cranwell, 'Sea Power and the Atomic Bomb,' in *Proceedings*, vol. 72, no. 10 (October 1946), pp. 1268, 1270; W. S. Parsons, 'Atomic Energy – Whither Bound?' in *Proceedings* vol. 73, no. 8 (August 1947), p. 905; H. B. Seim, 'Atomic Bomb, the X-Factor of Military Policy,' in *Proceedings*, vol. 75, no. 4 (April 1949), p. 393.

29. Walmer Elton Strope, 'The Navy and the Atomic Bomb,' in *Proceedings*, vol. 73, no. 10 (October 1947), p 1222; Cranwell, p. 1267.

30. C. C. Hughes Hallett, 'Naval Logistics in a Future War,' in *RUSI* vol. xcv, no. 578 (May 1950), p. 235.

31. Hezlet, *Submarine*, p. 241.

32. 'New Missiles,' in *RUSI*, vol. xcii, no. 566 (May 1947), p. 248; Robert E. Cushman, 'Amphibious Warfare: Naval Weapon of the Future,' in *Proceedings*, vol. 74, no. 3 (March 1948), p. 305.

33. Frank R. Uhlig, Jr., 'The New Battle Cruisers,' in *Proceedings*, vol. 75, no. 1 (January 1949), pp. 33–7.

34. Pratt, p. 2.

35. Ibid., p. 6.

36. Ibid., p. 9; and Eller, p. 1166. It is interesting that in his *Sea Power of the State*, Gorshkov made a similar argument. He discussed this in terms of the sophistication of naval power, in that it represented the potential vice the actual application of military power. Gorshkov argued that through such sophisticated applications, navies could achieve Soviet goals in crisis situations without firing a shot. He believed that this was not possible with the deployment of troops into crisis arenas.

37. Smith, 'Naval Future', p. 494; and Pratt, p. 10.

38. Ryan, p. 8: 'Navy Notes,' in *RUSI*, vol. xciii, no. 569 (February 1948), p. 151; 'International Situation,' in *RUSI*, vol. xciv, no. 575 (August 1949), p. 460; and (November 1950), p. 612. See

also: Stephen G. Xydis, 'The Genesis of the Sixth Fleet,' in *Proceedings*, vol. 84, no. 8 (August 1958), p. 41–50.

39. Ryan pp. 8–9; and Hugh H. Goodwin, 'The Significance of Japan's Collapse As a World Power,' in *Proceedings*, vol. 73, no. 12 (December 1947), p. 1443. The US Navy was unopposed as it contained communism by ruling the seas.

40. US Department of the Navy, *Annual Report of the Secretary of the Navy for the Fiscal Year 1946* (Washington, DC: GPO, 1947), pp. iii, 2.

41. US Department of the Navy. *Annual Report of the Secretary of the Navy for the Fiscal Year 1947*, (Washington, DC: GPO, 1948), pp. 1–2, 3, 4, 10, 12.

42. 'The price of a ship in 1939 only covers a fraction of the cost today.' US Department of the Navy, *Annual Report of the Secretary of the Navy for the Fiscal Year 1948* (Washington, DC: GPO, 1949, pp. iii, 2.) The Secretary of Defense took office as head of National Military Establishment on 17 September 1947, and the National Security Act of 26 July 1947 took effect on 18 September. Unification dominated naval affairs during the year (p. 1).

43. Ibid., pp. 3, 12, 34, 38, 39.

44. Ibid., pp. 212–3, 220. Wainwright claims that modern advances make the mine almost unsweepable and were best used to bottle-up enemy forces, particularly submarines. See: R. C. P. Wainwright, 'Changes in Naval Warfare Owing to New and Modern Weapon', in *RUSI*, vol. xciii, no. 570 (May 1948), p. 192.

45. *Conway's All the World's Fighting Ships, 1947–1982, Part I: The Western Powers* ed R. Gardiner (hereinafter referred to as *Conway's Part I*) (Annapolis, MD: Naval Institute Press, 1985), p. 184.

46. Middleton, p. 115; and Hezlet, *Submarine*, pp. 243–4.

47. Wainwright, p. 189; Ryan, p. 11; 'Navy Notes,' in *RUSI*, vol. xcii, no. 565 (February 1947), p. 140; Malcolm W. Cagle, 'The Jets Are Coming,' in *Proceedings*, vol. 74, no. 11 (November 1948), pp. 1343, 1349.

48. 'Navy Notes,' in *RUSI*, vol. xciii, no. 570 (May 1948), p. 315; 'Professional Notes,' in *Proceedings*, vol. 74, no. 4 (April 1948), p. 504.

49. *Conway's, Part I*, pp. 200–1; 'Navy Notes,' in *RUSI*, vol. xciii, no. 572 (November 1948), p. 663; Professional Notes,' in *Proceedings*, vol. 75, no. 4 (April 1949), p. 485.

50. Labayle Couhat, pp. 721–2, 732; *Conway's, Part I*, p. 194; 'Navy Notes,' in *RUSI*, vol. xcii, no. 565 (February 1947), p. 141; and (November 1948), p. 663; (February 1948), p. 151; and (February 1949), p. 132; 'Professional Notes,' in *Proceedings*, vol. 74, no. 10 (October 1948), p. 1438; Wainwright, p. 191.

51. C. R. Brown, 'The Principles of War,' in *Proceedings*, vol. 75, no. 6 (June 1949), p. 625.

52. Ryan, p. 13.

53. Guy Richards, 'The Riddle of Combined Arms: 1949,' in *Proceedings*, vol. 75, no. 8 (August 1949), no. 882, 888–9.

54. Cushman, pp. 302, 304–7.

55. Ryan, p. 11; 'Navy Notes,' in *RUSI*, vol. xciv, no. 575 (August 1949), p. 481.

56. *Second Report of the Secretary of Defense*, pp. 9, 220–1. For additional discussion on the incident, see: George Quester, ed., *Sea Power in the 1970s* (New York: Dunellen, 1975).

57. Ibid., pp. 205, 220–1; 'Navy Notes,' in *RUSI*, vol. xciv, no. 575 (August 1949), p. 481; February 1950), p. 144; and (May 1950), p. 328.

58. Labayle Couhat, p. 704: 'Navy Notes,' in *RUSI*, vol. xciv, no. 575 (August 1949), p. 481; and (May 1950), p. 328; *Second Report of the Secretary of Defense*, pp. 219–20; M. J. Manesergh, 'Naval Aviation,' in *RUSI*, vol, xcv, no. 580 (November 1950), p. 571.

59. 'Navy Notes,' in *RUSI*, vol. xciv, no. 575 (August 1949), p. 481; (November 1949), p. 671; and (August 1950), pp. 520–1.

60. Ibid., pp. 268–9.

61. Ibid. (May 1947), p. 293; and (May 1948), p. 310.

62. H. E. Felser Paine, 'An Indian Ocean Pact,' in *RUSI*, vol. xcv, no. 577 (February 1950), pp 72–3.

63. 'Navy Notes,' in *RUSI*, vol. xcii, no. 566 (May 1947), p. 293; and *Proceedings*, vol. 74, no. 3 (March 1948), pp. 377–8. It is true, for example, that there were increases. The Navy Estimates for 1950–51, presented to Parliament on 9 March 1950, were for 193 million pounds, 3.7 million pounds more than 1949–50. However, when these estimates were presented, it was noted that the increase was due to higher prices, pay increases, replacement of depleted stocks, and other administrative expenses. The number of people in naval service was to be reduced from 140,000 to 127,500. Also noteworthy was the great emphasis placed on ASW. The estimates placed the strength of fleet at one fleet carrier, four light carriers, fourteen cruisers, 34 destroyers, 27 frigates, 32 submarines, and ten minesweepers. Also of significance was the fact that, while the estimates claimed that ongoing construction included two light carriers, seven light fleet cruisers, three cruisers, and eight destroyers, work on three cruisers had been suspended, and other work was proceeding very slowly. 'Navy Notes', in *RUSI*, vol. xcv, no. 578 (May 1950), p. 323.

64. 'International Situation,' in *RUSI*, vol. xci, no. 561 (February 1946), pp. 121–2; and (May 1949), pp. 273–6. A further indication of both British and Allied resolve occurred in June and July 1949, when Great Britain, France, the Netherlands, and Belgium conducted exercises in the Straits of Dover, English Channel, and Bay of Biscay. The exercises included cross-Channel convoy operations, minesweeping exercises, bombardment, and air defense maneuvers. Nearly 50 warships and auxiliaries, including five carriers from France and Great Britain, participated. ('Western Union Naval Exercises, 1949,' in *RUSI*, vol. xciv, no. 575 (August 1949), pp. 430–3.)

65. D. Trimingham, 'The Composition and Design of Our Post-War Fleet,' in *RUSI*, vol. xci, no. 561 (February 1946), pp. 73, 76.

66. P. D. H. R. Pelly, 'The Pattern of a Future War,' in *RUSI*, vol. xcv, no. 578 (May 1950), pp. 222–4.

67. Hezlet, *Submarine*, p. 242.

68. Ibid.; and *Conway's, Part I*, p. 127.

69. Hezlet, p. 243.

70. *Conway's, Part I*, p. 127.

71. Ibid., pp. 142–6; and Labayle Couhat, p. 204.

72. Ibid., pp. 150, 152; 'Navy Notes,' in *RUSI*, vol. xciv, no. 570 (May 1949), p. 297; (November 1949), p. 665; (August 1950), p. 516; (November 1950), p. 632; and (February 1950), p. 140.

73. Vice-Admiral Sir Arthur Hezlet, *Electronics and Sea Power* (New York: Stein and Day, 1975), p. 268.

74. 'Navy Notes,' in *RUSI*, vol. xcii, no. 565 (February 1947), p. 140.

75. Ibid., (February 1947), p. 140; (November 1947), p. 614; (November 1948), p. 662; (August 1948), p. 483; (August 1949), p. 480; (August 1950), p. 520; and (November 1950), p. 636; and 'Western Union Naval Exercises,' pp. 430–3.

76. 'Navy Notes,' in *RUSI*, vol. xcii, no. 565 (February 1947), p. 140.

77. Ibid. (February 1950), p. 143; and (May 1950), p. 327; *Conway's, Part I*, pp. 1, 12, 78, 92; *Conway's, Part II*, p. 377.

78. Ibid. (May 1948), p. 315; (February 1949), p. 131; and (November 1949), p. 671.

79. Ibid. (May 1948), p. 315; (November 1949), p. 671: (November 1947), p. 614; and (August 1949), pp. 480–1, *Conway's, Part I*, pp. 53, 102, 107, 119; and 'Professional Notes: United States Navy plans for 1949,' in *Proceedings*, vol. 74, no. 3 (March 1948), pp. 384–5.

80. *Conway's, Part I*, pp. 5, 7.

81. Ibid. (May 1949), p. 297; and (February 1947), p. 140; and *Conway's, Part II*, pp. 393, 401–3, 407.

82. *Conway's, Part II*, pp. 338–9, 353; and 'Navy Notes,' (August 1948), p 483; (February 1948), p. 150; (November 1948), p. 661; (August 1949), p. 480; (November 1949), pp 669–70; (November 1950), p. 635; and (February 1950), p. 143.

83. *Conway's, Part II*, pp. 326–9; and 'Navy Notes,' (November 1947), 614; (May 1948), p. 315; and (May 1949), p. 297.

84. *Conway's, Part I*, pp. 273–6, 281–2, and 'Navy Notes,' (May 1948), pp. 314–15; (August 1948), pp. 482–3; (November 1948); pp. 660–1; (February 1949), p. 130; (May 1949), p. 300; (February 1950), pp. 142–3; (August 1950), p. 519; and (November 1950), p. 635.

2
The Sides are Drawn, 1950–6

THE EFFECTS OF THE INFLUENCING FACTORS

Political Events

In many ways, the interaction of the five influencing factors made the period from 1950 to 1956 the most significant one in post-war naval development. Concerning political factors, from 1950 to 1953, the Soviet Union remained under Stalin's influence, still believing that Western aggression was a real danger. It protected itself from this by continuing to encourage the exaggeration of its naval expansion, thereby inflating the threat that it posed against the West, and by encouraging conflicts such as the Korean War that would direct Western attention away from the Soviet Union.

For the West, the Korean War was a turning-point for two reasons. First, it elevated the communist threat to that of a clear and present danger, prompting the reversal of the disarmament that had been taking place from 1945 to 1950. Second, in the United States, it demonstrated the importance of sea power, negated the arguments of Stuart Simington and others that naval power had seen its day, and prompted such a reversal of the existing American shipbuilding policy that the early 1950s would see a renaissance in US shipbuilding.

Stalin's death in 1953 would usher in a re-evaluation of existing Soviet policies. The result, the policy of peaceful coexistence, would be in total accord with the views Lenin expressed in 1920. It would view the Second World War as a phenomenon that had resolved temporarily those animosities– *Germany versus Europe*, *America versus Europe*, and *America versus Japan*– that had dominated international affairs before 1939. It would also see that the same war had brought Lenin's two remaining animosities–*the emerging nations versus their colonial masters*, and *capitalism versus communism (the United States versus the Soviet Union)*–into such vivid relief that they were the major themes in post-war international affairs. Both themes would convince Moscow that it needed a modern navy, which it began creating in 1956.

Technological Progress and the Importance of the Seas

Because of the technological progress that was developing, the period from 1950 to 1956 stands as the most significant period in post-war naval development. All the major problems concerning aircraft carriers and submarine nuclear propulsion systems were solved, thus assuring that these would remain as the two most important naval systems of the post-war era. Likewise, the advances that the US Navy made in these two systems would assure it decisive naval superiority for the next decade.

Naval Activity

The Western naval operations that were conducted during the Korean War were so effective that they not only reversed the decline in US naval power that had been taking place from 1945 to 1950, but so impressed the Eisenhower administration of sea power's importance that it would support a major shipbuilding program built around aircraft carriers and nuclear-powered submarines. Related to this changing perception of the value of sea power was an increased awareness of the importance of the seas. Eisenhower realized the sophistication of sea power, in that, unlike land-based power, it could be detailed to crises arenas without making hostilities a certainty and that, through the potential use of naval power, US policy objectives could be achieved. Admiral Sergei Gorshkov would make a similar case in the 1970s when he argued for his Soviet Navy, but Eisenhower realized it by 1952, and would use the Navy as a major foreign policy instrument throughout his tenure as President. Indeed, while the US responses to Suez in 1956 and Lebanon in 1958 were the high points of such use, before 1956, the Sixth Fleet had become the policeman of the Mediterranean. Eisenhower had detailed US naval power so often to crisis arenas 'to protect US lives and property' – code-words that were used to sell the use of naval power to uphold US interests in a shrewd policy of realpolitik–that such announcements became commonplace national news. And Eisenhower's use of such naval power was astute and effective, especially when one considers that his two major fiascos, Hungary and the U-2 incident, were among the few times that he could not use US naval power in crisis situations.

From 1950 to 1953, Soviet naval operations were limited to coastal naval activity and some sorties out into the nation's maritime approaches. The distribution of available power remained weighted toward the Baltic Fleet to defend it against any Western forces that attempted to attack the nation's major industrial centers, located in that region. These conformed to Stalin's concept of sea power usage and contributed to the Western impression of expanding Soviet naval power.

After Stalin's death in 1953, there was a re-evaluation of naval strategy. As part of the decision to build a new navy that not only would defend the nation, but also would protect Soviet foreign policy initiatives under Khrushchev's policy of peaceful coexistence, it was realized that concentrating sea power in the Baltic was undesirable. This was true because, although such a concentration was excellent for defense, the same area was a poor location for offensive operations. Deploying ships had to transit along the German, Danish, and Norwegian coasts where they were subject to scrutiny in peacetime and to potential attack in wartime, and then were very vulnerable as they passed through the very narrow Baltic approaches. Thus, Soviet naval power was shifted to the Northern Fleet where, although deployed submarines were vulnerable to detection as they passed southward through the Norwegian

1. The battleship USS *New Jersey* (BB 62), still going strong after four decades of service, leads her task group in the Pacific Ocean. She saw action during the First World War and the Korean War, was reactivated in April 1968 for duty off Vietnam, decommissioned again in December 1969 before becoming operational in December 1982 after a $326 million modernization that included Tomahawk and Harpoon missiles, and modern communications and engineering equipment. Since that time, her operations have taken her to the Pacific Ocean and the Caribbean Sea, and then off Lebanon as part of the US naval response.

2. The battleship USS *Missouri* (BB 63) aboard which the Japanese formally surrendered at the end of the Second World War. She was the third ship in a program that involved modernizing and recommissioning four *Iowa*-class battleships. An explosion in one of the turrets aboard *Iowa* in April 1989 killed 47 men and prompted many to ask whether these ships were simply too old for further service. Nevertheless, they have provided excellent shore bombardment and have served in autonomous battle groups, augmenting carrier forces by carrying out independent missions.

I

2

3. The *Forrest Sherman* class destroyer USS *Barry* (DD 933) is seen under way. The *Forrest Sherman*s comprised the only post-Second World War US general-purpose gun-armed destroyers. A re-evaluation of US combatant shipbuilding in the 1950s resulted in terminating this class at eighteen ships in favour of the missile-armed *Charles F. Adams* class. *Barry*, completed in 1956, was later modified to a test ship for the bow-mounted SQS-23 sonar.

4. USS *Skate* (SSN 578), lead ship of her class, is seen under way on the surface. This class was the first US attempt at a production model of nuclear-powered submarine. Smaller than *Nautilus* and with about half her power, they were about the size of the earlier *Tang* class. Production was discontinued in favour of the much faster *Skipjack* class.

5. This Polaris A-3 missile, seen emerging from its underwater launch, and others like it, had a 2,500 nautical mile range. The fact that it could travel 1,000 miles further than the Polaris A-2 meant that Polaris patrols could now be conducted in the Pacific and also complicated vastly the Soviet ASW problem. The success of the SSBN program prompted a major investment in these submarines, diverting funds from other naval development.

6. The *Charles F. Adams*-class guided-missile destroyer USS *Henry B. Wilson* (DDG-7) is seen under way. The *Adams* class was originally designed as a modified version of the *Forrest Sherman*-class destroyer, but the sonar, weapons and electronics were such that the ship had to be lengthened and considerably redesigned. Further production was terminated in favour of a newer design to accommodate the expected Typhon missile system.

7. USS *Enterprise* (CVN 65), in service in November 1961, was the world's first nuclear-powered aircraft carrier. An extensive refit in the late 1980s and periodic overhauls have assured that *Enterprise* is equipped with the latest electronics and weapons.

8. The USS *Long Beach* (CGN 9) is shown conducting operations off Catalina Island, California. She was the first US surface combatant to have nuclear power, and was originally intended to carry Regulus, then Polaris missiles. *Long Beach* has extensive flag facilities and her weapons suite has been modernized to include Tomahawk and Harpoon SSMs and the Mk 15 Vulcan/Phalanx CIWS.

9. The *Iwo Jima*-class amphibious assault helicopter carrier USS *New Orleans* (LPH 11) is seen anchored off Vietnam during the closing days of the war. Their greatest drawback was that they could not operate landing craft, and therefore could not attack or support troops on the beach in rough weather. The ships represented a culmination of the Marine Corps' development of vertical assault. Their troop spaces could accommodate 2,000 troops and they had excellent medical facilities.

10. USS *Bainbridge* (CGN 25), laid down in 1959 and in service in 1962, was intended as a nuclear-powered frigate (DLGN) and was built as a prototype escort. She was subsequently redesignated as a cruiser and the nuclear-powered surface combatant program moved on to *Truxun* (CGN 35) and then to larger ships. Her AAW suite was improved markedly during a refit and modernization that was completed in 1977, and even more significant improvements, to include improved fire control, sonar, electronics and the addition of two Mk 15 Vulcan/Phalanx 20mm AA CIWS, were made during a refit that was completed in 1985.

11. Two Terrier surface-to-air missiles are seen on the aft launcher of the USS *Leahy* (CG 16). *Leahy* was subsequently overhauled and currently is armed with Harpoon SSMs, the 20mm Mk 15 CIWS, ASROC and torpedoes.

11

12. These three *Skoryy*-class destroyers are seen while visiting Portsmouth in October 1955. Seventy-two *Skorrys* were built from 1950 to 1953, and twelve were still active in 1983. Six were converted to a Modified-*Skoryy* configuration, involving modifying the weapons suite, but there was no general conversion or modernization of the entire class. The *Skoryy* destroyers were a successful design and were deployed often to the Mediterranean Fleet in the 1960s and early 1970s. Some of the units were transferred to Egypt, Indonesia, and Poland.

13. The successor to *Skoryy*, the highly successful *Kotlin* class, built from 1953 to 1957, was the last conventional destroyer class to be built by the Soviet Navy. Note the raked bow, flush deck, and the pronounced forward sheer. Four were completed with surface-to-surface missiles as the *Kildin* class. Concerning armament, compared to *Skoryy*, the *Kotlins* had a true dual-purpose capability. In the 1960s and 1970s, eight *Kotlins* were converted to SAM-*Kotlins*, and another eleven were modified. Like the *Skoryys*, the *Kotlins* were used as general-purpose destroyers and were deployed extensively in the 1960s and early 1970s for duty with the Mediterranean Fleet.

13

14. Of the 24 of these *Sverdlov* cruisers that were ordered in Stalin's post-war building program, fourteen were completed. Huge, gun-armed cruisers, they were part of a Stalinist fleet of heavy surface combatants that were inappropriate for the changing naval scene of the post-war years. By 1961, *Dzerzhinskiy* had been converted to an experimental missile cruiser, being equipped with the Army's SA-2 surface-to-air missile. Two other *Sverdlov*s, *Admiral Senyavin* and *Zhdanov*, were given extensive electronics suites and converted to command cruisers in 1972, and modifications were made to other units as they were overhauled in the 1970s.

15. Five of these *Echo I* nuclear-powered cruise-missile submarines were built from 1960 to 1962. Equipped with the SS-N-3 missile, they could not accommodate the requisite mid-course command guidance radar and they were later converted to attack submarines from 1970 to 1975. One had an accident in the Pacific in August 1980 in which several of the crew perished.

16. The *Kynda*-class cruisers that were built from 1959 to 1965 provided the Soviet Navy with its first blue-water anti-carrier capability. Each was equipped with a pair of quadruple trainable SS-N-3 launchers. The *Kynda* also had a helo pad for the Ka-25 Hormone helicopter, which could be launched to provide mid-range over-the-horizon guidance for the missiles she fired. *Kynda* was used heavily in the Mediterranean in the 1960s and 1970s as a component of the Soviet anti-carrier task group.

17. The *Kresta I* and *Kresta II* were direct descendants of the *Kynda* guided-missile cruisers. *Kresta I* was armed with four, rather than eight, SS-N-3 missiles that were carried in fixed-train elevating tubes under the bridge, SA-N-1 missile launchers forward and aft, and a Hormone helicopter. *Kresta II*'s armament and configuration emphasized anti-submarine warfare (ASW), with her bow sonar and eight SS-N-14 ASROC-like missiles in place of the SS-N-3 system on *Kresta I*. Like *Kynda*, *Kresta I* was often used as a component of Soviet anti-carrier task groups. The ten *Kresta II*s were used as important components of Soviet ASW forces.

18. The *Centaur*-class aircraft carrier HMS *Bulwark* (R 08) was one of a class of eight that were planned. Four were actually built, but the fourth was so different that she amounted to a separate class. Almost as soon as they were completed the ships were modified with angled decks. After the Suez Crisis of 1956, they were given steam catapults and stronger arrester-wires. The class proved to be too small for the aircraft coming on line, and *Bulwark* was converted to a commando carrier by removing the catapults and arrester gear, and by providing helicopters and landing craft.

19. HMS *Dainty* (D 108), a *Daring*-class destroyer of the immediate post-war period, was one of an eight-ship class. These ships were manned as light cruisers. Beginning in 1963, the class was modernized, which involved removing the torpedo tubes and upgrading the electronics and sensors. Subsequently, when they became too small for more modern weapons and

sensors, several were transferred or sold abroad, while *Dainty* and three others were retired.

20. *Hermes*-class fleet carrier HMS *Hermes* (R 12) was radically redesigned during the period when the *Centaur*-class aircraft carriers were being built, and when she was built she was significantly different from the three *Centaurs*. She had a 6.5° angled deck, a side lift, an enlarged superstructure, reduced armament and improved electronics. Her main difficulty was that when she was commissioned in 1959 she could only operate 28 aircraft, and later could not operate the new F-4K Phantom which replaced the Sea Vixen. In 1971 she became a commando carrier and in 1977, an ASW carrier. Subsequently she was converted to operate a squadron of Sea Harrier STOVL aircraft, and she was the flagship for the Falklands Task Force in April–June 1982. She was stricken in 1985, was transferred to India, and was commissioned as *Viraat* in May 1987.

19

21. The nuclear-attack submarine, HMS *Valiant* (S 102), entered service in July 1966 as the lead unit of a five-unit class. Her diving depth is 300 metres, and she is armed with six 533mm torpedo tubes that can also fire Harpoon.

22. The ballistic-missile submarine HMS *Resolution* (S 22), lead unit of a four-unit class, entered service in October 1967. Her propulsion, navigation, and launching and guidance systems characteristics are very similar to the US *Lafayette* class. Each carried sixteen US Polaris A3TK missiles with six Cheveline MRV warheads of British design.

23. This *County*-class guided-missile destroyer, HMS *Fife* (D 20), entered service in June 1966. The *County* class had major innovations. Together with the *Tribal* class, they were the first British ships to have the combined steam and gas turbine (COSAG) propulsion system, and were of the first design to have provision for a helicopter. *Fife* and the other three later ships of the 8-ship class were given Exocet missile systems.

22

23

24

24. The guided-missile cruiser *Colbert* (C 611) entered service as a cruiser in 1959. She was converted to a SAM cruiser in the early 1970s. The excellent command facilities were enhanced in the 1970s, and Exocet SSMs were installed in 1980. She is also armed with SAMs and AA guns. She currently serves as the flagship of the French Mediterranean Squadron and is scheduled for disposal in 1997.

25. The *Surcouf* (T 47) class anti-aircraft destroyer *Cassard* (D 623) was third in a class of twelve ships that were clearly in a line of succession to French pre-war construction and were intended to protect the new carriers. Initially little attention was given to ASW, but four triple banks of torpedo tubes were added to the design. *Cassard* was retired in 1976.

25

26. The aircraft carrier *Clemenceau* (R 98), lead ship of a two-ship class, entered service in November 1961. These angled-deck carriers can carry 36 aircraft and two helicopters. With a reinforced flight deck and bridge superstructure and armored spaces, she and her sister, *Foch* (R 99), are very much in the European aircraft carrier design tradition. *Clemenceau* is nearing the end of her service life and the French Navy intends to replace her with *Charles de Gaulle* (R 91).

27. The *Köln*- (Type 120) class guided-missile frigate *Karlsruhe* (F 223) of a six-ship class, was launched in October 1959, and was transferred to Turkey in December 1982. She is currently the Turkish frigate *Gelibolu* (D 360), and serves in the Turkish Navy with her sister, *Gemlik* (D 361), the ex-*Emden* (F 221). These ships are armed with dual-purpose and AA guns, ASW torpedoes and an ASW rocket-launcher, and can carry up to 82 mines.

27

28

28. The *Albatros*-class corvette, *Alcione* (F 544) entered service in October 1955. Five others went to Denmark and the Netherlands. However, the Dutch returned their single unit in 1961, and she was renamed *Aquila*. The original armament was replaced with newer equipment in 1963, but even when they were first built they were too slow for hunting submarines, and were used primarily as fishery protection vessels. *Albatros* was decommissioned in April 1986.

29. The guided-missile destroyer *Impavido* (D 570) was completed in 1963. Slightly larger than the *Impetuoso* class, she carried newer AA gun armament and a single Tartar SAM launcher. Both *Impavido* and *Intrepido* (D 571) were modernized in the mid-1970s, and received SM-1 standard missiles for the Mk 13 SAM launcher in place of Tartar. They are to be replaced by the *Animoso*-class destroyers.

29

Sea and then through the Greenland–Iceland–United Kingdom (GIUK) gaps, they enjoyed greater security than in the Baltic. This shift was reported by Norway, and contributed further to Western uneasiness concerning Soviet naval expansion.

Traditional Theories of Sea Power

While the theories themselves were not stressed in the 1950s, the Western use of sea power conformed to Mahan's postulations. The importance of the sea lanes through the North Atlantic and the threat that the Soviet submarine fleet posed against them were recognized, and a substantial naval effort was made to improve the Western ASW capability in that region. Likewise, in the Pacific, the Korean War demonstrated the effectiveness of US naval power in influencing regional affairs and the United States would continue to use its Seventh Fleet to exert its influence in the region.

Thus, the post-war Western sea power reductions were stopped after June 1950, as the West reacted to the outbreak of the Korean War. During the next six years, the world's major sea powers discerned that the Soviet–American superpower rivalry was spreading to the seas and each adjusted its sea power accordingly. The threats were evaluated, the responses were significant, and the results were both dynamic and restrictive; dynamic because that rivalry prompted a great deal of naval development, and restrictive because each side developed its naval power to counter the threat it perceived from the other.

THE KOREAN WAR

By 1950, Europe had settled firmly into the Eastern and Western camps as the cold war was continued. In the East, the Soviet Union continued to develop its military power, and in the West, the Marshall Plan and NATO brought the European nations out of ruin and together in order to face the perceived communist threat. Soviet policy continued to attempt to magnify the threat it posed against the West and to attempt to direct attention away from Europe. Donald Treadgold avers that, based on the evidence, the North Korean invasion in June 1950 was carried out with Moscow's concurrence.[1] If that were so, the motive might have been to embroil the West in the conflict in order to preoccupy it, thereby giving Moscow additional time to strengthen her defenses. Whether this was in fact the case and how much influence Moscow exerted both remain undetermined. One thing is certain, however, – the war did preoccupy the West for three years and the Soviet military was strengthened considerably during that time.

Soviet troops had been withdrawn from Korea by December 1948 and the last 500 US troops left in July 1949, but the Soviets had armed the North Koreans, who had 90,000 troops, 180 tanks, and 175 aircraft on 25 June 1950, the day they invaded South Korea. Initially successful, they soon reached the River Han and took Seoul. By August, North Korean forces had captured all but the peninsula's south–eastern corner. The South Korean capital had been moved to Taegu and UN forces managed to hold Pusan. On 15 September, a counter-offensive was begun, when more than 260 ships took part in the landing at Inchon. From here, the main thrust was at Seoul, while other forces broke out of the Taegu perimeter to form a pincer movement. By October, the US Army was operating under two independent commands, with Major General Walker and the US Eighth Army on the west, and Major General Almond and the US X Corps on the east, and overall command was exercised by General MacArthur from Tokyo. In December when Walker was killed in a jeep accident in Seoul, Lieutenant General Matthew Ridgway was ordered to Korea to take command of all forces, and on 11 April 1951, when MacArthur was relieved by President Truman, Ridgway went to Tokyo to be replaced by Lieutenant General Van Fleet in Korea.[2]

Overall naval command was exercised by Commander Naval Forces Far East (COMNAVFE), VADM Joy, US Navy, headquartered in Tokyo. Under him were four task forces that were generally distributed so that the US Navy operated on Korea's eastern coast and the other navies operated on the western coast under British control. This arrangement was not rigid and units were detailed to either coast as they were needed.

COMNAVFE assumed operational control of the Seventh Fleet and additional US ships were sent to Korea. A cruiser, four destroyers, and two transports with Marines were sent from the Mediterranean, and the *Missouri*, a carrier, eight destroyers, a destroyer tender, transports, and various small ships were detailed from the Atlantic. Canadian, Australian, New Zealander, Dutch, French, and South Korean naval ships were also provided to the UN force. This response was extremely prompt, and in the first year alone, the US Navy and Marine Corps flew about 70,000 combat sorties, 44,000 of which were from carriers, while 23,000 were from shore bases. The United States fought a major conflict. At war's end, 54,000 Americans had been killed, another 103,000 had been wounded, and $20 billion had been spent. While the US Navy accomplished the bulk of the war's naval operations, the British effort was considerably more substantial than is often reported. Admiral Scott-Moncrieff, Royal Navy, commanded the British Far Eastern Fleet, consisting of two carriers, two cruisers, eight destroyers, eight frigates, and auxiliaries, from April 1951 to September 1952. There were also Commonwealth forces, including three destroyers from Canada, two from Australia, and, for part of the time, a carrier and a destroyer from New Zealand. He also controlled a US carrier, several US destroyers, and rocket, tank landing, and mining ships, a Dutch destroyer, and several South Korean naval units. His primary duty was to enforce a blockade. On the east coast, US carrier-based aircraft provided direct support to the Army, while *Missouri*'s 16in guns were used in direct support of the Army's front line, with great effectiveness. Such operations were more difficult from the west coast, because of the great coastal tidal variations. However, effective aerial bombardment by carrier-based aircraft, first from *Triumph* and subsequently from *Theseus* and other ships, and close air support to ground troops was provided continually. Additional missions included island warfare, combined air and gun strikes, minesweeping, shore bombardment, and mine-clearing operations.[3]

The British effort was substantial in the face of strong combat threats. In August 1953, HMS *Mounts Bay* was the twelfth British ship to be hit by shore battery fire in a nine-month period. The intensity of British operations was also notable. For example, by September 1952, HMS *Belfast* had steamed more than 80,000 miles, fired 8,000 6in shells, and spent 404 days at sea. In November 1952, HMS *Ocean* could boast that she had conducted 123 sorties in one day (the record for Commonwealth carriers), averaged 76 sorties daily for a total of 79 flying days, had used 420 1,000lb bombs, 3,454 500lb bombs, and 1,500,000 rounds of 20mm ammunition, destroying a host of enemy targets, including 196 bridges and 69 gun positions and killing more than 1,000 of the enemy.[4]

The war also demonstrated the value of amphibious warfare forces. The landing at Inchon stands among the greatest amphibious operations in history and vividly demonstrated that amphibious warfare had become more, not less, important, given the international climate. Additionally, it validated all that Lieutenant Colonel Robert Cushman had argued concerning the link between amphibious operations and base acquisition.[5]

THE UNITED STATES

The war had several effects on American naval development. It reversed the previous naval reduction and it spawned naval growth because it validated the Navy's views concerning the value of force projection, carrier task forces, and amphibious warfare in the post-war nuclear era. Its assertions about the value of sea power as the ideal power projection force and the value of overseas naval bases were also proven. The result was that the American leadership candidly admitted that many of its defense and disarmament policies had been incorrect and a resurgence in US naval development began.

Naval Strategy
Traditional Themes On the eve of the Korean War, naval strategists continued to espouse the traditional themes, as they tried to determine the atomic bomb's significance to warfare, with inconclusive results.[6] The Soviet submarine force was often discussed and the consensus remained that, although the number of submarines could not be determined precisely, enough were being built to pose a significant danger and that carrier task forces were the ideal means of countering them. There was a greater realization of the Navy's relevance to a variety of cold war scenarios.[7] The dispute with the other military branches continued, as well as naval arguments against the integration of the armed forces, as the Navy waged a rearguard action against a *fait accompli*.[8] The defense against air power advocates continued, noting that it was too restrictive, and that only naval power would provide the flexibility necessary to win many types of wars. Concerning Europe, sea power proponents believed that the Mediterranean's importance in the cold war was not fully realized and that this might be the place where the next war would begin. The Navy continued to formulate its justification for its Sixth Fleet operations and, by 1951, it was generally accepted that the fleet's purposes were to keep the Soviet Union out of the Mediterranean, bolster national free will, train crews in Mediterranean conditions, deter aggression, and help the Mediterranean

states develop their naval power. Elsewhere, the Navy believed that the Pacific Ocean's importance to US security was underrated as it tried to determine how best to influence the region. Some believed that British sea power and a wise British policy traditionally had been effective and that with its advanced sea power, the United States also could control the area *if* it pursued an enlightened foreign policy. Most agreed that the United States was not adequately protecting its Pacific frontier and many called for the strengthening of Formosa and Guam. It was generally agreed that, while the Soviet Union was a presence in Northeast Asia, Soviet transportation and logistical systems to the Far East were very meager and that US sea and air superiority gave America an advantage. This would not change because any shift of Soviet forces to Asia would reduce her strength in Europe and therefore would not occur.[9]

US Naval Operations, 1950-5 The war was not the only requirement on the US Navy and from 1950 to 1955 it responded to many incidents. From June to December 1950, there was a response to Lebanon and from March to December 1951, there was a reaction to Yugoslavia. By late 1951, the Sixth Fleet had been built up to between 60 and 70 ships, doubling its size of the previous year. In July 1953, the Navy conducted visits to Turkey as part of a policy to counter Soviet pressure on Ankara, and when the USSR exploded a nuclear weapon that year, a new role was seen for submarines as the Polaris program was begun. In May and June 1954, there was a response to the crisis in Guatemala and in July there were a series of incidents involving the People's Republic of China. These began when a British Cathay civilian aircraft was shot down, and continued on 7 July when Chinese planes attacked a US naval reconnaissance aircraft over Formosa Strait. It escaped without damage. On 26 July, two Red Chinese aircraft attacked a US Navy Skyraider and were shot down. Congress then passed the Formosa Resolution in January 1955, giving President Eisenhower power to defend Taiwan and, when the United States was asked to evacuate Chinese Nationalists from the Aachen Islands, which were then under attack, the Navy evacuated 24,000 people, 8,600 tons of equipment, 166 heavy guns, and 100 vehicles in 85 hours.[10]

The communists were also active in Vietnam. In 1950, President Truman approved $15 million in aid to the newly formed states of Vietnam, Laos, and Cambodia and, in March, USS *Stickell*, with Commander, US Seventh Fleet, VADM Russell S. Berkey, embarked, and USS *Anderson*, arrived in Saigon for a port visit, while 60 aircraft from USS *Boxer* flew over the city in a highly visible show of support. A plan to save the French at Dien Bien Phu never reached the operational stage, however, and on 7 May 1954, Viet Minh troops overwhelmed French forces. The Geneva Accords were subsequently signed on 20 July 1954, dividing Vietnam at the 17th parallel. When many Vietnamese in the north wanted to come southward, the Navy was called upon to assist and Operation 'Passage to Freedom', a ferry service, ran from the north to Saigon and other cities. The evacuation, begun on 16 August, involved 113 ships, evacuated 304,740 refugees, and tons of cargo and vehicles.[11]

The Effect of the War on the Themes As important as these other operations were, it was the Korean War that was the primary factor in reversing the US naval decline because it substantiated traditional naval theories and it broke America's preoccupation with Europe and NATO's defense. Now America would also consider events in the non-European world. This was particularly relevant in light of the fact that, beginning in 1956, the Soviet Union would pursue a policy of active involvement in the same region. Although the lines of these policies were not fully defined until much later, US perceptions of their importance began at this time. First to go was the push-button war and the attack on amphibious operations, since Inchon stood as one of history's greatest amphibious operations, representing a continuation of the great amphibious tradition of D-Day and the Pacific operations against Japan. Thus Korea, in demonstrating the error of the push-button war theory, was a defeat for air power advocates, as the Marines were now perceived to be as important as they had been in the past. Contemporary discussion also was centered on crisis management and Korea provided the necessary evidence for sea power advocates.[12] Inchon, thousands of carrier-based aircraft sorties, minesweeping, blockade, and shore bombardment missions, the Marine Corps' extremely impressive performance, and a host of other activities proved beyond a doubt the importance of sea power in general and the absolute necessity of the Marine Corps and the attack carriers in particular. Thus the war had a most positive effect on naval development and greatly influenced the types of systems that were created.

The Official Policy Position

The war's first effect was to reverse the naval reduction. The Navy's initial combat missions were to: provide transport and protect Americans being evacuated by sea; provide naval forces to assist in the war; prevent the possible invasion of Formosa by the Chinese communists; and enforce a blockade of the Korean coast. This role grew into complex, intense carrier and shore bombardment operations and the Navy was expanded so that it could fulfill these missions. Table 2.1 shows the Navy's growth from 1951 to 1956. By July 1951, the United States had successfully accomplished the first stages of rebuilding its navy and the mistakes of the post-war demobilization were being rectified. In the next year, three large *Midway*, and five *Essex* carriers were converted to carry heavier aircraft, eleven light and escort carriers were converted, and nine reserve destroyers and two reserve escorts were modernized. In 1951, the Secretary of Defense noted that 'communist aggression in Korea marked the beginning of a new policy for the United States,' and had triggered the rebuilding of the US Armed Forces. However, by 1954, the war's negative effects were also evident. The Navy's operating tempo had been horrendous, with obvious effects on its ships, and the Secretary of the Navy expressed concern over the fleet's increasing obsolescence, noting that it would cost much more to maintain it in the future. If such funds were not provided, the Navy would experience block obsolescence in which large numbers of aged ships would wear out at roughly the same time, thereby sorely depleting the inventory.[13] As the war ended and the United States maintained its defenses, there were slight reductions and the traditional theme of peacetime disarmament again began to gain favor. Believing that great reductions were imminent, the Navy fully developed the theme of the Soviet naval threat. Since this theme would dominate the Navy's budget defense for decades, it deserves close attention.

Table 2.1
Order of Battle – US Navy, 1951–6[a]

	Year					
	51	52	53	54	55	56
Strategic Missile Submarines	1	1	2	2	1	2
Submarines	83	104	108	108	108	108
Large Aircraft Carriers	17	19	19	20	21	22
Light and Escort Carriers	9	10	10	7	3	2
Battleships	3	4	4	4	3	3
Cruisers	15	19	19	18	17	16
Command Ships	0	0	0	0	0	1
Destroyers	206	243	247	247	249	250
Frigates	38	56	56	57	64	70
Mine Warfare	91	114	121	117	112	113
Patrol Vessels	40	29	23	22	15	11
Amphibious Vessels	208	189	226	223	175	139
Auxiliaries	269	309	287	288	262	236
Totals	634	980	1122	1113	1030	973

[a]US Department of the Navy, *US Navy Ship Force Levels, 1917–1989* (Washington, DC: Ships History Branch, Naval Historical Center, Department of the Navy, 1989), p. 5.

The Navy's reliance on the Soviet threat to defend its cause is a very complex and significant phenomenon because of the Navy's motives, its implementation, and its effects. In its first full public discussion of the threat in 1954, the Navy noted that: the Soviet Navy was expanding very rapidly; it had risen from seventh most powerful in the Second World War to third; the new Soviet ships were versatile and rugged; and minelaying was being stressed.[14] Its main weaknesses were that it was not a balanced fleet and that it lacked a sea-based air capability. In 1956, the threat was placed at 400 submarines, 24 cruisers, 100 destroyers, and 3,500 modern naval aircraft.[15] These views, in retrospect, were made from incomplete information about a largely unknown navy that was seen as the enemy at a time when the US Navy was facing cutbacks. It was also made about an evolving Soviet Navy that was using outdated construction concepts – one that was less than ideal for the post-war environment.

The argument inevitably maximized the Soviet naval threat, and its effects on subsequent US naval development cannot be overstated, since it tied the US Navy's cause to Soviet naval developments. Using the Soviet naval threat was so successful that the need for further justification was not necessary for decades. This meant that the US–Soviet naval relationship would be symbiotic because advances in one force would be used to justify advances in the other.

The result was significant sea power development, but inhibited, because it focused on the threat that each perceived from the other.

Secondly, the argument was so convincing that the Navy had little reason to scour its ranks further to justify its requests. The effects were most pronounced in the evolution of naval strategy within the Navy's ranks, which atrophied significantly after the retirement of Arleigh Burke, only to enjoy occasional brief revivals when individuals such as Elmo Zumwalt, John Lehman, and C. A. H. Trost rose to prominence. In essence, justifications were reduced to the all-important bean count, as the significance behind Soviet developments was examined only superficially. Thus the political purposes behind and the benefits enjoyed from the Soviet Navy were too seldom understood, because an awareness of such matters was unnecessary to a Navy that sold the Soviet threat so well.[16]

When this threat projection was mated with Mahan's concepts of force projection, the resulting emphasis was accorded priority in roughly the following order. The highest priorities were given to submarine and aircraft carrier development and ASW. Anti-air and electronic warfare, and command, control, and communications were also stressed, since these were vital to the submarine and carrier defenses. Much less attention was paid to amphibious warfare and non-force projection forces such as mine warfare ships, patrol craft, and other small ships.

Naval Construction, 1950-6

Submarines The post-war submarines were vastly superior to those of the Second World War with improvements that involved electronics, underwater endurance, habitability, and fighting capability. The most dramatic advances were in nuclear propulsion and in weapon systems. In propulsion, the submarine was unique to the extent that nuclear power vastly increased its range.[17] The second great advance was in missiles and nuclear warheads, because these made the submarine a strategic system that could attack and devastate land targets deep within enemy territory. While the submarine-launched missile was still in its earliest stages in the early 1950s, there were some who foresaw its future and saw that the first use of rocket-firing submarines in exercises in October 1949 marked the beginning of a new era.[18]

Since opposition to the Navy's nuclear submarine program had been less than that to its carrier program, it advanced rather smoothly. Under Admiral Rickover's guidance, progress came rapidly. On 21 August 1951, the Navy awarded the contract for the first nuclear-powered submarine to the Electric Boat Company, while Westinghouse received a contract for the propulsion machinery. Work proceeded so successfully that, in January 1952, Congress was asked to authorize a second nuclear-powered unit. On 14 June, the keel was laid for *Nautilus*, the first nuclear-powered submarine, and on 15 May 1953, the keel of *Sea Wolf*, the second nuclear submarine was laid, as *Nautilus* was almost completed. On 21 January 1954, *Nautilus* was launched. At 4,092 tons, her speed was expected to be about 23 knots, and she would be armed with six torpedo tubes. She was commissioned on 30 September, her nuclear reactor was operational on 30 December, and the propellers were turned for the first time on 5 January 1955. After completing her sea trials, she joined the fleet in April.[19] This was perhaps the greatest accomplishment of the entire post-war era and it made this period the era's most significant years. What many had said was impossible had been accomplished, nuclear power had been applied to the submarine, providing a submersible with virtually unlimited underwater endurance. It only remained to apply ICBMs, no mean problem, to produce the world's most protectable strategic missile system.

A strength of the submarine program was its imagination, and submarines were considered for a wide assortment of roles, including surveillance and as transports and tankers, and for other duties.[20] While most of these concepts were not accepted, the submarine did become a first-rate ASW weapon. In 1951 the Secretary of the Navy said that USS *Grouper (SSK 214)*, the first ASW submarine conversion, had been completed, killer submarines (SSKs) 1, 2, and 3, designed specifically for ASW, had been launched, and progress was being made toward the goal of 100 units. Work on USS *Grenadier* (SS 525), the first of a new class of fleet submarine, and on USS *Guavina* (SSO 362), the first unit to be converted to a tanker submarine, progressed. The Navy also tested *Tang*, an attack and killer submarine, and planned for five more boats. On 28 October, a 344-ship building and conversion program was begun to improve the submarine and ASW fleets.[21]

Even these impressive accomplishments paled when, in response to the perceived threat from the Soviet Navy, President Eisenhower, on 2 December 1955, announced that the United States would develop a reliable naval missile system quickly. The Chief of Naval Operations, Admiral Arleigh Burke, ordered Admiral William F. Rayborn to develop a fleet ballistic missile, giving him *carte blanche* to accomplish the assignment. With Edward Teller's help, Rayborn concentrated on the Polaris ballistic missile, which was 25 feet long, 5 feet in diameter, weighed 15 tons, and had a range of 1,500 nautical miles.[22]

Meanwhile, other naval programs that would impact on Polaris were progressing. The 7,773-ton *Triton*, a nuclear-powered radar picket submarine with a high surface speed, and *Halibut*, which carried several Regulus missiles but still had to surface to fire them, were laid down in 1956 and 1957. *Tullibee*, a nuclear-propelled killer submarine was begun. Nuclear power did not alter the roles of these submarines but drastically influenced their ability to fulfill them. Finally, an experimental unit, *Albacore*, was built. While her purpose was hydrodynamic research, she was significant because she proved the theory that a submarine with a short, fat, streamlined shape and a single screw offered the best speed. From then on, submarines were built to this form, resulting, for example, in considerable increases in speed in *Skipjack* and other classes.[23]

Aircraft Carriers The nadir of the Navy's aircraft carrier program was reached when Louis Johnson and Stuart Symington were successful in their effort to reduce the carrier force level to only seven large carriers in 1950. However, their value in the Korean War so impressed the Eisenhower administration that four *Forrestal*-class carriers and *Enterprise*, the first nuclear carrier, were commisioned between 1955 and 1961. Thus the Navy's carrier program thrived because of the war. On 26 July 1950, the Navy put nine more carriers and 39 other ships into service and, on 26 October, it announced that 17-ton AJ-1 attack bombers, which could carry atomic bombs, had landed on a carrier for the first time.[24] On 8 January 1951, the $2 billion naval bill which Carl Vinson, Chairman of the House Armed Services Committee, introduced into Congress included a new 60,000-ton carrier and the conversion of six *Essex* carriers. The carrier would take more than three years to build, but the conversions would be completed in two years.[25] In February, the escort carrier *Kula Gulf* was recommissioned, while *Hornet* was taken out of reserve. On 13 March, President Truman signed the $2 billion naval construction and conversion program bill. Meanwhile, as part of a $78 million ASW program, work progressed on five ASW carriers. On 28 June, the Navy took two *Essex* carriers out of reserve, on 12 July, it issued a contract for *Forrestal*, and on 21 August, it began converting four more *Essex* carriers.[26]

To provide a logistic network to support sea projection forces built around attack carrier task groups, the Navy moved quickly to gain access to forward bases around the world. On 20 August 1950, the base on Midway was reopened and in January 1951, the Navy decided to retain Yokuska. With its six drydocks, it would be a major repair facility. In October, an aircraft squadron was stationed at Malta to bolster the Mediterranean fleet and in 1952, Port Lyautey in North Africa was developed and then used in accordance with an agreement with France.[27]

The war had also demonstrated the helicopters' potential. For the first time, the Marines used them to move troops, which increased significantly the mobility of amphibious forces. In 1951, an automatic pilot was developed which allowed their use from carriers at night and in bad weather.[28]

Other research established the carrier as a strategic system, capable of delivering nuclear strikes on land-based enemy targets. On 25 October 1951, Secretary of the Navy Daniel Kimball said that the Sixth Fleet now had nuclear weapons and was capable of delivering them and, on 6 December, Admiral William M. Fechteler, the Chief of Naval Operations, stated that nuclear weapons could be delivered from anywhere on the seas to 600 miles inland, the radius of carrier-based aircraft.[29]

The operational experience of the war continued to influence the program. The fleet had used both propeller-driven and jet aircraft in Korea and had experimented with turbo-prop aircraft. Korea confirmed the need for stronger, better-equipped carriers to handle the new aircraft. Part of the problem was solved by converting Second World War carriers, but this was only a stop-gap until the *Forrestal* carriers were operational. In January 1952, the Navy announced plans to build a 60,000-ton aircraft carrier each year for ten years and hoped that the later ones would be nuclear-powered. On 29 April, it began adapting the British aircraft catapult to US ships, installing the first one on USS *Hancock*. By 31 July, a nuclear plant for large surface ships, such as aircraft carriers, had been ordered and, on 16 December, the keel was laid for *Saratoga*.[30]

In 1952, three new jet fighters were accepted, including two swept-wing models, and the Navy adopted the angled deck for its aircraft carriers. In 1953, new pilot ejection systems were developed. By January 1954, significant progress had been made: construction had continued on *Forrestal* and

Saratoga, and planning continued for *Ranger*. In 1954, the first conversion program of the *Essex* carriers, involving strengthened flight decks and larger elevators, was completed and two *Essex* carriers completed a second conversion program, involving catapults. A water washdown system had been perfected to protect ships from nuclear radiation. Four new aircraft were also developed. In 1955, *Forrestal* was completed and a fourth *Forrestal* carrier, *Independence*, was laid down. The program continued into 1956: *Forrestal* and *Saratoga* joined the fleet, two more carriers, *Kitty Hawk* and *Constellation* were laid down, and preparatory work for the first nuclear-powered carrier, *Enterprise*, was continued.[31] These accomplishments assured the US Navy of having the world's strongest sea projection capability for decades.

Major Surface Combatants Progress was made on other types of surface combatants in order to provide a balanced fleet. The greatest advances were in ASW and anti-air warfare. The 1951 naval bill provided for the building of 80 naval ships and the modernization of another 250. Included were two missile-armed ships, the conversion of two cruisers to missile-armed cruisers, and the provision of 194 destroyers with modern ASW equipment.[32]

Space had become a premium as electronics and weapon systems now required more room and the Navy developed a new type of ship, the frigate or destroyer leader. Smaller than a cruiser but larger than a destroyer, the destroyer leader was to provide a greater ASW capability. The initial class of the type, *Mitscher*, was a mixed success. Originally designed from 1944 to 1946, these 493-foot, 3,650-ton ships had extensive spaces for embarked flag officers. However, the operations spaces for the flag officer's staff were co-located with the ship's combat information center and were too small, often creating confusion between the flag's and ship's staffs. Also, she was provided with Weapon Alfa, an ASW rocket-launcher which was positioned just forward of the bridge. When fired, it emitted a horrendous blast of fire that certainly destroyed the night vision of the bridge watch and would singe the hair of those unlucky enough to be on the bridge wings. *Mitscher* was later modified with a hangar deck, but the development of DASH drone helicopters lagged, so that the helicopters deployed were often unreliable. Finally, the name was confusing, since traditionally, frigates were a ship type that was smaller, not larger, than a destroyer. Two of a four-ship class, *Mitscher* and her sister, *John S. McCain*, were commissioned in 1953 and served in the fleet for thirteen years. Following *Mitscher*'s 1965 Mediterranean tour, she and *McCain* were converted to guided missile destroyers and were recommissioned, while the two remaining ships of the class were decommissioned in 1969. The destroyer leader was eventually dropped as later guided missile destroyers were even larger. Still, *Mitscher* was a significant advance and provided much feedback that spawned improvements in later classes.[33]

The USS *Dealey* (DE-1006), first of her class, was completed in 1954, while three *DD-931*-class destroyers, two destroyer escorts, and 32 other ships were included in the 1954 budget, and five destroyers and eight escorts were included in the 1955 budget. In 1955, the new *Forrest Sherman*-class destroyer and the newly converted guided missile cruiser *Boston*, armed with the new Terrier surface-to-air missile, entered the fleet, and a second cruiser, the *Canberra* was commissioned in 1956.[34]

Anti-submarine Warfare (ASW) The Soviet submarine threat to the Atlantic sea lanes and naval combatants prompted further research and development, and in 1950, funding for ASW increased by 200 per cent, a number of destroyers were converted for ASW operations, and research and development in snorkelling and in carrier-based ASW aircraft and helicopters continued. In tactics, ways to enable ASW ships and aircraft to prosecute enemy submarines before they took to the seas were examined. A $78 million ASW program continued into 1951, as work progressed on long-range patrol aircraft, sonobuoys, submarine attack planes, a 6,000-ton light cruiser, five ASW carriers, ASW destroyers, and ASW torpedoes and rockets. This improved the ASW capability, and escort destroyer divisions were composed of ships specifically configured for ASW. By 1953, ahead-thrown weapons had been developed, allowing a destroyer to attack as she approached a submarine, to continue the attack with other weapons while she was over the contact, and to use still other weapons as she passed away. Fire control systems that could predict a submarine's future positions, based on existing locating data, vastly improved the tracking capability, and new electrically powered, acoustic homing torpedoes provided much more effective weapons.[35]

Guided Missiles and Anti-air Warfare (AAW) The first guided missile went into mass production in 1951. The emphasis had been on surface-to-air missile (SAM) development to alleviate the air problem, but many realized that there were other uses for missiles. In October 1951, the Office of Guided Missiles was created to improve the lagging US effort and, in November, the Navy began to convert a cruiser to a guided missile cruiser. A new air-to-air/air-to-surface missile was approved for production in 1953.[36]

In air defense, improved radars, other early warning devices, and better fire control radars were developed. Digital computers were used for aircraft acquisition, and fire control systems were improved. Higher muzzle velocities and rates of fire were provided in AAW guns, as new 3in AAW batteries replaced the lighter ones of the Second World War.[37]

Command, Control, and Communications (C³) and Electronic Warfare While much of the research and development in command, control, and communications (C³) and in electronics would result in the advanced systems of the late 1950s and the 1960s, several inprovements reached the fleet at this time. Among the most important were the development of fixed underwater hydrophone arrays, comprising the Sound Surveillance System (SOSUS). These could detect submarines at considerable distances, depending on the noise generated by the submarine, ocean conditions, and signal processing techniques. Since the positions provided by the early arrays were rather imprecise, long-range patrol aircraft such as the P-2 Neptune and P-3 Orion were developed to reacquire and prosecute targets.[38]

In 1951, improved radars were installed on ships to improve their AAW capabilities and the Navy turned to computers to acquire, track, and target incoming enemy aircraft more rapidly. Advances in air control allowed for the more rapid scrambling of aircraft from carriers, and both ship conversions and new construction included spaces for electronic gear to improve a combatant's ASW capabilities. The advances in electronics were of such magnitude that they required the complete reorganization of a combatant's operations spaces. In 1952, the Navy began testing a new combat information center in the fleet.[39] ***Amphibious Warfare and Mine Warfare*** The Marine Corps continued to develop its amphibious operations. Six landing ships were included in the $2 billion naval bill of 1951, and nine tank landing ships (LSTs) were built in 1954, as the Navy gained approval for a prototype LST and two landing ship docks (LSDs).[40]

While a lower priority had been assigned to mine warfare, the situation improved slightly when the Navy's Bureau of Ordinance assumed responsibility for controlled mines from the Army 1949. Despite steady improvements in controlled mining, offensive mining, and minesweeping, however, four minesweepers were sunk and three destroyers were damaged by mines in Korea in 1950 and early 1951. Further progress was made when the Navy included 52 minesweepers in its 1951 naval construction bill, and three more were approved in 1954.[41]

Conclusions

The Korean War reversed the continuing naval reduction as America rebuilt its maritime power. This program conformed to Alfred Mahan's concepts to the extent that force projection forces received priority over shore defense, minesweeping, and patrol forces. Aircraft carriers and submarines continued to receive the highest priorities, and the most revolutionary advances were developed or planned during this period. For the carrier, the flight deck was completely redesigned and the angled deck of today's carriers resulted. Its size was increased markedly, catapult and arresting systems were developed, and modern electronic air control systems were devised and perfected. Finally, planning was completed as work progressed on *Enterprise*, the world's first nuclear-powered aircraft carrier. Aircraft with swept wings, capable of carrying enormous bomb loads were produced, so that such aircraft, if armed with nuclear weapons, made the carrier a strategic as well as a conventional weapon system. For the submarine, the hull was completely redesigned, a nuclear propulsion system which permitted virtually unlimited underwater endurance was perfected, and work was begun on strategic missiles. While the result, the nuclear-powered ballistic missile-equipped submarine, truly a strategic weapon system, would not be operational until the late 1950s, the major problems were considered and solved by Admiral Rickover's team at this time. Henceforth, in both the aircraft carrier and the submarine, refinements would result and higher endurance aircraft, longer-ranged missiles, and improved propulsion plants would be made, but much of this would be improvements on the very significant breakthroughs that were made at this time.

GREAT BRITAIN

The revision of Great Britain's maritime strategy was completed and articulated by 1951; henceforth, she perceived NATO to be an alliance that would counter Soviet expansion. The Navy's goal was to control sea communications, which meant: ensuring friendly use of the sea lines of communication (SLOCs); denying the enemy use of his SLOCs: protecting the transport of army and air forces over water to combat arenas; preventing the enemy from doing the same; and providing support for the initial assault of friendly land forces and flanks of the land battle. These were traditional British goals, but the methods and tactics for achieving them had changed considerably, since the greatest threats were now from aircraft and submarines, to be defeated by aircraft carriers and ASW and AAW units.[42] The relevant portion of the Navy's order of battle is shown in Table 2.2. As in the US Navy, its size was increased in response to the Korean War and a higher inventory was maintained in the post-war years.

Submarines

The Navy's submarine force suffered two disasters in the early 1950s. On 12 January 1950, HMS *Truculent* sank in the Thames estuary east of Sheerness, England after colliding with the Swedish tanker *Divina*. There were fifteen survivors while 64 men were lost. The second disaster occurred on 17 April 1951, when HMS *Affray* sank in the English Channel and 75 men were lost. The cause was believed to be a poorly welded snorkel mast which had caused flooding. Unlike the US Navy, the Royal Navy conducted a sustained research and development effort in hydrogen peroxide propulsion systems for submarines, and launched *Explorer* and *Excaliber*, submarines with hydrogen peroxide plants, in March 1954 and February 1955. Earl Mountbatten, who became First Sea Lord in 1955, ended the expensive and controversial program and authorized Britain's first nuclear submarine, *Dreadnought*.[43]

Table 2.2
Selected Force Levels – Royal Navy, 1951–6

	Year						
	50	51	52	53	54	55	56
Submarines	32	35	39	38	37	40	44
Fleet Aircraft Carriers	1	2	2	2	1	2	2
Light and Escort Carriers	4	4	3	3	2	2	2
Battleships	0	1	1	1	1	0	0
Cruisers	13	12	12	11	10	10	9
Destroyers	28	34	31	29	26	27	29
Frigates	36	38	36	35	33	30	28
Minesweepers	13	26	46	42	38	38	37

Surface Combatants

In 1950, as HM Queen Elizabeth launched the *Ark Royal*, the emphases on aircraft carriers and ASW and AAW were continued. HMSS *Formidable* and *Indomitable* were modernized to carry aircraft that could carry nuclear weapons, and the remaining *Daring* destroyers were launched from 1950 to 1952. And this heavy investment in sea power was continued. The Navy Estimates for 1950-1 reflected an ambitious program involving the carrier *Hermes*, and construction of minesweepers and ASW frigates. Six destroyers were converted to ASW frigates in 1950, with more in 1951, and HMS *Victorious* was reconstructed from 1951 to 1957 so that she could carry heavier aircraft. On 8 November 1950, the swept-wing Supermarine 510 jet fighter made its first deck landings on HMS *Illustrious*, thereby proving that aircraft with swept-wings of as much as 40° could maintain control at low speeds and could therefore land on carriers.[44]

The Korean War's expense and this ambitious program were reflected in the Navy Estimates for 1951-2. They totalled 278,500,000 pounds, an increase of 85.5 million pounds over the previous year, and a supplementary estimate pushed them even higher. An order of battle was presented (see the figures for 1951 in Table 2.2), and it was noted that two fleet carriers, seven light fleet carriers, three cruisers, eight destroyers, four frigates, and 41 minesweepers were being built or modernized, and an additional 232 ships, including aircraft carriers, destroyers, frigates, and patrol boats were planned in the next three years. If this program were completed, the Navy would have eighteen aircraft carriers, plus three in the Commonwealth, in contrast to the eleven that it had during the war.[45]

Largely in response to the Korean operations, on 7 March 1951, the Navy began bringing 60 ships–two destroyers, two frigates, three submarines, 30 minesweepers, two fast minelayers, and 21 smaller craft–out of reserve, while a light fleet carrier, a destroyer, a landing ship, and three ASW frigates were brought forward for trials and training. This was an impressive and sustained shipbuilding program which produced a remarkable number of ships. For example, Great Britain launched twelve ships each in June and September 1954, and in 1955 71 ships were launched, in a program that approached the output of the Second World War. It also amounted to a considerable cost and did not begin to decline until the 1956-7 estimates, which were still a considerable £401,670,000.[46]

Aircraft Carriers In carrier developments, on 3 May 1950 the *Ark Royal* was launched. Similar to *Eagle* (which was then fitting out), but with many improvements, she had a 53,060-ton displacement, was 804 feet long, had a 113-foot beam and a complement of 2,750 men. Provisions had been made for her to carry jet aircraft. The Navy also began using helicopters for communications between ships, and air-sea rescue. In August, the new sea-based fighter, Sea Venom, equipped with radar and carrying a crew of two, went into series production and into service alongside the single-seat jet fighters Sea Hawk and Attacker. On 22 August 1951, the first operational squadron of naval jet aircraft was established. Composed of eight Attacker aircraft, it would be embarked in *Eagle*, which was commissioned in October and accepted into service on 1 March 1952. The first operational night landings of jet aircraft were made on board *Theseus* and in February 1952, the Navy developed a new catapult capable of 'launching the most modern carrier-borne aircraft'. In 1953, it developed an angled flight deck. The angle, about eight degrees off the centreline, allowed incoming aircraft to fly off the carrier without altering course if they failed to land properly. On 16 February, the carrier *Hermes*, fourth of the *Centaur*s but radically resdesigned, was launched. *Centaur* was completed in 1953, and *Albion* and *Bulwark* were completed and accepted into service in 1954.[47]

Cruisers In 1951, the Navy opted to complete three *Tiger*-class cruisers, *Tiger*, *Lion* and *Blake*, which had been launched in 1944 and 1945. A new design was developed and they were completed from 1959 to 1961. Although they were excellent ships, their 6in guns were no longer valuable for AAW and, therefore, their missions were restricted to shore bombardment and surface warfare. Their excellent command facilities made them ideal for task group flagship assignments. Meanwhile, designs for a *Minatour*-class cruiser were developed in 1947 and refined in 1951, and design studies for a series of large, medium, and small '1960' cruisers were completed in 1948 and 1949. However, their projected expense and the Navy's changing mission priorities prevented any of these ships from being built.[48]

Other Major Surface Combatants Notable advances also were made concerning the ASW and AAW surface combatants that were so necessary to defend the aircraft carriers. In February 1952, the first two *Daring* destroyers were accepted into service, and the program was continued until the eighth and last unit was accepted in March 1954.[49] From 1953 to 1961, all eight *Cavendish* destroyers were modernized as general-purpose destroyers.

In frigates, Second World War destroyers were converted as frigates in the 1950s. The results were very successful and these ships were used heavily. In 1961 the Navy began to retire them. In new frigate construction, the trend was toward specialization because it was believed that a single frigate could not carry all the equipment needed for modern combat. There were four new types of frigate, two for ASW, a third for AAW, and a fourth for air direction. On 25 June 1953, *Salisbury*, the first of the new air direction frigates, was launched, and on 25 September, HMS *Dundas*, the first of the *Blackwood* ASW frigates, was launched. The *Blackwood*s were of all-welded construction, could be built quickly, were highly manoeuverable and could maintain high speeds in heavy seas during submarine searches.[50] The first two units, *Whitby* and *Torquay*, of a second type of ASW frigate that was designed for locating and detecting submarines, the *Whitby*-class, were launched in 1954. The first AAW frigate, *Puma*, of the *Leopard*-class, was launched on 30 June 1954.[51]

Finally, in all surface combatants, progress was made in shipboard propulsion systems, resulting in greater endurance and speed with much smaller systems. These were necessary because the newer shipboard electronics and weapons systems took up so much room that space was at a premium.[52]

Minesweepers and Minor Combatants The Navy devoted considerable attention to the mine threat. In the early 1950s, two classes of inshore minesweepers, *Ham* and *Ley*, were built. The *Ham*s proved to be too small for the latest equipment and were either downgraded to inshore minesweepers or transferred to other nations. Most of the *Ley*s were designed for minehunting. In May 1952, the first of the *Ton* coastal minesweepers, *Bickington*, was launched. The Navy's mine warfare program was assisted considerably when, on 13 March 1953, the United States signed an $11 million contract for minesweepers that would be allocated to NATO nations as needs dictated.[53]

FRANCE

The importance of the French experience in Vietnam cannot be overstated. Nationally, it tore the nation apart, as the French empire in south-east Asia crumbled when she withdrew in defeat from the bloody conflict. Regionally, her withdrawal left instability in South Vietnam and a nascent US commitment replacing the French role. Additionally, the West's refusal to support France more actively created great bitterness in Paris, particularly against the United States, a factor that certainly played in De Gaulle's later decision to leave NATO. Finally, the cost of the war was so high that France simply did not have the funds necessary to develop a large navy.

The results of Vietnam were extremely important because of the influence they had on events in the 1960s and 1970s. One problem was that very few Americans, President Eisenhower and General MacArthur among them, viewed accurately the interaction between Korea, Formosa, Vietnam, and Malaysia. Eisenhower proposed a UN General Headquarters to deal with the Korean, Indo-Chinese, and Malaysian problems collectively, but war-weary America, frustrated with less than complete victory in Korea, simply would not support actively the cause in Indo-China. Additionally, certain aspects of the US policy were at odds with the French one. For example, when America granted $385 million in military aid against communist aggression in Asia in 1953, it stated that it supported the right of self-determination of all peoples, clearly a slap at French colonialism. Washington exerted great pressure on the French to end the conflict in Indo-China in 1954, and an agreement was reached concerning the partitioning of Vietnam. The resultant vacuum left by the French led to political chaos, as Ngo Dinh Diem fought for control.[54]

Naval Construction
This terribly costly and humiliating war, while it spawned French naval innovation also detracted from the funds available for such development. Concerning innovation, the war prompted a revision in French naval thinking. Aircraft carriers on loan from the United States proved so useful in Vietnam that the entire French naval effort was built around them. This led to the belief that the carrier had replaced the battleship as the key force projection ship, and France subsequently began to develop a navy around carrier task groups.

However, developing such a force was difficult due to a lack of funds. In December 1949, the expense of the war necessitated decommissioning several naval units to save money. Three cruisers, two destroyers, two frigates, and three hydrographic ships were decommissioned, and the *Richelieu* and the *Jean Bart* were manned with only skeleton crews. The Navy's missions had not decreased and it tried to make do with what it had. The French continued to participate in NATO and sent ships to take part in NATO exercises, such as Exercise 'Symphonie' which involved British and French manoeuvers near Malta in February and March 1950. In September, the French announced their naval construction plans, which included building four submarines, four escorts, three gunboats, and completing two other submarines. However, even these plans appeared too ambitious for the economy to bear and other NATO states attempted to help France prop up her naval inventory. In the winter of 1950,

Table 2.3
Selected Force Levels – French Navy, 1951–6

	Year						
	50	*51*	*52*	*53*	*54*	*55*	*56*
Submarines	16	19	19	24	24	24	26
Light and Escort Carriers	2	3	3	3	4	4	4
Battleships	2	2	2	2	2	2	2
Cruisers	8	8	6	6	6	5	5
ASW and AAW Leaders[a]	0	0	2	2	2	2	2
Destroyers	17	16	15	15	22	22	21
Frigates	22	21	22	23	20	28	38
Minesweepers	28	38	62	91	121	135	135
Escorts	24	26	26	22	22	24	24

[a]Two *Châteaurenault*-class cruisers were reclassified as anti-submarine and anti-aircraft leaders.

two US-funded destroyer escorts entered the French Navy under NATO's Mutual Defense Assistance Program and, on 1 August 1951, Great Britain lent France four submarines for four years.[55]

A 28 December 1951 revision to the construction plan was quite ambitious. The new 34 billion franc program would produce 15,600 tons of light ships: four anti-aircraft escorts, and 46 minesweepers. The escorts were associated with the new emphasis on carriers and were intended to provide the necessary AAW and ASW protection. The cruiser *De Grasse* was completed but was redesigned as an anti-aircraft cruiser, to provide substantial AA protection and command facilities. War prizes and generous United States aid enabled the French Navy to pass through this difficult financial period.[56]

In 1951, France was able to proceed on naval modernization. *Surcouf*, the lead ship in a twelve-unit series of *Surcouf* (T 47) class destroyers, was laid down in July 1951. The class, which was completed in June 1957, was designed to provide AAW support to French carrier forces. A similar class, *Duperré* (T 53), which provided improved air tracking and controlling capabilities, was laid down in November 1954. Five ships were completed in a run that ended in July 1958. Meanwhile, in October 1951, the four-ship *Le Corse* (E 50) destroyer escort class was begun. It was to provide ASW support for convoy protection. Improvements were made to the *Le Corse* design and the 13-ship *Le Normand*-class was begun when the lead unit was laid down in July 1953. In 1951, *Narvel*, the first of a new class of 1,910-ton long-range submarines, was laid down. Six were built in a program that ended in 1960. *Narval* incorporated the technology of the German Type XXI program and was intended for operations in the world-wide French empire. In mine warfare, improvements were made through Allied assistance. From December 1954 to November 1955, fifteen *Hasse* minesweepers built in Britain with US funding were transferred to France under the US Offshore Procurement Program and several more were provided by the United States.[57]

Conclusions

While the Indo-Chinese War was among the factors that stifled France's naval development, it also prompted a change in French naval thinking to one which saw the aircraft carrier as the key force projection system. French construction was retarded as France recovered from the war and fought the war in Indo-China but the new ships of the early 1950s reflected intentions to develop carrier task forces and to build a modern navy.

THE SOVIET UNION

The End of the Stalin Period, 1950-3

The Stalinist shipbuilding program was continued until his death in 1953. Shrouded in secrecy, it created uneasiness in the West, as analysts attempted to discern Soviet intentions. One analyst argued that the USSR had two aims, the defense of the homeland and eastern European gains, and world domination. In this context, Soviet imperialism had replaced Soviet communism as the motive behind her foreign policy, and in pursuing the latter goal, she would wage a policy of brinkmanship in order to make further gains. Within this overall strategy, her Baltic strategy was intended to deny Allied access to the Baltic in wartime, a denial that would be based on mine warfare, in which the minefields would be defended by surface combatants and submarines.[58]

In estimating actual Soviet naval construction and fleet distribution, the reports were indeed confusing. In December 1949, the editors of *Jane's* admitted difficulty in determining the size of the Soviet fleet and, in August 1951, *Revue de Defense Nationale* also expressed uncertainty about the fleet's numbers. The Soviets contributed to such confusion. In January 1950, there were reports that the battleship *Sovietski Soyuz* had been completed; in March, it was noted that the Soviets appeared to be building up their Pacific Fleet and were upgrading the facilities at Vladivostok and Petropavlovsk; and, in July, Soviet Navy Day Speeches emphasized the need for bases, particularly in the Northern and Pacific Fleets.[59]

Other reports discussed Soviet naval assertiveness. In October 1950, the naval installations on the Estonian islands in the Gulf of Riga which could be used for offensive action against Finland and Sweden were fortified. In the same month, British and Scandinavian fishing ships near the Soviet coast were seized repeatedly after the USSR extended her territorial waters from three to twelve miles. Meanwhile, there were continued reports of a Soviet naval build-up. *La Revue Maritime* reported that Russia spent 19 per cent of her

Table 2.4
Selected Force Levels – Soviet Navy, 1951–6[a]

	Year						
	50	51	52	53	54	55	56
Submarines	202	278	319	330	335	335	397
Battleships	4	4	3	3	3	3	3
Cruisers	17	17	18	21	25	30	32

Destroyers	67	70	74	78	128	150	178
Frigates	43	22	28	37	42	47	55
Minesweepers	80	210	292	293	350	350	350

ᵃVarious sources, including *Combat Fleets of the World, Conway's All the World's Fighting Ships, 1947–1982, Part II: The Warsaw Pact and Non-Aligned Nations,* and *Jane's Fighting Ships.* The data are based on incomplete information. The Soviets shrouded their programs in secrecy and attempted to maximize the perceived threat in an attempt further to deter Western actions. None the less, the figures are valuable for indicating trends in Soviet construction.

defense 1950 budget on her Navy (about 15 billion roubles). This figure did not include construction, armament, and naval shore establishment expenses. The fleet was believed to consist of a battleship, ten cruisers, 66 destroyers, and 250 submarines. Emphasis was placed on submarine and aircraft production in an ambitious program that was to be completed in 1956. It focused on completing those ships under construction while providing them with newer arms wherever possible. *La Revue Maritime* concluded that reports of an aircraft carrier, while they could not be substantiated, could not be ignored. *Jane's* continued to express concern about the lack of complete information. On 20 December 1950, it said that there were about 350–370 Soviet submarines in service and believed that this figure might eventually reach 1,500 units.[60]

Such concern continued into 1951. In April, a Soviet naval build-up in the Baltic that included minesweepers, small craft, minelayers, and small transports was reported. The goal appeared to be to close the Baltic in wartime. In May 1951, *La Revue Maritime* reported that the Soviet defense budget for fiscal year 1951 was 96.4 billion roubles, of which the Navy would receive 22 billion roubles, seven billion more than the previous year. On 23 July, Moscow announced that Vice-Admiral N. G. Kuznetsov, a noted proponent of big ships, had been appointed Soviet Minister of the Navy, succeeding Admiral I. S. Yumashev, who had been relieved of his duties at his own request.[61]

Fears of Soviet expansion in the Baltic and Far East continued to appear in the Western press. In the Pacific, there was believed to be great concord between the Soviets and Chinese, as these communist nations were viewed as a bloc. In 1952 and 1953, Mao Tse-tung spoke of liquidating Chang's stronghold on Formosa, and the British felt that he might press for a US withdrawal from the island. By 1953, the West viewed the defense of Korea as a success and believed that the communists no longer hoped for victory, but in Indo-China, where the French had fought for eight years, the situation was viewed with concern. There was also continued concern about the Soviet shipbuilding program. In March 1953, when the British First Lord introduced the Navy Estimates, he stated that the Soviet Navy had a very ambitious naval construction program and now had twenty cruisers, more than 100 destroyers, and more than 350 submarines, making it the world's second strongest navy. On 27 July, when the cease-fire agreement was signed in Korea, the Secretary of the Navy noted that the following new Soviet ships had been or were being built: 24 cruisers, including the new *Sverdlov*-class, which were good as commerce raiders; more than 100 destroyers, including units of the *Otlichnyy* and *Skoryy* classes; more than 100 submarines, many of which were large long-distance boats, and some of which were equipped with missiles; and hundreds of mine and patrol craft for coastal defense.[62]

In reality, these estimates slightly exaggerated Soviet construction. The Soviets incorporated German submarine technology and design concepts to produce two classes of boats in the early 1950s. The *Whiskey* was built from 1950 to 1957. With a 1,350-ton submerged displacement, she was considered to be a medium- to long-range submarine. While the Soviets built 236 *Whiskey*s, they built 26 *Zulu*-class boats in a production run from 1951 to 1955. *Zulu* was larger–2,350 tons submerged, and had a greater operational radius. Both classes were successful and some units of each were later converted for other purposes. From 1954 to 1957, 30 *Quebec*-class short-range submarines were also built.[63]

In surface combatants, two classes of frigates appeared in the early 1950s. Six *Kola* frigates were built in 1950 and 1951, and the first of 64 *Riga* frigates was begun in 1952. Both fitted in well with Stalin's coastal defense strategy.[64]

After *Skoryy*, the next destroyer to appear was *Tallin*, built in 1953-4. She was considerably larger than *Skoryy* and her unique features included a flushed deck in order to obtain a higher freeboard at the forecastle. Only one *Tallin* was built because Krushchev cancelled the programme.[65]

Twenty-seven *Kotlin* destroyers were built between 1953 and 1957. Very similar to *Tallin*, *Kotlin* had the same flushed deck and other traits. However, her superstructure was quite different and, at 3,500 tons, she was lighter than *Tallin* and was capable of 34 knots. Fast, versatile, and heavily armed, she, and the *Skoryy*, were mainstays of the Soviet destroyer force in the 1950s and 1960s.[66]

The *Skoryy–Tallin–Kotlin* progression demonstrated two enduring and significant characteristics of the Soviet naval construction program. It was pedestrian to the extent that the progression from one class to another was slow and laborious with less incremental technological advances between classes than that of ships designed in the West. Conversely, when a class such as *Tallin* proved undesirable, the program was dynamic, stopping production of a failed design in favor of producing a subsequent class that met mission requirements. We will see other instances of both these characteristics in subsequent decades.

In cruisers, *Sverdlov* represented a continuation of Stalin's big, gun-armed ship concept. Displacing 17,200 tons, *Sverdlov* was 656 feet long and was heavily armed with surface and AAW guns, torpedo tubes, and from 140 to 250 mines. Twenty keels were laid but only sixteen ships were launched from 1950 onward, because the program was stopped with the appointment of Admiral Gorshkov as Commander-in-Chief in 1956. Only fifteen units had been completed by 1955. *Dzerzhinski*, was converted to carry the Guideline missile in 1961 and 1962, and two, *Admiral Senyavin* and *Zhdanov*, were subsequently provided with extensive electronic suites and became command cruisers in the Pacific and Black Sea Fleets. The other *Sverdlov*s were gradually phased out of the Soviet inventory.[67]

The Reorientation, 1953-6

The year 1953 was truly a watershed because it gave birth to influences that would eventually alter the complexion of the Soviet fleet remarkably. To begin with, Stalin died in that year, and with him went the insistence on a fleet of heavy, gun-armed combatants. Also, the major post-war Soviet policy themes – Europe, China, and Korea – which had continued to place emphasis on the Soviet Army and regions contiguous to Soviet borders, had reached resolution. Henceforth, Soviet policy-makers would examine new themes and possibilities. This exercise was played out in the larger context of the succession crisis which occurred after Stalin's death and was resolved by 1956. The results, codified by the Twentieth Party Congress in 1956, were of the greatest importance to the Soviet Navy. First, Nikita Khrushchev made his famous 'secret speech', in which he signalled the shifting of the Soviet focus away from the old themes and toward the developing world. He indicated that the Soviet–American superpower rivalry was a major theme that dominated international relations, and stated that the Soviet Union would pursue a policy of 'peaceful coexistence' in which it would compete for influence in the developing world.[68]

This policy shift back to Leninist themes influenced subsequent Soviet naval development for two reasons. First it identified the United States as a major maritime power and the USSR's major competitor. The US Navy enjoyed two advantages. It could overwhelm any Soviet naval force deployed for crisis response operations, and it could conduct operations directly against Soviet territory. In order to compete, the Soviet Union had to counter both US naval advantages by securing the sea routes that led to the Soviet Union and by building crisis response forces that could compete with the US Navy. Admiral Gorshkov accurately understood this situation when he stated that NATO was essentially a maritime alliance in which the US Navy was the key military force. Countering this force meant a very definite shift in Soviet naval construction. One of the earliest signs of this shift appeared in July 1954, when the new plan for 'transforming the armaments of the Navy' was adopted. Now the main basis of the Navy was to be submarine, and while the theme remained sea denial rather than sea control, the aim would be to counter US carriers and Polaris submarines rather than massive invading armadas.[69]

The second factor was the arena of conflict. No longer was Soviet attention focused on nations along her borders. Now it was on the developing world, in areas that were physically isolated from her. This meant that the political utility of the Soviet Army, which had proven to be so effective in its occupation of eastern Europe and had had a potential effect in China during the Chinese revolution and in Korea during the Korean War, was greatly restricted, because the arenas of conflict would be in distant areas that were unaccessible to Soviet ground-based forces.[70] The 'relevant military power', as Admiral Elmo Zumwalt would say, became naval power, a factor that would prompt naval development and would exert great influence on the types of naval ships that were built. Thus, although defense of the sea lanes was the Navy's top defense priority, it would also have to be able to project power outward to offset the US naval advantage in conflict arenas.

Other events reflect this realization. On the eve of the Twentieth Party

Congress, Admiral Sergei Gorshkov was appointed as Commander-in-Chief of the Soviet Navy, replacing Admiral Kuznetsov, who was a 'big-ship' proponent. Additionally, the Congress approved the new five-year plan that contained the funds to build the new Soviet Navy. The result of this would be a new generation of surface combatants, including the *Kynda* and *Kresta I* and *Kresta II* guided missile cruisers and *Kashin* guided missile destroyer, and new classes of submarines. Khrushchev's penchant for nuclear missiles would affect the fleet's composition and the themes would first be anti-carrier warfare and then ASW.[71]

OTHER NATIONS

Elsewhere, the post-war trend of buying Second World War ships at bargain prices or receiving them at no cost from the major powers had virtually ended by 1950, as the world's sea powers had depleted their excess inventories. The early 1950s were hallmarked by a shifting of naval power among the NATO and other non-communist allies and by indigenous naval construction elsewhere in the world.

Europe

In Europe, the major naval theme remained the perceived Soviet threat. The submarine, air, and mining threats were still the primary dangers and ships were shifted among the western European nations to provide an adequate defense. In 1950, the United States transferred twelve destroyer escorts to NATO nations and, on 5 September 1951, the US Senate approved the transfer of 24 destroyers to foreign nations with which America had mutual defense agreements. In the latter program, one ship was to go to Great Britain, eight each to France and Brazil, three to Peru, and two each to Denmark and Uruguay, although many of these ships were never delivered.[72]

In northern Europe, developments in Norway, Sweden, and West Germany were noteworthy. In 1950, Norway announced plans to have a naval force of five destroyers, two escort destroyers, eleven submarines, thirteen motor torpedo-boats, and a number of smaller craft within five years, and intended to move its submarine base from Trondheim to Bergen. The Navy considered this barely adequate for the nation's maritime defense and reacted when the government announced its 1951-5 program on 21 February 1951. Norway would procure only three submarines, two minelayers, and thirteen motor torpedo-boats (which would replace the British motor torpedo-boats that had been borrowed). Three destroyers might also be modernized and the Navy might also receive a number of British *Hunt*-class destroyers. Viewing this as insufficient, the Navy publicly criticized the Army and Air Force's receiving the lion's share of the defense budget. It did receive four *Hunt*-class destroyers on loan from Great Britain.[73] Alarm was also expressed in the Swedish Navy. In 1950, it had three cruisers, twelve destroyers, and twenty submarines, which the Commander-in-Chief of the Navy felt was inadequate. Twenty destroyers were needed, and while the two destroyers and five torpedo craft that were being built, and the proposed three submarines and four torpedo craft would help, they clearly were not an adequate defense. The situation worsened when the Soviets began seizing Swedish fishing boats inside their newly claimed twelve-mile territorial limit.[74] In West Germany, on 15 April 1951, the United States announced that it was organizing a West German naval force, commanded by US Naval personnel but manned primarily by Germans. Minesweepers, cutters, and torpedo-boats, all from the former German Navy, were refitted and commissioned. In 1956, Bonn asked Great Britain to sell seven frigates and asked the United States for twelve destroyers until Germany could afford to provide these ships for itself.[75]

Elsewhere in northern Europe, the Belgian and Dutch navies were strengthened. After the remaining five of six minesweepers were delivered by Great Britain in 1950 and 1951, the Belgian Navy consisted of two frigates, two high-speed minesweepers, and six minesweepers.[76] In the Netherlands, the cruiser *De Zeven Provincien* was launched by Queen Juliana in August 1950. She and her sister ship, *De Ruyter*, had been laid down in 1939 and were finally commissioned on 17 December and 18 November 1953, respectively. Two destroyer escorts were transferred to the Dutch Navy as the first of the transfers under the Mutual Defense Assistance Program. The Netherlands' naval budget for 1951 was announced soon thereafter; it would amount to 6.6 per cent of the national budget. The Dutch naval order of battle then consisted of a light aircraft carrier, two cruisers, six destroyers, submarines, and lighter units. Two more cruisers, and twelve destroyers also were building. These increases were depleted slightly when three submarines on loan from Great Britain since 1948 were returned.[77]

In the Mediterranean, the most significant naval activity occurred in Italy and Spain. In December 1949, Italy said that it would build six 2500-ton destroyers, two small AAW ships, an anti-air cruiser, a dispatch ship, and a few coastal speed-boats. By 9 November 1950, Italy was building two 2,400-ton destroyers, a 300-ton gunboat, two 150-ton motor-boats, and a small gunboat. In April 1951, the United States transferred three destroyer escorts under the NATO military aid plan and, on 6 December, two US destroyers and six gunboats were received under the provisions of the North Atlantic Treaty. Such assistance was continued when the submarine USS *Barb* was transferred on 14 December 1954.[78]

In Spain, the naval budget was increased in September 1950. She had been successful in building smaller units, but a lack of raw materials had delayed the completion of larger ships. In January 1951, the Navy received a 1,635-ton destroyer, *Liniers*, and launched another. In the same month, the Navy conducted its first large-scale naval manoeuvers in years. Taking place between Cadiz and the Canary Islands, the exercise involved 45 ships and more than 10,000 men, and the scenario included convoy operations and combating a naval force staging from North Africa. Three more destroyers were launched on 4 September. The ambitious Spanish naval program was expensive, and in light of the favored position of the Army in defense spending, funds were restricted. However, this problem was alleviated with US aid. In 1954 and 1955, Spain received three US minesweepers, but even greater assistance had been provided in 1953, when Spain, after two years of negotiations, agreed to establish US air and naval bases on her territory. This gave the United States a large share of defense of the Western Mediterranean and provided funds for future naval development.[79]

In Greece, initially there was little change other than the return, on 1 June 1952, of two British submarines that had been on loan since 1943. Soon after the Spanish agreement in 1953, however, a US-Greek agreement was signed in which America would improve and jointly use Greek airfields and naval installations. As in the Spanish agreement, this accord increased Greek security significantly because it obligated the United States to a share of the Eastern Mediterranean's defense and to upgrading Greek defense installations and bases.[80]

There also was an increase in Turkey's naval posture when two American submarines were received in December 1950. This brought the total number of US ships given to six submarines, four destroyers, sixteen minesweepers, and four auxiliaries. The United States also developed a naval base at Iskanderun and transferred it to Turkey on 20 October 1953.[81]

In North Africa, there was continued development in both the Arab and Israeli navies. In August 1951, *La Revue Maritime* said that the Israeli Navy had a frigate, two or three corvettes, three ex-American coast guard cutters, two ex-American patrol craft, and assorted small craft, while the Egyptian Navy had two older destroyers, six older frigates, an LST, three minesweepers, eight coastal minesweepers, and assorted small craft and auxiliaries. Egypt bought two Z-class destroyers from Great Britain in 1955. Further southward, South Africa purchased the *Wessex*, a *Wager*-class destroyer, in February 1950. It became the nucleus of a new fleet, as South Africa then had only three obsolete frigates and some minesweepers. It bought another destroyer from Great Britain in 1953, and in 1955 London began to transfer control of Simonstown naval base to South Africa.[82]

Canada

The Canadians took the Soviet naval threat very seriously in 1950, and responded accordingly. In the summer, there were widespread reports that Soviet submarines had patrolled along Canada's east coast and intruded within the three-mile limit. Although it is highly doubtful, the Canadians claimed that there were two submarines involved, one that penetrated the Gulf of St. Lawrence and a second in the Bay of Fundy. On 6 February 1951, the Canadian Ministry of Defense released its defense plan for the next three years. A $5 billion program, it would produce almost 100 ships for the Navy by building new ships and reactivating ships in reserve. The program's objectives were to defend Canada and the United States from direct attack, honor Canadian commitments to NATO, and create the organization necessary to build up the nation's strength. Canada purchased the *Majestic*-class aircraft carrier, *Powerful*, to replace the HMCS *Magnificent*. In November 1950, it laid down the *St. Laurent*, the first in a seven-ship destroyer construction program that would be completed in 1956. A second seven-ship program, the *Restigouche*-class, was begun in July 1953. Both classes were influenced by the British *Whitby*-class, supplemented with Canadian and US electronics.[83]

Latin America

In Venezuela, three *Nueva Esparta*-class destroyers were ordered from Great Britain. The first of these ships was launched in November 1952, and the second on 29 June 1953, the same day that the keel of the third was laid. Ecuador bought two *Hunt*-class frigates from Great Britain in 1955.[84]

The most important regional event involved territorial rights to the Falkland Islands Dependencies, an issue that would continue to fester until it erupted in 1982. From November 1950 to April 1951, Chile established a base on British Antarctic territory in the Falkland Islands Dependencies and the British protested. On 30 April 1951, Argentina announced that it had established a permanent detachment in Grahamland, in the Argentine Antarctic sector. Great Britain protested this and the earlier settlement, and Argentina rejected the protest. On 6 April 1952, Argentina announced that it had established a sixth naval base in the 'Argentine Antarctic sector' of British Antarctica. It now had six bases in British Antarctica, five of which had not been authorized by Great Britain.[85]

The Indian Ocean

The major regional naval development centered on India. In 1953, London lent three *Hunt* frigates to India for three years, transferred two *Ham* minesweepers in 1955, and sold it the 6in gun cruiser *Nigeria* in 1957, thereby providing its navy with a second cruiser. The transfer of a cruiser and four British destroyers to Pakistan worked to maintain the Indo-Pakistani balance.[86]

The Pacific Ocean

Pacific activity was dominated by the Korean War and the perceived communist threat. Much attention was paid to Red Chinese designs on Formosa. By 1950, it was generally accepted that China was building a navy and an air force in order to attack Formosa, and in 1951 Taiwan claimed that Soviet submarines were operating from a naval base on Hainan Island in the South China Sea, that the base could support four submarines, and that the Russians also had given the Chinese several warships and had sent Soviet naval officers to Canton to train Chinese naval personnel.[87]

These events caused concern among the other nations of north-east Asia. In 1954, Japan asked the United States to supply thirteen ships, including destroyers and a light aircraft carrier, for its new Defense Forces. However, they had their greatest effect on Australia, where the two-ship Modified British *Battle*-class program, producing *Tobruk* and *Anzac*, was completed in 1951. In August 1950, five British Second World War destroyers on loan to Australia were transferred permanently without charge, to be converted to ASW frigates by the Australian Navy. Australia also continued its *Daring* destroyer program.[88]

CONCLUSIONS

Because of technological advances, the six-year period from 1950 to 1956 stands as the most dramatic interval of the entire post-war period. Politically, the sides were drawn and both camps came to realize the importance of sea power. Henceforth, each would develop and maintain maritime forces as an integral part of the defense.

Technologically, the period witnessed the creation of the first nuclear-powered submarines and the resolution of the major problems associated with the attack aircraft carrier. Other projects – nuclear-powered aircraft, submersible aircraft carriers and the like – either proved unfeasible or too costly. Only one further breakthrough, the application of ballistic missiles to submarines, remained. Thus, in future years, with the exception of the ballistic missile, refinements – more capable aircraft for the carriers, better operating techniques, and improved designs and propulsion plants for nuclear-powered submarines – would dominate further progress in naval construction. Conversely, it was in other fields – command, control and communications (C^3), electronic warfare, ocean surveillance satellites, and naval intelligence systems – that there were to be dramatic breakthroughs. The future was filled with crises and the cost of further naval development was so high that in most cases progress occurred more slowly. The one exception was the missile-equipped patrol combatant, an important aspect of naval development that is discussed in Chapter 4.

NOTES

1. Donald W. Treadgold, *Twentieth Century Russia*, 6th ed. (Boulder, CO: Westview Press, 1987), p. 410.

2. A. S. Bolt, 'HMS *Theseus* in the Korean War, and Some Special Problems of Naval Aviation in that Theatre,' in *RUSI*, vol. xcvi, no. 584 (November 1951), pp. 548-50. The British viewed this as unusual, since there did not appear to be a great deal of co-ordination among the two forces, thereby creating confusion for US forces operating in the central portion of the peninsula. They are quick to point out, however, that no such confusion existed in the command of the naval forces deployed. See: Bolt, p. 549.

3. Of the British forces, one light fleet aircraft carrier, two cruisers, six destroyers, eight frigates, and eight auxiliaries were actually involved in the war. US Department of Defense, *Semiannual Report of the Secretary of Defense and Semiannual Reports of the Secretary of the Army, Secretary of the Navy, and Secretary of the Air Force January 1 to June 30, 1951* (Washington, DC: GPO, 1951), pp. 149-50. See also: US Department of Defense, *Semiannual Report of the Secretary of Defense and Semiannual Reports of the Secretary of the Army, Secretary of the Navy, and Secretary of the Air Force July 1 to December 31, 1951* (Washington, DC: GPO, 1952). Paul B. Ryan, *First Line of Defense: The U.S. Navy Since 1945* (Stanford, CA: Hoover Institution Press, 1981), p. 16; 'British Commonwealth Naval Operations During the Korean War–Part II,' in *RUSI*, vol. xcvi, no. 584 (November 1951), p. 609; and Part III, vol. xcvii, no. 586 (May 1952), pp. 219, 223, 245. For an excellent discussion of the evolution of Allied co-operation in the Far East, see, E. A. Whiteley, 'Allied Defence Cooperation in the Far East,' in *RUSI*, vol. c, no. 600 (November 1955), pp. 532-49; and 'British Commonwealth Naval Operations During the Korean War–Part IV,' in *RUSI*, vol. xcviii, no. 589 (February 1953), p. 113.

4. 'British Commonwealth Naval Operations During the Korean War–Part V,' in *RUSI*, vol. xcviii, no. 590 (May 1953), pp. 279-81; Part VI, vol. xcviii, no. 592 (November 1953), pp. 606-8; Part VII, vol. xcix, no. 593 (February 1954), pp. 102-9; A. K. Scott-Moncrieff, 'Naval Operations in Korean Waters,' in *RUSI*, vol. xcviii, no. 590 (May 1953), pp. 218-26; and S. M. Raw, 'The Fleet Train,' in *RUSI*, vol. xcix, no. 593 (February 1954), pp. 31-3.

5. R. Stanbury, 'Some Naval Aspects of an Assault Landing,' in *RUSI*, vol. xcvi, no. 581 (February 1951), p. 120; and Robert E. Cushman, 'Amphibious Warfare: Naval Weapon of the Future,' in *Proceedings*, vol. 74, no. 3 (March 1948), pp. 301-7.

6. See, for example, Richard B. Creecy, 'Military Applications of Atomic Energy,' in *Proceedings*, vol. 76, no. 7 (July 1950), p. 751. Creecy argued

that much more had to be understood and conveyed to the public about nuclear weapons. He believed that even policy-makers did not have an accurate appreciation for the weapons, and that the result was dangerous.

7. Martin E. Holbrook, 'A Review of Post-War Construction,' in *Proceedings*, vol. 76, no. 11 (November 1950), p. 1234; Field Marshal The Viscount Montgomery of Almein, 'A Look Through a Window at World War III,' in *RUSI*, vol. xcix, no. 596 (November 1954), pp. 507-20; Bern Anderson, 'Russia's New Kind of War,' in *Proceedings*, vol. 76, no. 11 (November 1950), pp. 1175, 1177; W. D. Puleston, 'Dimensions and Characteristics of a Future War,' in *Proceedings*, vol. 76, no. 6 (June 1950), pp. 594, 605; and Thaddeus V. Tuleja, 'The Historic Pattern of Russian Naval Policy,' in *Proceedings*, vol. 77, no. 9 (September 1951), pp. 966-7. One noted commentator, however, argued an interesting alternative position. Admiral Sir Gerald Dickens believed that Stalin did not have a true understanding of sea power and that this would prove fatal to the Soviet Union should war occur. The shift in Soviet naval construction in 1956 supports his position on Stalin's outdated views. See: Gerald Dickens, 'Sea Power in a War with Russia,' in *Proceedings*, vol. 76, no. 10 (October 1950), p. 1072.

8. Perhaps the most profound of these arguments was stated by George F. Eliot, who contended that the integration of the services of other nations in history meant that the army was traditionally in control, that a land strategy was adopted, and that if the nation was a sea power, then the war was lost. See: George Fielding Eliot, 'How to Lose a War,' in *Proceedings*, vol. 76, no. 7 (July 1950), pp. 707-14. See also: J. D. Hittle, 'Sea Power and a National General Staff,' in *Proceedings*, vol. 75, no. 10 (October 1949), pp. 1091-1103.

9. W. R. Kintner, 'Political Limitations of Air Power,' in *Proceedings*, vol. 76, no. 3 (March 1950), pp. 249, 251-2, 255; Ernest M. Eller, 'Will We Need a Navy to Win?' in *Proceedings*, vol. 76, no. 3 (March 1950), pp. 237-47; Charles R. Brown, 'American National Strategy,' in *Proceedings*, vol. 76, no. 4 (April 1950), pp. 355, 358-9, 363; James K. Eyre, 'Naval Power and the American Destiny,' in *Proceedings*, vol. 77, no. 3 (March 1951), pp. 297-307; Anthony Talerico, 'Sea of Decision,' in *Proceedings*, vol. 76, no. 9 (September 1950), pp. 943, 949; Leon B. Blair, 'Mediterranean Geopolitics,' in *Proceedings*, vol. 77, no. 2 (February 1951), p. 136; 'United States–Mediterranean Fleet Missions,' in *Proceedings*, vol. 76, no. 7 (July 1950), pp. 804-5; and Harold G. Bowen, Jr., 'Naval Aspects of the Mission to Turkey,' in *Proceedings*, vol. 77, no. 10 (October 1951), pp. 1043, 1044, 1048. Some very cogent, incisive comments on the Mediterranean command are provided in Admiral the Earl Mountbatten of Burma, 'Allied Naval and Air Commands in the Mediterranean,' in *RUSI*, vol. c, no. 598 (May 1955), pp. 171-83; William H. Hessler, 'Air-Sea Power on the Asian Perimeter,' in *Proceedings*, vol. 77, no. 10 (October 1951), pp. 1026-7; Edward E. Wilcox, 'Back Door in the Pacific,' in *Proceedings*, vol. 76, no. 2 (February 1950), p. 189; and M. L. Deyo, 'How Far Can the Bear Walk,' in *Proceedings*, vol. 76, no. 11 (November 1951), pp. 1203, 1205.

10. 'Navy Notes,' in *RUSI*, vol. xcvii, no. 585 (February 1952), p. 123; Ryan, pp. 18-22; and US Department of Defense, *Semiannual Report, January 1 to June 30, 1955* (Washington, DC: GPO, 1955), p. 146. See also: US Department of Defense, *Semiannual Report, July 1 to December 31, 1955* (Washington, DC: GPO, 1956).

11. Ryan, pp. 17-18; and US Department of Defense, *Semiannual Report, January 1 to June 30, 1955*, p. 146.

12. Hittle, pp. 1289-1290, 1297. Additionally, it was averred that the success of amphibious operations was due to two factors: surprise and concentration of force, and traditionally America had relied on concentration over surprise. See also: Robert Hugh Williams, 'Amphibious Warfare–Two Concepts,' in *Proceedings*, vol. 77, no. 5 (May 1951), p. 467; Joseph L. Howard, 'The Navy and National Security,' in *Proceedings*, vol. 77, no. 7 (July 1951), pp. 749-53; John E. McAuley, 'The Navy's Role in International Affairs,' in *Proceedings*, vol. 77, no. 1 (January 1951), p. 19; and H. B. Seim, 'The Navy and the "Fringe" War,' in *Proceedings*, vol. 77, no. 8 (August 1951), p. 841.

13. US Department of Defense, *Semiannual Report, January 1 to June 30, 1950* (Washington, DC: GPO, 1950), p. 107; US Department of Defense, *Semiannual Report, July 1 to December 31, 1950* (Washington, DC: GPO, 1951); US Department of Defense, *Second Report of the Secretary of Defense and the Annual Reports of the Secretary of the Army, Secretary of the Navy, and Secretary of the Air Force for the Fiscal Year 1949* (Washington, DC: GPO, 1950), p. 112; *Semiannual Report, January 1 to June 30, 1951*, p. 2; and US Department of Defense, *Semiannual Report, January 1 to June 30, 1954* (Washington, DC: GPO, 1954), pp. 156, 163.

14. Western views on Soviet mine warfare proved to be very accurate, as this was stressed in the Soviet Navy. See: Donald Mitchell, 'Russian Mine Warfare: The Historical Record,' in *RUSI*, vol. cix, no. 633 (February 1964), pp. 32-9.

15. *Semiannual Report, of the Secretary of Defense, January 1 to June 30, 1954*, pp. 160-1; *Semiannual Report, July 1 to December 31, 1956* (Washington, DC: GPO, 1957), pp. 161-2; *Semiannual Report, July 1 to December 31, 1954* (Washington, DC: GPO, 1955).

16. Indeed, in one of the US Navy's leading operational intelligence centers in 1975 an analyst spent considerable time in determining the motives behind Soviet naval operations along the

coast of West Africa. Since the analysis was based on 'soft' political factors rather than the harder empirical justification of 'beans', the analyst's supervisor was predictably suspect. 'Do you really believe this stuff?' was his question. Since such 'political analysis' was perceived to be under the purview of the Central Intelligence Agency, it was subsequently deleted from the report. This ignorance and disdain of strategy was not limited to the US Navy, but was prevalent in NATO as well. See, for example, the comments in R. E. Walters, 'The Submersible Fleet of the Future,' in *RUSI*, vol. cxi, no. 644 (November 1966), pp. 317-22. For an excellent progression of naval strategy since Mahan, see: Clark G. Reynolds, 'Sea Power in the Twentieth Century,' in *RUSI*, vol. cxi, no. 642 (May 1966), pp. 132-9.

17. Vice-Admiral Sir Arthur Hezlet, *The Submarine and Sea Power* (New York: Stein and Day, 1967), p. 246. On surface ships, it proved to be far more expensive, while it offered a minor improvement in the power-weight ratio, and little space savings. For submarines, however, the contribution was great because the increases in speed and endurance while totally submerged were dramatic improvements.

18. In a very profound and accurate piece, he argued that the 1949 exercise was a decisive step in the application of nuclear missiles to submarines, creating the strategic systems of today. See: Holbrook, pp. 47-51.

19. *Conway's, Part I*, p. 230; 'United States–Atomic Sub Planned,' in *Proceedings*, vol. 76, no. 6 (June 1950), p. 688; 'Navy Notes,' in *RUSI Journal*, vol. xcvi, no. 584 (November 1951), p. 660; (May 1952), p. 282; (August 1952), p. 462; (May 1955), p. 313; (November 1953), p. 639; and (November 1955), p. 639; US Department of Defense, *Semiannual Report, January 1 to June 30, 1954* (Washington, DC: GPO, 1954), pp. 4, 192; Drew Middleton, *Submarine: The Ultimate Naval Weapon – Its Past, Present and Future* (Chicago: Playboy Press, 1976), pp. 130-1; and US Department of Defense, *Semiannual Report, January 1 to June 30, 1955*, pp. 178-9. See also: US Department of Defense, *Semiannual Report, July 1 to December 31, 1954* (Washington, DC: GPO, 1955).

20. On 21 September 1949, the USSR accused the United States of spying. It stated that the USS *Cochino*, which had exploded and sunk 'not far from Murmansk', was spying on the Northern Fleet. US Navy officials were unavailable for comment on this matter. See: 'USSR – *Cochino* Accused of Spying,' in *Proceedings*, vol. 75, no. 11 (November 1949), pp. 1309-10.

21. *Conway's, Part I*, p. 230; US Department of Defense, *Semiannual Report, January 1 to June 30, 1951*, p. 147; '1951 Subs,' in *Proceedings*, vol. 77, no. 6 (June 1951), pp. 667-8; and 'Naval Program,' in *Proceedings*, vol. 77, no. 1 (January 1951), p. 97.

22. Ryan, pp. 25-6.

23. *Conway's, Part I*, pp. 232, 233, 237; and Hezlet, *Submarine*, p. 246.

24. John Lehman, *Aircraft Carriers: The Real Choices*, The Washington Papers, no. 52, Center for Strategic and International Studies, Georgetown University (Beverly Hills, CA: SAGE Publications, 1978), p.7; 'Oriskany,' in *Proceedings*, vol. 76, no. 5 (May 1950), pp. 573-4; and 'Navy Notes,' in *RUSI*, vol. xcv, no. 580 (November 1950), p. 637.

25. Vinson noted that Secretary of Defense Johnson had halted earlier plans for a carrier in 1949, but he emphasized that the proposed legislation had been approved by Secretary of Defense George Marshall, the Joint Chiefs of Staff, and the Bureau of the Budget.

26. 'Navy Notes,' in *RUSI*, vol. xcvi, no. 581 (February 1951), p. 175; (May 1951), p. 333 and (August 1951), p.512; '1951 Subs,' in *Proceedings*, vol. 77, no. 6 (June 1951), pp. 667-8; US Department of Defense, *Semiannual Report, January 1 to June 30, 1951* (Washington, DC: GPO, 1951), p.152; and 'Modernization Program,' in *Proceedings*, vol. 77, no. 11 (November 1951), p. 1236.

27. 'Navy's European Base,' in *Proceedings*, vol. 76, no. 11 (November 1950), pp. 1268-9; 'Far East Base,' in *Proceedings*, vol. 77, no. 2 (February 1951), p. 213; and 'Navy Notes,' in *RUSI*, vol. xcvi, no. 584 (November 1951), p. 660 and (February 1952), p. 123.

28. Edward L. Barker, 'The Helicopter in Combat,' in *Proceedings*, vol. 77, no. 11 (November 1951), pp. 1207, 1209; *Semiannual Report, January 1 to June 30, 1951*, p. 172; and *Semiannual Report, January 1 to June 30, 1952*, p. 156.

29. 'Navy Notes,' in *RUSI*, vol. xcvii, no. 585 (February 1952), p. 123.

30. *Conway's, Part I*, p. 203; *Semiannual Report, January 1 to June 30, 1952*, p. 156; *Semiannual Report, January 1 to June 30, 1951*, pp. 148-9, 151; and 'Navy Notes,' in *RUSI*, vol. xcvii, no. 586 (May 1952), p. 282; (August 1953), p. 483; (August 1952), p. 462; (November 1952), p. 615; and (February 1953), p. 142.

31. *Semiannual Report, January 1 to June 30, 1954*, pp.193-6. *Saratoga* was launched on 8 October 1955. 'Navy Notes,' in *RUSI*, vol. ci, no. 601 (February 1956), p. 135; and (February 1955), p. 137; *Semiannual Report, January 1 to June 30, 1956* (Washington, DC: GPO, 1956), p. 3; and *Semiannual Report, January 1 to June 30, 1957*, p. 230.

32. 'Navy Notes,' in *RUSI*, vol. xcvi, no. 581 (February 1951), p. 175; (November 1952), p. 615; and (August 1951), p. 512; and 'Modernization Program,' in *Proceedings*, vol. 77, no. 11 (November 1951), p. 1236.

33. Based on personal experience; *Conway's, Part I* p. 212; and *Semiannual Report, January 1 to June 30, 1955*, p.181. See also: W. D.

Brinckloe, 'A Page from the New Navy: The Frigate,' in *Proceedings*, vol. 84, no. 3 (March 1958), pp. 154-5.

34. Labayle Couhat, p. 740; *Conway's, Part I*, pp. 209, 217, 224; *Semiannual Report, January 1 to June 30, 1954*, pp. 191-4; *Semiannual Report, January 1 to June 30, 1953* (Washington, DC: GPO, 1953), pp. 208-9; and 'Navy Notes,' in *RUSI*, vol. ci, no. 601 (February 1956), pp. 135-6.

35. *Second Report of the Secretary of Defense*, pp. 113-14; '1951 Subs,' in *Proceedings*, vol. 77, no. 6 (June 1951), pp. 667-8; and *Semiannual Report, January 1 to June 30, 1953*, pp. 221-2.

36. *Semiannual Report, January 1 to June 30, 1952*, pp.149-50, 172; 'Missiles Super-Agency,' in *Proceedings*, vol. 77, no. 1 (January 1951), p. 97; 'AA Cruiser,' in *Proceedings*, vol. 77, no. 1 (January 1951), p. 98; and *Semiannual Report, January 1 to June 30, 1953*, p. 220.

37. *Semiannual Report, January 1 to June 30, 1950*, p. 114; *Semiannual Report, January 1 to June 30, 1951*, p. 152; and *Semiannual Report, January 1 to June 30, 1953*, pp. 219-20.

38. *Conway's, Part I*, p. 184.

39. *Semiannual Report, January 1 to June 30, 1951*, pp. 151-3, 169, 171; and *Semiannual Report, January 1 to June 30, 1952*, p. 147.

40. *Second Report of the Secretary of Defense*, p. 4; 'Navy Notes,' in *RUSI*, vol. xcvii, no. 587 (August 1952), p. 462; (February 1951), p. 175; and (November 1952), p. 615; and *Semiannual Report, January 1 to June 30, 1954*, pp. 191-2, 194.

41. *Second Report of the Secretary of Defense*, p. 115; *Semiannual Report, January 1 to June 30, 1950*, pp. 169; *Semiannual Report, January 1 to June 30, 1951*, p. 153; and *Semiannual Report, January 1 to June 30, 1954*, p. 194.

42. J. M. Spaight, 'Pax Atlantica.' in *RUSI*, vol. xcvi, no. 583 (August 1951), pp. 434, 439; R. M. J. Hutton, 'The Future of Maritime Power,' in *RUSI*, vol. xcvi, no. 582 (May 1951), pp. 222, 224-6; and 'Great Britain – Britain's Revitalized Navy,' in *Proceedings*, vol. 77, no. 2 (February 1951), p. 214-15.

43. 'Navy Notes,' in *RUSI*, vol. xcvi, no. 582 (May 1951), p. 328; (August 1951), p. 508; (May 1954), p. 298: and (May 1955), p. 309; and Hezlet, *Submarine*, p. 249.

44. *Conway's, Part I*, pp. 145, 152; 'Great Britain – Carrier Launching,' in *Proceedings*, vol. 76, no. 6 (June 1950), p. 690; 'Aviation–Britain's Sub Killers,' in *Proceedings*, vol. 76, no. 10 (October 1950), p. 1160; 'Britain's Fleet,' in *Proceedings*, vol. 76, no. 10 (October 1950), p. 1155; 'Great Britain–New Destroyer,' in *Proceedings*, vol. 76, no. 11 (November 1950), p. 1270; and 'Navy Notes,' in *RUSI*, vol. xcvi, no. 581 (February 1951), pp. 169-71.

45. 'Navy Notes,' in *RUSI*, vol. xcvi, no. 582 (May 1951), pp. 329-30; 'Great Britain – Naval Program,' in *Proceedings*, vol. 77, no. 5 (May 1951), pp. 555-6; 'Great Britain–Britain's Revitalized Navy,' in *Proceedings*, vol. 77, no. 3 (March 1951), p. 330; and 'Great Britain – Naval Program,' in *Proceedings*, vol. 77, no. 1 (January 1951), p. 99.

46. 'Navy Notes.' in *RUSI*, vol. xcvi, no. 582 (May 1951), p. 321; (November 1954), p. 619; (February 1956), pp. 131-2; and (May 1956), p. 287.

47. *Conway's, Part I*, p. 145; 'HM Aircraft Carrier Ark Royal', in *Proceedings*, vol. 76, no. 8 (August 1950), pp. 927-8; 'Navy Notes,' in *RUSI*, vol. xcvi, no. 582 (May 1951), p. 327; (August 1951), p. 508; (November 1951), p. 656-7; (February 1952), p. 120; (May 1952), p. 279; (February 1953), p. 142; (May 1953), p. 307; and (February 1955), p. 133; 'Great Britain–Carrier Completion,' in *Proceedings*, vol. 77, no. 9 (September 1951), p. 1236; and 'Great Britain: Royal Navy 1950,' in *Proceedings*, vol. 77, no. 4 (April 1951), pp. 439-40.

48. *Conway's, Part I*, pp. 149, 150, 151.

49. 'Navy Notes,' in *RUSI*, vol. xcvii, no. 586 (May 1952), p. 279; (May 1951), p. 327; (August 1952), p. 459; (February 1953), p. 141; (February 1954), p. 138; and (May 1954), p. 297.

50. *Conway's, Part I*, pp. 158-9; Labayle Couhat, pp. 216-17; and 'Fast Frigates for Royal Navy,' in *The Times*, London, 13 March 1956.

51. *Conway's, Part I*, p. 151; 'Navy Notes,' in *RUSI*, vol. xcviii, no. 589 (February 1953), p. 141; (August 1953), p. 478; (November 1953), p. 636; (February 1954), p. 138; (February 1955), pp. 133-7; and (August 1954), p. 470. See also: 'Navy Notes,' (May 1955), p. 309; (August 1955), p. 480; and (November 1955), p. 636.

52. 'Navy Notes,' in *RUSI*, vol. c, no. 597 (February 1955), p. 133; and C. P. Gallimore, 'The Development of Propulsive Machinery for Surface and Submarine Warships,' in *RUSI*, vol. xcvi, no. 583 (August 1951), p. 393.

53. *Conway's, Part I*, p. 180; Labayle Couhat, p. 225; and 'Navy Notes,' in *RUSI*, vol. xcix, no. 595 (August 1954), p. 470; (August 1952), p. 459; (February 1953), p. 141; (May 1953), p. 307, 310; and (May 1954), p. 297. For an excellent discussion on contemporary views concerning mine warfare, see: J. S. Cowie, 'Minelayers,' in *RUSI*, vol. c, no. 600 (November 1955), pp. 601-10.

54. A. K. Chesterton, 'The International Situation,' in *RUSI*, vol. xcviii, no. 589 (February 1953), p. 122; (August 1953), p. 460; (November 1953), p. 618; (February 1954), p. 120; (May 1954), pp. 279-80; (August 1954), p. 449; (November 1954), p. 602; (February 1955), p. 112; (May 1955), p. 288; (August 1955), p. 461; (November 1955), p. 619; (February 1956), p. 102; and (May 1956), pp. 271-2.

55. 'France – Naval Reductions,' in *Proceedings*, vol. 76, no. 3 (March 1950), p. 342; 'France – Manoeuvers in Mediterranean,' in *Proceedings*, vol. 76, no. 7 (July 1950), p. 688; 'France – Exercise "Symphonie",' in *Proceedings*, vol. 76,

no. 8 (August 1950), pp. 928-9; 'France – French Five-Year Plan,' in *Proceedings*, vol. 76, no. 12 (December 1950), p. 1387; and 'Navy Notes,' in *RUSI*, vol. xcvi, no. 584 (November 1951), p. 659; (August 1952), p. 462; and (November 1952), p. 614.

56. *Conway's, Part I*, pp. 20-1.

57. *Conway's, Part I*, pp. 34-5, 39-40, 43; 'France,' in *Proceedings*, vol. 77, no. 5 (May 1951), pp. 557-8; and 'Navy Notes,' in *RUSI*, vol. xcviii, no. 592 (November 1953), p. 638; (February 1955), p. 136; and (February 1956), p. 134.

58. S. Le H. Lombard-Hobson, 'Communism and Cold War Policies,' in *RUSI*, vol. xcvi, no. 584 (November 1951), pp. 624-6; and 'USSR–Baltic Strategy,' in *Proceedings*, vol. 77, no. 4 (April 1951), p. 442. See also: Alvary Gascoigne, 'Russian Policy Since 1945,' in *RUSI*, vol. c, no. 597 (February 1955), pp. 24-31; and T. Gerhardt Bidlingmaier, 'The Strategic Importance of the Baltic Sea,' in *Proceedings*, vol. 84, no. 9 (September 1958), pp. 23-31.

59. 'USSR – Conflicting Reports on Soviet Navy,' in *Proceedings*, vol. 76, no. 3 (March 1950), pp. 342-3; 'USSR – Soviet Navy,' in *Proceedings*, vol. 76, no. 12 (December 1950), pp. 1389-90; 'USSR – Soviets Commission a New Battleship,' in *Proceedings*, vol. 76, no. 3 (March 1950), p. 343; 'USSR – Sea Power Increasing,' in *Proceedings*, vol. 76, no. 5 (May 1950), pp. 576-8; and 'USSR – Soviet Navy Eyes Arctic and Pacific,' in *Proceedings*, vol. 76, no. 10 (October 1950), pp. 1156-7.

60. 'USSR–Red Gibraltar,' in *Proceedings*, vol. 76, no. 12 (December 1950), pp. 1388-9; 'USSR–Soviet Navy,' in *Proceedings*, vol. 77, no. 3 (March 1951), pp. 333-5; and 'USSR–Undersea Fleet,' in *Proceedings*, vol. 77, no. 3 (March 1951), p. 335.

61. 'USSR – Baltic Build-up,' in *Proceedings*, vol. 77, no. 8 (August 1951), pp. 897-8; 'USSR – Defense Budget,' in *Proceedings*, vol. 77, no. 8 (August 1951), p. 898; and 'Navy Notes,' in *RUSI*, vol. xcvi, no. 584 (November 1951), p. 660.

62. 'International Situation,' in *RUSI*, vol. xcviii, no. 591 (August 1953), pp. 459-60; 'Navy Notes,' in *RUSI*, vol. xcviii, no. 590 (May 1953), p. 310; and *Semiannual Report, January 1, 1954 to June 30, 1954*, pp. 153, 161-4.

63. *Conway's, Part II*, pp. 492-4; *Jane's Fighting Ships, 1971–1972*, pp. 603-6.

64. Ibid., p. 632; and *Conway's, Part II*, pp. 489-90.

65. *Conway's, Part II*, p. 487; *Jane's Fighting Ships, 1972-1973*, pp. 153, 629; Siegfried Breyer, *Guide to the Soviet Navy* (Annapolis, MD: US Naval Institute, 1970), pp. 25-6, 41, 51, 86-7, 89-91, 93-4, 96; and Wilhelm Hadeler, 'The Ships of the Soviet Navy,' in *The Soviet Navy*, M. G. Saunders, ed. (New York: Frederick A. Praeger, 1958), pp. 150-1, 153.

66. Labayle Couhat, p. 616; *Conway's, Part II*, pp. 487-8; Hadeler, p. 153; Breyer, pp. 50-1, 67-8,

88-9, 90, 92-4, 96, 270; and *Jane's Fighting Ships, 1972-1973*, p. 628.

67. *Jane's Fighting Ships, 1971-1972*, pp. 611-13.

68. For excellent discussions of peaceful coexistence and the Western responses, see: 'Sea Power in Competitive Coexistence,' in *Proceedings*, vol. 82, no. 11 (November 1956), p. 1172; and Malcolm W. Cagle, 'Sea Power and Limited War,' in *Proceedings*, vol. 84, no. 7 (July 1958), pp. 23-7.

69. John Erickson, 'The Soviet Naval High Command,' in *Proceedings*, vol. 99, no. 5 (May 1973), pp. 66-87.

70. Ibid., p. 69.

71. *Conway's, Part II*, pp. 465-6; and Middleton, p. 146.

72. 'Navy Notes,' in *RUSI*, vol. xcvi, no. 584 (November 1951), p. 660; and 'Twelve DEs to Pact Countries,' in *Proceedings*, vol. 76, no. 5 (May 1950), p. 574.

73. 'Norway,' in *Proceedings*, vol. 76, no. 3 (March 1950), p. 344; and 'Navy Notes,' in *RUSI*, vol. xcvi, no. 582 (May 1951), pp. 332-3; and (November 1952), p. 615. The first two units, *Zetland* and *Beaufort*, were transferred in September 1954. See: 'Navy Notes,' in *RUSI*, vol. xcix, no. 596 (November 1954), p. 622.

74. 'Sweden,' in *Proceedings*, vol. 76, no. 3 (March 1950), pp. 344-5; and vol. 76, no. 8 (August 1950), pp. 930-1; 'Sweden–Admiral Stromback and the Baltic Situation,' in *Proceedings*, vol. 76, no. 9 (September 1950), p. 1043; and 'USSR – International Rights in the Baltic,' in *Proceedings*, vol. 76, no. 9 (September 1950), p. 1043. In February 1950, Vice-Admiral Helge Stromback, then Commander-in-Chief of the Swedish Navy, estimated that the Soviet Baltic Fleet and Eastern bloc fleets had a battleship, five cruisers, 25 destroyers, 100 motor torpedo-boats, 100 submarines, 200 minesweepers, and a naval air force of 600 to 800 planes. See: 'USSR – Baltic Navy,' in *Proceedings*, vol. 76, no. 5 (May 1950), pp. 576-8.

75. 'Navy Notes,' in *RUSI*, vol. xcvi, no. 583 (August 1951), p. 512; and (May 1956), p. 292.

76. 'Belgium,' in *Proceedings*, vol. 76, no. 2 (February 1950), p. 225; 'Navy Notes,' in *RUSI*, vol. xcvi, no. 583 (August 1951), p. 511; and (November 1951), p. 659.

77. 'Belgium – The Belgian Navy,' in *Proceedings*, vol. 76, no. 9 (September 1950), p. 1042; 'Navy Notes,' in *RUSI*, vol. xcviii, no. 591 (August 1953), p. 482; (February 1954), p. 138; and (November 1953), p. 639; 'Netherlands,' in *Proceedings*, vol. 76, no. 5 (May 1950), p. 579; vol. 76, no. 8 (August 1950), p. 929; 'Holland,' in *Proceedings*, vol. 77, no. 4 (April 1951), pp. 443-4; vol. 76, no. 12 (December 1950), p. 1390.

78. 'Italy,' in *Proceedings*, vol. 76, no. 3 (March 1950), p. 344; vol. 77, no. 2 (February 1951), p. 217; vol. 77, no. 10 (October 1951), p. 1125; 'Navy Notes,' in *RUSI*, vol. xcvi, no. 581 (February 1951), p. 174; (May 1951), p. 332;

(February 1952), p. 122; and (February 1955), p. 136. In July 1951, *La Revue Maritime* reported that the Italian Navy had two battleships, three cruisers, 33 escorts, 626 coastal units, and sixteen minesweepers.

79. 'Navy Notes,' in *RUSI*, vol. c, no. 597 (February 1955), p. 137; (August 1955), p. 484; (May 1951), p. 333; (November 1951), p. 660; and (February 1955), p. 137; 'Spain,' in *Proceedings*, vol. 76, no. 11 (November 1950), p. 1274; vol. 76, no. 12 (December 1950), p. 1391; vol. 77, no. 4 (April 1951), p. 444; and A. K. Chesterton, 'International Situation,' in *RUSI*, vol. xcviii, no. 592 (November 1953), p. 616. Subsequent reports indicated just how substantial this agreement was. In essence, the United States agreed to provide Spain with a modern navy. Much of this was to be accomplished by modifications to existing Spanish combatants, and the rest through ship transfers; see: 'Navy Notes,' in *RUSI*, vol. c, no. 599 (August 1955), p. 484. The cost of this program had reached $30 million by the summer of 1955; see: 'Navy Notes,' in *RUSI*, vol. c, no. 600 (November 1955), p. 639.

80. 'Navy Notes,' in *RUSI*, vol. xcvii, no. 587 (August 1952), p. 462; and A. K. Chesterton, 'International Situation,' in *RUSI*, vol. xcviii, no. 592 (November 1953), p. 616.

81. 'Navy Notes,' in *RUSI*, vol. xcvi, no. 581 (February 1951), p. 175; and (February 1954), p. 142.

82. 'Egypt,' in *Proceedings*, vol. 77, no. 11 (November 1951), p. 1242, 1244; 'Navy Notes,' in *RUSI*, vol. c, no. 600 (November 1955), p. 638; (May 1953), p. 309; and (November 1955), p. 638; 'Destroyer for South Africa,' in *Proceedings*, vol. 76, no. 5 (May 1950), p. 576.

83. *Conway's, Part I*, pp. 7-8; 'Submarine Reconnaissance,' in *Proceedings*, vol. 76, no. 6 (June 1951), p. 669; 'Navy Notes,' in *RUSI*, vol. xcvi, no. 582 (May 1951), p. 331; (August 1951), pp. 509-10; (November 1952), p. 615; (August 1953), p. 481; (November 1955), p. 638; and (February 1956), p. 133; and 'Canada,' in *Proceedings*, vol. 77, no. 4 (April 1951), p. 443.

84. *Conway's, Part II*, pp. 401-7, 416, 428; 'Navy Notes,' in *RUSI*, vol. xcvi, no. 581 (February 1951), p. 175; (November 1951), p. 660; (February 1952), p. 123; (February 1953), p. 144; (August 1953), p. 483; and (November 1955), p. 638; and 'Brazil,' in *Proceedings*, vol. 76, no. 8 (August 1950), p. 929.

85. 'Navy Notes,' in *RUSI*, vol. xcvi, no. 582 (May 1951), pp. 331-2; and (August 1952), p. 461.

86. *Conway's, Part II*, pp. 339-40, 351-2; and 'Navy Notes,' in *RUSI*, vol. xcviii, no. 589 (February 1953), p. 143; (August 1953), p. 481; (May 1954), p. 300; and (August 1954), pp. 470-3.

87. 'China,' in *Proceedings*, vol. 75, no. 11 (November 1949), p. 1310; and 'USSR: Hainan Base,' in *Proceedings*, vol. 77, no. 4 (April 1951), p. 441.

88. *Conway's, Part I*, pp. 275-7; and 'Navy Notes,' in *RUSI*, vol. xcix, no. 595 (August 1954), p. 472.

3
From the Suez Crisis to the Six Day War, 1956–67

THE EFFECTS OF THE INFLUENCING FACTORS

The major factors influencing naval development from 1956 to 1967 were political events and technological advances; the former justified the continued need for naval forces, while the latter made building them increasingly costly. In one sense they concentrated existing naval power because the world became more polarized and the US–Soviet superpower rivalry became more pronounced, prompting both nations to invest heavily in their navies.[1] Navies also became increasingly costly, prompting nations such as Great Britain to curtail naval development. In another sense, there was a dispersing force since the leading nations exported naval ships to less affluent nations, creating regional navies that would come to play a role in maritime affairs. The great exception to this was France, which chose to resign from NATO and become an independent military power.

As naval development occurred, naval operations continued to reflect the importance of seas and importance of sea power, as the traditional theories of sea power remained valid. The period opened with the Suez Crisis and continued with other crises in which maritime power was relevant. The carrier was still seen as a most important system, but advances in submarines and guided missiles, coupled with the carrier's expense, limited further growth in her size. Conversely, battleships were almost extinct and heavy cruisers were becoming obsolete, as only the Soviet Navy had built a large number of them recently. Light cruiser, destroyer, and frigate designs had become overlapped with little distinction between displacements, armaments, and speeds. The emphasis on specialization that prevailed in the 1950s yielded to a need for general-purpose ships that could respond to all tasks. Quality was stressed over quantity, resulting in smaller navies, due to the expense involved.[2]

POLITICAL EVENTS AND NAVAL OPERATIONS

The Suez Crisis

The Suez Crisis affected Soviet and US naval development and prompted Great Britain and France to reconsider their sea power needs. The Canal had been a contentious issue for Great Britain and Egypt in the early 1950s, but, when talks led to the withdrawal of British troops, it seemed that conflict had been averted. However, Nasser's nationalization of the Canal on 26 July 1956 prompted a British–French–Israeli joint action in October. The plan called for an Israeli invasion of the Sinai which would give Great Britain and France a pretext to intervene and take control of the Canal. The Israeli offensive began on 29 October, but British and French ground forces did not arrive until 5 November, four days after the United States introduced a UN cease-fire resolution.[3]

The United States, which opposed such military action against Egypt, used its naval power skillfully to thwart the operation. Ships were deployed from the US west coast to the central Pacific, those in Hawaii were moved westward, and Seventh Fleet ships were ordered southward into the South China Sea. From there some of them, including amphibious forces, were sent to the Arabian Sea, within striking range of the Red Sea and the Persian Gulf. Concurrently, ships were deployed from the US east coast to an area south of the Azores, and ships from the Sixth Fleet were moved eastward in the Mediterranean. In effect, there was a general convergence of US naval power world-wide on Suez. US amphibious forces evacuated Americans from Alexandria, Egypt, Israel, and other nations as the Sixth Fleet, located southeast of Crete, helped stabilize the situation as hostilities were terminated.[4]

Although Egypt was soon to be a client of the Soviet Union, the USSR was unable to come to its defense, because it did not have adequate naval power to send into the Mediterranean, and even if it had had such power, it lacked the strategic strength to confront the United States. Thus, its role was limited to supporting Egypt in the UN debates.

The effects of Suez were significant. To America, it showed the value of its naval power. To the Soviet Union, it showed the correctness of the decisions made at the Twentieth Party Congress earlier in the year to build a modern ocean-going navy. To Egypt and the Arab world, while the Soviet Union did not respond with naval power, it still was perceived as a possible counter to US power in the Mediterranean. Finally, to the British and French, it showed the necessity of maintaining one's navy, because no matter how closely allied nations might be, there would be times when one's own naval forces would be indispensable.

In many respects, then, Suez was the beginning of an era. While the United States would use its sea power to react to crises, the Soviet Union, now convinced of the value of naval power, would proceed quickly to develop a world-class navy. For France, Suez was another stinging US action, following closely the humiliation in Vietnam, and it would later choose an independent course and resign from NATO. Finally, for Great Britain, Suez caused her to re-evaluate following the US lead, particularly when it came to supporting Israel.

The Lebanon Crisis, 1958

The outcome of Suez prompted further unrest – the Jordanian and Syrian crises in 1957 – as Arab nationalists tried to use Nasser's model as a means to influence their governments. This climaxed in Lebanon in 1958, when a bloody pro-Egyptian *coup d'état* in July caused additional violence as factions demanded that Lebanon join the United Arab Republic. Lebanese President

Camille Chamoun invoked the Eisenhower Doctrine and asked the United States to send in troops. By 16 July, the first of 15,000 US Marines had landed without incident. They remained until late October, after General Fuad Chebab was elected.

To the Soviet Union, still unable to deploy sufficient naval power, Lebanon was a fiasco. Limited again to making threats in international fora, Moscow's failure to react militarily prompted disillusionment in the Arab world, and she was no longer seen as a counter to US naval might. To compensate this setback, she began stationing submarines at Valona, Albania in the summer of 1958. At first eight, then ten, and finally twelve submarines were deployed, and in the West, these were perceived as a minor threat to the US Sixth Fleet.[5] The deployments were noteworthy and included a widely publicized naval exercise in the Ionian Sea in 1960. When the Sino–Soviet split occurred, however, dogmatic Albania sided with dogmatic China against revisionist Moscow and expelled the Soviet Navy from Valona. The departure was not a peaceful one, as Albanian forces fired on Soviet naval men, killing several and seizing two Soviet submarines. The loss of Valona was devastating. Without access to its logistical facilities, the Soviet Navy could not maintain a Mediterranean force, and unable to gain access to Arab ports, it had to cease its operations until the summer of 1964.

Quemoy and Matsu, August-October 1958

The year 1958 was a test of the power of US naval forces because while conducting the Lebanon landings, they also had to react to a crisis over the islands of Quemoy and Matsu. As tension increased, USS *Essex* sailed from the Mediterranean through the Suez Canal and onward to the China Sea, and a Marine amphibious task group was redeployed from Singapore. On 23 August, Chinese communists began shelling Quemoy and Matsu and conducted torpedo-boat attacks, as they threatened an invasion. Responding US forces defuzed the crisis; Beijing accepted an offer to resume negotiations on 6 September and announced a cease-fire on 5 October. Great Britain, while her naval commitments were such that she could not respond actively, had four carriers in the Mediterranean and one in the Persian Gulf that contained these regions as the United States reacted to China.[6] For the Soviet Union, this was another setback, since her inability to respond contributed to a deteriorating Sino-Soviet relationship.

British Naval Operations, 1958

While America responded to Lebanon, Jordan asked for British help against Iraq. As British troops were flown into Amman under air cover provided from HMS *Eagle*, carriers transported Marines to Malta, HMS *Bulwark* moved into the Gulf of Aqaba and other British naval ships were positioned to bring power to bear. The troops were removed after the situation had settled down. Later, in Oman in 1958, the Royal Navy supported Middle East Air Forces as they conducted operations and, in June 1961, Kuwait asked for assistance against an anticipated attack from Iraq. Aircraft and 5,700 personnel were dispatched and subsequently, the *Victorious* arrived to provide air cover. British forces remained until the threat of invasion had passed.[7]

The Bay of Pigs and the Cuban Missile Crisis

Communist insurgency and US–Soviet friction continued to influence international affairs. There were the Panama patrols in 1959, the U-2 crisis which scuttled a Soviet-American summit conference, and a crisis in the Congo in July 1960. In September the US Sixth Fleet was bolstered in response to a Berlin crisis and, in November, the Navy responded to Cuban-sponsored activity in Guatemala and Nicaragua. From February to April 1961, there was a reaction to Laos, and in June there was a response to events in the Dominican Republic. In September, a US carrier and cruiser entered the Black Sea to counter Soviet pressure. From May to July 1962, there was an intervention in Thailand, then threatened from Laos, and, in June and July, there was a build-up of Chinese forces opposite Formosa. However, it was Cuba rather than any of these reactions that was to have the greatest impact on subsequent affairs.

Prior to the Bay of Pigs operation, Moscow remained aloof from Havana, because her policy required that regimes resulting from successful national-liberation operations prove themselves before they could enjoy a close relationship with Moscow. This made the Soviet Union more immune to accusations of adventurism and minimized confrontations with the West. In Cuba's case, Moscow apparently believed that the United States would not permit a communist government to exist so close to its shores and expected it to overthrow Castro. This assessment was accurate, as Washington was almost obsessed with Castro. The response was the Bay of Pigs. Not wishing to be directly implicated, however, Washington did not provide sufficient support and the invading forces were stopped on the beaches. Castro had survived and, henceforth, the USSR was willing to support him more actively.

The Soviet response, to base medium- and long-range ballistic missiles and Beagle strike aircraft in Cuba, was scheduled to occur during the campaigning for the US Congressional elections in 1962, when Khrushchev felt that Kennedy, who needed greater Democractic Party representation in Congress, would not react militarily for fear of an adverse public reaction. However, this was a miscalculation, because Kennedy's reaction was assertive. The Soviets ultimately failed because although their nuclear weapons in Cuba gave them strategic power there, their conventional power was insufficient to defend this strategic outpost and they were forced to remove the missiles.[8] In retrospect, the crisis ended an era because, except for Vietnam, it was the last time that Moscow would not use her Navy to respond to a relevant crisis. Henceforth, she would deploy the new combatants that would become operational in the early 1960s in responses that supported her clients.

Allied Naval Operations, 1962-7

The Allied navies also reacted to several incidents in the 1960s. The US Navy reacted to a dispute between the Dominican Republic and Haiti in the spring of 1963, to the Cyprus crisis in 1963 and 1964, and to an Indo-Pakistani dispute in 1965. In 1962, Royal Navy forces participated in suppressing the Brunei

Rebellion by sea-lifting forces and assuring air cover. In January 1964, the British were asked to assist Tanganika, Kenya, and Uganda in quelling mutinous troops. HMS *Centaur* provided air cover as troops landed at Dar-es-Salaam to subdue a mutiny that threatened to spread throughout East Africa. The exercise was accomplished quickly and successfully, and order was restored.[9]

In 1965, US naval forces responded to a crisis in the Dominican Republic in April and USS *Boxer* was ordered to evacuate US citizens. Since their safety could not be guaranteed, forces were landed in western Santiago and a corridor was established between contending forces. By mid May, 23,850 troops were ashore, while 38 naval ships were offshore, as 6,500 people from 46 nations were evacuated. There were other alerts in 1965 and 1966, but the situation gradually returned to normal.[10]

Meanwhile, the British Navy was also busy. In 1966, HMS *Eagle* and then *Ark Royal* constantly patrolled the Mozambique Channel to ensure an embargo on shipments of oil to Rhodesia, and 40,000 troops were detailed to Singapore, where Great Britain supported Malaysia in its confrontation with Indonesia.[11]

Vietnam

A more enduring theme was Vietnam. What had begun as a moderate US commitment by Eisenhower became firmer under Kennedy and a major effort under Johnson. Attacks on the USS *Maddox* in August 1964 prompted Congress to pass the Gulf of Tonkin Resolution, which began a major US commitment to South Vietnam's defense. US naval activity, involving carrier operations, river patrols, and a host of other operations, became intense, tying up US naval assets and retarding naval development as the war drained available defense funds.[12]

In 1965, even before facilities were available for large-scale land-based air operations, the Navy's carriers provided a strike capability. Five carriers were assigned, and three were constantly on station. Naval gunfire support provided by cruisers and destroyers began in May 1965, expending more than 10,000 rounds of ammunition per month. In March, Operation 'Market Time', an anti-infiltration patrol to stop seaborne deliveries of supplies to the Viet Cong, was begun, and Operation 'Game Warden', involving more than 100 river patrol boats, Seal Teams, and Navy helicopters, was begun in April 1966 to deny the Viet Cong use of the rivers of the Mekong Delta. In October 1966, the Seventh Fleet was directed to conduct Operation 'Sea Dragon', intercepting enemy ships and craft along the North Vietnamese coast. Meanwhile, aircraft from three carriers staged more than 92,000 sorties and, in an average month, more than 5,000 tons of bombs and 30,000 rockets were used on enemy targets.[13] These operations showed again the value of US naval might because, while the Soviet Union closed the US – Soviet naval gap during the Vietnam period, America had so much military power in South-east Asia that Moscow could not hope successfully to intervene militarily and staged only one naval action in the early 1970s. Thus, at great cost, the US Navy fulfilled its missions in Vietnam.

France – Leaving NATO

After his re-election in 1965, Charles De Gaulle declared that the French were 'a race created for brilliant deeds', and felt that these could only be achieved if France were out from under foreign influence. His goal was to make France the leader of a European alliance independent of US and Soviet control. Among his first steps were to create an independent French nuclear weapons program, to remove all French troops from NATO, and to demand that all NATO military bases and troops be removed from France by April 1967.

The British East of Suez Policy

Several factors played in the British decision to adopt the East of Suez policy. The diminishing empire, the increasing cost of British colonial operations, and the uncertainty of retaining the remaining colonies were among the major political factors. However, equally important were economic considerations and events in Europe. Great Britain had initially opted not to join the European Common Market, but when the Market appeared as if it might succeed, Britain applied for admission. Primarily due to the opposition of France's De Gaulle, who considered Great Britain a rival for leadership in Europe and believed that London's US ties would give America too much influence, her request was denied. This exacerbated her financial difficulties and further justified adopting the East of Suez policy.

Although the policy was not adopted until later, the Defence White Paper of 1966 was definitive, so weakening the British military that the policy had to be adopted. And once it was adopted, there was less reason to continue the world-class Navy of the past. Now the nation's maritime demands were more regional, pertaining to the protection of British ports and sea lines of communication. As she tailored her Navy to meet these less rigorous demands, her naval construction was reduced accordingly.

Soviet Naval Operations, 1956-67

Soviet naval activity also was a factor compelling the West to continue its naval development. The shift of resources from the Baltic to the Northern Fleet was continued in order to position the Navy more ideally for operations on the high seas. Admiral Gorshkov's decision to send the fleet to sea created hardship as the Navy learned through on-the-job training. Accustomed to coastal operations, the Navy's knowledge of even the fundamentals of operating away from home waters was superficial. In one reported incident, a submarine that was familiar only with operating away from the pier for a day or at best a few nights was ordered to put to sea for a more lengthy patrol. Since canning, freezing, and other food preserving procedures were still primitive, an adequate amount of food – mostly fresh provisions – was brought to the pier alongside the boat as she prepared for sea. The crew dutifully loaded the food, fully filling compartment after compartment from deck to overhead and bulkhead to bulkhead, with no consideration of a balanced meal. While at sea, the crew literally ate its way through the compartments, ingesting one staple after another. One can imagine that the procedure created particular difficulties as the crew ate and digested the cabbage ration. In another report, a submarine captain complained that Soviet canning did not consider the problem of submarine pressure changes due to snorkelling. These changes created a cacophony of noise as can after can contracted and expanded, causing a continuous, deafening popping. The situation was so bad that some of the crew went berserk and had to be sedated.

In spite of these difficulties, the Navy fulfilled Gorshkov's orders and operated more frequently in the Norwegian and North Seas. Meanwhile, intelligence-collectors were detailed to the world's oceans – the US east coast, the British North Sea coast and elsewhere – to monitor Allied naval developments. In 1960, an impressive naval exercise was conducted in the Norwegian Sea, and Soviet submarines operated out of Albania from 1958 to 1961. It became obvious that the Soviet Navy was expanding on to the high seas as it attempted to establish sea control over a zone outward from the coast that was wider than the range of US Polaris missiles. These activities were duly reported by Western intelligence, adding further credence to threat projections.

The Six Day War, June 1967

The June 1967 War was the end of the era of the US Navy's domination in international crises. Since the Soviet Navy had renewed its Mediterranean naval operations in the summer of 1964 and had a sizeable force there in 1967, the war was the first test of its crisis management capability. The fleet was composed of modern surface combatants and submarines and had practised its operating techniques and command and control procedures, so that in June 1967, the US Sixth Fleet faced the greatest opposing force of ships since the Second World War. While the Soviet fleet was strong, however, it was not invincible. It was untested in combat, but its presence meant that Moscow no longer intended passively to permit unilateral US naval crisis reactions. Just before the war, the fleet was bolstered with ten ships from the Black Sea, and further arrivals eventually provided a fleet of more than 70 ships and submarines. The Soviets used this fleet conservatively by assigning missions that never taxed the capabilities of the fleet or of individual units. Thus, the response was limited to assertive operations such as penetrating US naval screens and cutting off ships; more complex, sophisticated missions were not attempted. For its part, the US Navy was employed less assertively than in the past. Those ships in port remained there, and the Sixth Fleet was centered north of Crete, considerably farther away from the crisis arena than it had been in the past. America learned two things from the war: that the Soviet naval presence in the Mediterranean was expanding, and that the contraction of British forces east of Suez was to have a significant impact. British augmentation during the crisis had been only an aircraft carrier and three frigates.[14]

The war had important effects. The Suez Canal, interdicted during the war, remained closed until 1974, necessitating a drastic shift in merchant marine operations world-wide. For the Soviet leadership, who had sought to extend their influence over the Canal, this was a major setback. Offsetting this, however, was their gaining naval access to Mediterranean ports, which had been denied since the expulsion from Albania in June 1961. Subsequent Soviet use of both Egyptian and Syrian ports was extensive, allowing an increase in the fleet's force level.

Conclusions

These political events had great influence on contemporary naval development. Perceiving that the Soviet Union was a major threat that was developing her naval power and that naval power was valuable in a variety of crisis responses, the United States continued its naval development. The Vietnam War, while it took its toll on ships, did not impact significantly as US naval development until the late 1960s. Meanwhile, the Soviet naval response to the June 1967 war was a harbinger of even greater naval reactions in the future. Great Britain gradually accepted the end of her empire, began to realize that it was necessary to abandon her commitments east of Suez, and started to become more regionally oriented, which affected adversely her subsequent naval development. France left NATO and began building a stronger navy. Elsewhere, there was a shift of power among the NATO nations as a response to the perceived Soviet – Warsaw Pact threat, and the supply of naval ships and systems to the world's nations as more and more navies developed.

GREAT BRITAIN – TWILIGHT OF THE QUEEN OF THE SEAS

The Political Context

In 1956, Britain reviewed the Suez crisis. 'What are the results? The overall result is that Great Britain has suffered one of the most shattering and humiliating defeats of her history. Her power in the Middle East has almost vanished.'[15] None the less, the government acted purposefully. It concluded that the Navy's missions were to prevent war by being able to meet hostilities on a global scale and to bring power quickly to bear on peacetime emergencies or limited hostilities.[16] A most significant reversal of British maritime policy was to occur, however, as the nation came to accept that the days of the empire were about to end, a realization that led gradually to accepting the East of Suez policy.

Restricted defense spending had begun to affect British maritime development even before 1956, although the problem's severity was not evident to many until the 1960s. We noted earlier that there was much innovation and activity in British naval construction after the war, but the problem was not in the numbers, but in the *types* of ships. In 1956, the nation had no nuclear-powered ships and had ordered no new large warships since the war. The aircraft carriers that were started during the war and the *Daring* destroyers were completed, but since the war Great Britain had concentrated on frigates, converting destroyers into fast ASW frigates, and building large numbers of minesweepers and fast patrol boats.

This would not sustain a world-class navy. And yet the signals were mixed in the mid 1950s. The 1956-7 Navy Estimates stated that design for a new guided missile cruiser was progressing, and the fleet escorts that had been ordered in the 1955-6 estimates were to be armed with guided missiles instead of AA guns. Conversely, the estimates were a reduction of £40,000,000 and, while the 1958-9 Estimates had an increase of 24 million pounds, most of this merely covered inflation. Many ships were scrapped – the carriers *Glory*, *Ocean*, *Theseus*, and *Unicorn*, the battleships *King George V*, *Howe*, *Anson*, and *Duke of York*, the cruisers *Cleopatra*, *Liverpool*, *Cumberland*, *Dido*, *Euryalus*, *Phoebe*, and *Sirius*, six destroyers, forty frigates, a monitor, six submarines, and a host of minesweepers, motor torpedo-boats, and other minor combatants. The angled-deck carrier *Warrior* was sold to Argentina. By 1961, the Navy had only ten cruisers – *Blake*, *Lion*, *Tiger*, *Bermuda*, *Belfast*, *Swiftsure*, *Mauritius*, *Gambia*, *Kenya*, and *Sheffield*, and only five carriers – *Ark Royal*, *Hermes*, *Centaur*, *Eagle*, and *Victorious*.[17] The Navy Estimates for 1962-3 provided for only one assault ship and two replenishment tankers, prompting the observation that the '. . . record of new construction . . . during these seventeen years is two guided missile armed destroyers, forty frigates, fourteen submarines and 200 coastal and inshore minesweepers . . .'[18] Planning for a carrier was approved in 1963, but the one was to replace two. This was in vivid contrast to the position of the 1950s which had proposed a new generation of carriers.[19] This prompted a comment from R. V. B. Blackman, editor of *Jane's Fighting Ships*:

> Britain's defence priorities are crystal clear and absolutely imperative to all except those of parsimonious or misdirected bent or in permanent blinkers. These priorities are new aircraft carriers, more frigates, and a steady replacement of our old, conventionally powered submarines by nuclear-powered hunter-killer submarines.
>
> Without new aircraft carriers the Fleet Air Arm will die and with it . . . Britain's power East of Suez, and Britain's voice in world counsels.
>
> Without more frigates Britain will die in wartime. . . .
>
> Without nuclear-powered submarines, the Navy itself will die. . . .
>
> . . . .Trincomalee is gone, Malta has been written off, Gibraltar is vulnerable to both air attack and foreign nationalism, Simonstown could deny access, Aden is insecure, Singapore is suspect after succession, and Hong Kong is only tenable by grace of the mainland giant.
>
> The British Commonwealth cannot continue to depend on the USA. . . . lest it find itself bereft of active US support as it was at the beginning of both wars.[20]

Planning was continued on the new carrier. When the government announced in August 1965 that it might give up its base in Aden, many commented that British defense must rely on *either* carriers *or* bases and that to give up both was illogical. Full realization of this contradiction came in 1966, however, when a Defence White Paper cancelled the aircraft carrier, called for a running down of the carrier force, substituting land-based aircraft working from island bases in the Indian Ocean and leaving British Guiana, the South African Territories, Nicosia, Aden, and Malta. This dictated the East of Suez policy, because without either carriers or bases, Great Britain could not provide air cover to protect her colonies. The carriers were to be retired as they wore out.[21]

The government's policy began an inter-service internecine fight that was just as brutal and debilitating as the one that raged in the US military during the late 1940s. The Navy, arguing that the carrier had provided relevant power in almost every recent British response, believed that the nation should reduce drastically or eliminate the Army, completely integrate the services into five or six well-defined commands, and rely on nuclear power at sea. The Army argued against continuing the Marines, while Air Marshall Heath, speaking for the Air Force, denigrated the carriers, claiming that they were not as responsive as the Air Force. He also argued that there was little need for air power east of Suez.[22]

Concerning the nation's colonial commitments, the reduction in military power and economic problems prompted the East of Suez discussion. Many argued that her commitments were not in London's vital interests, since East of Suez accounted for only 7 per cent of her trade. They averred that Britain should be a leader in a rapprochement between Asia and the West, thereby becoming a strong influence, but she should abandon the idea of being a great power.[23] It was in this context of restricted defense spending and a diminishing world role that British maritime development took place.

Submarines

The British nuclear-powered submarine program progressed when a proto-type, the 4,000-ton *Dreadnought*, was ordered in March 1957. Laid down on 12 June 1959, she was completed on 17 April 1963. Her power unit was purchased from Westinghouse, which shortened the construction time considerably. While reliance on a US plant similar to the one in USS *Skipjack* dictated the external appearance aft, her forward part was a unique British design. She provided significant feedback that was vital in designing the *Valiant*-class, which was slightly larger, displacing 4,900 tons. Five of the class, *Valiant*, *Warspite*, *Churchill*, *Conquerer*, and *Courageous*, were built from January 1962 onward (see Table 3.1). With a length of 285 feet and a 33-foot beam,

Table 3.1
Selected Force Levels – Royal Navy, 1957–67[a]

	Year										
	57	58	59	60	61	62	63	64	65	66	67
Submarines	46	48	42	36	31	34	36	39	35	36	36
Carriers	6	7	8	5	3	3	4	4	4	4	3
Commando Ships	0	0	0	0	1	1	2	2	2	2	2
Cruisers	9	9	8	7	5	4	3	2	2	1	0
Missile Destroyers	0	0	0	0	0	1	4	4	4	6	6
Destroyers	31	29	27	24	20	15	13	10	10	9	14
Frigates	28	30	31	32	33	42	52	53	60	56	49
Mine Warfare	38	42	46	50	54	58	62	61	58	58	56

[a]Various sources, including *Combat Fleets of the World, 1988–89*; *Conway's All the World's Fighting Ships, 1947–1982, Part I: The Western Powers*; *RUSI, The Soviet Union and the NATO Powers: The Military Balance* (London: Institute for Strategic Studies, 1959); *RUSI, The Military Balance* for the years 1961–1967; and *Jane's Fighting Ships*.

she was 20 feet longer and a foot wider than *Dreadnought* and was an excellent

ASW system.[24]

In February 1963, the government announced that it would build a fleet of five nuclear-powered ballistic missile-equipped submarines and that the first would begin operational patrols in 1968. Since it could afford only one system, it justified its decision by noting that the Royal Air Force's airborne Skybolt program had proven too expensive and that deploying the land-based Minuteman would make the British Isles' targets subject to destruction in a general war. The missiles would be bought from the United States, while the warheads would be of British design, and the fleet would be based at Faslane, about seven miles from Holy Loch. The result, the *Resolution*-class, provided a significant capability of 64 Polaris A-3 missiles in the four submarines, *Resolution*, *Repulse*, *Renown*, and *Revenge*, that were actually built. *Resolution* put to sea for trials on 22 June 1967, prior to beginning operational patrols in 1968.[25]

In conventionally powered submarine developments, in 1956, HMS *Porpoise*, namesake of a class of eight boats, was launched. The first operational submarine to be designed since the war, she provided a significant regional ASW capability. With great speed, diving depth, and endurance, these 2,303-ton boats were armed with eight 21in torpedo tubes. The 2,450-ton *Oberon*-class, which could conduct patrols in any part of the world, supplemented *Porpoise* in the late 1950s. *Oberon*, the lead unit, was laid down in 1955, and later units of this class were the first to have fiberglass in their superstructures.[26]

Aircraft Carriers

While no new carriers were built, Great Britain went to significant lengths to modernize existing units. The rebuilding of *Victorious*, which included an angled deck, steam catapults, and a modern aircraft arresting system, begun in 1950, was completed in 1957, and she joined the fleet in 1958. *Eagle's* modernization was completed, and *Hermes'* construction, begun in 1944, was finished in 1959. The *Centaur* carriers *Bulwark* and *Albion* were converted to commando carriers. Each could carry a commando detachment and had helicopters that could embark and unload the detachment's vehicles and could also be used for ASW. Both carried sufficient supplies to support commando operations ashore, providing much greater versatility and independence to commando forces.[27]

Cruisers

Since the Navy considered the battleship obsolete and scrapped the last one, *Vanguard*, in 1960, the cruiser was to be among the largest types in the fleet. Cruiser construction progression was similar to the carrier program – to modernize existing units but not build new ones. In 1959, *Belfast* was recommissioned after extensive refit and modernization. Work on the *Tiger*-class ships, *Blake*, *Lion*, and *Tiger*, which had begun in 1941-2, was completed when *Blake* was finished in 1961. Since their armament was of limited value in AAW and because they had excellent command facilities, *Blake* and *Tiger* were refitted with a flight deck for four helicopters. *Blake* was refitted from

1965 to 1969, and *Tiger*'s refit was begun in 1968.[28]

Destroyers

The deceleration in shipbuilding was most obvious in destroyers. The conversion of Second World War units to fast ASW frigates ended in 1956, with only 32 of 45 destroyers completed. Several *Weapon*- and *Battle*-class destroyers were converted to radar pickets.[29]

The *County*-class destroyer program was begun on 9 March 1959, when *Devonshire*, the first of eight units, was laid down. Construction was extremely slow, however, and the last two units, *Norfolk* and *Antrim*, were not completed until 1970. Armed with Seaslug and Seacat missiles, these 6,800-ton destroyers were capable of 32.5 knots, making them excellent for convoy duties, as components in a task force, and for crisis response operations world-wide. Given the lengthy construction period, improvements were made to the later units, including reconfiguring the mast in *Kent* and *London*. All were fitted with ASW helicopters.[30]

A follow-on to *County*, four *Type-82*-class destroyers were planned for in the mid 1960s. Built around the Seadart SAM system, the 7,700-ton *Type-82* was armed with an Ikara ASW launcher, Limbo depth-charge mortars, and 4.5in guns. Capable of 30 knots, it would improve significantly the Navy's ASW and anti-air capabilities. However, only one of these ships was ordered as a trials ship, while the remaining three fell victim to economic stringency. Laid down on 15 November 1967, HMS *Bristol* was launched on 30 June 1969. The cancellations prompted R. V. B. Blackman to comment, 'Only one of the four Type-82 will be built. Will other destroyers be sacrificed on the altar of economic penury like the long promised but now cancelled new aircraft carrier, the approved but subsequently rescinded fifth Polaris submarine, and the Type 82 in plural?'[31]

Frigates

Construction of four specialized classes of frigates – *Leopard*, *Whitby*, *Blackwood*, and *Salisbury* – ended when the last unit, the *Salisbury*-class frigate *Lincoln*, was completed on 7 July 1960.[32] However, since the frigate was not only cheaper to build, but also seemed more suited to the regional NATO role that many in government wanted to play, there was more construction in this class than in larger ships. In 1957, the *Rothesay*-class, was begun. Basically a modified *Whitby*, she displaced 2,560 tons and had the same dimensions and armament as *Whitby*. Nine of the thirteen planned units were built and all were later converted to carry a helicopter.[33]

In January 1958, *Ashanti*, the first of seven *Tribal* frigates, was begun in a production run that would end with the completion of *Zulu* in April 1964. These 2,700-ton, 27-knot ships were 360 feet long and were armed with Seacat SAMs, surface and AA guns, a Limbo ASW mortar, and a helicopter.[34]

In 1959, *Leander*, a new class of general-purpose frigate was begun. At 2,860 tons, she was larger and represented a return to more versatile, less specialized ships. With a length of 360 feet, *Leander* had impressive armament, including Seacat SAMs, guns, a Limbo ASW mortar, and a helicopter. At 28.5

knots, she was suited for ASW, AAW, anti-surface warfare, and radar picket duty, a fast and versatile asset for North Atlantic and European operations. Seven units were ordered initially, but *Leander* was such a successful design that 26 were built in a program that ended in 1973. The last ten are sometimes considered to be a separate class, called the *Broad Beam Leander*s. Their beams were 43 feet vice 41 feet in *Leander*, and they were modern.[35]

Assault Ships

In response to perceived changing responsibilities, the Navy built two *Fearless*-class assault ships, *Fearless* and *Intrepid*, completed in 1965 and 1967, to support amphibious operations. Each was armed with missiles and conventional guns, carried landing craft, heavy tanks, and helicopters and could launch craft by flooding her well deck astern. She combined the roles of a landing platform dock (LPD), landing ship infantry ship (LSI), and landing ship headquarters/fighter direction ship (LSH/LSF). Her mission was to land troops up to brigade strength together with armored fighting and transport vehicles and to provide the command facilities needed for such operations.[36]

THE UNITED STATES

The Soviet military threat continued to prompt US naval development and the construction plans were impressive. The 1959 plan included a nuclear-powered guided missile destroyer leader, six guided missile destroyer leaders, five guided missile destroyers, a nuclear-powered guided missile submarine, and four nuclear-powered attack submarines. In 1960, the Navy announced that its plans for 1960-70 were: 150 nuclear-powered ships, 200 SAM ships, arming all ships with ASW missiles or ASW aircraft by 1967, and a fleet of 75 nuclear-powered submarines, 40 of which would have ballistic missiles. The programs for the following years were similarly ambitious, although in 1962 it was decided that a new carrier would be conventional rather than nuclear-powered. Conversely, the perennial problems of cost and obsolescence continued to haunt the Navy. In 1958, the Chief of Naval Operations, estimating 20-year lives for aircraft carriers, fifteen years for destroyers, and thirteen years for submarines, stated that more than half the Navy's 900 ships were becoming obsolete. Some of this was cleared away when 26 small escort carriers, 23 cruisers, five battleships, and several old amphibious ships and submarines were scrapped in 1959. The block obsolescence problem remained, however, and the Navy's solution was the Fleet Rehabilitation and Modernization (FRAM) program which would extend a ship's life for five to eight years.[37] In this way, it was able to get the new submarines and surface combatants it needed by postponing replacement of existing ships.

Submarines

Under Admiral Rickover, the Navy's nuclear program had progressed so remarkably that by 1956, it had proven that nuclear-propulsion in submarines was feasible. The Navy had developed two types of plant, a water-cooled plant that was placed in *Nautilus*, and a sodium-cooled one in *Sea Wolf*. The records that these two units set were amazing. In 1957, *Nautilus* was refuelled for the first time after cruising 62,560 nautical miles, and she had travelled more than 1,280,000 nautical miles by August 1958. In a 1957 polar voyage, she came within 180 nautical miles of the North Pole, and in 1958, twin polar voyages by *Nautilus* and *Sea Wolf* were made with *Nautilus* reaching the North Pole on 3 August, and *Sea Wolf* reaching the Pole on 12 August. While these operations were so successful that US policy declared that all new submarines would be nuclear-powered, it was determined that *Sea Wolf*'s sodium-cooled reactor was not as efficient, and in 1959 it was replaced.[38]

Experiments with hull forms and types of submarines continued. *Skate* was commissioned in December 1957, and in 1958, thirteen nuclear-powered submarines were building or were on order. Seven had the *Albacore* shape and *Triton*, a radar picket submarine, launched in August, was at 5,963 tons, the largest submarine that had ever been built. She had two nuclear reactors and her purpose was to screen task forces against attack. She set a record in 1960 when on 10 May, she completed a round-the-world underwater voyage of 36,000 nautical miles in 84 days. *Swordfish* and *Sargo*, the fourth and fifth nuclear submarines, were commissioned in 1958, and *Halibut* the first nuclear-powered guided missile submarine, was completed in 1960.[39]

Having proven the feasibility of nuclear propulsion, it remained to demonstrate that a ballistic missile could be fully integrated into the submarine. If accomplished, it would have become a strategic nuclear system. As in other aspects of this amazing program, the projected schedule for a ballistic missile-equipped nuclear-powered submarine (SSBN) was shortened significantly. Polaris was to be operational in 1962. Flight tests for the solid propellant two-stage rocket began on 27 September 1958. Meanwhile, *George Washington*, the first SSBN, was launched on 9 June 1959, was commissioned on 30 December, successfully accomplished Polaris test launchings on 20 July 1960, and began her first operational patrol on 15 November, two years ahead of schedule. In doing so, the final goal had been achieved; henceforth until MRV and MIRV, progress would be in ranges, payloads, and accuracy, as the basic system had been built successfully. Polaris A-1 had a 1,200-mile range, A-2 a 1,500-mile range, and A-3 a 2,500-mile range. In 1961, A-2 was almost ready for production, and A-3 was in development.

The program was now helped significantly by politics. In his 1960 campaign, President John Kennedy claimed that America was behind in missile development, and the 'missile gap' became a major issue. Once President, he directed that there be a total of 29 Polaris submarines by December 1964, two years earlier than previously scheduled.[40]

Larger classes were built until the 41st SSBN, *Will Rogers*, was commissioned in 1967 (see Table 3.2). Five were of the 6,700-ton *George Washington*-class. Five were of the 7,844-ton *Ethan Allen*-class, commissioned from August 1961 to January 1963, and equipped with the 1,500-mile Polaris A-2. Finally there were 31 8,250-ton *Lafayette*-class units. The first eight were provided with Polaris A-2, while 24 carried the 2,500-mile Polaris A-3. Each SSBN carried sixteen missiles, for a total of 656 missiles. When the longer-ranged Polaris A-3 was developed, it allowed for patrols in the Pacific. Agana

Harbor, Guam was chosen as the staging site for Pacific-deployed SSBNs, and the first Pacific patrol, by *Daniel Boone*, was begun on 25 December 1964. Progress continued after the goal of 41 units was achieved. Older units were retrofitted with newer missiles, and planning for Poseidon, a more advanced missile, was begun in 1965. In January 1967, it was decided to deploy Poseidon and to retrofit it on the Polaris boats.[41]

In nuclear-powered attack submarine (SSN) developments, SUBROC, an anti-submarine rocket that could be launched by patrolling SSNs was developed. Eleven 4,311-ton *Permit*-class attack submarines were built from July 1959 until December 1967. They were powered by a single nuclear reactor, and were armed with SUBROC and four 21in torpedo tubes.[42] The lead ship, *Thresher*, was lost while conducting trials on 10 April 1963, and the *Permit*s were scrutinized during the Navy's SUBSAFE program that followed *Thresher*'s loss. They were soon followed by 42 4,777-ton *Sturgeon*-class units that were built from June 1961 to August 1975. *Sturgeon* was slightly larger, had a different sail, and incorporated the results of the SUBSAFE program. She was capable of 30 knots while submerged and had the same weapons as *Permit*.

Aircraft Carriers
The remaining three *Forrestal* units, *Saratoga*, *Ranger*, and *Independence*, were commissioned in April 1956, August 1957, and January 1959, respectively. 1,039 feet long, 250 feet wide, and with a maximum speed of 33 knots, they each had four acres of flight deck, four steam catapults, and four deck-edge elevators. *Kitty Hawk*, an improved *Forrestal*-class, was then begun. Displacing 80,945 tons, these were slightly heavier and longer than the *Forrestal*s. Their lengths and beams varied from unit to unit as new concepts and systems were incorporated, and they had smaller islands on their flight decks, improved elevators, and other innovations. *Kitty Hawk*, *Constellation*, and *America* were commissioned in April and October 1961, and January 1965, respectively. The fourth, *John F. Kennedy*, delayed by a debate as to whether she should be nuclear powered, was commissioned in September 1968.[43]

Meanwhile, work continued on *Enterprise*, and she was commissioned on 25 November 1961. Her eight reactors gave her a speed of 32 knots, and at 89,084 tons, a length of 1,040 feet and a 133-foot beam, she was the largest ship built to that time. While *John F. Kennedy* was not a nuclear-powered attack carrier (CVAN), a second CVAN, *Nimitz*, was authorized in 1967, and

Table 3.2
Order of Battle – U.S. Navy, 1957–67[a]

	Year										
	57	58	59	60	61	62	63	64	75	66	67
Ballistic Missile Submarines	2	2	4	7	10	14	17	23	30	37	41
Other Submarines	113	109	109	106	105	104	102	102	104	104	105
Attack Carriers	22	24	23	23	24	26	24	24	25	23	23

Battleships	2	0	0	0	0	0	0	0	0	0	0
Cruisers	16	15	12	13	12	13	14	14	14	14	13
Command Ships	1	1	1	1	1	1	2	2	2	2	2
Destroyers	253	245	237	226	223	240	226	225	234	232	237
Frigates	84	71	61	41	41	68	40	40	39	42	46
Mine Warfare	104	77	82	81	83	84	84	84	84	84	83
Patrol Vessels	12	12	6	4	4	2	0	0	0	0	3
Amphibious Ships	134	121	120	113	110	130	132	133	135	159	162
Auxiliaries	224	213	205	197	206	218	216	212	213	212	216
Totals	967	890	860	812	819	900	857	859	880	909	931

[a]US Department of the Navy, *US Navy Ship Force Levels, 1917–1989* (Washington, DC: Ships History Branch, Naval Historical Center, Department of the Navy, 1989), pp. 5–6. From 1963 until 1967, the former DLG and DLGN types appear under the types of cruisers or destroyers to which they were assigned on 30 June 1975, in the following manner: the DLG 6-class appears under destroyers; and the DLG 16-class and DLG 26-class (which became CGs), and the DLGN 25-, 35-, and 36-classes (which became CGNs) appear under cruisers.

some funds were appropriated for a third in 1968.[44]

Battleships and Cruisers

All four battleships had been decommissioned by 1958, but while other nations scrapped them, the Navy refused to let them die. In 1967, *New Jersey* was reactivated for use in Vietnam.[45]

Boston and *Canberra* joined the fleet in 1956. Armed with Terrier, a 20-mile-ranged, mach 2.5, beam-riding, proximity-fuzed surface-to-air missile (SAM), these cruisers improved the fleet's AAW capability considerably. Similarly, six *Cleveland* cruisers were converted to carry Tartar or Talos SAMS and were recommissioned between May 1958 and March 1960. Meanwhile, *Long Beach* (CGN-9), initially intended to be a frigate, was approved as the first nuclear-powered cruiser. Laid down in December 1957 and launched on 14 July 1959 at Quincy, Massachusetts, she was commissioned on 8 September 1961. Her two reactors provided a maximum speed of 30 knots and her armament included Talos and Tartar SAMs. At 16,602 tons and with a length of 721 feet, she had a crew of 1,107. She was the first ship to down an enemy aircraft with Talos missiles in combat. While she was a successful design, the Navy found it much harder to justify nuclear propulsion for surface ships than it did for submarines, and thus did not build additional CGNs for several years. While she was the only US cruiser built since the Second World War, with the converted cruisers the Navy had *Long Beach*, three *Albany*-class, two *Boston*-class, and six *Cleveland*-class units, for a total of twelve guided missile cruisers.[46]

Destroyer Leaders

The Navy continued to build destroyer leaders or frigates. *Bainbridge*, the first nuclear-powered guided-missile frigate (DLGN), was laid down in 1959 and commissioned in 1962. The armament on this 7,982-ton, 550-foot ship included Terrier SAMs, 3in AA guns, ASROC, and torpedo tubes. A second DLGN, *Truxun*, was laid down in 1963 and commissioned in May 1967. At 8,927 tons, she was larger than *Bainbridge*, and, in addition to *Bainbridge*'s armament, had a 5in 54-caliber dual-purpose gun, a newer ASROC/Terrier launcher, and two more torpedo tubes.[47]

Progress was also made on DLGs. The first of ten *Farragut* ships were laid down on 1 March 1957, in a program that would end in 1961. The armament on the 5,648-ton *Coontz* included Terrier SAMs and ASROC and torpedo tubes, making her a very capable AAW and ASW combatant. She was smaller than the nine 7,590-ton *Leahys* that were built from 1959 to 1964. These ships were 'double-enders', meaning that they had missile-launchers forward and aft in a design that was intended to screen fast carrier task forces. Armed with Terrier, 3in guns, ASROC, and torpedoes, she was a vast improvement to the carrier's security. The nine ships of a third class of DLGs, the *Belknap*, were built from 1962 to 1967. At 7,890 tons, these were larger than the *Leahys*. *Belknap*'s armament provided her with excellent ASW and AAW capabilities.[48] *Belknap* was damaged severely in a collision with *John F. Kennedy* in the Mediterranean in November 1975, was rebuilt and subsequently became the Sixth Fleet flagship.

Destroyers

Eighteen *Forrest Sherman* ships were built from 1953 to 1959. These, the first destroyers to be designed since the war, were 418 feet long and displaced 4,916 tons. Armed with 5in guns, some later received ASROC and other ASW systems. Four were converted to guided-missile destroyers from 1965 to 1968, having been given a single Tartar launcher aft and improved ASW systems, but plans for converting the other ships were dropped. A second class, *Charles F. Adams*, improved on the *Forrest Sherman* design. Built between June 1958 and August 1964, these 23 ships were larger and were armed with SAMs, 5in guns, torpedo tubes, and ASROC, making them excellent general-purpose destroyers.[49]

To maintain the fleet quantitatively, the FRAM (Fleet Rehabilitation and Modernization) Program was begun with the goal of extending a combatant's life by five to eight years in order to avoid block obsolescence. The program provided for the complete rehabilitation of the hull and machinery and modernization of the weapons and equipment. The primary emphasis was on ASW, and DASH was provided on the conversions. The prototype ship, *Perry*, was completed in 1959 and, at a cost of $6 million each, dozens of *Gearing* ships had undergone FRAM-I by the spring of 1965. FRAM-II provided similar modernization to *Sumner* and some *Gearing*-class destroyers.[50]

Destroyer Escorts

Four 1,916-ton *Claud Jones* destroyer escorts, built between 1957 and 1960, were an attempt to develop an economical system but they were succeeded by the more successful *Garcias*. These ten 3,371-ton escorts, built from 1962 to 1968, weighed as much as many of the world's destroyers, but were classified as escorts because of their single propeller and limited speed. Concurrently, six *Brooke* DEGs were built from 1962 to 1967. *Brooke* was identical with

Garcia except that a Tartar launcher and a different electronics system were provided. Both classes were followed by the 4,066-ton *Knox*, a highly successful but very expensive 46-unit class that was similar to *Garcia* and *Brooke*, but was larger.[51]

Amphibious Ships

In 1956, construction of seven *De Soto County*-class tank landing ships (LSTs) was begun. They had better sea-keeping ability than the *Terrebonne Parish*-class LST, which was completed in 1954, but, because of their slow speed, they were succeeded by the larger 8,342-ton *Newport*-class LST, which was built between 1967 and 1972. At 20 knots they were much faster than earlier classes, but had to forego the traditional bow doors in order to provide a hull form that could sustain the speed. Three classes of dock landing ships also were built. Three 13,745-ton *Raleigh*-class ships, which had both helicopter decks and floodable well decks, were built from 1960 to 1963. Twelve 16,900-ton *Austin*-class ships, built from 1963 to 1970, and five 13,700 *Anchorage*-class ships were significant developments in amphibious warfare. These ships were as big as cruisers, and carried helicopters, landing craft, tanks, troops, and cargo. They had both landing decks and docks, were armed with a battery of AA guns, and could operate independently like cruisers. The most significant advance, however, was the *Iwo Jima* amphibious assault ship (LHA). An entirely new type of amphibious ship, the LHA was a combination of an LPH (helicopter or amphibious assault ship) and dock landing ship that displaced 18,004 tons, was 602 feet long, and was armed with missiles and AAW guns. Seven such ships were built from 1959 to 1969.[52]

Missiles and ASW Weapons

Progress was also made in non-strategic missiles. In SAMs, Terrier, Tarter, and Talos were installed on surface combatants. Terrier had a 12-mile range and, like Talos, began its flight as a beam-rider, and then used semi-active homing for its final phase. Tartar, like the British Sea Dart, used computer imputs in first stage of flight, and then used semi-active homing. The 75-mile Talos, operational in January 1959, could be armed with a high-explosive or a nuclear warhead. In the early 1960s, the Navy considered the long-range Typhon system to provide fleet protection against the future long-range aircraft threat, but opted in favor of developing a smaller, less complex, cheaper system in 1964.[53]

In air-to-air missiles, the 12-foot, 300-pound Sparrow I supersonic missile was operational in 1956. It had a solid-fuel rocket motor and a velocity of more than 1,500mph. Advancements were made and Sparrow III was operational in 1960.[54]

In ASW developments, the antisubmarine rocket (ASROC) was perfected and delivered to the fleet. Able to deliver either a nuclear depth-charge or homing torpedo well beyond the range of Weapon Alfa, it was a dramatic ASW improvement and was placed on most new combatants and on FRAM ships. In 1959, improved sonobuoy systems, Julie and Jezabel, were installed on aircraft, and the P-3 Orion became operational in July 1962. A highly successful design, the Orion, a long-range, turboprop aircraft that could strike with depth-charges, torpedoes, special weapons and rockets, replaced the P2V Neptune, and became the ASW airborne workhorse. Meanwhile, DASH (Drone Antisubmarine Helicopter), a remotely controlled helicopter which could be flown from the deck of a ship, became operational in 1963.[55]

Electronics

The Ionospheric Forward Scatter and the Tropospheric Forward Scatter, developed in the 1950s, increased significantly the range of VHF and UHF communications. The single sideband technique was also developed and allowed for economizing power and the use of more channels. US photographic satellites, developed in the 1960s, were a great improvement over manned U-2 aircraft, since they were invulnerable to attack, and vastly improved US intelligence concerning Soviet naval developments. Finally, from 1958 to 1967, $18 million was expended in research in ELF (extra low frequency) communications, and a test cable was laid in the mountains of North Carolina and Virginia. The expense and public opposition retarded the program's progress.[56]

Several developments occurred in radar, sonar, and command and control. The SPS 39 three-dimensional radar was developed, and SPS 32 and SPS 33, the most advanced radars, were fitted on *Enterprise* and *Long Beach*. In 1960, new long-range radars, capable of operating in an ECM environment, and improved ECM receivers were deployed to the fleet. Further improvements were made, culminating in the AN/SPS-48 radar. In 1963, FRISCO (Fast Reaction Integrated Submarine Control) was initiated. It integrated all submarine command and control components into a single system. In sonars, the AN/SQS-23 and AN/SQS-26 sonars were integrated with various ASW weapons systems, including ASROC, DASH, and torpedoes, and were in the fleet by the mid-1950s.[57]

Conclusions

The Soviet military threat, the Suez, Lebanon, and Cuban missile crises, the Vietnam War, and political influences such as the missile gap issue sustained US naval development. While the great expense of maintaining a modern navy was realized, part of the cost was defrayed through FRAM. This was mortgaging the future, however, as FRAM ships would have to be replaced eventually, and an even greater expense would have to be faced. Additionally, the Vietnam War would continue and would eat into available defense funds. Finally, the Soviet Navy's performance in the June 1967 War and America's less incisive conduct were indicators of a future in which the United States and the Soviet Union would compete for naval influence. Thus, while the fleet was in good shape in 1967 and significant advances had been made, the Navy was about to enter a difficult period, which would affect adversely subsequent naval development.

THE SOVIET UNION

Admiral Gorshkov's leadership and substantial naval appropriations had a dramatic effect on the Soviet Navy. The major threats were seen as the developing US SSBN fleet and the aircraft carrier task groups. The response was multifaceted. Drawing on a rich submarine tradition, the Navy invested heavily in submarines in order to create an SSBN fleet of its own and a force of attack submarines. Concurrently, surface combatants and naval aviation were developed with the goal of establishing a sea denial perimeter along the Soviet coasts that would be deeper than the range of US Polaris missiles. As the range became longer with Polaris A-2 and A-3, the Soviets attempted to extend the perimeter farther outward in order to minimize this Polaris advantage.

The Navy provided other benefits and its use as a foreign policy instrument, so brilliantly described by Gorshkov in his articles, 'Navies in War and Peace,' and book, *Sea Power of the State*, was seen more frequently in the years from 1956 to 1967. The Navy was too weak to respond to Suez, Lebanon, or the Cuban Missile Crisis since the new ships were still being built, but it learned its lessons well as its reaction to the June 1967 Arab-Israeli War so vividly reflected.[58] In these years, defense concerns dominated naval construction. The goal was not sustained operations on the high seas or force projection. Rather it was to stop the Western naval forces that might advance on the Soviet Union in wartime, and the missile-armed combatants were built accordingly. With cramped living conditions and weapon systems that had little or no reload capacity, these ships were intended for a one-time shootout on the high seas.

Submarines

A priority after 1956 was the development of a force of ballistic missile-equipped submarines to balance the impending deployment of Polaris. After converting diesel attack submarines, the Navy built 22 *Golf*-class diesel-powered ballistic missile submarines (SSBs) from 1958 to 1965. These 2,700-ton submarines were armed with the SS-N-4 Sark missiles. Sark had a 300 nautical mile range and the submarine had to surface and conduct a time-consuming procedure in order to launch it. (Later, *Golf*s were provided with two 750-mile SS-N-5 Serb missiles, which greatly improved the capability.) Concurrently, six *Hotel* SSBNs were built from 1958 to 1962. She carried Sark, but in *Hotel II*, this was replaced with the SS-N-5 Serb, which could be fired while the submarine was submerged.[59] The Soviet SSBN program was accomplished with much less fanfare than the US program and there were rumors that it had encountered such difficulties that it was going to be discontinued, but US success drove Soviet builders onward until success was achieved. At any rate, the Soviets also achieved the remarkable – they placed a strategic missile in a nuclear-powered submarine, thereby creating a strategic weapon system. Admiral Gorshkov was correct when he said that this feat placed the Navy with the Strategic Rocket Forces, in the forefront of the branches of the Soviet military.

In 1960, the Soviets began their first nuclear-powered guided missile class, the *Echo-I* SSGN. Five boats were built; they were 360 feet long and displaced 5,500 tons. The *Echo I*s each had six Shaddock missile tubes, but could not carry the necessary mid-course guidance radar, and were later converted to attack submarines. More *Echo I*s were forsaken in favor of *Echo II*, 29 of which were built from 1961 to 1967. The *Echo II*s were 397 feet long, longer than *Echo I*, in order to allow for adding two additional Shaddock tubes and the mid-course radar.[60]

Their second class was the *Juliett* SSG, which appeared in 1962. Sixteen of these 2,500-ton diesel-powered boats were built, and each was armed with four SS-N-3 surface-to-surface missiles. She was a medium-sized long-range submarine that was used with aircraft or surface ships to protect against Western combatants. In a typical scenario, an aircraft or a surface combatant such as a SAM-equipped *Kashin* DDG would be a tattletale, shadowing a Western carrier or combatant and passing targeting data to an SSG/SSGNs and a missile-equipped surface combatant, such as a *Kynda* or *Kresta I*, that would be prepared to fire their missiles in a violent, short-lived conflict.[61]

The Soviets also built a fleet of attack submarines. Their first class, an improved version of *Zulu*, was the 2,400-ton *Foxtrot*, a highly successful diesel-powered submarine class which was used extensively in the Mediterranean in the 1960s and 1970s. Sixty-two were completed between 1958 and 1967. Concurrently with *Foxtrot*, the Soviets built their first nuclear-powered attack submarine, *November*, from 1958 to 1963. Fifteen *November*s were built. They displaced 5,300 tons, were armed with six 21in torpedo tubes, and could travel at more than 25 knots while submerged. One *November* was lost in the North Atlantic, and the class was deployed widely to support naval operations on the high seas in the 1960s and 1970s.[62]

In summary, the Soviet submarine program progressed more quietly and continually lagged behind the American program. Additionally, habitability was a low priority. For example, *Morskoy Sbornik*, the Soviet naval digest, reported that when a *Foxtrot* was at snorkel depth in the Mediterranean, interior temperatures could be as low as 35°F in the winter and well over 100° in the summer. Also, there were references to submarine crewmen with unsightly bald spots and skin ulcers – classic signs of radiation sickness – reflecting that the nuclear power plants in these early boats were not shielded properly. In spite of these shortcomings, which would have been unacceptable in the West, the program produced a credible threat against Western navies and an increasing strategic threat against the West.

Surface Combatants

In developing missile-equipped ships, the Soviets converted existing units and designed new ones. For their first new class, they built the highly successful *Kildin*. *Kildin* construction began in 1957, and four units were fitted with an SSN-1 Strela surface-to-surface missile (SSM) toward the stern. On a massive launcher, which could not be elevated above 15 degrees, Strela was a jet-propelled missile with a range of 30 miles. It had a radio and homing guidance system and could carry either a high-explosive or a nuclear warhead. If the missile flew over the horizon, mid-range relay stations, such as helicopters, submarines, or surface ships, continued to guide it. SAM-*Kotlin*s were converted from *Kotlin*s and were provided with the SA-N-1 Goa, a two-stage missile with a solid propellant booster, that had a range of thirteen to seventeen nautical miles and a maximum effective ceiling of 44,000 feet. Goa was a beam rider and had a high-explosive warhead. Nine SAM-*Kotlin*s were converted from 1961 onward, with variations between the first and the remaining eight. Integrative problems occurred, particularly with SAM-*Kotlin*, where topside weight reduced sea-keeping ability, but the units probably supplied technical feedback that was valuable in designing subsequent systems. Both classes were deployed extensively to the Mediterranean from 1967 onward.[63]

The *Krupnyy*-class was begun in 1958. While larger, her hull and superstructure were similar to *Kotlin*, but she had two Strela SS-N-1 missile-launchers, one forward and one aft, and an arsenal of twelve missiles, double that of *Kildin*. She had a helicopter platform, was a second experimental platform for Strela and, while she was similar to *Kildin*, she had greater firepower and better electronics. She reflected Soviet satisfaction with Strela and was an attempt to develop a better platform for the missile. She was used heavily in Soviet naval deployments to the high seas.[64]

The Soviets also began building the *Kashin* guided missile destroyer (DDG), one of their most successful ships. The last of the Soviets' general-purpose destroyers, she was a heavily armed combatant that was excellent for AA defense in which the missile system had been fully integrated into the ship's design. The first of twenty ships was completed in 1962 in a program that ended in 1972. She was armed with two fully trainable twin GOA (SA-N-1) missile-launchers forward and aft, each atop a missile magazine. The world's first all gas turbine propelled warship, she served as the tattletale in the anticarrier task group of the 1960s and 1970s. A conversion program was begun in 1972 which involved modernizing the weapons suite and adding a helicopter platform.[65]

The next combatant to appear was the 5,600-ton *Kynda* guided-missile cruiser (CG). Four were built from 1959 to 1965 as a response to Allied carrier task groups. *Kynda*'s armament included eight SS-N-3B SSM launchers in two quad mountings, with one reload per launcher. For air defense, she had a twin SA-N-1 launcher and a supply of sixteen missiles.[66]

Kynda was followed by four 7,500-ton *Kresta I* ships which were built from 1964 to 1968. At a length of 508 feet, this 32-knot ship was larger than her predecessor. The most significant advance was a hanger and deck for a Hormone helicopter, which meant that she could provide her own mid-range guidance for her surface-to-surface missiles, and did not require assistance. Her armament included two twin SS-N-3b SSM launchers and two twin SA-N-1 SAM launchers. She was an excellent general-purpose ship that was oriented against the attack carrier task group threat.[67]

In 1966, reflecting a program shift away from anticarrier warfare and to ASW, the Navy began building ten *Kresta II* cruisers in a program that would end in 1978. At 518 feet, she was slightly longer than her predecessor. Of greatest importance were her SS-N-14 dual-purpose ASW/anti-ship missile-launchers. She also carried SA-N-3 missile-launchers, other guns, ASW weapons, torpedo tubes, and a Hormone A helicopter.[68]

The *Kanin* guided missile destroyers were a conversion of *Krupnyy* and involved replacing the SS-N-1 surface-to-surface missile with the GOA (SA-N-1) SAM system. *Kanin* provided additional AA and ASW defense to operating forces, but was not a significant advance in naval technology.[69]

In summary, the development of Soviet missile-equipped ships progressed through the conversion of existing conventional units to the design and production of new ships. In engineering, the Soviets showed a great interest in gas turbine propulsion. The advantages here were the high speed available and that they were capable of the 'cold start'. (In contrast, a US ship had to wait from the time a unit was at cold iron watch to when sufficient pressure was available.) In size and weight, succeeding classes of ships tended to be larger than previous ones, but there were exceptions. Concerning mission, an initial emphasis on anticarrier warfare was later switched to ASW. Thus, advances in both anti-ship (SSM) and anti-air (SAM) missiles occurred concurrently, with emphasis on range, accuracy, fire power, and speed. Technology progressed on both high-explosive and nuclear warheads. The SSMs and SAMs provided a capability for ships to attack carrier task groups with SSMs and to defend themselves with SAMs from air attack. Finally, the lack of space, the limited missile reloads, and the habitability standard indicated that these ships had been built to defend against NATO forces in a quick, violent conflict. Larger, more self-sustaining ships for force projection and extended operations in remote areas of the world would come later. For now, the immediate goal was to counter Western naval power, and the surface combatants produced provided greater defense against Western forces that might advance toward Soviet territory.

Amphibious Ships and Missile Patrol Boats

In amphibious warfare, the Soviet Naval Infantry was abolished in the early 1950s, for reasons that still remain unknown. For equally obscure reasons, it was re-established in the early 1960s, just before the fall of Khrushchev. Unlike the US Marine Corps, the Soviet Naval Infantry was always a small, élite force that would operate in areas relatively close to Soviet territory where air cover was assured. Since it was not intended for operations world-wide, the ships built to support it were modest when compared to US amphibious ships. In this context, the Soviets made significant progress when they deployed the first of fourteen 4,700-ton *Alligator* tank landing ships (LSTs) in 1966. These were 370 feet long and had a 50-foot beam, large enough to transport 540 troops and their equipment. They were capable of sixteen knots and were used widely in the Mediterranean and Indian Ocean, and along the coast of West Africa. Fifty-five units of a smaller ship, the *Polnocny*, were built in Poland from 1963 to 1972, and were capable of carrying smaller numbers of troops.[70]

Progress in missile-equipped boats was revolutionary. The early classes, *Komar* and *Osa I* and *II* were built from the late 1950s onwards. *Komar* was armed with two and *Osa* with four SS-N-2 missiles. Small, fast, and armed with deadly missiles, they completely upset the traditional concept of equating a ship's fire power with her displacement. These boats would pose a great threat to navies operating on the high seas and would create the 'missile fever' of the late 1960s.[71]

Table 3.3

Selected Ship Types – Soviet Navy, 1957–67

	Year										
	57	58	59	60	61	62	63	64	65	66	67
Ballistic Missile Nuclear Submarines	0	0	0	0	0	1	1	1	2	3	6
Ballistic Missile Diesel Submarines	10	19	23	23	23	23	23	23	23	23	23
Guided Missile Nuclear Submarines	0	0	0	0	2	4	9	15	23	29	33
Guided Missile Diesel Submarines	0	1	2	3	5	12	16	18	20	22	25
Nuclear Attack Submarines	0	0	0	1	3	4	5	6	7	8	10
Diesel Attack Submarines	345	305	275	250	262	302	320	323	320	205	280
Carriers	0	0	0	0	0	0	0	0	0	0	1
Cruisers	31	30	30	26	21	21	22	22	21	21	21
Destroyers	170	140	120	109	111	112	112	116	116	110	103
Frigates	57	59	62	66	66	80	94	106	106	100	92

Conclusions

Contemporary reports of Soviet naval development noted a navy that was operating ever more frequently on the high seas. Intelligence collection patrols were begun off the US east coast and elsewhere, and their Mediterranean naval operations were duly noted. These operations were not without their mishaps. For example, when six Soviet submarines were sent to the Caribbean during the Cuban missile crisis, one had mechanical problems that prevented it from submerging except for short periods, and it eventually returned to the Baltic on the surface, accompanied by a trawler.[72] But the Navy was growing and staged an impressive response to the June 1967 Arab-Israeli War. It would play a major role in maritime development in the 1970s.

FRANCE

France's extrication from Indo-China improved her financial situation, but her involvement in Algeria continued to burden the treasury and the situation was still difficult in the late 1950s. The war in Indo-China had convinced the French that the carrier was the key force projection ship and she designed her future navy accordingly. Progress had been made when the *Surcouf* and *Duperre* destroyer classes were built and the 11,545-ton cruiser *De Grasse* was redesigned to provide AAW protection. These programs and the *Le Normand* frigate program were completed in the 1950s. Meanwhile, work continued on the heart of the new Navy, the carriers, *Clemenceau* and *Foch*, which were launched in December 1957 and July 1960. These 32,780-ton ships were very much in the European, vice the American, carrier tradition, in that they were smaller and more heavily armored. They were innovative and incorporated all the advances in carrier technology of the 1950s. Initially intended to carry 60 aircraft, they finally carried fewer, owing to the fact that newer aircraft needed more space. The *Clemenceau*-class was a successful design, providing France with the desired force-projection ships.[73]

In the latter part of the 1950s, the Navy was still encumbered with restricted financing. *Jean Bart* was laid up on 1 August, to be converted to a schools ship. She was obsolete and funds were not available to convert her to a guided-missile ship. In 1958, because of reduced appropriations, a 30,000-ton aircraft carrier and a guided-missile light cruiser were cancelled and, in 1961, France cancelled plans to build a guided-missile cruiser. These were minor setbacks, however, as France continued to develop a modern Navy. The 12,365-ton helicopter carrier *Jean d'Arc*, was laid down in July 1960 and completed in June 1964. She was very much in the European tradition and looked like a cruiser forward and a helicopter carrier aft. Capable of carrying both assault and ASW helicopters, she provided additional flexibility to the Navy.[74]

In other construction, an experimental destroyer, *La Galissonnière* (T 56), was completed in July 1962. Provided with a helicopter and the latest equipment, she provided valuable input for future classes, including the 6,090-ton *Suffren*-class, which was begun in December 1962. *Suffren* and her sister *Duquesne* were designed to provide AAW and ASW protection to the new carriers. They were France's first guided-missile destroyers, had a radically different design, were very innovative, and represented a departure from European concepts to a unique French design. Her influence was seen in *Aconit* (C 65), a single ASW ship that was laid down in 1967 and completed in 1973.[75]

France also devoted appropriate attention to her submarine fleet. On 29 June 1957, *Argonaute*, the first of four *Aréthuse*-class submarines, was launched. These were very innovative, since they were hunter-killer submarines and were a significant departure from the earlier *Narval*.[76]

Soon after *Aréthuse* was begun, the lead unit of the highly successful *Daphné* class was laid down. Very maneuverable, easy to maintain, and with a small crew, these quiet submarines were very popular and several were built for export. The French run of eleven units was completed in 1970.[77]

La Force de Dissuasion

Like the United States and Great Britain, France developed a strategic submarine fleet, and in her case, given the political circumstances, this was a significant feat. When Charles de Gaulle came to power in 1958, he began to extricate French forces from NATO, triggering a series of events that ended with the removal of all NATO facilities from France in 1969. An aspect of de Gaulle's program was that France could no longer exist under the US nuclear umbrella and had to develop a force of its own. The result, the *force de dissuasion*, was difficult to develop because France had alienated the United States, who refused to provide the requisite nuclear technology. France's solution was to schedule the force as follows: the first phase consisted of producing a force of 62 Mirage IV bombers; while the second involved placing intermediate-range missiles in hardened bunkers. However, these would be transitory to the third generation, which would be comprised of at least three nuclear-powered submarines carrying 48 500-kiloton IRBMs. The submarines would be operational in 1970, 1972, and 1974.[78]

Without US assistance, France faced a sizeable problem. An experimental submarine, *Gymnote*, was launched in 1958. Conventionally powered because France could not obtain the nuclear technology from America, she was equipped with the gear necessary to test the new ballistic missiles. Meanwhile, France did develop the necessary technology and, in 1964, *Le Redoutable*, France's first SSBN, was laid down. In a five-unit construction program that would continue into the 1980s, France produced a class that, while it was only mildly innovative, provided her with the desired strategic capability. Each carried sixteen missiles, initially the 500-kiloton, 2,500-kilometer M1. However, improved missiles, the 3,000-kilometer M-2 and then the one-megaton M-20 were provided in the third unit onward.[79]

Table 3.4
Selected Force Levels – French Navy, 1957–67

	Year										
	57	58	59	60	61	62	63	64	65	66	67
Submarines	25	25	23	21	19	24	24	22	22	21	21
Carriers	4	4	4	4	2	3	4	4	4	4	4
Battleships	2	2	1	1	1	0	0	0	0	0	0
Cruisers	5	5	5	4	4	2	2	2	2	2	2
ASW/AAW Leaders	2	2	2	2	1	0	0	0	0	0	0
Destroyers	20	20	20	20	19	18	18	18	18	18	18
Frigates	50	66	62	51	44	44	46	43	31	30	29
Mine Warfare	114	101	99	95	86	86	86	102	102	100	105
Patrol Craft	30	42	31	22	16	16	15	20	20	15	15
Amphibious Ships	8	6	6	5	8	6	6	8	8	9	9

Thus, while de Gaulle's policy created problems for the naval program, developments in submarine construction and additional classes of surface ships contributed, so that in 1967, France was developing a well-balanced fleet of combatants and support ships, an independent navy that Paris could use for its own purposes.

OTHER NATIONS

Europe

In 1956 Norway received three modernized *River*-class frigates from Canada. In 1967, she received the last eight *Kobben*-class submarines and, in 1966, the last of five *Oslo*-class frigates was completed. It perceived that aggressive Soviet military operations against it were psychological warfare that was part of a Soviet policy of exerting pressure on the wings of Europe. Likewise, Sweden perceived a threat and maintained a moderately sized navy. In 1956, its naval inventory was composed of three cruisers, fifteen destroyers, six frigates, 31 motor torpedo-boats, 24 submarines, two minelayers, 50 mine-sweepers, and nine auxiliaries, for a total of 140 ships. It ordered two large destroyers and six *Draken* submarines in 1957, but cancelled the destroyers and a minelayer in 1958. By 1960, its inventory was 182 ships, including 27 submarines.[80]

The German Navy was expanded significantly. In 1956, it received two US destroyers and began a large construction program so that, whereas there were 80 officers and petty officers and no non-rated enlisted at the end of 1955, there were 8,000 men and 70 vessels by the end of 1956, and 15,000 men and 100 ships by the end of 1957. In 1958, the new program included several destroyers, frigates, submarines, minelayers, minesweepers, motor torpedo-boats, and other ships. Additionally, Great Britain sold seven frigates to Germany in January 1958 and 1959. On 26 March 1960, the first German destroyer built since the war, the 4,330-ton *Hamburg*, was launched. The first of four such ships, she was armed with dual-purpose guns, torpedo tubes, and depth-charge mortars. In May 1963, the last of four *Hamburg*s was launched, and three slightly modified *Charles F. Adams* destroyers were ordered from the United States.[81]

The Dutch also maintained their naval power. In 1955, the last of four *Holland* destroyers were completed and, in 1958, the *Friesland* destroyer program was completed when the eighth unit, *Amsterdam*, was finished. From 1963 to 1967, six 2,850-ton *Van Speijk* frigates were built, and from 1959 to 1961, sixteen *Van Straelen* inshore minesweepers were built. In 1958, the conversion of the carrier *Karel Doorman*, which included an angled flight deck, a steam catapult, and a new AA battery, was completed. In submarines, the last of four triple-hulled *Dolfijn* submarines was completed in 1966.[82]

In southern Europe, Portugal maintained her navy by relying on transfers and purchases from other nations: four British *Bay*-class frigates were transferred in 1959 and 1961, and three US *Dealey*-class and four *Commandant Rivière*-class frigates were procured in the mid-1960s. Four French *Daphné* submarines were ordered in 1964. More significantly, Spain developed her navy through indigenous construction and US assistance. In 1956, she was nearing the end of her construction program of three fast frigates, nine ASW frigates, four submarines, and six corvettes. Shortly after *Rota* was completed in early 1960, Spain announced that she would receive two more US destroyers as part of her modernization program. The relationship was continued into the 1960s and, in 1965, the United States agreed to finance the building of five frigates in Spain for the Spanish Navy. To bolster her submarine force, she ordered four *Daphné* submarines from France in 1966.[83]

Italy's naval development was also notable. Two *Doria*-class helicopter cruisers, *Andrea Doria* and *Caio Duilio*, were laid down in 1958 and were completed in 1964. These were unique; they had very broad beams in relation to their length, were armed with guided missiles forward, and had helicopter decks aft. Two guided missile destroyers, *Impavido* and *Intrepido*, were completed in 1964. Two classes of frigates were also built. Four 1,650-ton *Bergamini* frigates were completed in 1962, while two *Alpino* frigates were launched in 1967. The *Toti*, a four-unit diesel submarine class, was begun in 1965 and completed in 1968. Three US *Balao* submarines were acquired in 1960 and 1966.[84]

Africa and the Middle East

Very significant naval development occurred in Egypt where, beginning with the Czechoslovakian Arms Agreement of 1955, it received naval assistance from the Warsaw Pact. By 1959, this aid included six *Whiskey* submarines, two destroyers, four minesweepers, and twelve torpedo-boats from the USSR, and six Yugoslav motor torpedo-boats. Of greater consequence was the provision of twelve *Osa* and eight *Komar* missile boats, which would have a dramatic impact after the June 1967 War. Partially to offset this Egyptian build-up, Israel bought two British submarines, *Springer* and *Sanguine*.[85]

Elsewhere, the corvette *Tobruk*, which had been built especially for Libya, was commissioned in 1966, and in Ghana, two minesweepers were commissioned in 1959. In Nigeria, the British minesweeper *Hare* was transferred and renamed *Nigeria* in 1959 and, in 1964 Nigeria bought a 2,000-ton frigate built in the Netherlands.[86]

More significant development began to take place in South Africa. In 1956, it bought the British ASW frigate *Wrangler* and renamed it *Vrystaat*, but cancelled an order for two more such ships. It also began an expansion program which included buying British minesweepers and seaward defense boats. On 2 April 1957, Simonstown, which had been a British naval base for 142 years, was transferred to South Africa. Subsequently, three *Rothesay* ASW frigates and several *Ton* coastal minesweepers and *Ford* seaward defense boats were bought from Great Britain and, in 1967, three *Daphné* submarines were bought from France.[87]

Canada and Latin America

Canada still took her defense responsibilities seriously in 1956. The light fleet carrier, *Bonaventure*, was received from Great Britain in January 1957 and the *St. Laurent* and *Restigouche* frigate programs were completed. By the end of 1958, the *River* frigate modernization and reconstruction program had been completed and construction had begun on *Mackenzie*, a new destroyer class that was an upgrade of the *Restigouche*. Four were built between 1958 and 1963. It was subsequently decided to equip two additional *Mackenzie* units, *Nipigon* and *Annapolis* with helicopter facilities. Two *St. Laurent*-class destroyer escorts, *St. Laurent* and *Assiniboine*, were converted to include adding VDS and facilities for ASW helicopters, and the remaining five were converted from 1963 to 1967. Meanwhile, Canada purchased three British *Oberon*-class submarines.[88] While this naval activity involved little innovation, it provided Canada with a significant naval force.

Farther southward, the relevant activity involved buying older ships from Europe and the United States. Argentina purchased the carrier *Warrior* from Great Britain in 1958 and renamed it *Independencia* and Venezuela bought seven British destroyers and three Italian light destroyers. Peru bought the British cruisers *Newfoundland* and *Ceylon*, while Brazil bought the British carrier HMS *Vengeance*, renaming it *Minas Gerais*. Brazil also received seven US *Fletcher* destroyers. Finally, Colombia bought two *Modified Halland* Swedish destroyers.[89]

The Indian Ocean

In the Indian Ocean, the most significant activity concerned India and Pakistan. Primarily through purchases and transfers from Great Britain, the Indian Navy evolved into an important regional naval force. It invested heavily in the specialized British frigates, purchasing a dozen of these ships, which gave her impressive AAW and ASW capabilities. Pakistan also invested in British ships to provide a defense capability and to offset Indian naval development. These included *Diadem*, a British *Bellona*-class cruiser and the *Battle*-class destroyers *Cadiz* and *Gabbard*. In 1958, the destroyers *Tariq*, *Tippu Sultan*, *Taimur* and *Turghil* began conversion to ASW frigates and two were completed in 1959. In 1958, the United States bought HMS *Charity*, a destroyer, and gave it to Pakistan, where it was renamed *Shah Jehan*. In 1964, the US *Tench*-class submarine *Diabolo* was transferred and, in 1966, four *Daphné* submarines were ordered from France. Finally, in Ceylon the British bases at Trincomalee and Katunayle were transferred from Great Britain to Ceylon in 1958. Ceylon bought two former Canadian *River* frigates from Israel and acquired three *Algerine* minesweepers.[90]

The Pacific Ocean

Malaysia received twelve British minesweepers in the late-1950s and 1960s. The most significant naval activity occurred in the People's Republic of China, which by 1957, had received several destroyers, submarines, and escorts from the USSR, and in the Republic of Korea, Japan, Australia, and New Zealand. Korea received several US ships including destroyer escorts and submarines.[91]

Japan invested heavily in her navy. By January 1957, she had built two *Harukaze* destroyers and four frigates (one *Wakaba*-, one *Akebono*-, and two *Ikazuchi*-class), had received eighteen frigates, a submarine, and 50 gunboats from the United States, and planned to build a large submarine, nine destroyers, nine minesweepers, and fifteen other combatants. In the late 1950s, she built seven *Ayanami*-, three *Murasame*-, and two *Akazuki*-class destroyers. On 25 May 1959, the 1,100-ton *Oyashio*, Japan's first post-war submarine, was launched. It was followed by three classes in the early 1960s, the two-unit *Hayashio*-class, the two-unit *Natsushio*-class, and the four-unit *Oshio*-class. *Hayashio* and *Natsushio* had limited range, but the *Oshio*s were much larger and more capable. The surface combatant program was also continued. A single *Amatsukaze*, Japan's first guided-missile destroyer, was completed in 1965. She was equipped with Tartar missiles. The first of six *Yamagumo*-class ASW destroyers was laid down in March 1964. This was such a successful design that construction was continued into the 1970s. A second class, *Minegumo* very similar to *Yamagumo* but substituting DASH for ASROC, was begun in 1967. Three ships were built. Finally, the first of four *Takatsuki* ASW destroyers was laid down in 1964. Like the *Minegumo*s, the *Takatsuki*s were meant to carry DASH, but when the DASH program was adjudged unsatisfactory, both classes were modified.[92]

Australia continued its building program. The last of the *Daring*-class destroyers was completed in 1959, and four *Yarra*-class ASW frigates, similar to the British *Whitby*, were built from 1957 to 1963. A modified *Yarra*, the *Swan*-class, was begun in 1965, and the second and last ship was completed in 1970. Australia bought three *Charles F. Adams* guided-missile destroyers in 1963. These were virtually the same as the US class, except that they carried the Ikara ASW system in place of ASROC. Naval activity in New Zealand was limited to replacing units: the *Whitby*-class frigates *Otago* and *Taranaki* were ordered from Great Britain.[93]

CONCLUSIONS

In many ways, June 1967 saw the end of an era. Henceforth, many existing, trends would mature to alter the naval scene significantly. Great Britain, contending with the Defence White Paper of 1966, would accept the East of Suez policy and tailor her Navy accordingly. The US Navy was overextended, given its obligations in Vietnam, and this would inhibit future naval development. It had mortgaged the future with FRAM and would have to pay the price. France, now independent, would have a greater impact on naval development, while the Soviet Navy, fresh from its success in the June War, would play more prominently in future years. Finally, the access of less affluent nations to cheaper naval systems—missile patrol boats and the like, would have a very great affect on future events. Thus, in July 1967, many of the world's navies looked forward to an uncertain future.

NOTES

1. James A. Nathan and James K. Oliver, *The Future of United States Naval Power* (Bloomington: University of Indiana Press, 1979), p. 9.

2. *Jane's Fighting Ships, 1958-1959* (New York: McGraw-Hill, 1958), p. iv; *1961-1962*, pp. iv-v; and *1964-1965*, p. iv; and William R. Kintner, 'American Responsibilities in the Nuclear Age,' in *Proceedings*, vol. 82, no. 3 (March 1956), p. 254. The issue of the carrier's vulnerability was still being fought in 1958. See: Laurence B. Green, 'A Case for the Attack Carrier in the Missile Age,' in *Proceedings*, vol. 84, no. 7 (July 1958), pp. 46-134; and 'Navy Notes,' in *RUSI*, vol. ciii, no. 610 (May 1958), p. 276.

3. A. K. Chesterton, 'The International Situation, in *RUSI*, vol. xcviii, no. 590 (May 1953), p. 289; (November 1953), p. 619; (May 1954), p. 281; (August 1954), p. 453; (November 1954), p. 603; (February 1955), p. 114; (November 1955), p. 620; and (February 1956), pp. 101-2; Ernest Stock *Israel on the Road to Sinai, 1949-1956* (Ithaca, NY: Cornell University Press, 1967), pp. 185, 206-7, 212-15; and Congressional Quarterly, *The Middle East*, 7th ed. (Washington: Congressional Quarterly, 1987), p. 17. For an insight into the legal issues involved, see: Charles W. Koburger, Jr. 'The Legal Background to the Suez Crisis,' in

Proceedings, vol. 83, no. 3 (March 1957), pp. 315-20.

4. J. C. Wylie, 'The Sixth Fleet and American Diplomacy,' in *Soviet-American Rivalry in the Middle East* ed. J. C. Hurewitz (New York: Frederick A. Praeger, 1969), pp. 55-6, A total of 2,200 Americans were evacuated from the Middle East from Alexandria, Haifa, Tel Aviv, Amman, and Damascus: 1,680 by the Navy and 533 by the Air Force. (US Department of Defense, *Semiannual Report, January 1 to June 30, 1957* (Washington, DC: GPO, 1957), p. 175.) See also: William Hessler, 'Sixth Fleet: Beefed Up for a Bigger Job,' in *Proceedings*, vol. 84, no. 8 (August 1958), pp. 23-30.

5. In 1957, there were reports that the Soviet Union was building a secret base on the island of Saseno, in the Bay of Valona. See: 'Soviet Base in Albania,' in *Deutsche Soldaten Zeitung*, March 1957.

6. Ryan, p. 21.

7. D. C. Watt, 'The Role of the Aircraft Carrier in Some Recent British Military Operations,' in *RUSI*, vol. cxi, no. 642 (May 1966), p. 129; Maurice Heath, 'The Balance in Britain's Air Power: Land-Based or Carrier-Borne?' in *RUSI*, vol. cxi, no. 642 (May 1966), p. 126; Peter Mangold, 'Britain and the Defence of Kuwait,

1956-1971,' in *RUSI*, vol. 120, no. 3 (September 1975), p.46; and Watt, p. 129.

8. Howe, p. 28.

9. US Department of Defense, *Annual Report for Fiscal Year 1964, Including the Reports of the Secretary of Defense, Secretary of the Army, Secretary of the Navy, and Secretary of the Air Force* (Washington, DC: GPO, 1965), p. 239; Heath, p. 126; T. M. P. Stevens, 'A Joint Operation in Tanganyka,' in *RUSI*, vol. cx, no. 637 (February 1965), p. 48-55; and Watt, p. 130.

10. US Department of Defense, *Annual Report for Fiscal Year 1965*, (Washington, DC: GPO, 1966), pp. 9-11, 260-1.

11. 'Notebook: Keeping Watch Off Beira,' in *Proceedings*, vol. 92, no. 8 (August 1966), p. 166.

12. On 2 August, North Vietnamese PT boats attacked the USS *Maddox*, which was on patrol in the Gulf of Tonkin. Aircraft from USS *Ticonderoga* warded off the attack and damaged all but three of the PT boats. On 4 August, two destroyers were attacked in the Gulf, and at least four PT boats sunk. Aircraft from *Ticonderoga* and *Constellation* then flew 64 sorties against North Vietnamese PT boat bases and oil storage depots. Twenty-five boats were sunk or damaged, and the facility was 90 per cent destroyed, while two US aircraft were lost and two were damaged. The incident is very significant because of its political effects. In the immediate aftermath, the Gulf of Tonkin Resolution was signed on 10 August 1964 and US personnel in southeast Asia increased from 16,500 to 60,000 in Fiscal Year 65. As the war dragged on, however, many in Congress would question the wisdom of the resolution. (US Department of Defense, *Annual Report for Fiscal Year 1965* (Washington, DC: GPO, 1966), p. 5.) The US build-up was very rapid. The US presence was increased significantly and Seventh Fleet ships with Marines embarked were moved into the immediate area when crises occurred. On 28 July 1965, the strength was raised from 75,000 to 125,000. By November, there were 153,000 and, by 30 June 1966, 267,000 personnel. At end of Fiscal Year 1966, there were 200 Navy ships and 47,000 Navy personnel in south-east Asia. (US Department of Defense, *Annual Report for Fiscal Year 1966* (Washington, DC: GPO, 1967), pp. 5-6, 11).

13. US Department of Defense, *Annual Report for Fiscal Year 1967* (Washington, DC: GPO, 1968), pp. 7, 303-4; and *Annual Report for Fiscal Year 1966* (Washington, DC: GPO, 1967), p. 293.

14. Based upon personal observation. See also: J. C. Wylie, 'The Sixth Fleet and American Diplomacy,' in *Soviet-American Rivalry in the Middle East*, edited by J. C. Hurewitz (New York: Frederick A. Praeger, 1969), pp. 57-60; Neil Sheehan, 'Admiral Says Soviet Shadowing Often Imperils Ships in Sixth Fleet,' in *New York Times*, 1 June 1967, p. 18; Peter Young, 'The Arab-Israeli War-I,' in *RUSI*, vol, cxii, no. 648

(November 1967), pp. 324-31; Peter Young, 'The Arab-Israeli War-II,' in *RUSI*, vol. cxii, no. 648 (November 1967), pp. 332-9; and Howe, p. 326.

15. A. K. Chesterton, 'The International Situation.' in *RUSI*, vol. cii, no. 605 (February 1957), p. 87.

16. Donald Barry, 'The British Navy in the Nuclear Age.' in *Proceedings*, vol, 83, no. 10 (October 1957), p. 1070.

17. B. B. Schofield, 'Britain's Postwar Naval Policy,' in *Proceedings*, vol. 84, no. 5 (May 1958), pp. 81-3; 'Navy Notes,' in *RUSI*, vol. ciii, no. 610 (May 1958), p. 274, and (November 1958), p. 583; *Jane's Fighting Ships, 1956-1957*, pp. v-vi; *1958-1959*, p. iv; and *1961-1962*, p. iv; and 'Future of Five British Battleships,' in *The Times*, London, 30 January 1956.

18. *Conway's, Part I*, pp. 133-5; Labayle Couhat, p. 225; and *Jane's Fighting Ships, 1962-1963*, p. v.

19. *Jane's Fighting Ships, 1963-1964*, p. v; and *1964-1965*, p. v.

20. *Jane's Fighting Ships, 1965-1966*, pp. vi, vii. See also: 'No More Bases,' in *Manchester Guardian*, 22 May 1956; Ronald Stead, 'British Reassess Singapore,' in *Christian Science Monitor*, 17 April 1956, pp. 3-4; Tom Pocock, 'We Must Go Down to the Sea Again: A Plea for a Return to a Maritime Strategy,' in *RUSI*, vol. cix, no. 633 (February 1964), pp. 23-6; and R. A. Clarkson, 'The Naval Heresy,' in *RUSI*, vol. cx, no. 640 (November 1965), pp. 316-20.

21. 'Notebook: British Carriers,' in *Proceedings*, vol. 87, no. 2 (February 1961), p. 148; 'Notebook: Britain May Give Up Aden Base,' in *Proceedings*, vol. 91, no. 10 (October 1965), p. 145; and Peter Gretton, 'The Defence White Paper, 1966,' in *RUSI*, vol. cxi, no. 642 (May 1966), p. 117.

22. Gretton, p. 118; Watt, pp. 128-31; L. E. S. H. Le Bailly, 'The Royal Navy's Role in the Defence Service of the 1980s,' in *RUSI*, vol. cxi, no. 646 (May 1967), pp. 137, 142; and Heath, pp. 124-7.

23. Alastair Buchan, 'Britain East of Suez: Part One–The Problem of Power,' in *RUSI*, vol. cxii, no. 647 (August 1967), pp. 209-15; and William Clark, 'Britain East of Suez: Part II–The Problem of Influence,' in *RUSI*, vol. cxii, no. 647 (August 1967), pp. 216-20.

24. Labayle Couhat, p. 209; *Jane's Fighting Ships, 1959-1960*, p. v; *1961-1962*, p. v; and *1971-1972*, pp. 336-7; 'Navy Notes,' in *RUSI*, vol. civ, no. 616 (November 1959), pp. 514, 516-18; (May 1959, p. 253; and (August 1960), p. 427; Hezlet, *Submarine*, p. 249; and Middleton, p. 141.

25. *Conway, Part I*, p. 172; Labayle Couhat, p. 208; Hezlet, *Submarine*, p. 252; 'British Select A-Sub Base,' in *Proceedings*, vol. 89, no. 7 (July 1963), pp. 156, 158; 'Britain Set to Build Four Polaris Subs,' in *Proceedings*, vol. 89, no. 7 (July 1963), pp. 156, 158; *Jane's Fighting Ships, 1971-1972*, p. 335; and 'Fifth Polaris Submarine Cancelled,' in *Proceedings*, vol. 91, no. 6 (June 1965), p. 168.

26. Labayle Couhat, p. 210; *Conway's, Part I*, pp.

170, 171; *Jane's Fighting Ships, 1956-1957*, pp. iv-v; *1958-1959*, p. iv; *1959-1960*, p. v; *1961-1962*, p. v; and *1971-1972*, pp. 338-9; 'Navy Notes,' in *RUSI*, vol. ciii, no. 611 (August 1958), p. 428; (February 1958), p. 126; (February 1959), p. 111; (November 1959), p. 514; (February 1957), p. 104; (August 1957), p. 421; (February 1960), p. 124; and (November 1960), pp. 575-6; and Hezlet, *Submarine*, p. 249.

27. *Jane's Fighting Ships, 1956-1957*, pp. v-vi; *1958-1959*, pp. iv-v; *1961-1962*, p. v; and *1959-1960*; p. v; 'Navy Notes,' in *RUSI*, vol. cv, no. 617 (February 1960), p. 124; and (May 1960), p. 292.

28. *Conway's, Part I*, p. 151; 'Navy Notes,' in *RUSI*, vol. cv, no. 620 (November 1960), p. 576; (November 1959), p. 514; and (May 1959), p. 253; and *Jane's Fighting Ships, 1956-1957*, pp. iv-v; *1958-1959*, p. iv; *1959-1960*, p. v; *1961-1962*, p. v; *1964-1965*, p. iv; *1966-1967*; and *1971-1972*, p. 342.

29. *Jane's Fighting Ships, 1956-1957*, p. v; and *1959-1960*, p. v.

30. *Conway's, Part I*, p. 154; *Jane's Fighting Ships, 1964-1965*, p. v; and *1971-1972*, pp. 346-7; and 'Navy Notes,' in *RUSI*, vol. cv, no. 618 (May 1960), p. 292.

31. *Conway's, Part I*, p. 155; and *Jane's Fighting Ships, 1967-1968*, p. v.

32. Desmond Whettern, 'Britain's New Frigates,' in *The Nautical Magazine* (September 1956); Desmond Wettern, 'Britain's New Frigates,' in *Proceedings*, vol. 83, no. 8 (August 1957), pp. 906-7; 'Navy Notes,' in *RUSI*, vol. cii, no. 605 (February 1957); p. 104; (May 1957), p. 253; (August 1957), pp. 420-1; (November 1957), p. 593; (February 1958), p. 125; (August 1958), p. 427; (November 1958), p. 583; (February 1959), p. 110; (November 1959), p. 514; (February 1960), p. 124; and (November 1960), p. 575; and *Jane's Fighting Ships, 1956-1957*, pp. iv-v; *1958-1959*, p. iv; and *1959-1960*, p. v.

33. *Conway's, Part I*, p. 163; 'Navy Notes,' in *RUSI*, vol. cv, no. 617 (February 1960), p. 124; (May 1960), p. 292; (August 1960), p. 427; and (November 1960), p. 575; and *Jane's Fighting Ships, 1961-1962*, p. v.

34. *Conway's, Part I*, p. 162; and *Jane's Fighting Ships, 1958-1959*, p. iv; and *1959-1960*, p. v; 1961-1962, p. v; and *1971-1972*, p. 356.

35. Labayle Couhat, p. 221; *Conway's, Part I*, pp. 164-5; and 'Navy Notes,' in *RUSI*, vol. ciii, no. 611 (August 1958), p. 428; and *Jane's Fighting Ships, 1961-1962*, p. v; and *1964-1965*, p. iv.

36. *Conway's, Part I*, p. 174; Labayle Couhat, p. 226; and 'Britain's Second Assault Ship Sails,' in *Proceedings*, vol. 93, no. 8 (August 1967), pp. 153-4.

37. *Jane's Fighting Ships, 1956-1957*, p. vi; *1958-1959*, pp. v-vi; *1959-1960*, p. vi; *1962-1963*, p. vi; *1963-1964*, p. v; *1964-1965*, p. v; and *1966-1967*, p. v.

38. US Department of Defense, *Semiannual Report, January 1 to June 30, 1957* (Washington,

DC: GPO, 1957), pp. 4, 232; US Department of Defense, *Annual Report, July 1 1959 to June 30, 1960* (Washington, DC: GPO, 1961), p. 22; '"Nautilus" Sets Many Marks,' in *New York Times*, 9 August 1958; 'Navy Notes.' in *RUSI*, vol. ciii, no. 612 (November 1958), p. 585; and *Jane's Fighting Ships, 1956-1957*, p. vi.

39. *Conway's, Part I*, pp. 230, 232, 237, 240; *Semiannual Report, January 1 to June 30, 1958*; *Jane's Fighting Ships, 1958-1959*, pp. iv, vii; *1956-1957*, p. vi; and *1959-1960*, p. vi; 'The First Fifty Years of US Submarines,' in *Proceedings*, vol. 82, no. 11 (November 1956); p. 1215; 'Professional Notes,' in *Proceedings*, vol. 82, no. 6 (June 1956); pp. 667-70; 'Navy Notes,' in *RUSI*, vol. cv, no. 619 (August 1960), p. 429 and (November 1957), p. 595; and *Semiannual Report, January to June 1957*, p. 178.

40. *Jane's Fighting Ships, 1958-1959*, p. iv; and *Annual Report, 1958-1959*, pp. 16, 220, 245; *Annual Report, 1959-1960*, p. 245; Paul B. Ryan, *First Line of Defense: The US Navy Since 1945* (Stanford, CA: Hoover Institution Press, 1981), p. 27; and *Annual Report, 1960-1961*, pp. 7-8. In view of this accelerated program, it was believed that SSBNs would provide adequate security, and the installation of Polaris on *Long Beach* was cancelled.

41. *Jane's Fighting Ships, 1966-1967*, p. v; and *1967-1968*, p. v; J. L. M. McGeoch, 'Submarine Developments,' in *RUSI*, vol. cxi, no. 643 (August 1966), p. 202; 'Guam Chosen as Home Site for Pacific Fleet Polaris Subs,' in *Proceedings*, vol. 88, no. 12 (December 1962), p. 143; *Annual Report, 1965*, p. 14; and *Annual Report, 1967*, p. 14.

42. US Department of Defense, *Annual Report, July 1960 to June 1961*, p. 238; *Annual Report, 1964*, p. 20; *Annual Report, 1965*, p. 267; and *Jane's Fighting Ships, 1971-1972*, p. 415.

43. John Bunker, ' U.S. Navy Outgrows "Jeep" Escort Carrier,' in *Christian Science Monitor*, 2 March 1956; *Semiannual Report January to June, 1956*, *Semiannual Report January to June 1957*, p. 4.; *Semiannual Report, January to June 1958*, p. 7; *Annual Report, July 1 1960 to June 30, 1961*, p. 197; *Annual Report, 1967*, p. 316; *Jane's Fighting Ships, 1956-1957*, p. vi; *1958-1959*, pp. vi, vii; *1960-1961*, p. v; and *1971-1972*, pp. 434-6, 439-40; 'Navy Notes,' in *RUSI*, vol. cii, no. 608 (November 1957), p. 595; (May 1959), p. 255; W. D. Brickloe, 'A Page from the New Navy: The *Forrestal*-Class Attack Carrier,' in *Proceedings*, vol. 84, no. 7 (July 1958), p. 145.

44. Labayle Couhat, p. 699; *Jane's Fighting Ships, 1956-1957*, p. iv; *1958-1959*, p. vi; *1959-1960*, p. vi; *1965-1966*, p. v; *1966-1967*, p. iv; and *1967-1968*, p. v; 'Navy Notes,' in *RUSI*, vol. cii, no. 606 (May 1957), p. 256 and (November 1960): p. 577; *Semiannual Report, January to June 1957*, p. 230; and *Annual Report, 1967*, p. 316.

45. *Jane's Fighting Ships, 1965-1966*, p. v; and *1967-1968*, p. v.

46. Labayle Couhat, pp. 726-7; *Conway's, Part I*, p. 209; *Semiannual Report, January 1 to June 30, 1956*, p. 4; David A. Anderton, 'Terrier-Armed Cruiser to Defend Navy's Atlantic Fleet Task Forces,' in *Aviation Week*, 7 November 1955; *Semiannual Report, January to June 1958*, pp. 7, 11; *Annual Report, July 1959 to June 1960*, p. 265; 'Navy Notes,' in *RUSI*, vol. civ, no. 616 (November 1959), p. 518; *Semiannual Report January to June 1957*, p. 233; *Jane's Fighting Ships, 1956-1957*, pp. iv, vi; *1958-1959*, p. vii; *1959-1960*, p. iv; *1961-1962*, pp. iv, v; *1965-1966*, p. v; and *1971-1972*, p. 452.

47. Labayle Couhat, pp. 725-6; *Conway's, Part I*, pp. 211, 214; and *Jane's Fighting Ships, 1959-1960*, p. vi; *1961-1962*, p. v; *1967-1968*, p. v; and *1971-1972*, pp. 455, 457.

48. Labayle Couhat, pp. 729-31; *Conway's, Part I*, pp. 213-15; *Annual Report, July 1958 to June 1959*, p. 241; *Annual Report, July 1960 to June 1961*, p. 230; M. E. Bustard, 'A Page from the New Navy: USS *King* (DDG-10),' in *Proceedings*, vol. 87, no. 3 (March 1961), p. 161-6; and *Jane's Fighting Ships, 1960-1961*, p. vi; and *1971-1972*, p. 456.

49. Labayle Couhat, pp. 735-6; *Conway's, Part I*, pp. 217-18; 'New Destroyers Use Aluminium Parts,' in *Marine Journal* (May 1956); *Annual Report for 1967*, pp. 319-20; *Semiannual Report, January to June 1956*, p. 203; *Jane's Fighting Ships, 1959-1960*, p. vi; *1960-1961*, p. v; and *1971-1972*, pp. 463-7; and L. D. Carey, 'A Page from the New Navy: The USS *Henry B. Wilson* (DDG-7),' in *Proceedings*, vol. 87, no. 7 (July 1961), pp. 152, 154.

50. *Conway's, Part I*, pp. 223-4; and *Annual Report, July 1960 to June 1961*, pp. 206, 209; and *Annual Report, July 1959 to June 1960*, p. 266.

51. Labayle Couhat, pp. 741-4; *Conway's Part I*, pp. 225, 226; and *Jane's Fighting Ships, 1959-1960*, p. vi; and *1971-1972*, pp. 480, 481, 483, 485.

52. Labayle Couhat, pp. 758-9; *Conway's, Part I*, pp. 241, 244, 245, 246; *Annual Report, July 1958 to June 1959*, p. 219; *Annual Report, 1962*, p. 204; *Annual Report 1964*, p. 251; and *Jane's Fighting Ships, 1959-1960*, p. vi; *1961-1962*, p. v; *1965-1966*, p. v; and *1971-1972*, pp. 508-9; 511-12.

53. Labayle Couhat, pp. 755-8; Vice-Admiral Sir Arthur Hezlet, *Electronics and Sea Power* (New York: Stein and Day, 1975), pp. 273-4; *Semiannual Report, January to June 1958*, p. 7; *Annual Report, July 1958 to June 1959*, p. 18; *Annual Report, July 1960 to June 1961*, p. 242: 'Talos Soon to Join Land and Sea Missile Arsenal,' in *Evening Star* (Washington), 7 March 1956; and John G. Norris, 'Navy Missile, Talos, Unveiled,' in *Washington Post*, 18 June 1957.

54. 'New Guided Missile Now in Service,' in *Douglas Air View News*, 16 April 1956; *Semiannual Report, January 1 to June 30, 1958*, p. 11; *Annual Report, July 1, 1958 to June 30, 1959*, pp. 10-11, 20; and *Annual Report, July 1, 1959 to June 30, 1960*, p. 8.

55. *Annual Report, July 1, 1958 to June 30, 1959*, p. 250; *Annual Report, July 1, 1959 to June 30, 1960*, p. 274; *Annual Report, July 1, 1960 to June 30, 1961*, p. 209; *Annual Report, 1963*, p. 206; and *Annual Report, 1964*, p. 248.

56. Vice-Admiral Sir Arthur Hezlet, *Electronics and Sea Power* (New York: Stein and Day, 1975), pp. 207-1; and Lowell L. Klessig and Victor L. Strite, *The ELF Odyssey: National Security Versus Environmental Protection* (Boulder, CO: Westview Press, 1980), p. xxi.

57. Hezlet, *Electronics*, p. 272; *Annual Report, July 1 1960 to June 30, 1961*, pp. 200, 209-10; *Annual Report, 1967*, pp. 318-20; and *Annual Report, 1963*, p. 199.

58. Many observers point to the Cuban Missile Crisis as the turning-point, but Norman Polmar astutely placed the turning-point at Suez in 1956, noting that it would take considerably longer than two years to make the decisions to build missile-armed combatants and then to undertake the research, development, test and evaluation necessary to produce the sophisticated missile-armed units that appeared in 1963-5.

59. One *Hotel* was converted to a *Hotel III* in 1970, a test platform to test the SS-N-8 missile. Labayle Couhat, p. 584; *Conway's, Part II*, pp. 494-5; and *Jane's Fighting Ships, 1971-1972*, pp. 595, 598; and *1986-1987*, pp. 538-9.

60. Labayle Couhat, pp. 586-7; *Conway's, Part II*, pp. 495, 496; and *Jane's Fighting Ships, 1971-1972*, p. 595; and *1986-1987*, pp. 542.

61. Labayle Couhat, p. 587; and *Jane's Fighting Ships, 1971-1972*, p. 598; and *1986-1987*, pp. 543.

62. Labayle Couhat, pp. 591-3; *Conway's, Part II*, p. 494; and *Jane's Fighting Ships, 1971-1972*, pp. 597, 602; and *1986-1987*, pp. 550, 553.

63. Labayle Couhat, pp. 614-15; *Conway's, Part II*, pp. 487-8; 'USSR: Missiles,' in *Aviation Week and Space Technology*, vol. xcviii, no. 12 (March 19, 9173), p. 121; Breyer, pp. 58-62, 98-101, 272-3; and *Jane's Fighting Ships, 1971-1972*, pp. 626, 627; and *1986-1987*, pp. 574, 575.

64. *Conway's, Part II*, p. 489; Norman Polmar, *Soviet Naval Power: Challenge for the 1970s* (New York: National Strategy Information Center, 1972), p. 99; Breyer, pp. 71, 100; and *Jane's Fighting Ships, 1971-1972*, pp. 624-5.

65. Labayle Couhat, pp. 611-14; *Conway's, Part II*, p. 489; F. M. Murphy, 'The Soviet Navy in the Mediterranean,' in *Proceedings*, vol. xciii, no. 3 (March 1967), p. 41; Polmar, p. 38; Breyer, pp. 99, 106, 274-5; and *Jane's Fighting Ships, 1971-1972*, pp. 621-2; and *1986-1987*, pp. 570-1.

66. Labayle Couhat, pp. 604-6; *Conway's, Part II*, p. 482; and *Jane's Fighting Ships, 1971-1972*, pp. 619-20; and *1986-1987*, pp. 566.

67. Labayle Couhat, pp. 603-4; *Conway's, Part II*, p. 483; and *Jane's Fighting Ships, 1971-1972*, pp. 617-18; and *1986-1987*, p. 565.

68. Labayle Couhat, pp. 601-3; *Conway's, Part II*, p. 483; and *Jane's Fighting Ships, 1971-1972*, pp.

616; and *1986-1987*, p. 565.

69. Labayle Couhat, pp. 614-15; *Conway's, Part II*, p. 489; Breyer, pp. 274-5; and *Jane's Fighting Ships, 1971-1972*, pp. 622-3; and *1986-1987*, pp. 573.

70. Labayle Couhat, pp. 638-9; *Conway's, Part II*, p. 550; Pritchard, pp. 28-30; and *Jane's Fighting Ships, 1986-1987*, pp. 594-5.

71. Labayle Couhat, pp. 630-1; *Conway's, Part II*, pp. 503-4; and *Jane's Fighting Ships, 1971-1972*, pp. 638-9; and *1986-1987*, p. 586.

72. Labayle Couhat, pp. 129-30; 'Soviet Trawler *Vega* of Murmansk Photographed Off the East Coast,' in *Proceedings*, vol. 89, no. 4 (October 1960), p. 152; and Hanson W. Baldwin, 'Soviet Submarine Lag,' in *New York Times*, 18 April 1963.

73. *Conway's, Part I*, pp. 28, 33-4.

74. Labayle Couhat, p. 130; *Conway's, Part I*, pp. 29-30; 'The "De Grasse" Commissioned,' in *La Revue Maritime* (November 1956); 'Navy Notes,' in *RUSI*, vol. cii, no. 606 (May 1957), p. 255; (August 1957), p. 423; 'Launching of the Carrier: *Clemenceau*,' in *Bulletin d'Information de la Marine Française*, 17-24 December 1957; 'Steam Catapult in French Carriers.' *Bulletin d'Information de la Marine Française*, 3 January 1957; and *Jane's Fighting Ships, 1956-1957*, p. vii; *1958-1959*, p. vii; *1959-1960*, p. vi; *1961-1962*, p. vii; *1962-1963*, p. v; and *1963-1964*, p. v.

75. *Conway's, Part I*, pp. 36-7.

76. Ibid., pp. 43-4.

77. Labayle Couhat, p. 135; and *Conway's, Part I*, p. 44.

78. *Conway's, Part I*, pp. 20-21.

79. Labayle Couhat, pp. 133-4; *Conway's, Part I*, pp. 44-5; 'French Progress on a Nuclear Force,' in *Proceedings*, vol. 93, no. 11 (November 1967), pp. 154-5; and *Jane's Fighting Ships, 1966-1967*, p. iv.

80. *Conway's, Part II*, p. 381; O. P. Araldsen, 'Norway and Soviet Pyschological Warfare,' in *RUSI*, vol. cvi, no. 624 (November 1961), pp. 582-8; 'Sweden's Sea and Coastal Defense,' in *Marinens Pressdetalj* (Stockholm) (July 1956); Roger L. Simons, 'Sweden's Defense Problem,' in *Proceedings*, vol. 84, no. 11 (November 1958), p. 68; *Jane's Fighting Ships, 1956-1957*, p. vii; *1958-1959*, p. vii; and *1968-1969*, pp. 205-6.

81. Labayle Couhat, pp. 176-7; *Conway's, Part I*, pp. 259-61; Friedrich Ruge, 'The Postwar German Navy and Its Mission,' in *Proceedings*, vol. 83, no. 10 (October 1957), p. 1037; 'Navy Notes,' in *RUSI*, vol. ciii, no. 610 (May 1958), p. 276; (February 1959), p. 114; (November 1959), pp. 514, 516-17; (August 1958), p. 430; and (May 1960), p. 294; and *Jane's Fighting Ships, 1956-1957*, p. vii; *1958-1959*, p. vii; *1959-1960*, p. viii; *1960-1961*, p. v; *1962-1963*, pp. v, vii; *1963-1964*, p. v; *1965-1966*, p. v; and *1967-1968*, p. vii.

82. *Conway's, Part I*, pp. 78-91; 'Steam Catapult in French Carriers,' in *Bulletin d'Information de la Marine Française*,' 3 January 1957; 'French Sub-

marine Fleet,' in *Bulletin d'Information de la Marine Française*, 3 January 1957; and *Jane's Fighting Ships, 1956-1957*, p. vii; *1958-1959*, p. vii; and *1959-1960*, p. viii.

83. Herbert L. Matthews, 'US Speeds Work on Spanish Bases,' in *New York Times*, 9 August 1956; *Jane's Fighting Ships, 1956-1957*, p. vii; 'Navy Notes,' in *RUSI*, vol. cii, no. 607 (August 1957), p. 421; (November 1959), p. 517; and (August 1960), p. 429; and 'South Africa Lets Submarine Contract,' in *Proceedings*, vol. 93, no. 12 (December 1967), p. 154.

84. Labayle Couhat, p. 304; *Conway's, Part I*, pp. 68-70, 73; 'Italy: Additions to the Fleet,' in *La Revue Maritime* (July 1957); *Jane's Fighting Ships, 1956-1957*, p. vii; *1958-1959*, p. vii; *1959-1960*, p. vii; *1963-1964*, p. vii; and *1966-1967*, p. vi.

85. *Conway's, Part I*, p. 301; *Jane's Fighting Ships, 1956-1957*, p. vii; Ernest M. Eller, 'US Destiny in the Middle East,' in *Proceedings*, vol. 82, no. 11 (November 1956), p. 1169; and 'Navy Notes,' in *RUSI*, vol. cii, no. 607 (August 1957), p. 424; and (February 1959), p. 114.

86. *Conway's, Part II*, pp. 306-7, 314; and 'Navy Notes,' in *RUSI*, vol. cv, no. 617 (February 1960), p. 126; and (November 1959), p. 516.

87. *Conway's, Part II*, pp. 318-20; 'South Africa Lets Submarine Contract,' in *Proceedings*, vol. 93, no. 12 (December 1967), p. 154; 'Navy Notes,' in *RUSI*, vol. cii, no. 605 (February 1957), p. 106; and (May 1957), p. 255; and *Jane's Fighting Ships, 1956-1957*, p. v; *1958-1959*, p. v; and *1959-1960*, p. vi.

88. *Conway's, Part I*, pp. 7-11; *Jane's Fighting Ships, 1956-1957*, p. v; *1958-1959*, p. v; and *1959-1960*, p. v; 'Navy Notes,' in *RUSI*, vol. cv, no. 619 (August 1960), p. 429; and (August 1960), p. 429; and 'Royal Canadian 1962 Summary,' in *Proceedings*, vol. 89, no. 4 (April 1963), pp. 163-5.

89. *Conway's, Part II*, pp. 394-5, 411, 422; 'Navy Notes,' in *RUSI*, vol. civ, no. 613 (February 1959), p. 113; (February 1959), p. 113; and (February 1957), p. 106; *Jane's Fighting Ships, 1956-1957*, p. vii; and 'Colombia Soon to Take Delivery of Two Modern Swedish-Built Destroyers,' in *Proceedings*, vol. 84, no. 8 (August 1958), p. 140.

90. 'Navy Notes,' in *RUSI*, vol. cii, no. 605 (February 1957), p. 106; (May 1957), p. 255; (August 1957), p. 423; (November 1957), p. 594; (February 1958), p. 127; (May 1958), p. 276; (August 1958), p. 430; (November 1958), p. 584; (February 1959), p. 113; (November 1959), p. 516; and (May 1960), p. 293; *Conway's, Part II*, pp. 353-5; and *Jane's Fighting Ships, 1956-1957*, p. v; *1958-1959*, p. v; and *1959-1960*, p. vi. See also: Hayaud Din, 'The Pakistan Navy,' in *Proceedings*, vol. 84, no. 9 (September 1958), pp. 59-63; and 'South Africa Lets Submarine Contract,' in *Proceedings*, vol. 93, no. 12 (December 1967), p. 154.

91. *Conway's, Part II*, pp. 330-4, 346-8, 351; 'Navy Notes,' in *RUSI*, vol. civ, no. 614 (May 1959), p. 254; (May 1960), p. 293; and (August 1960), p. 429; *Jane's Fighting Ships, 1956-1957*, p. vii; and Maurice H. Hellner, 'Sea Power and the Struggle for Asia,' in *Proceedings*, vol. 823, no. 4 (April 1956), p. 361.

92. Labayle Couhat, p. 329; *Conway's, Part II*, pp. 284-9; *Jane's Fighting Ships, 1956-1957*, p. vii; *1958-1959*, p. vii; *1959-1960*, p. viii; *1960-1961*, p. vii; *1961–1962*, p. vii; *1962-1963*, p. vii; *1963-1964*, p. vii; and *1966-1967*, p. vii; and 'Navy Notes,' in *RUSI*, vol. civ, no. 616 (November 1959), p. 517.

93. Labayle Couhat, pp. 334-5; *Conway's, Part I*, pp. 276-8, 282; *Jane's Fighting Ships, 1956-1957*, p. v; *1958-1959*, p. v; and *1959-1960*, pp. v-vi; 'Navy Notes,' in *RUSI*, vol. cii, no. 605 (February 1957), p. 106; (May 1957), p. 255; (February 1959), p. 113; (May 1959), p. 254; and (November 1959), p. 516; 'Australia's New Navy,' in *Proceedings*, vol. 89, no. 11 (November 1963), pp. 155-6; and Geoffrey Rawson, 'Problems of Australian Defense,' in *Proceedings*, vol. 84, no. 6 (June 1958), p. 63.

4
Vietnam, East of Suez, Gorshkov, and Those Nasty Little Boats, 1967–79

THE EFFECTS OF THE INFLUENCING FACTORS

Technological and political forces and naval operations caused a drastic change in the complexion of world maritime power from 1967 to 1979, resulting in a dichotomy in which much naval power was amassed in the behemoth US and Soviet navies, while the remaining power was atomized among the less affluent nations. The importance of the seas and sea power and the traditional maritime theories remained valid and operative during the period. Modern technology made ships very costly, forcing all but the most resolute nations to temper their naval construction plans. For example, in 1968, France, Italy, Germany, and Japan all assessed their programs with an eye to economy. Conversely, technology brought forth a very economical, potent naval system – the missile-equipped fast attack boat – and when Egypt sank the Israeli destroyer *Eilat* in October 1967 with missiles from Soviet-supplied boats, the result was the 'missile fever' of the late 1960s. Traditionally, a combatant's fire power had been equated to its displacement – the heavier a ship, the greater its firepower. Now these light craft completely challenged that conventional wisdom, with far-reaching effects. For nations with large navies, this was a dangerous threat which they were unprepared to handle. For poorer nations, it provided a tremendous opportunity to affect the naval balance because these economical boats, under certain conditions, could combat much larger ships. The result was tantamount to a stampede, as less affluent nations armed themselves with fleets of boats, and by 1971, many navies, including those of Norway, Sweden, Germany, Denmark, Israel, Italy, Greece, Algeria, China, Malaysia, Brunei, Cuba, Egypt, Finland, East Germany, Indonesia, Poland, Romania, Yugoslavia, Syria, and Libya, had them.[1]

Political forces caused a dramatic change in the US – Soviet naval balance. *Jane's* and other defense journals were rife with reports of Soviet naval expansion. By 1971, many agreed that the US Navy retained a decisive advantage only in aircraft carriers and henceforth, many would claim that it was impossible to judge whether the US or the Soviet Navy was stronger. The Soviet program was most impressive, producing a balanced navy of aircraft, surface ships, and submarines which quickly negated the advantages the US Navy had previously enjoyed. But this Soviet growth, in itself, did not account entirely for the almost complete negation of the West's naval advantage. Two other factors, Vietnam and Western views of sea power, account for the rest of the shift.

The US Navy's operations in Vietnam which had begun to cause problems in the late 1960's became critical in 1971. Several factors contributed to the problem. The FRAM program merely postponed the block obsolescence problem until the early 1970s, when dozens of combatants became worn out and were retired. The Vietnam operations were intensive, and while they did not affect a ship's obsolescence, they certainly were hard on the ships, especially the carriers, escorts, and amphibious and auxiliary ships. Finally, the war's expense was such that shipbuilding was restricted in order to economise, shrinking the fleet from 931 to 533 ships between 1967 and 1979. These factors, plus an increasingly assertive, anti–military Congress, created a critical situation for the US Navy which would have existed even if the Soviet Navy had not developed so rapidly. To make matters worse, many European nations curtailed their naval development, preferring to rely on US naval power for their defense; and when US naval construction was restricted while Soviet naval power developed significantly, the result was a major Soviet naval threat by 1971.[2]

POLITICAL FORCES AND NAVAL OPERATIONS

The North Korean seizure of the USS *Pueblo* in January 1968, and the deliberate Israeli attack on another communications ship, USS *Liberty*, during the June 1967 Arab-Israeli War, prompted many to question why a nation with the world's strongest navy could not defend two lightly armed intelligence trawlers operating in international waters. Indeed, there appeared to be limits to the value of massive naval power.

The British East of Suez Policy

Admiral Mahan warned that democracies tended to neglect their naval power and, in 1919, Sir Halford Mackinder said that a democracy 'refuses to think strategically unless and until compelled to do so for purposes of defense'.[3] Both views proved to be true in British and US actions concerning the British withdrawal from east of Suez. With few exceptions, US naval leaders had not appreciated the importance of naval strategy. Everything was reduced to the US – Soviet naval rivalry and, within this context, the counting of beans – the comparing of quantitative naval strengths. This meant that America saw the Royal Navy primarily in terms of its size, concluding that the British were making only a moderate contribution and that, while London's withdrawal from Asia might place an additional burden on the US Navy operationally, this would be offset by the fact that making all decisions in Washington would provide a unity of purpose. Few realized the traditional benefits that were provided by the British and their views were simply not heeded by a Washington that had difficulty thinking strategically in maritime matters.

Across the Atlantic there also was some very muddled thinking. What was taking place was the dissolution of 350 years of British rule as the empire ended, which would certainly have widespread strategic ramifications. The first issue was whether it had to happen at all. The answer appears to be that the empire had to end, but that the means by which this was to be achieved were not based in profound thinking. In March 1969, one commentator stated, 'Future researchers may well marvel at the decision to abandon our friends for so small a financial saving. Having lost an Empire, they may say, Britain was offered a role but declined to play it.'[4] Indeed, everything seemed to be viewed in the simplistic black and white – East of Suez was a liability and should therefore be lopped off and forgotten. The resulting policy amounted to a staggering from one position to another, in which an initial determination that 'everything must go' gave way to a fall-back policy of maintaining some influence at minimal expense. That this policy was piecemeal and myopic is reflected in the fact that as late as 1975, one informed observer commented, 'There appears to be no actual strategy concerning the protection of British shipping through the Indian Ocean.'[5]

The second question was whether Great Britain profited in terms of her defense. If the answer to this question were yes, then regardless of how ill-conceived the policy was, it could still be justified in terms of national security. However, the answer unfortunately was no. In 1968, Admiral Terrance T. Lewin, Commander-in-Chief, Naval Home Command, commenting on the future composition of the Navy after Suez, said that it was composed of: amphibious forces that would be used on the NATO'S northern and southern flanks; cruisers that provided a defensive versatility through their afloat control spaces that were needed to control land-based air power; destroyers that provided area anti-missile, ASW, and AA defense; and submarines, including ballistic missile-equipped units for strategic defense, and attack units. Eight years later, in a statement that obviously showed the dominance of tactical over strategic considerations, Lewin allowed that reducing fixed commitments had enabled the Navy to operate more effectively in task groups, rather than as single ships obligated to fulfill commitments.[6]

The core issue was the decision to build Polaris submarines. One commentator summarized the issue, saying,'I believe that it will prove to have been a mistake for us to have gone in for Polaris submarines. We live in a world in which a strategic nuclear balance has been reached, with sufficiency between the two great Powers. We should have spent the Polaris money more effectively in other ways.'[7] The United States would certainly maintain the strategic balance, and the British SSBNs never figured prominently in US strategic planning. None the less, her strategic security was assured by America and this cost her nothing. Still, her Navy opted to build Polaris and pursued other very expensive programs, many of which did not bear fruit. While there was a certain prestige to be gained from having an SSBN force in that it placed Great Britain in a group of five nations that had them, it provided little real defense benefit and consumed great resources that could have been spent on carriers and other units necessary to maintain a more substantial presence East of Suez. Failing to pursue this policy reflects the fact that many British leaders had lost the understanding of the true value of naval power. Here, two tenets were most important. Political influence rested on military presence, and the Suez decision abrogated existing defense agreements. Their end spelled the end of 150 years of British influence in Asia and the Persian Gulf and Indian Ocean, removing a factor that acted toward excluding the

Soviets from the Gulf and controlling the relations among an area's nations, a most effective deterrent to regional aggression.[8]

However, this position still begs the question of whether US sea power could be substituted for British sea power. Again, the answer requires an understanding of the subtle benefits that British sea power offered. It was a traditional influence and would surely be less provocative to the Soviet Union than the initial appearance of US naval power, which would probably prompt a Soviet response, thereby spreading the Soviet–American superpower rivalry into another ocean area.[9]

One also should consider the expense involved in a continued British military presence. Here again, nuances are important. The British presence and her traditional willingness to use force to attain her goals meant that she enjoyed a reputation that significantly curtailed challenges to her desires. Through bases and mobile naval forces, the presence was rather economical. By both reducing the number of bases and restricting shipbuilding, however, the entire balance was disrupted, making a future presence much more costly and the entire system unmanageable. One observer, seeing the myopia of the approach, stated, 'One cannot escape the feeling that this is the end result of many years of wrong decisions and muddling through.'[10]

Finally, if the regional security arrangements that London tried to develop to supplant her withdrawal were successful, one might still justify the British policy. The arrangement in the Pacific was to be built around Australia and concerned Malaysia and Singapore. SEATO figured prominently. But SEATO failed and Australia was simply unwilling to assume the intended role. In 1973, its Labour Party stated that the nation's interests were not served by adhering to a cold war posture and it hoped gradually to decrease Australia's role in SEATO and to cease a forward defense of stationing forces in Malaysia and Singapore.[11]

And what of British designs in the Indian Ocean? Here the security arrangement was to be built around an alliance of India, Pakistan, Ceylon, (Sri Lanka) and, from the American side, Iran. Hindsight reveals that it was successful in that the Soviets were considerably excluded from the Persian Gulf, their presence being limited to a few port visits and an occasional patrol in the Strait of Hormuz. But the containing of regional animosities was considerably less successful. The Indo–Pakistani War resulted in the fatal crippling of any type of Indo–Pakistani alliance. India became a major client of the Soviet Union, although this did not include the internal spread of Soviet influence. US reliance on the Shah may have been a factor behind the major changes in Iran that contributed to the Shah's fall from power, to be replaced by a radical Islamic fundamentalist anti-Western regime. There were major disputes in Dofar and the Yemen, a major war between Ethiopia and Somalia, a very serious attempted *coup d'état* in the Seychelles, and a host of disturbances in Africa and Southern Asia. While it is unfair to lay all these at Parliament's doorstep, one can neither ignore the fact that such unrest continually disrupted regional political life, nor fail to ponder the possible effect London might have had if she had maintained a more substantial presence.

Finally, when one considers that Great Britain consciously acted to divest herself of her colonies in order to assume a more appropriate role in international affairs, one must ask whether this transition was successful. Specifically, while curtailing her empire, she also resized her Navy into a regional force that would contribute to NATO, and, through her SSBN force, would assure her strategic security. The reorientation was unsuccessful to the extent that after Suez, Great Britain was not respected. Rather she was denigrated and considered prey by nations that hitherto had not dared to challenge her wishes. This was obvious in the Cod War, and when London misinterpreted that message, it was brought home brutally in the Falklands War.

The 1975-6 Cod War

The 1975-6 Cod War over the rich Icelandic fishing grounds began on 15 October 1975, when Iceland began enforcing a unilaterally declared 200-mile fishing limit around its coast. When it dispatched seven gunboats to disrupt British fishing, London sent frigates to protect the fishing boats. From 25 November to 30 May 1976, 21 frigates were asssigned, with a maximum force of six frigates at any one time. Fifteen frigates were involved in 49 collisions with Icelandic craft, and two were so badly damaged that they required extensive repair. The resulting agreement involved considerable British concessions: British fishermen would be allowed to fish in areas at least 20 to 30 miles from the Icelandic coast and not more than 24 trawlers could fish per day. This was a 50 per cent reduction in the annual British catch (67,000 tons vs. 130,000 tons in 1973). Also, the war cost £2,914,000, the agreement adversely affected the fishing industry by driving up the price of British cod, and involved a considerable loss of British face.[12]

Naval Reactions to Crises

The Era of US–Soviet Crisis Responses While Great Britain reduced her Navy's size and the US Navy faced a hostile Congress, the expanding Soviet Navy acted more assertively on the high seas. Its response to the June 1967 Arab–Israeli War began a new phase in crisis reactions. No longer would the United States have the advantage of being the only nation to react to such crises. Now the Soviet Navy would also deploy in a period that can be characterized as one of bilateral naval responses. Five of six of the reactions in this period occurred in the Mediterranean, while one was in the Indian Ocean. This one exception happened during the Indo–Pakistani War of 1971, when both the Soviet and US navies reacted, but the US force, centered around USS *Enterprise*, arrived much earlier and enjoyed superiority throughout the war. The weak, tardy Soviet response indicated that their force projection into the Indian Ocean needed much work. For its part, the United States proceeded to build a base on Diego Garcia.[13]

The situation was quite different in the Mediterranean, where steady Soviet progress was made. The first of five crisis responses occurred during the Jordanian Crisis of 1970. Superficially, the reaction did not seem to be that relevant. The Soviet Fleet had been bolstered in a recent exercise, and it reacted as People's Liberation Organization and Syrian forces fought King Hussein's troops. The US Sixth Fleet was bolstered, Jordan prevailed, and the crisis subsided. However, Admiral Thomas Moorer, then Chief of Naval Operations, warned that the Sixth Fleet was over-extended in the Mediterranean and cautioned against any land-based US involvement in the Middle East. His successor, Admiral Elmo Zumwalt, was even more adamant, stating that the situation was critical and that the Sixth Fleet could no longer uphold US interests in the region. Proof of these statements came in the Yom Kippur War in October 1973, when the Soviet Fleet was almost doubled in size, peaking at 95 ships. While the showing of more than 70 ships in June 1967 had been impressive, the ships in this response were even more capable, a most dangerous threat to the Sixth Fleet. The Soviet naval missions were increased accordingly, as the Navy showed impressive command and control procedures, protected the sea lanes to Syria and Egypt, transported Arab troops, and performed other tasks. However, its most important mission was sea denial – establishing power sufficient to deny the US Navy the ability to accomplish all of its missions. Whether the Soviets actually accomplished this goal or not was debatable, but one thing is certain. On 23 October, when it appeared that the Soviets were about to deploy troops to Egypt, the United States declared DEFCON 3, an increased defense condition, in order to convince Moscow that Washington would not permit the airborne deployment of Soviet troops. Admiral Moorer and others have stated that raising the defense condition was necessary because America simply did not have enough naval power in the Mediterranean to persuade the Soviets not to make the deployments. This was a further testament to Soviet progress.[14]

The subsequent Mediterranean crises, Cyprus in 1974 and Lebanon in 1975, were not as dramatic, since neither Washington nor Moscow was as committed to the belligerents. In 1974, both US and Soviet forces patrolled off Cyprus, as each nation evacuated its civilians. Likewise, in Lebanon, while naval forces from both nations were deployed off the coast, the intensity of the activity between them was quite low.

The Era of Unilateral Soviet Responses A period of intense US introspection followed Vietnam, an anti-military era in which US military power was neglected. This reduced the number of US crisis responses, giving rise to a period of unilateral Soviet responses – an era of easy wins as America ignored its responsibilities. Three crises occurred during this period. The first was the Angolan Civil War in 1975. As Soviet-sponsored Angolan forces approached victory, Holden Roberto, leader of the opposition forces, ordered that Soviet ships delivering arms to his enemies be interdicted. The Soviets responded quickly and established a seven-ship force which staged out of Conakry, Guinea and operated along the Angolan coast. Since Congress prohibited US involvement, the Soviet force, while modest, was enough to establish sea control, insure that Soviet arms carriers were not attacked, and provide navigational and other assistance to convoys carrying Cuban troops to Angola.

Another reaction occurred a year later in Ethiopia. A disastrous Soviet policy toward Ethiopia and Somalia resulted in Moscow's supporting two contending Marxist nations after Ethiopian Marxists deposed Emperor Haille Selassie. Attempting to assuage both sides as it desperately tried to defuze a conflict that it had earlier encouraged, Moscow alienated Somalia. It then threw its support completely behind Ethiopia, conducting a very complex and successful multi-service response. For its part, the Soviet Navy was deployed off Massawa, protecting seaborne shipments of supplies and shelling advancing Eritrean forces, while Soviet ships ferried Cuban troops from Cuba and Angola to Ethiopia.

The final reaction was the Sino–Vietnamese War in 1979. Realizing that Beijing was unpredictable and resolute, Moscow proceeded cautiously. It amassed its Ground Forces, conducting exercises along the Sino-Soviet border with a great deal of fanfare, and deployed 29 ships from Pacific Fleet ports. Some of these ships operated off the Chinese coast due east of Shanghai, while others were detailed to Vietnamese ports to protect them from possible Chinese air attacks. While this was sufficient to protect reconnaissance flights along the Chinese coast and an airlift of supplies to Vietnam, Moscow also realized that it had exerted only a limited influence on Beijing. Thus there was a significant increase in Soviet military power in the Pacific during the years following the war, while Soviet naval access to Vietnamese ports after the war enabled the Navy to establish a significant presence in south-east Asia.[15]

Conclusions

From 1967 to 1979, the Soviet Navy acted increasingly assertively on the high seas as it responded to several relevant crises. Concurrently, Great Britain withdrew most of her forces from east of Suez and the United States was preoccupied with introspectively assessing the Vietnam débâcle. The result was that the Soviet Navy demonstrated its value as a political vehicle, thereby upholding the theories of Admiral Gorshkov. This was of the greatest importance in Soviet naval construction because it allowed the Navy to design and build more complex ships capable of sustained operations on the high seas, the elements needed for a navy with global range, that would contribute to an even more capable force in the 1980s. However, while this was happening, the Navy also fought and lost an interservice political battle that would affect its future dramatically.

SOVIET UNION – THE RISE AND (POSSIBLY) THE FALL OF A NAVAL POWER

Political Influences

Very early in a nation's life, it identifies its defense concerns – the threats to its existence and, possibly, the opportunities for expansion – as either land-based or maritime in nature. If this choice is based on an accurate assessment of its strategic situation, it stands a good chance of surviving. If not, it will probably fail to survive. Once having identified itself as a land power, a nation might experiment in sea power, as did the Romans or more recently Nazi Germany, but when it is faced with a risk to its national survival, such experiments are usually discarded as it turns again to its army, which has always seen it through in the past. Just such a progression occurred in the Soviet Union.[16] For centuries, Russia had relied on her armies for protection and for the power that allowed her to be a great leader. In 1956, a Khrushchevian policy of peaceful coexistence made the arena of conflict the Third World, which was isolated from the Soviet land mass, and identified the US Navy as the enemy's key force. A Red Navy rapidly developed and soon the USSR became one of the world's two most powerful maritime nations.

The Navy displayed great confidence in these years as it advanced rapidly on to the high seas. Table 4.1 shows the Soviet out-of-area presence from 1956 to 1989, computed on the basis of the out-of-area ship day, which is a day or a portion of a day that a ship spends operating on the high seas outside local waters. The Soviet Mediterranean Fleet's presence virtually doubled from 1967 to 1970, and reached an all-time high in 1973, owing to the reaction to the October War. Combatant deployments to the Caribbean began in 1969, to be continued at least annually. A naval presence was established along West Africa at Conakry in 1970 and was expanded to Angola after the Angolan Civil War. Indian Ocean Squadron operations were begun in 1969 and the Navy gained access to Vietnamese ports after the Sino-Vietnamese War of 1979, allowing it to develop a substantial presence in south-east Asia. Another excellent indicator of Soviet naval progress was exercise activity. In 1970, a large exercise, *Okean-70*, amounted to deploying a sizeable number of ships on to the high seas, but controlling their activities rigidly from Moscow. However, in *Okean-75*, held only five years later, more than 200 ships were deployed to the world's major oceans where they conducted a variety of operations and demonstrated a much improved command and control arrangement.[17]

The Navy reflected confidence in these years, as it moved aggressively outward on to the world's oceans to challenge Western naval power. This

Table 4.1
Soviet Out-of-Area Naval Presence on the High Seas, 1956–87[a]

Year	Atlantic Ocean	Caribbean Sea	Mediterranean Sea	Pacific Ocean	South China Sea	Indian Ocean	Total
1956	500	0	100	200	0	0	800
1957	1,500	0	600	200	0	0	2,300
1958	1,300	0	1,000	900	0	0	3,200
1959	2,100	0	4,100	900	0	0	7,100
1960	1,600	0	5,600	400	0	200	7,800
1961	2,200	0	2,300	700	0	0	5,200
1962	4,300	0	800	1,400	0	100	6,600
1963	5,300	0	1,800	2,000	0	0	9,100
1964	5,400	0	3,700	2,500	0	0	11,600
1965	5,500	0	5,400	2,800	0	0	13,700
1966	5,800	0	8,800	3,600	0	200	18,400
1967	5,900	0	11,700	4,200	0	1,200	23,000

1968	9,600	300	15,400	5,900	0	4,100	35,300
1969	13,600	700	17,400	7,100	0	4,900	43,700
1970	14,800	700	18,700	6,200	0	4,000	44,400
1971	14,500	1,900	17,700	5,900	0	8,900	48,900
1972	13,000	1,400	20,600	6,300	0	8,900	50,200
1973	13,900	1,200	20,200	7,400	0	10,500	53,200
1974	13,200	1,100	20,000	6,800	0	7,100	48,200
1975	14,000	1,000	18,600	6,500	0	7,300	47,400
1976	15,800	1,200	16,300	7,500	0	6,700	47,500
1977	16,100	1,300	16,600	6,900	0	8,500	49,400
1978	16,200	1,100	16,600	9,900	0	7,600	52,600
1979	16,800	800	16,500	11,800	0	11,800	57,800
1980	17,000	1,200	16,900	11,100	0	11,000	55,200
1981	16,800	1,300	16,200	12,800	0	10,200	56,900
1982	18,100	1,200	17,600	6,200	9,000	8,800	60,900
1983	18,400	1,200	15,600	8,400	9,100	9,200	61,900
1984	16,600	1,600	16,500	7,300	9,400	7,800	59,200
1985	16,500	1,200	15,900	7,800	9,600	9,000	60,000
1986	14,900	1,100	14,500	7,800	9,000	9,000	56,300
1987	15,500	900	13,000	4,700	9,300	7,500	50,900
1988	14,700	1,200	11,900	4,500	8,800	8,100	49,200
1989	12,300	1,400	12,500	4,200	9,300	8,500	48,200

[a]Assembled from several sources, including Bruce W. Watson, *Red Navy at Sea* (Boulder, CO: Westview Press, 1982); Bruce W. Watson and Susan M. Watson, eds., *The Soviet Navy: Strength and Liabilities* (Boulder, CO: Westview Press and Arms & Armour Press, 1986); and Bruce W. Watson and Susan M. Watson, eds., *The Soviet Naval Threat to Europe: Military and Political Dimensions* (Boulder, CO: Westview Press, 1989).

confidence was reflected in both its naval writings and construction. In 1975, Admiral Gorshkov, the Navy's Commander-in-Chief, codified the Navy's position in his *Sea Power of the State*. He presented a comprehensive theory on the evolution of sea power and then challenged the Soviet Ground Forces for right of place by asserting that its SSBN force placed the Navy up with the Strategic Rocket Forces, in the forefront of the five branches of the Soviet military.[18] While masterfully presented, his position was not accepted by the Ground Forces-dominated General Staff. He was attacked for advocating an independent naval strategy when a unified military strategy had been accepted by the Party as the only acceptable approach. He was being accused of heresy – his opponents were playing ideological hardball. Forced to issue a retraction, the scrappy admiral was equal to the task. He noted that the unified military strategy was the correct strategy, but said that within it, each branch maintained its own identity and, in any conflict, one branch was ideally equipped to respond and the other branches should assist as necessary. Modern weapons, because of their range and accuracy, had made theater warfare concepts obsolete, and it was now proper to think in larger terms – in environments that encompassed both lands and seas but in which one type of military power would prevail. He conceded that Europe was a land environment, where the Ground Forces were the ideal force and the other branches should be supportive, but distinguished this from maritime environments, in which the Navy was the ideal force. However, Gorshkov failed to identify other land environments and, by omission, implied that the rest of the world was maritime, in which his Navy should prevail. It was a brilliant gambit, the product of naval genius that approached that of Alfred Mahan. But ultimately it failed. In the early 1980's, Gorshkov was attacked in a series of articles that appeared in *Morskoy Sbornik*. He was retired, to be succeeded by Admiral Chernavin, an officer who had made it clear that he was a team player, content to see the Navy relegated to its traditional role of faithful assistant to the Soviet Ground Forces. One observer saw Gorshkov as a consistent figure in Russian history:

> His consistency is that of exception to the rule, the aberration that occurs with a certain lonely regularity. He was the great flash of naval brilliance that finally died for lack of the right cultural tinder. Gorshkov joins the ranks of the other brief, bright naval lights in a hostile professional environment – Ushakov, Nakhimov, and Makarov – the great professional sailors and warrior admirals of Russia. The naval promise of Russia seemed to share the mortality of their own lives because the continental lodestone denied the navy the necessary attention that would have institutionalized their example.[19]

Thus, in a brief period from 1967 to 1979, the Soviet Navy appeared on the maritime stage, delivered a brilliant but limited performance, and then possibly faced retirement, to assume its traditional role as a supportive force. This progression has the greatest relevance to our investigation, because it is here that the Navy made its greatest contribution, both in producing capable, innovative ships and in prompting responsive Western maritime development. Although the Navy had been supported adequately from 1956 onward, it was not until 1967 that this investment had an impact and yielded returns. Likewise, although Gorshkov and, with him, the Navy may have lost the battle in 1979, given the nine- to eleven-year lead time necessary to conceptualize, design, test, build, arm, and outfit ships and then train crews, some of the gains made by Gorshkov and his colleagues would not be operational until well into the 1990s. Still, many interesting, innovative classes became operational from 1967 to 1979, the golden era of Soviet naval operations.

Submarines

Dramatic advances were made in submarines. The thirty-four 10,000-ton *Yankee* ballistic missile submarines (SSBNs), built between 1963/64 and 1974, were a very significant advance. These units were armed with sixteen SS-N-6 missiles, with ranges varying from 1,300 miles for Mod 1 to 1,600 miles in the Mod 3, which also had an MRV capability. *Yankee*'s significance was that the range of its missiles allowed it to patrol much farther from US shores, while a submerged launch capability made it less vulnerable than previous classes.[20] *Yankee* patrols, which began off the US east and west coasts in 1969 and 1971, provided missile coverage of almost the entire country.

While a dramatic advance, *Yankee* was still vulnerable because it had to travel to the US coasts, where it could be prosecuted by ASW forces. Even this liability was compensated for in the 11,750-ton *Delta I*. Built from 1969 to 1977, the eighteen *Delta*s were armed with twelve SS-N-8 missiles. The SS-N-8 Mod 1 had a range of 4,200 miles, and Mod 2, 4,900 miles, which meant that the *Delta*s could patrol in heavily defended Arctic sanctuaries where they could be protected by submarines, surface combatants, and aircraft. This represented such a major shift in the strategic balance of power that its importance is hard to exaggerate. It certainly justified Gorshkov's claim concerning the Navy's strategic importance. This was true, because in wartime, Western ASW forces no longer enjoyed the advantage of being able to attack undefended Soviet SSBNs on patrol in the Atlantic. Now they would have to penetrate the Norwegian Sea and face heavy submarine, surface, and air opposition as they attempted to destroy the SSBNs in the Arctic bastions. Two later classes, *Delta II* and *Delta III*, were larger and, while the four *Delta II*s each carried four more of the SS-N-8s carried by *Delta I*, the SS-N-18 on the fourteen *Delta III*s were innovative. Mods 1 and 3 delivered three and seven MIRVs to a range of 3,500 miles, while Mod 2 delivered a single 4,300-mile warhead.[21]

Significant advances were also made in guided missile-equipped submarines. The 4,900-ton, 311-foot *Charlie I*, built between 1967 and 1973, was equipped with eight 35-mile SS-N-7 missiles. These twelve submarines were much quieter and had longer-ranged missiles than their predecessors, thereby increasing greatly the threat to US carrier task groups. The 5,100-ton *Charlie II* was 340 feet long and larger than *Charlie I*. A single *Papa* SSGN was completed in 1970. Whether it was a test platform or an unsuccessful design remains undetermined.[22]

In attack submarines, fourteen *Victor I*s, completed from 1968 to 1975, were a great advance over *November*. The 5,100-ton *Victor I* was armed with six 21in torpedo tubes. (Some were provided with SS-N-15 missiles together with the torpedoes.) *Victor I* was succeeded by seven *Victor II*s which were completed from 1972 to 1978. An enlarged *Victor I*, the 5,700-ton *Victor II* could dive to 1,300 feet and both *I* and *II* could achieve 30 knots. *Victor II* had six tubes for 21in or 25.6in torpedoes, and was also equipped to carry the SS-N-15 or -16 in place of some torpedoes. The 5,800-ton *Victor III*s were built beginning in 1978 to carry the SS-N-16 A/B. Another SSN class, *Alfa*, had a strange history. The prototype, completed in 1967, was scrapped in 1974, but the program was continued until 1983. The seven additional *Alfa*s were 267 feet long, displaced 3,680 tons, and were a most significant advance because of their speed and diving depth. Capable of speeds of 43 to 45 knots and depths of 800m, the titanium-hulled *Alfa* was one of the fastest, deepest-diving submarines ever built and a very critical submarine threat for the West.[23]

The Navy continued building diesel target submarines. Four 2,900-ton *Bravo* target submarines armed with six torpedo tubes were built from 1968 onward. The 3,900-ton *Tango*, built to replace *Foxtrot*, had eight 21in torpedo tubes. Built from the early 1970s onward, the 18 *Tango*s were used extensively in the Mediterranean. In 1979, the Soviets began producing more *Kilo*s, 2,900-ton submarines armed with eight 21in torpedo tubes. A single 3,000-ton research submarine was begun in 1979, about the same time that two *India*-class rescue submarines were built.[24]

Surface Combatants

Impressive progress was also made in surface combatant shipbuilding. The Navy initially opted to build systems to combat US attack carriers and later designed air-capable ships of its own. It first produced the *Moskva* helicopter carrier. *Kiev* construction ran from 1970 to 1986 (see Table 4.2). She displaced 43,000 tons, was 902 feet long, and could carry 32 aircraft, a mixture of Forger aircraft and Hormone or Helix helicopters. Built in the European carrier tradition, *Kiev* looked somewhat similar to *Moskva*, a carrier forward and a cruiser aft. She was heavily armed with surface-to-surface and surface-to-air missiles (SSMs and SAMs), guns, and ASW weapons.[25] She was a successful design and a logical step in the sea-based air program. *Kiev* was detailed to the Northern Fleet, while the second and third units, *Minsk* and *Novorossiysk*, were sent to the Pacific. *Baku* has remained in the Northern Fleet.

In 1973, the Navy began building *Kirov*, a nuclear-powered guided-missile cruiser. Except for aircraft carriers, it was the largest surface combatant built by any nation since the war. She displaced 28,000 tons, was 814 feet long, and had a 94-foot beam. Capable of 33 knots, *Kirov* and her sisters had slightly different armament, including SS-N-14s and -19s, SA-N-6, SA-N-4, and SA-NX-9 SAMS, 100mm guns (on *Kirov*) or 130mm guns (on *Frunze*), 30mm Gatling guns, 21in torpedo tubes, and ASW weapons.[26] A very capable, heavily armed ship, *Kirov* was a remarkable advance in maritime technology in contrast to the Western trend of not building large surface combatants.

Two other cruiser programs were also conducted. In 1969, the first of seven 9,700-ton *Karas* was begun in a program that ended in 1980. A logical advance from her predecessor, *Kresta II*, she was armed with SAMs, SSMs, guns, and ASW weapons. A much greater technological advance was made in *Slava*. Unlike the previous *Kynda-Kresta-Kara* generation, the 32-knot *Slava* represented a new generation of ships that were capable of sustained operations for lengthy periods on the high seas. At 12,500 tons, she was more spacious, allowing for better habitability.[27] She was armed with SS-N-12, SA-N-4, and SA-N-6 missiles, 130mm guns, 30mm Gatling guns, 21in torpedo tubes, and ASW weapons.

Table 4.2
Selected Force Levels – Soviet Navy, 1968–79

	Year											
	68	69	70	71	72	73	74	75	76	77	78	79
Submarines												
Ballistic Missile Nuclear	10	15	21	27	33	39	45	52	59	67	69	69
Ballistic Missile Diesel	22	22	22	20	20	20	20	20	18	19	18	16
Cruiser Missile Nuclear	35	36	38	39	41	42	43	42	43	44	44	45
Cruiser Missile Diesel	25	27	27	27	27	25	25	25	25	23	23	20
Nuclear Attack	12	15	20	20	22	25	28	35	38	40	42	47
Diesel Attack	274	258	260	257	254	248	224	206	160	162	163	162
Surface Combatants												
Carriers	0	0	0	0	0	0	0	0	1	1	2	2
Helo Carriers	1	2	2	2	2	2	2	2	2	2	2	2
Cruisers	22	24	23	24	26	28	28	30	32	33	35	35
Missile Destroyers	20	15	35	36	40	38	38	37	36	36	36	36
Gun-Armed Destroyers	86	76	70	66	64	60	59	57	55	52	50	49

Frigates	90	106	116	121	128	134	139	138	141	143	152	159
Missile Corvettes	0	0	0	0	6	6	8	10	14	17	16	19
Missile Boats	150	150	150	150	147	127	125	125	125	125	120	125
Coastal/Patrol	600	600	525	500	475	450	410	375	360	344	389	340
Mine Warfare	280	280	295	305	305	295	295	295	310	330	335	350
Amphibious Ships	100	100	80	105	105	100	100	100	100	100	95	93

The design philosophy of producing ships for sustained operations, such as *Slava*, was also seen in two new specialized guided-missile destroyers that were meant for specific types of warfare. The 7,840-ton *Sovremennyy* destroyers, which were begun in 1976, were intended for surface warfare. They were armed with SS-N-22 and SA-N-7 missiles, 130mm guns, 30mm Gatling guns, 21in torpedo tubes and ASW weapons. The second class, the 8,100-ton, 30-knot *Udaloy*, was slightly larger and was intended for ASW. She carried SS-N-14 and SA-N-9 missiles, 100mm guns, 30mm Gatling guns, 21in torpedo tubes, and two Helix A helicopters.[28] Like *Slava*, *Sovremennyy* and *Udaloy* had reloads for many of their weapons, qualifying them for sustained combat operations. Together with *Kiev* and *Kirov*, they reflected Admiral Gorshkov's philosophy of building ships capable of extended operations world-wide in defense of the nation and its national interests.

The Navy began building 3,900-ton, 405-foot Krivak guided missile frigates in the late 1960s. Three variants, I, II, and III, were built, with Krivak III intended for the KGB. These ships could sustain 29 knots and were extremely smart in appearance, were armed with SAMs and SSMs, guns, and ASW weapons. They still are used extensively in the Mediterranean. A second frigate, the 1,600-ton *Koni*, was designed specifically for export. Armed with SAMs, guns, and ASW weapons, they were exported to East Germany, Yugoslavia, Algeria, and Cuba.[29]

Amphibious Ships and Missile Patrol Boats

Two missile-armed fast corvettes were also produced. The 32-knot, 685-ton *Nanuchka*, heavily armed with SS-N-9 and SA-N-4 missiles, was designed primarily for coastal defense duties, although it was occasionally deployed to the Mediterranean. Later, the 480-ton, 36-knot *Tarantul* appeared. She was slightly smaller and faster. Twenty-one *Tarantul*s were built. They were armed with SS-N-2c or SS-N-22 and SA-N-5 missiles, a 76mm gun, and 30mm Gatling guns.[30]

From 1974 onward, at least 25 *Ropucha* LSTs were built. At 3,600 tons, they were about three-fourths the size of the *Alligator* LSTs. Greater progress was made in *Ivan Rogov*, a 13,000-ton landing platform dock capable of carrying a battalion of naval infantry and 20 tanks. With a floodable well and a helicopter deck, she was a very capable ship. Whether the Navy was unhappy with *Rogov*'s design or whether amphibious warfare was given a low priority in the allotment of available resources is uncertain, but construction was extremely slow, with only two units operational in the mid 1980s, and a third completed in 1989.[31]

Finally, the Navy made dramatic progress in intelligence collection and ocean surveillance. Gone were the small converted trawlers, replaced by large intelligence factories, capable of processing and analyzing intelligence before forwarding it to Naval Headquarters. Two types of satellite were also developed: radar-equipped ocean reconnaissance satellite (RORSATS), and ELINT ocean reconnaissance satellite (EORSATs). These and other Soviet satellites provided a much more complete picture of Allied naval activities and programs.[32]

Conclusions

The years from 1967 to 1979 were exciting ones and comprised an era when strategy, construction, and operations came together to produce the golden era of the modern Soviet Navy. Many innovative classes of ships and submarines were built, amounting to a major contribution to naval development. While the Navy proved its value, however, the continental mentality of the Soviet military leadership inhibited naval expansion. The failure of the Gorshkov gambit created a feeling of uneasiness in 1979, as the Navy hoped to continue the expansion that it had enjoyed over the past several years.

THE UNITED STATES

While the Soviet Navy enjoyed unprecedented support, the US Navy faced the post-Vietnam anti-military syndrome in which it had to fight for every penny. Such an atmosphere was most damaging to naval innovation as the Navy tried to maintain its carrier and submarine forces, while designing less capable, cheaper destroyers and escorts.

Table 4.3
Order of Battle – US Navy, 1967–79[a]

	Year												
	67	68	69	70	71	72	73	74	75	76	77	78	79
Ballistic Missile Submarines	41	41	41	41	41	41	41	41	41	41	41	41	41
Submarines	105	105	100	103	100	94	84	73	86	74	77	81	80
Carriers	23	23	22	19	19	17	16	14	15	13	13	13	13
Battleships	0	1	1	0	0	0	0	0	0	0	0	0	0
Cruisers	13	13	13	10	28	27	29	26	27	26	26	28	28
Command Ships	2	2	2	2	2	0	0	0	0	0	0	0	0
Destroyers	237	240	222	176	173	132	138	108	102	99	92	95	97
Frigates	46	50	43	47	61	66	71	64	64	64	64	65	65
Mine Warfare	83	84	74	64	59	31	34	34	34	25	25	25	25
Patrol Vessels	3	6	7	15	17	16	14	14	14	13	6	3	3
Amphibious	162	157	153	97	95	77	65	65	64	65	65	67	67
Auxiliaries	216	210	207	171	177	153	148	135	123	116	114	113	114
Totals	931	932	885	743	752	654	640	574	570	536	523	531	533

[a]US Department of the Navy, *US Navy Ship Force Levels, 1917–1989* (Washington, DC: Ships History Branch, Naval Historical Center, Department of the Navy, 1989), pp. 6–7. The former DLG and DLGN types appear under the types of cruisers or destroyers to which they were assigned on 30 June 1975, in the following manner: the DLG 6-class appears under destroyers; and the DLG 16-class and DLG 26-class (which became CGs), and the DLGN 25-, 35-, and 36-classes (which became CGNs) appear under cruisers.

The period began with the intense Vietnam operations that were waged by a force that was partially composed of FRAM ships that were nearing the end of their useful lives. Since the available funds were diverted to the war's prosecution, needed construction was deferred again. Such penury continued with years of Congressional rebellion to the war and, in a larger sense, to the military, and with a phase of intense American introspection in which the military was scrutinized and funding was restricted. Thus, the great deal of construction necessary for the Navy to maintain its power was denied. After exhaustive discussions, the size of the fleet was first set at 850, then 770, and finally at 600 ships, a figure that would later be accepted by President Reagan. Ship designs and capabilities were scaled down in order to produce more hulls. In short, quality gave way to quantity in some of the classes produced. Even this concession was not enough. As Table 4.3 demonstrates, from 1967 to 1979, there was an overall reduction of 398 ships, or 42 per cent. While the ballistic missile submarine force was kept at 41 units, attack submarines were reduced considerably from 105 to 80 units. Likewise, the carrier force was reduced from 23 to 13, two below the minimum that the Navy needed to fulfil its missions. The greatest reductions occurred in destroyers, from 237 to 97, as the FRAM destroyers were retired; in mine warfare ships, from 83 to 25; and in auxiliaries, from 216 to 114.[33]

Submarines

Generally speaking, the least damage occurred in submarines. Construction proceeded, the designs were successful, and an acceptable force was maintained. In 1962, the first of forty-two 4,640-ton *Sturgeon* units was laid down in a run that ended in 1974. The 292-foot *Sturgeon*, larger than *Thresher*, became the backbone of the attack submarine force.[34]

Two *Sturgeon* submarines were noteworthy. *Narwhal* was a test platform for the S5G natural circulation reactor plant. The second, *Glennard P. Lipscomb*, had a turbine-electric plant and was built to develop techniques for quieting submarines. The advances made in *Lipscomb* were applied in the *Los Angeles*. At 6,900 tons and 360 feet, she was a very successful design. The first unit was laid down in 1972 and at least 62 were planned.[35]

In ballistic missile submarines, missile advances were made and, on 1 April 1971, *James Madison* (SSBN 627) was the first SSBN with multiple nuclear warhead missiles to go to sea on patrol. The provisions of SALT I limited the United States to 41 SSBNs and 656 missiles, with an option of substituting three more submarines and 54 missiles for 54 Titan land-based missiles. The Soviet Union was allowed 62 submarines and 960 missiles. Since the agreement limited the total number of missiles, they prompted a redirection of research toward developing newer, more capable missiles, so that a more formidable threat was posed while complying quantitatively to the treaty. Thus, on 16 May 1972, Secretary of Defense Melvin Laird announced that ten Tridents would be built in the late 1970s to replace the ageing Polaris units and in April 1976 the 18,700-ton, 560-foot *Ohio*-class was begun. Her 24 Trident I missiles, with their 4,350-mile range and MIRV capability, significantly increased the strategic threat to the Soviet Union, because not only could these boats patrol much further away from the Soviet coast where they were more difficult to locate and could be protected more capably, but their MIRVs made the Soviet targeting problem vastly more complex as multiple warheads would have to be intercepted.[36]

Aircraft Carriers

The intensive Vietnam operations justified additional carriers and, in 1968 and 1970, the first two *Nimitz* carriers, *Nimitz* and *Dwight D. Eisenhower*, were laid down. The dimensions of the class varied from unit to unit as new advances were incorporated, but generally, they were 1,088 feet long, displaced about 91,440 tons, and could carry more than 90 aircraft.[37] The *John F. Kennedy* decision was not repeated; these ships were nuclear-powered. When mated with nuclear-powered escorts, they composed task groups that had unprecedented mobility, sustainability, speed, and fire power, the epitome of power projection and ideal for operations in the huge Pacific and Indian Oceans.

The fleet's size became a major issue toward the end of the 1960s. In addition to the block obsolescence problem, the new ships were larger, more capable, and much more costly than those they replaced. When 195 ships were retired in 1969 and 1970 the net total was 769 ships, but replacements could not be made on a ship-for-ship basis and the fleet's size had to decrease. In this milieu, attention naturally centered on the nuclear-powered aircraft carrier. In March 1972, the *Washington Post* reported that the Air Force had launched a behind-the-scenes counter-attack on, in its perception, excessive Navy demands on the defense budget. Much of the discussion rehashed old arguments, but some comments were incisive. Heated discussion occurred over the fact that they made such lucrative targets, vulnerable because long-range Soviet air-to-surface missiles could hit them, satellite and long-range airborne surveillance aircraft could locate them, and strikes against land targets would tie them down while sensitive sonars on high-speed submarines allowed for more deadly submarine attacks. Of the pro-carrier arguments, the most profound and incisive was John Lehman's, which categorically rebutted the major tenets of the anti-carrier argument. Concerning the carrier's value, Lehman called upon Admiral Elmo Zumwalt who attested to the fact that in all the major international crises during his tenure as Chief of Naval Operations, the carriers had been the primary crisis management tool. Lehman argued that carriers were needed for both deterrence and war-fighting and noted that crisis management/deterrence involved presence, direct but limited confrontation with the USSR, and protecting US interests against Third World countries. Further, war-fighting involved protecting Allied SLOCs, denying the enemy use of his SLOCs, and attacking enemy targets. Concerning the economy of carriers, he argued that they were better than overseas bases because bases were expensive, were a source of loss in exchange payments, and were vulnerable to political changes. Also, if unoccupied, they could not be activated quickly and, if forward deployed, they were vulnerable. By contrast, Lehman demonstrated that, short of a direct hit, the carrier was the least sinkable ship that had ever been built.[38]

A major problem with carriers was their expense and this gave rise to Admiral Zumwalt's high–low argument. Concerned with the fleet's shrinkage, he argued that large, expensive ships limited unacceptably the size of the fleet and that, no matter how good a ship was, she could only be in one place at one time. He recommended building more, smaller, ships and proposed the sea control ship (SCS). Conversely, Admiral Rickover argued for the mobility that nuclear power provided. According to Zumwalt, Secretary of Defense James Schlesinger and Rickover reached an agreement in which Schlesinger would support nuclear propulsion for carriers and Rickover would support the SCS – the low part of the high–low mix. In April 1971, the fourth CVAN had been delayed because of a lack of money, but, with Zumwalt's support and after a three-year battle, the Navy gained approval for it in July 1972, and *Carl Vinson*, the third of the six-unit *Nimitz*-class, was laid down in October 1975. Zumwalt claimed that Rickover reneged on his part of the agreement with Schlesinger and the SCS and smaller forces were never built.[39]

There was evidence to support both positions. The nuclear-powered carriers were the epitome of force projection. But they were very expensive and therefore prevented the building of greater numbers of smaller ships. Additionally, they obligated tremendous resources to a single item that could be cut easily from budgets, as President Carter did when he cut a CVN in 1979.[40] The 'putting all your eggs in one basket' held true – but not in the sense that carriers were excellent targets on the high seas. Rather, they were excellent game for those hunting for reductions in budget appropriations.

Other Surface Combatants

The battleship *New Jersey* was recommissioned in 1968 to provide shore bombardment in Vietnam, but was decommissioned in December 1969. Two *California*-class CGNs, *California* and *South Carolina*, originally classified as destroyer leaders, were begun in 1970. Provided with two water-cooled reactors, these 30-knot, 10,150-ton, 596-foot ships, armed with Harpoon, ASROC and Mark 32 torpedo tubes, and having provisions for Tomahawk, were excellent additions to the nuclear-powered carrier task groups. A third unit was cancelled in favor of four 11,000-ton, 585-foot *Virginia*-class ships, *Virginia*, *Texas*, *Mississippi* and *Arkansas*. They were armed with Harpoon, 5in mounts, and Phalanx, an excellent anti-air weapon, and they had provisions for Tomahawk. Completed from 1976 to 1980, these ships were also ideal for nuclear-powered task groups.[41]

There was a definite attempt to limit the cost of combatants. Thus quality yielded to quantity in a strategy aimed at producing a number of versatile hulls, such as the 7,800-ton *Spruance*. which could be more heavily armed later. The program began as *Spruance* was laid down in 1972 and ended with *Hayler*'s commissioning in 1983. A major modernization to upgrade the ASW capability was begun in 1976. *Spruance* was criticized for having so little armament for a ship of her displacement. She was armed with 5in mounts, Harpoon, ASROC, and torpedoes, with provision for adding Tomahawk. Four units, built for Iran but cancelled after the Shah's fall from power, were built to the original plans and were general-purpose vice ASW destroyers. They became the 9,574-ton *Kidd*-class, the most powerful guided-missile destroyers in the fleet, and were armed with Harpoon, ASROC, Phalanx, Mark 32 torpedo tubes, 5in mounts, and LAMP helicopters.[42]

Two frigate classes also appeared. The 438-foot *Knox* displaced 4,260 tons. Forty-six were built in a run which began in 1965 and ended with *Moinster's* commissioning in 1974. *Knox* was armed with Harpoon, Sea Sparrow (later replaced by Phalanx) and torpedo tubes.[43] In 1975, the 3,486-ton *Oliver Hazard Perry* was laid down. The early *Perrys* were oriented toward ASW, while later ones were equipped with Phalanx, which was retro-fitted in the earlier units. Armament, includes torpedo tubes, a 76mm gun, Phalanx, and Harpoon.[44]

In amphibious forces, in 1967, work began on the first of two 19,200-ton *Blue Ridge* amphibious command ships which had extensive command and control facilities for integrating sea, air, and land warfare. *Blue Ridge* and *Mount Whitney* became the flag ships of the Seventh and Second Fleets. In 1971, the first of five 39,300-ton *Tarawa* multi-purpose amphibious assault ships was begun in a program that ended with *Peleliu* in 1978. Capable of 24 knots, she carried both helicopters and Harriers and had a well deck and extensive command and medical facilities.[45]

The Navy's approach was intelligent in that it built several versatile hulls which, while lightly armed, were upgraded later, thereby providing a strong fleet. In essence, in the lean Carter years of great Congressional opposition and lukewarm White House support, it gambled on a brighter future. The gamble paid off, because with the Reagan administration's ambitious ship-building program, these hulls were available for upgrading. None the less, through no fault on the Navy's part, this program, imposed by the necessity of political reality, was less ideal than a more consistent, adequately funded program would have been, and could not help but inhibit US naval innovation.[46]

Other Naval Developments

Because of the problems with Tartar-Terrier-Talos, the Secretary of Defense ordered the development of a new system. While developing such a missile, the Navy also developed the Harpoon (66-mile range, active radar terminal acquisition system) and Tomahawk (300-mile range) cruise missiles. In 1979, these were proving very successful. In naval gunnery, considerable progress was made against the close-in air and surface threats with Phalanx. In 1978, the Secretary of Defense praised Phalanx highly because of its effectiveness and reasonable cost. In other systems, the Air ASW Tactical Support System (ASTACS) was initiated in 1970, to manage automated support for analyzing ASW data and assigning weapons. The Mark 48 wire-guided, acoustic homing torpedo, a great improvement over older torpedoes, was sent to the fleet in 1972. Finally, progress was made in towed sonar arrays, and in 1978, the Secretary of Defense proclaimed them as 'the most important surface ship ASW development in a generation'. The SQR-18 Surface Ship Tactical Towed Array Sonar (TACTAS) system was backfitted on *Knox* frigates. Together with LAMPS, it extended significantly the range at which submarines could be detected and prosecuted.[47]

GREAT BRITAIN

The Political Context
The East of Suez Policy adversely affected British maritime development. Concerning a presence in the Indian Ocean, the Navy had considered island basing in the mid 1960s and believed that Diego Garcia, midway between Africa and Australia, offered the greatest advantages. However, these plans were abandoned, to be assumed by the United States and, by the end of 1971, with minor exceptions, the British had withdrawn from their bases east of Suez. Their residual presence in 1971 amounted to five frigates and destroyers on station east of Suez, one army battalion group, a detachment of Nimrod long-range reconnaissance aircraft and several Whirlwind helicopters. However, this withdrawal did not have the anticipated result of establishing a greater presence closer to home.[48]

This had an obvious impact on naval construction. Gone were plans for a fleet of carriers or even one carrier. Ideas of colonial responsibility, world leadership, and force projection were replaced with policies intended to cut defense to the bone, as the nation grappled with her economic problems. A Polaris fleet was built, but these submarines were so expensive that they left little money for other shipbuilding. *Hermes*, the newest of the carriers, was made into a commando carrier, while the fate of *Centaur* was even more ignoble – she was scrapped in 1971. And the cuts kept coming as the nation relied more and more on the United States for her security. Throughout, the Navy tried desperately to balance restricted funding against mission requirements, but not all of its programs were successful. A $13.2 million project failed to produce a successful torpedo and the Navy had to turn to the United States for its torpedoes. Such failures in an unhealthy climate could not help but further demoralize naval planners as they attempted to cope with an impossible situation. In 1971, London announced that it would buy more than $120 million of French Exocets. This was a wise move – Exocet was an excellent weapon, but this is not what one would expect if the nation were in the forefront of technology. The situation worsened. In 1975, the one remaining carrier was scheduled for disposal, a number of other ships were cut, and building programs were reduced.[49] In this adverse environment, it is amazing that the Navy survived as well as it did.

Submarines
The lion's share of the attention was paid to submarines, as the ballistic missile submarines (SSBNs) related directly to the nation's defense, and the attack submarines (SSNs) related to SLOC protection and port security. The SSBN fleet was maintained and two classes of SSNs were designed. The six-unit 4,500-ton, 272-foot *Swiftsure*-class was begun in 1969 and completed in 1981. She had a pressurized water-cooled reactor which provided 28 knots. The subsequent class, the seven-unit, 5,208-ton *Trafalgar*, was slightly larger and was begun in 1979 in a program that was to continue into the 1990s.[50]

Aircraft Carriers

East of Suez had significant impact on the Navy's carriers. Initially it was decided that they would be retired, but this was modified when London decided to keep one carrier until the end of the 1970s.[51] *Ark Royal* was never as mechanically reliable as *Eagle* and was finally retired in 1978 and broken up in 1980. Meanwhile, the long and complex story of a new carrier, which had begun in the early 1960s, was finally resolved in the *Invincible*-class light aircraft carriers. The lead ship, *Invincible* was laid down in 1973 and was completed in 1980. Her sisters, *Illustrious* and *Ark Royal*, were begun in 1976 and 1978. On a length of 675 feet and with 115-foot beam, these 19,500-ton ships could provide both combat power and extensive command, control, and communications (C³) facilities for conducting an assortment of operations. They could accommodate both V/STOL aircraft and helicopters and were provided with Sea Harriers and Sea King helicopters. Their armament included a twin Sea Dart SAM launcher and Phalanx CIWS.

Cruisers

The refitting of the *Tiger*-class cruisers *Blake* and *Tiger* were completed in 1969 and 1972. A lack of funds prevented refitting the third unit, *Lion*, which was cannibalized and then broken up in 1975. *Blake* and *Tiger* proved valuable, but when *Hermes* and *Bulwark* were recommissioned as ASW helicopter ships, these cruisers, with their big crews and high maintenance costs, were retired in 1979 and 1980.[52]

Destroyers and Frigates

The *Type 42* or *Sheffield* destroyer, initially meant to provide air defense for a task force, was built in three batches of four, with the lead ship, *Sheffield*, being laid down in January 1970. The initial displacement and dimensions, 4,350 tons and a 410-foot length, were increased in Batch 3 in a significant design change. Gas turbine-powered, the 30-knot *Sheffield*'s armament included Sea Dart SAMs (SSM capable). The Falklands War showed vividly both the strengths and weaknesses of these ships. Designed primarily for ASW, *Sheffield* was used out of necessity for airborne early warning, where she was vulnerable to air attack. After she was hit by Exocet missiles, her wiring burned producing noxious gases and the aluminum superstructure actually melted and burned in areas where the fires were most intense. She sank. Much study was devoted to the reasons behind her loss and subsequent ship designs were adjusted accordingly.[53]

Construction of the *Broadsword* frigate was similar to the *Sheffield* in that three batches were built, with the later ships incorporating feedback from the Falklands War experience. These ships initially were 430 feet long and displaced 4,600 tons. The armament varied, but included Exocet missiles (Harpoons in Batch 3). Each of these gas turbine-powered, 30-knot ships had the Lynx Mark 2 helicopter which could carry Sea Skua ASMs and ASW torpedoes. Construction of fourteen units took place in three batches and was begun with *Broadsword* in 1975.[54]

Table 4.4
Selected Force Levels – Royal Navy, 1968–79

	Year											
	68	69	70	71	72	73	74	75	76	77	78	79
Ballistic Missile Submarines	3	3	3	4	4	4	4	4	4	4	4	4
Nuclear Attack Submarines	3	3	3	3	6	6	7	8	9	9	10	11
Diesel Attack Submarines	30	22	21	17	24	22	21	20	19	18	17	16
Carriers	3	2	2	2	1	1	1	1	1	1	1	0
Commando Carriers	3	2	2	2	3	2	1	2	0	0	0	0
Assault Ships	2	2	2	2	2	2	2	2	2	2	2	0
ASW Carriers	0	0	0	0	0	0	0	0	1	2	2	2
Cruisers	2	1	1	1	2	2	2	2	2	2	2	1
Missile Destroyers	6	6	3	7	9	9	10	10	11	11	11	12
Destroyers	8	2	2	2	3	0	0	0	0	0	0	0
Frigates	51	54	55	48	57	58	60	60	59	57	55	54
Mine Warfare	48	45	44	47	44	44	43	43	43	43	38	37

Conclusions

Political factors dominated the Royal Navy's shipbuilding in the 1970s. Abandoning a world-wide colonial empire, the nation accepted a more regional role and tailored its Navy accordingly. The majority of available funds went into building a fleet of SSBNs, and the conventional fleet suffered. Aircraft carriers and cruisers were retired and destroyers and frigates were designed to operate in the European environment, where land-based air power could be provided. This had a significant and adverse effect on innovation in British shipbuilding and, while they were successful designs that fulfilled mission requirements, the classes that were produced did not contribute significantly to the advancement of naval technology.

FRANCE

Submarines

After leaving NATO, France reorganized her Navy and moved her naval headquarters from Toulon to Brest. The paramount task was the nation's strategic security, in which a fleet of SSBNs was to play the major role. The SSBN program began with the first unit, *Le Redoubtable*, in 1964, and she was operational until 1971. None the less, the program succeeded. These submarines were initially armed with sixteen relatively low-yield ballistic missiles, but most were refitted with the M-4, which had six 150-kiloton MIRVs that could be delivered to 2,500–3,000 miles.[55] Representing phase three of France's strategic program, they increased her strategic security significantly.

Nuclear-powered attack submarines also were built, beginning with the *Rubis* (SNA 72) in 1976. This 2,670-ton, 237-foot unit was among the smallest

SSNs ever designed. Capable of 25 knots, she was armed with SM 39 missiles, an adaptation of the 50-mile MM 38 Exocet, and four 21in torpedo tubes. This was a very innovative and successful program that would continue into the 1980s. The 1,725-ton, 222-foot *Agosta* diesel attack submarine on which the *Rubis* design was based, was begun in 1972, and ended when the fourth unit, *Ouessant*, was completed in 1978.[56]

Surface Combatants

As Table 4.5 shows, France maintained the size of her navy, replacing older ships with new designs. Qualitatively, there was great improvement. The *Aconit* (C65) destroyer was succeeded by the three-unit *Tourville-* (F 67) class,

Table 4.5
Selected Force Levels – French Navy, 1968–79

	Year											
	68	69	70	71	72	73	74	75	76	77	78	79
Ballistic Missile Submarines	0	0	0	1	2	2	3	3	4	4	4	4
Other Submarines	19	19	20	19	19	19	19	19	20	21	21	21
Carriers	3	3	2	2	2	2	2	2	2	2	2	2
Helicopter Carriers	0	1	2	2	1	1	1	1	1	0	1	1
Cruisers	2	2	2	1	1	2	2	2	2	2	1	1
Command Ship	0	0	0	0	1	0	0	0	0	0	0	0
Missile Destroyer Leaders	2	2	2	2	2	1	1	1	1	0	0	0
Missile Destroyers	4	4	4	4	4	6	7	8	9	9	9	11
Destroyers	14	14	13	12	13	10	11	11	11	11	9	9
Frigates	24	24	27	27	29	25	24	24	27	22	28	24
Mine Warfare	54	54	80	89	91	53	50	46	49	38	35	32
Amphibious Ships	10	10	9	7	5	7	7	7	5	2	7	7

which carried helicopters. The lead ship, *Tourville*, was laid down in 1970, beginning a production run that would end in 1977. An equally significant development was the *Type C 70*-class, which had ASW and AAW variants. The lead ASW unit, *Georges Leygues*, was laid down in 1974, in a seven-ship series that would continue into the 1990s. At 456 feet, this 4,200-ton ASW destroyer was very innovative and quite versatile. Her propulsion was a gas turbine-diesel arrangement, in which she could make 18 knots on her diesels, and 30 knots overall. She was extremely well-armed for a ship of her size, carrying Exocet, a Crotale EDIR, torpedo-launchers and ASW helicopters. A superb design, this class would support the Navy into the 21st century. For coastal operations, beginning in 1972, France produced 17 *D'Estienne D'Orves* (Type A 69) corvettes, and three more were sold to Argentina. Some of these 1,250-ton, 262-foot ships were armed with Exocet but had limited ASW capabilities.[57]

OTHER NATIONS

Northern Europe

Divergent forces influenced naval development in Sweden and the European NATO nations. On the one hand, the expense of modern combatants and US protection prompted nations to restrict naval development. Conversely, the Soviet naval threat prompted them to invest in naval forces. The responses were varied. Norway took its defense and the Soviet threat seriously. In November 1972, it reported that a submarine had been seen in Sognefiord, north of Bergen, inside Norwegian territorial waters. Government sources later said that the submarine was a Soviet *Whiskey* or *Foxtrot* and that it had been allowed to escape in order to avoid an international incident. Similar intrusions often occurred, prompting Norway to seek US assistance in detecting Soviet submarine intrusions into its fiords. This and other factors made Norway sensitive to the Soviet threat.[58] It continually emphasized the threat in NATO counsels and sought greater security for the flanks of NATO. Realizing that it was responsible for its coastal SLOCs, it invested in its Navy. Table 4.6 shows that the Navy's size remained rather constant from 1968 to 1979. It maintained its fleet of *Kobben* diesel submarines, *Oslo* frigates, and *Sleipner* corvettes, and developed a force of missile-armed coastal craft. In 1970, the first of six 138-ton *Snögg* fast attack craft, armed with Penguin missiles, was commissioned, supplementing two other classes, *Storm* and *Hauk*, that also carried Penguins.[59] While Norwegian naval leaders said that this was barely an adequate defense for Norway's long and vulnerable coast, it none the less contributed to NATO's northern flank security.

Table 4.6
Selected Force Levels – Norwegian Navy, 1968–79

					Year						
	68	69	70	71	72	73	74	75	76	77	78	79
Submarines	15	15	15	15	15	15	15	15	15	15	15	15
Frigates	5	5	5	5	5	5	5	5	5	5	5	5
Corvettes	2	2	2	2	2	2	2	2	2	2	2	3
Mine Warfare	14	15	15	15	14	15	15	14	14	14	12	12
Coastal Craft	45	46	47	47	46	40	46	46	44	42	46	55

Table 4.7
Selected Force Levels – Swedish Navy, 1968–79

					Year						
	68	69	70	71	72	73	74	75	76	77	78	79
Submarines	24	23	23	23	22	22	22	22	20	17	17	16
Cruisers	1	1	1	0	0	0	0	0	0	0	0	0
Destroyers	8	8	8	8	8	8	8	8	6	6	6	6
Frigates	8	8	7	7	5	5	5	5	5	6	4	2
Mine Warfare	40	40	48	36	37	40	45	48	46	42	42	42
Coastal Craft	66	42	42	42	43	45	65	74	76	82	86	90
Amphibious Craft	23	23	23	48	48	48	126	123	123	142	147	144

Outside the NATO umbrella, Sweden had to provide for its own defenses. It also suffered from Soviet submarine intrusions, but until 1980, these boats if detected quickly made for the open sea. Table 4.7 shows that Sweden reorganized its Navy in the late 1970s. Deciding that large surface combatants were too vulnerable and too costly, it focused on fast attack craft, mine warfare ships, and submarines. The destroyers and frigates were virtually retired in 1979, as Sweden organized its maritime defense around its *Draken, Sjöormen*, and *Näcken* submarines and a fleet of missile-armed fast attack craft composed in part of *Hugin* and *Spica* missile-armed boats.[60] The validity of this defense would be tested sorely in the 1980s.

Table 4.8
Selected Force Levels – West German Navy, 1968–79

	Year											
	68	69	70	71	72	73	74	75	76	77	78	79
Submarines	11	11	11	11	15	18	24	24	24	24	24	24
Missile Destroyers	0	2	3	3	3	3	3	3	3	3	3	3
Destroyers	8	8	8	8	8	8	8	8	8	8	8	8
Frigates	8	8	6	8	6	6	6	6	6	6	6	6
Corvettes	6	6	6	6	6	6	6	5	5	5	5	5
Mine Warfare	77	73	72	74	58	61	64	57	75	60	59	58
Coastal Patrol	40	40	40	40	40	40	39	39	40	42	42	50
Amphibious Units	24	24	24	24	24	24	22	19	18	20	22	21

Given the Liberal-Greens political opposition and its ground and air defense responsibilities as a front-line NATO nation, it was impressive that West Germany took its maritime obligations most seriously. Table 4.8 shows a slight shrinkage in the navy's size, but a strong force was maintained. The highlights were building *Type 205* and 18 *Type 206* coastal submarines, acquiring several classes of fast attack craft, fitting *Hamburg* destroyers with Exocet missiles and starting *Bremen* frigates in 1979. This 3,800-ton ship, a modification of *Kortenaer*, was armed with Harpoon and Sea Sparrow missiles.[61]

The Dutch Navy evolved into a more regional force that emphasized air defense, ASW, and port security, as the Dutch abandoned their colonial empire and became accustomed to their role as a modest European nation. The highlight was the building of twelve Harpoon-armed *Kortenaer* frigates which, while modestly innovative, were reliable additions to NATO defenses. Two more were sold to Greece. Belgium's Navy stressed mine warfare, but besides building a fleet of mine hunters and sweepers, it built four 2,430-ton *Wielingen* frigates in the mid 1970s.[62]

Southern Europe
Portugal, while attentive to her maritime responsibilities, was able to do little more than pare down her navy as her empire diminished in the 1970s. She did complete two classes of frigates comprising four *de Andrada* ships built from

1972 to 1976, and six *Joao Coutinho* ships built from 1968 to 1971. While these classes were modestly innovative, they bolstered Portugal's maritime defenses.[63]

Table 4.9
Selected Force Levels – Spanish Navy, 1968–79

	Year											
	68	69	70	71	72	73	74	75	76	77	78	79
Submarines	4	4	4	4	4	8	10	10	10	10	10	8
Helicopter Carrier	1	1	1	1	1	1	1	1	1	1	1	1
Cruisers	1	1	1	1	1	1	1	1	0	0	0	0
Destroyers	16	19	22	16	13	13	13	13	13	13	13	11
Frigates	6	6	4	8	8	8	10	10	15	14	15	16
Corvettes	6	6	6	6	2	3	4	4	—	—	—	—
Mine Warfare	25	31	31	31	17	20	23	23	22	22	16	15
Coastal Craft	20	20	20	20	20	20	20	20	21	25	25	25
Amphibious Craft	11	11	8	8	18	16	15	16	16	16	18	18

By far the most significant naval activity along NATO's southern flank occurred in Spain and Italy. Through US aid, foreign purchases, and indigenous design and construction, Spain developed an excellent navy. Its approach was very shrewd, because, while it had to permit a US presence on its soil in return for extensive naval assistance, this insured that America would assume a considerable portion of Western Mediterranean defense, thereby furthering Spanish security. Additionally, the United States paid a high price and Spain worked to limit the value of this presence as potential Soviet targets in wartime. In a Treaty of Friendship and Cooperation, Spain required that Rota-based US SSBNs be relocated by July 1979, necessitating a significant revision in US operating schedules. Table 4.9 shows that the Navy's size was rather consistent. The power of the submarine fleet was maintained by buying two more *Daphné* submarines in 1970 and four *Agosta* submarines in the mid 1970s. The surface combatant force was maintained by replacing older units with five US *Gearing* destroyers in the early 1970s and building five *Baleares* guided-missile and six other guided-missile frigates. These designs were innovative and well armed.[64]

Italy's vigorous program produced several innovative designs which maintained the navy quantitatively and provided a strong regional naval force capable of operating outside the Mediterranean if the necessary air support were provided. The submarine force was maintained as Italy acquired two US *Tang* submarines, another two US *Balao* submarines, and built four 1,641-ton *Sauro* diesel-powered boats (see Table 4.10). Fitted with 21in torpedo tubes, the *Sauro*s were excellent additions to her defense. In combatants, two 4,400-ton *Audace* guided-missile destroyers, completed in 1972, four 2,500-ton *Lupo* frigates begun in 1974, and eight 3,040-ton *Maestrale* frigates, begun in 1978, were excellent designs. *Maestrale* and *Lupo* had SAMs, surface-to-surface missiles and ASW weapons, making them excellent general-purpose ships.[65]

Table 4.10

Selected Force Levels – Italian Navy, 1968–79

Year

	68	69	70	71	72	73	74	75	76	77	78	79
Submarines	10	9	10	10	9	9	10	10	9	9	9	9
Cruisers	4	4	4	4	3	3	3	3	2	1	3	2
Destroyer Leaders	2	2	2	1	1	—	—	—	—	—	—	—
Missile Destroyers	2	2	2	2	6	8	9	9	9	6	7	7
Destroyers	4	4	4	5	5	—	—	—	—	—	—	—
Frigates	16	13	12	13	10	10	15	18	15	12	12	14
Corvettes	23	23	23	20	16	8	12	12	13	13	8	8
Mine Warfare	61	61	61	61	61	61	60	55	45	44	44	41
Coastal/Patrol	12	8	15	15	16	12	13	13	11	11	16	10
Amphibious Ships	0	7	7	5	3	4	3	2	2	2	2	2

Table 4.11

Selected Force Levels – Greek Navy, 1968–79

Year

	68	69	70	71	72	73	74	75	76	77	78	79
Submarines	3	2	2	2	2	7	7	7	6	6	7	9
Destroyers	8	8	8	8	8	9	11	11	11	11	12	12
Frigates	4	4	4	4	4	4	4	4	4	4	4	4
Mine Warfare	18	18	14	22	22	22	22	19	16	16	16	16
Coastal Craft	13	13	14	19	20	24	21	24	29	29	31	28
Amphibious	16	14	23	23	23	22	22	22	22	22	35	70

Greek and Turkish naval developments became increasingly important because of their nations' strategic locations on the south-eastern flank of NATO and because of the animosity between them. As Greece came to believe that the Soviet threat against it was exaggerated, it focused on the Turkish threat. Frustrated when their forces were unable to contain the Turks in Cyprus, the Greeks withdrew them from NATO on 14 August 1975.

Table 4.12

Selected Force Levels – Turkish Navy, 1968–79

Year

	68	69	70	71	72	73	74	75	76	77	78	79
Submarines	10	10	10	12	10	15	15	16	14	15	14	14
Destroyers	10	10	10	10	10	14	14	13	12	12	12	12
Frigates	0	0	0	0	2	2	2	2	2	2	2	2
Corvettes	15	15	14	8	6	8	5	5	0	0	0	0
Mine Warfare	23	23	23	25	26	27	29	29	32	34	33	30
Coastal Craft	44	44	40	35	25	25	45	50	55	55	66	70
Amphibious Ships	0	0	0	0	0	40	45	50	55	58	65	70

However, Greece was able to influence US naval assistance first by permitting the home-porting of US ships in Pyraeus in 1972 and the stationing of US military personnel on Greek soil, and then through pressure from the American Greek lobby which was able to establish a favorable ratio concerning military aid to Greece and Turkey. Greece maintained a relatively modern navy through US ship transfers and by acquiring eight US *Fletcher*, *Sumner*, and *Gearing* destroyers, two Dutch frigates, eight *Type 209* submarines and German, Greek, and French fast attack craft. Table 4.11 shows a growing fleet, with the greatest gains in amphibious units, useful for operations around Cyprus, and in coastal craft, useful for warfare in the Aegean.

The United States also provided aid to Turkey. Despite the creating of periodic tension, *Fletcher*, *Sumner*, and *Gearing* destroyers and *Balao* submarines were provided, and Turkey also acquired five German *Type 209* submarines.[66] Table 4.12 shows that its navy also grew, with the greatest increases in coastal craft and in amphibious units that would also be valuable in a Greco–Turkish conflict.

Africa and the Middle East

Along the Mediterranean littoral, after the June 1967 War, the Soviet Union provided naval aid to Egypt and Syria and used their ports extensively for its naval purposes. By 1971, the Soviets had supplied the Egyptian Navy with six *Romeo* and six *Whiskey* submarines, four *Skoryy* destroyers, twelve mine-sweepers, twelve *Osa* and eight *Komar* missile patrol boats, 42 other patrol craft, three *Polnocny* medium landing ships, and fourteen other landing craft (see Table 4.13). For its part, Syria was given fourteen *Osa*s, nine *Komar*s and

Table 4.13
Selected Force Levels – Egyptian Navy, 1968–75

	Year							
	68	69	70	71	72	73	74	75
Submarines	12	12	12	12	12	12	12	12
Destroyers	6	6	5	5	5	5	5	5
Frigates	5	4	3	2	2	4	3	3
Osa Missile Boats	12	12	12	12	12	12	8	8
Komar Missile Boats	8	8	8	8	7	7	5	5
Mine Warfare	8	8	8	6	11	12	12	12
Amphibious Units	24	20	20	20	14	14	14	14

several other ships. This threat became most important in October 1967, when Egypt used Soviet-supplied missile boats to fire missiles, sinking the Israeli destroyer *Eilat*. This single incident shook the international naval community, prompting the 'missile fever' of the late 1960s, as less affluent nations bought the cheap but very potent missile boats for defense against larger navies, while the larger navies spent billions developing electronic and weapon systems to defeat the missiles and destroy the high-speed craft.[67] The Soviet-Egyptian relationship deteriorated after President Anwar Sadat came to power. Resolute Soviet support in the October 1973 War did little to reverse this trend. The Soviet Navy was expelled from Egyptian ports in April 1976, abruptly ending Soviet assistance. Conversely, its relationship with Syria was continued into the 1990s.

Although Israel did not invest as heavily in its navy as it did in its army and air force, it acquired *Reshef* and *Saar* fast attack boats, *Dabur* patrol craft, helicopter corvettes, and three *Type 205* submarines to counter the growing Arab threat.[68]

After Libya ordered *La Combattante II* fast attack missile craft, the Soviet Union delivered six *Foxtrot* submarines and *Osa* missile boats. Algeria also received twelve Soviet *Osa*s. Farther southward, South Africa bought three *Daphné* submarines, but the UN ban on arms sales to South Africa restricted its access to French *Agosta* submarines and other foreign ships, forcing it to develop an indigenous surface ship-building capability.[69]

Canada and Latin America

The high point in Canadian naval development was the *Iroquois* helicopter destroyer program. These 4,700-ton, 423-foot, 29-knot ships were armed with Sea Sparrow missiles, a 5in gun, ASW weapons, and two ASW helicopters. Built between 1969 and 1973, they were well-designed, sorely needed replacements for a depleting naval order of battle.[70]

In Latin America, most naval activity was in response to a rapidly growing Brazilian Navy which acquired three British *Oberon* and seven US *Guppy* submarines and minesweepers and six *Niteroi* frigates. Colombia acquired two *Sumner* destroyers and a *Dealey* escort in the early 1970s, and two West German *Type 209* submarines in 1975. Chile acquired the Swedish cruiser *Gota Leon* and two *Leander* frigates in 1971, and later received two British *Oberon* submarines. Peru developed an impressive inventory which included the Dutch cruisers *De Zeven Provincien* and *De Ruyter*, three *Lupo* frigates, and four German *Type 209* and US *Guppy* submarines. Venezuela gained two *Sumner* destroyers, six Italian *Lupo* frigates, four German *Type 209* and two *Guppy* submarines and six British-built fast attack craft. Ecuador acquired two *Type 209* submarines, a US *Gearing* destroyer, six Italian corvettes, and some missile craft. Farther northward, Cuba received Soviet aid, including twenty *Osa*s, three *Foxtrot* submarines, nine *Yevgenya* minesweepers, and many *Zhuk* patrol craft. However, the most significant development occurred in Argentina, given the imminence of the Falklands War. It had bought the British *Modified Colossus*-class carrier *Karel Doorman* in 1968, and subsequently acquired four *Sumner* and four *Fletcher*, a *Gearing*, and two *Sheffield* destroyers, three *Meko* frigates, six *Meko* corvettes, three French *Type A 69* corvettes, and two German *Type 209* submarines. In 1977, it contracted for German *TR 1700* submarines.[71]

The Indian Ocean

The Indo-Pakistani War of 1971 highlighted regional activity. India dominated the naval scene, inflicting great damage on East Pakistani (Bengali) ports and establishing itself as a formidable regional power capable of intensive combat. As its relationship with the Soviet Union grew, it drew on both the East and the West for its naval ships. The USSR supplied *Foxtrot* submarines, *Kashin*

30. The USS *Horne* (CG 30) was of the nine-ship *Belknap* class which entered service from 1964 to 1967. Originally designated as frigates, the *Belknaps* were redesigned as cruisers in July 1975. The *Belnap* (CG 26) was severely damaged in a collision with USS *John F. Kennedy* (CV 67) in the Mediterranean in November 1975, and was subsequently repaired. All the ships have been modernized considerably and currently are armed with Harpoon, ASROC, the Mk 15 CIWS and torpedoes. All but one of the ships also have a LAMPS helicopter.

31. USS *America* (CV 66), the last of three *Kitty Hawk*-class ships, entered service in January 1965. The *Kitty Hawk*s were a vast improvement over the earlier *Forrestal* class, on which their design was based. Capable of carrying 88 aircraft, *America* is a vital component of the US sea projection capability, and is scheduled for the Service Life Extension Program (SLEP) in 1996, which will assure her continued operations well into the next century.

32. The *Austin*-class amphibious transport dock USS *Ogden* (LPD 5) is one of eleven ships that entered service from 1965 to 1971. The class is a lengthened version of the *Raleigh*-class LPD. Either an LCU or several LCMs or LVTs can be carried in the well deck, and up to six helicopters can be carried for brief periods. However, the small hanger, which was placed on only some of the units, can accommodate only one utility helicopter.

33. The tank landing ship USS *Newport* (LST 1179) is seen under way in the Delaware River. Each can carry up to 500 tons of cargo and 431 troops. The 34-metre mobile aluminium ramp forward is linked to the tank deck by a second ramp. The ramps can carry 75 tons.

34. The *Sturgeon*-class nuclear-powered submarine USS *Finback* (SSN 70) is seen operating off Virginia in the late 1960s. Intended for ASW, they were equipped with torpedoes, but later modifications added Harpoon and Tomahawk.

35. The escort ship USS *Knox* (FFG 1052) is shown operating off Hawaii. The ASROC system, which has an automatic reloading magazine, is also used to stow Harpoon missiles. The armament on these ships varies, but includes Harpoon, Sea Sparrow and the Mk 15 CIWS. Many are also equipped with a hangar for the LAMPS-1 helicopter. Several of the units have been sent to the Naval Reserve and others are scheduled to enter that force.

36. This ship, the USS *Schenectady* (LST 1185), is the seventh of the twenty-ship *Newport* class of tank landing ships that entered service from 1969 to 1972. Note the helicopter platform aft. There is also a stern door for loading and unloading vehicles. These 8,450-ton ships (fully loaded) can sustain 20 knots.

37. The amphibious command ship USS *Blue Ridge* (LCC 19), seen here, is the flagship of the Seventh Fleet. She and her sister, USS *Mount Whitney* (LCC 20), entered service in 1970 and 1971, respectively. Having a good cruising speed of 20 knots and equipped with excellent satellite communications and analysis systems, these 19,290-ton ships (fl) have excellent command and control facilities.

38. The *Spruance*-class guided-missile destroyer USS *Spruance* (DD 963) is the lead ship of a 31-unit class, the largest post-Second World War US destroyer program. Her hull and engineering plant have served as the basis for the *Kidd* (DD 993) and *Ticonderoga* (CG 47) designs. The gas turbine propulsion system is extremely quiet and the ships are highly automated, thereby allowing for a rather small crew, given the ships' size. *Spruance* is seen with the ASROC launcher forward, but this was replaced with a 61-cell group Mk 41, Mod. 0 vertical launcher that can hold up to 45 Tomahawks or sixteen vertical-launch ASROC missiles.

38

39. The *Kashin* guided-missile destroyer was the first large surface combatant in the world to be powered by turbine power plants. She was also the last Soviet general-purpose destroyer. Since her SA-N-1 launchers and excellent speed provided her with a modicum of air defense, she was often used as a 'tattletale', trailing and targeting Western naval ships for SSM-equipped surface combatants and submarines. *Kashin* production was completed in 1972, and six were converted to the Modified-*Kashin* class from 1973 onward. Among the additions were four SS-N-2 missile launchers aft, which enhanced the ship's 'tattletale' capability. In 1979, one *Kashin*, *Provornyy*, was seen with the SA-N-7 semi-active radar-guided missile system and was probably a test bed for that missile. Subsequently, three more were built for the Indian Navy, with the first being delivered in 1980.

40. Fourteen *Alligator* tank landing ships were built from 1964 to 1977. They are provided with bow and stern ramps and three cranes (the later ships have only one crane). In the late 1960s and early 1970s, an *Alligator* and two *Polnocny* medium landing ships comprised the Soviet Mediterranean Fleet's amphibious contingent stationed at Port Said, Egypt. *Alligators* were also used extensively in the Navy's West African contingent at Conakry, Guinea, and were deployed to the Indian Ocean Squadron as well.

41. This is a close-up of a *Victor II* nuclear-powered attack submarine (SSN). Slightly larger than the *Victor I*, *Victor II* carries the SS-N-15 missile. Seven units were completed from 1972 to 1978. A subsequent class, *Victor III*, was even larger, and is believed to carry the SS-N-15 and/or SS-N-16 missile.

42. Thirty-four Yankee ballistic missile-equipped nuclear-powered submarines (SSBNs) were built from 1967 to 1974. Initially equipped with the 1,300 nautical mile SS-N-6 missile that could be fired while she was submerged, *Yankee* was a vast improvement over *Hotel* and *Golf*, which had to surface in order to fire their missiles. *Yankees* were used for patrols off the US east and west coasts, and her basic configuration figured heavily in the Delta SSBN. One unit was converted to a *Yankee II*, being equipped as a test bed for the SS-N-17 missile, and the Soviets began withdrawing and converting them to SSNs in 1980 in order to comply with the provisions of SALT II. One unit was lost while on patrol off Bermuda in 1986, after suffering a fire in her missile bay area.

43. The *Krivak II*-class frigate *Pytlivyy* is seen at sea in 1986. Designated by the Soviets as patrol ships, the *Krivaks* are very smart in their appearance. The eleven *Krivak II*s that entered service from 1975 to 1982, have larger VDS housings on their sterns, and each has a single 100mm gun as opposed to the two 76.2mm guns on *Krivak I*. A third class, *Krivak III*, was built for the KGB.

44

44,45. This *Kiev*-class V/STOL carrier *Minsk* is seen operating in the Pacific. Four *Kievs*: *Kiev*, *Minsk*, *Novorossiysk* and *Baku* were built, with *Baku* having significant changes including additional launchers and the USSR's first fixed planar array radar system. In service from 1975 onward, the *Kievs* provided a much greater sea-based air capability than the earlier *Moskva* helicopter ships. The ships' aircraft complements consist of Forger A/B VTOL aircraft and Hormone or Helix helicopters.

45

46

46. The Type 12 frigate *HMS Rothesay* (F 107) entered service in April 1960. The *Rothesay* class was an improved version of the highly successful *Whitby*-class design, and all nine ships were modernized from 1966 to 1972, being given the Sea Cat missile system and a helicopter facility.

47. HMS *Ark Royal* was the largest aircraft carrier to see service with the British Navy. She was first commissioned in 1955 and was finally paid off in 1979. Originally scheduled to be scrapped in the mid-1970s, she was granted a reprieve and kept in service by obtaining spares from her redundant sister ship HMS *Eagle*. *Ark Royal* is seen here in June 1976 about to launch a Buccaneer strike aircraft from her angled deck. Also seen on deck are more Buccaneers (right), Phantom fighters (left) and Gannet AEW aircraft just forward of the super-structure.

48. Seen here when first commissioned in 1969, the *Leander*-class frigate HMS *Charybdis* was armed with twin 4.5-inch guns, the Sea Cat anti-aircraft missile system, a Limbo ASW mortar and a Wasp helicopter. In 1982 she completed a major conversion and was re-equipped with the Sea Wolf anti-aircraft missile system, Exocet anti-ship missiles, ASW torpedoes, 20mm AA guns and a Lynx helicopter, making her a much more formidable fighting ship. Four other frigates of the *Leander* class were also converted in the same manner during the early 1980s.

49. Amphibious warfare assault ships HMSS *Fearless* (L 10) and *Intrepid* (L 11) were built in the 1960s to provide the Royal Marines with a greater capability. The principal advantage over existing LSTs was their seaworthiness, range and capability. Each could carry 400 troops, fifteen tanks and 27 vehicles. Both served in the Falkland Islands War, but have since been retired as part of defence cutbacks.

49

50. This *Oberon*-class patrol submarine, HMS *Osiris* (S 13), is the seventh in an eleven-ship series, having entered service in January 1964. The *Oberon* was a successful design and several additional units were built for other nations. *Osiris* and three others were modernized, being given a modern sonar, a passive towed array, and modern electronics. The remaining seven were stricken and sold to other nations.

50

51. The *Daphné*-class diesel attack submarine *Doris* (S 643), of an eleven-unit class, entered service in August 1964. Armed with twelve torpedo tubes and able to submerge to 300 metres, these submarines were very popular and units were sold to Portugal, Pakistan and South Africa. Spain built four units with French assistance.

51

52. The helicopter carrier *Jeanne d'Arc* (R 97) entered service in June 1964 and currently serves as a training ship. In this capacity, she reflects the French approach of conserving a naval capability at minimal cost; in wartime she would be used for amphibious assault, as a troop transport, or for ASW missions. Her electronics were modernized during an upgrade in 1983–4.

53. *U12* (S 191), a *Type 205* submarine, is seen on the surface. Difficulties with the class centered on the hull coating. Corrosion on two of the boats led to the coating of the first six units with a poor quality anti-magnetic steel, which created severe operational restrictions. Construction of the remaining boats was postponed until a new non-magnetic steel could be produced. The first six subsequently were retired.

54. This Type 206-class submarine, *U 17* (S 196), was the fifth in a class of eighteen boats and was launched in October 1972. The class was initially intended as replacements for the earlier Type 205 boats, and the interiopr arrangement resembles the Type 201 and Type 205 with some improvements. The Type 206 can not only carry sixteen mines in place of its torpedoes, but can carry 24 mines in an external container, thereby allowing the boat to deploy with both mines and torpedoes.

55. The *Hamburg*-class missile destroyer *Hamburg* (D 181), lead ship of a four-unit class, was completed in March 1964. From 1975 to 1977 each was modernized; the boilers were modified, the mainmast was replaced, and a 100mm gun was replaced by two MM38 Exocet twin launchers. In 1978, the bridges were enclosed, and subsequently the torpedo tubes were replaced.

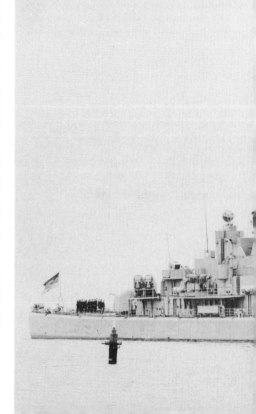

53

54

55

56, 57. The helicopter cruiser *Vittorio Veneto* (C 550) was completed in July 1969. Originally, a third unit of the earlier *Doria* class of helicopter cruiser was planned, but when it was realized that her design was too small, there were several redesigns, resulting in the much larger *Vittorio Veneto*. At 9,500 tons (full load), she is capable of 30 knots. She underwent modernization from 1981 to 1983, in which Ottomat missiles and 40mm AA gun systems were added. Her helicopters are housed in a hangar that is served by two elevators from the flight deck.

58. This *Enrico Toti*-class diesel attack submarine, *Enrico Dandalo* (S 513), was the third of a class of four boats. The first Italian submarines to be built after the Second World War, they entered service in 1968 and 1969. Their great manoeuvrability made them ideal for operations in the Mediterranean, but their small size (593 tons submerged) permitted only a limited number of reloads for their four 533mm torpedo tubes.

59. *Arashio* (SS 565), an *Oshio*-class submarine. The *Oshio* class was the first fleet submarine class constructed by the Japanese after the Second World War, and was completed between 1965 and 1969. These 2,150-ton (submerged) submarines were armed with eight 21-inch torpedo tubes. *Arashio* was the last of the class of five to be retired, in 1986.

59

60. The *Amatsukaze*-class guided-missile destroyer *Amatsukaze* (DDG 163) was the first guided-missile destroyer built in Japan, and was completed in 1965. Initially she carried the Tartar SAM system, ASROC (with no reloads), torpedoes, and Hedgehog and was refitted with Mk 32 torpedoes and an improved radar in 1967. The planned addition of OTO Melara 76mm compact mountings in a subsequent refit was never carried out.

61. This 56-foot patrol boat, *Dastoor*, is one of five that were built by Vosper Thornycroft, Singapore for Kuwait. Armed with two 7.62mm machine-guns, these 25-ton boats are capable of speeds up to 30 knots.

62. This British-made Vosper Mk 7-class frigate, *Dat Assawari*, was in service in 1973. She began refitting in Italy in 1979 and was damaged by a bomb in 1980. She was repaired and was re-commissioned in 1983. She is currently equipped with a 4-cell Albatros SAM launcher, Ottomat SSMs, and an ASW system for A244 torpedoes.

destroyers. *Nanuchka* guided-missile corvettes, *Petya* corvettes, *Osa* fast attack craft, and *Natya* minesweepers.[72]

Elsewhere, Bangladesh procured British *Salisbury* and *Leopard* frigates and several types of patrol craft; Pakistan received four US *Gearing* destroyers and four French *Daphné* and two *Agosta* submarines, Iraq and Ethiopia received several Soviet *Osa* missile patrol boats, and Saudi Arabia began developing a moderate naval force. Iran's development was confused, however, as it broke its relationship with the United States. It was expected that the Shah's Iran would become a regional naval power providing stability in the Gulf. The United States provided considerable naval assistance to help it attain this goal. It ordered six *Spruance* guided-missile destroyers and twelve French *La Combattante II* fast attack missile craft. However, after the break, the US ships were cancelled. In 1978, its order of battle included three destroyers, four frigates, four corvettes, 21 coastal craft, three amphibious ships and craft, and five minesweepers.[73]

The Pacific Ocean
In north-east Asia, Chinese naval progress slowed after the rift with the Soviet Union. The *Luda* guided-missile destroyer progressed slowly, yielding ships that provided a reliable if modest coastal defense capability. The Chinese penchant for copying proven designs yielded successful classes, but none with significant innovation.[74]

Japan dominated regional naval development. The US reaction to this was inconsistent, contradictory, and slightly insulting. On the one hand, it made it clear that it wished Japan to take a greater role in its maritime defense. This position was supported by those who claimed that US protection provided Japan with an undeserved economic advantage since its defense was at US expense. Conversely, many expressed fears that Japan would remilitarize and threaten the United States. None the less, the Japanese program proceeded steadily (see Table 4.14), producing ships that were much more innovative than those it built prior to 1941 and providing many valuable additions to the Maritime Self-Defense Force.[75] Noteworthy were several classes, including *Hatsuyuki-*, *Shirane-*, *Haruna-*, and *Tachikaze*-classes of destroyers, *Chikugo* and *Ishikari* frigates, and *Uzushio* and *Yushio* submarines. Here, the Japanese innovatively applied domestic and foreign technology to produce a capable force with impressive regional scope.

Table 4.14
Selected Force Levels – Japanese Navy, 1968–79

	Year											
	68	69	70	71	72	73	74	75	76	77	78	79
Submarines	8	10	10	11	11	13	14	15	15	15	15	14
Missile Destroyers	0	0	1	1	1	1	1	1	2	2	2	3
Gun Destroyers	24	28	26	37	27	28	28	29	28	28	29	30
Frigates	16	16	13	12	12	14	16	16	16	15	15	15
Corvettes	—	—	—	—	—	20	20	20	18	15	14	12
Mine Warfare	44	44	37	39	44	44	41	41	37	37	37	36

| Coastal Craft | 35 | 35 | 30 | 25 | 25 | 15 | 9 | 14 | 15 | 15 | 11 | 9 |
| Amphibious | 52 | 52 | 52 | 52 | 52 | 53 | 50 | 50 | 50 | 50 | 50 | 50 |

Table 4.15

Selected Force Levels – Royal Australian Navy, 1968–79

| | Year | | | | | | | | | | | |
	68	69	70	71	72	73	74	75	76	77	78	79
Submarines	3	3	4	4	4	4	4	4	4	4	6	6
Carriers	1	1	1	1	1	1	1	1	1	1	1	1
Missile Destroyers	2	3	3	3	3	3	3	3	3	3	3	3
Destroyers	5	3	9	5	4	4	2	2	2	2	2	2
Frigates	5	4	1	6	6	6	6	6	6	6	6	6
Mine Warfare	6	6	6	6	6	6	6	3	3	3	3	3
Coastal Craft	5	20	20	20	20	20	15	12	15	12	12	13

Elsewhere in north-east Asia, South Korea and the Republic of China both received US naval assistance. Aid to Taiwan included twenty-four destroyers, including the USS *Maddox*, the destroyer of the 1964 Tonkin Gulf incident, and two *Guppy II* diesel submarines. Korea benefited greatly from US naval ship transfers. In 1974, its naval inventory included seven destroyers, eight frigates, ten mine warfare units, 36 coastal craft, and twenty amphibious units.[76]

In the South Pacific, Australia and New Zealand so curtailed their naval spending that, in 1974, the editor of *Jane's Defence Weekly* asserted that their navies were barely able to protect their own shores (see Table 4.15).[77] This situation improved somewhat when Australia began ordering *Oliver Hazard Perry*-class frigates from the United States in 1976.

CONCLUSIONS

As the year 1979 ended, global naval development faced an uncertain future. The Soviet Navy was experiencing a golden era, when new ships of great innovation became operational and the Navy proved its worth both in strategic defense and as a vehicle of state policy. The fact that Admiral Gorshkov had to issue a revision to his *Sea Power of the State*, however, implied that there was opposition to the Navy's prosperity and that this might affect its future. The US Navy had suffered through the stormy post-Vietnam War period in which cost became so important as to have a significant impact on the innovation in US naval designs, but President Ronald Reagan's election in 1979 indicated that the situation might improve in the 1980s. Across the ocean, Great Britain had grossly curtailed her commitments in Asia and the Indian Ocean, but had invested in very expensive Polaris submarines, which, while they provided strategic defense and a degree of prestige, considerably inhibited innovation in other types of naval combatants. It appeared that she would not increase her naval appropriations significantly in the 1980s. In the Pacific, Japan continued balanced and impressive naval development and emerged as a strong regional naval power. Finally, China, France, Germany and other nations designed economical combatants that provided good area defense and were popular with the world's less affluent navies.

NOTES

1. 'Jane's Moore Makes a Case for Fast Attack Craft,' in *Proceedings*, vol. 102, no. 7 (July 1976), p.106; and *Jane's Fighting Ships, 1967-1968*, p.iv; and *1970-1971*, p. 153.

2. 'Navy to Retire 19 Ships from the Seventh Fleet,' in *Proceedings*, vol. 97, no. 1 (January 1971), p. 101; 'Carrier Capacity Seen Stretched,' in *Proceedings* vol. 95, no. 1 (January 1969), p. 146; 'CNO Tells Congress USN Still Number One – But Barely,' in *Proceedings*, vol. 102, no. 4 (April 1976), p. 114; *Annual Report of the Secretary of the Navy, Fiscal Year 1969* (Washington, DC: Department of the Navy, 1969), pp. 1-3; '"Mayday" for the *Mayaguez*,' in *Proceedings*, vol. 102, no. 11 (November 1976), pp. 93-111; 'Soviet/UAR Aircraft Eye Sixth Fleet,' in *Proceedings*, vol. 94, no. 12 (December 1968), p. 157; *Jane's Fighting Ships, 1969-1970*, pp. 74-6, 79; *1970-1971*, p. 80; *1978-1979*, p. 127; and *1970-1971*, p. 86. In 1969, *Jane's Defence Weekly* noted that the NATO allies had barely enough power to fulfill their missions. In 1970, the Netherlands and Canada had disposed of their aircraft carriers at a time when the US Navy said that it needed fifteen carriers to meet its commitments. It is unclear whether the Navy considered the loss of the NATO carriers when it computed this figure.

3. Paul M. Kennedy, 'British Defence Policy Part II: An Historian's View,' in *RUSI*. vol. 122, no. 4 (December 1977), p. 15.

4. 'Editor's Notes.' in *RUSI*, vol. 114, no. 653 (March 1969), p. 1. See also: William Luce, 'Britain's Withdrawal from the Middle East and Persian Gulf,' in *RUSI*, vol. 114, no. 653 (March 1969), p. 4.

5. Peter Walker, 'The Opposition's View of British Defence Policy,' in *RUSI*, vol. 120, no. 2 (June 1975), p. 5.

6. Terence T. Lewin, 'The Royal Navy in the Next Decade,' in *RUSI*, vol. cxiii, no. 651 (August 1968), pp. 205-6; and Terence T. Lewin, 'The Royal Navy – Its Contribution to National and Western Defence,' in *RUSI*, vol. 121, no. 3 (September 1976), p. 7.

7. J. M. Dougary, 'Comments Concerning a Lecture by Rear-Admiral T. T. Lewin titled "The Royal Navy in the Next Decade",' in *RUSI*, vol. cxiii, no. 651 (August 1968), p. 209.

8. Luce, pp. 7-8.

9. Ibid., p. 8.

10. Ibid., p. 12; and 'Editor's Notes,' in *RUSI*, vol. cxiii, no. 651 (August 1968), pp. 189-90. See also: Peter Mangold, 'Britain and the Defence of Kuwait, 1956-1971,' in *RUSI*, vol. 120, no. 3 (September 1975), p. 44; L. W. Martin, 'Sea Power and Modern Strategy,' in *RUSI*. vol. cxiii, no. 651 (August 1968), p. 196; Lewin, 'The Royal Navy in the Next Decade,' in *RUSI*, vol. cxiii, no. 651 (August 1968), p. 205; and T. B. Millar, 'Developments in the Far East and South-East Asia Following the British Withdrawal,' in *RUSI*, vol. cxiii, no. 653 (March 1969), p. 11.

11. An ANZUK force was composed of Australian, New Zealand, and British forces. However, judging from the tardiness of the British response to Australian needs during the Second World War and the severe cutbacks in British defense spending, the Australians were justified in questioning the promptness and potency of any future British response. Lord Carrington, 'British Defence Policy,' in *RUSI*, vol. cxviii, no. 3 (September 1973), p. 6; and Robert J. O'Neill, 'Australian Defence Policy Under Labour,' in *RUSI*, vol. cxviii, no. 3 (September 1973), pp. 30-6.

12. O'Neill, pp. 50-1.

13. 'Building of Indian Ocean Base is Well Underway by US Navy,' in *Proceedings*, vol. 97, no. 11 (November 1971), p. 109; 'Navy Hopes for Expansion of Forces in Indian Ocean,' in *Proceedings*, vol. 97, no. 2 (February 1971), p. 109; and 'Diego Garcia: The Seabees at Work,' in *Proceedings*, vol. 105, no. 8 (August 1979), pp. 53-61.

14. Isaac C. Kidd, Jr. 'View from the Bridge of a Sixth Fleet Flagship,' in *Proceedings*, vol. 98, no. 2 (February 1972), pp. 26-7. In spite of this resolute support for Egypt, the Soviet Union was unable to reverse the decline in Soviet–Egyptian relations and the Soviet Navy was finally expelled from Alexandria in 1976. For excellent discussions on this break, see the articles by Robert O. Freedman in *Naval War College Review*: 'Soviet Policy Toward Sadat's Egypt from the Death of Nasser to the Fall of General Sadek,' vol. 26, no. 3 (Nov–Dec 1973), pp. 63-79; 'The Soviet Union and the Middle East: The High Cost of Influence,' vol. 24, no. 5 (January 1972), pp. 15-34; 'Soviet Policy Toward the Middle East from the Exodus of 1972 to the Yom Kippur War,' vol. 27, no. 4 (Jan–Feb 1975), pp. 32-53; 'Soviet Policy Toward the Middle East since the October 1973 Arab–Israeli War,' vol. 28, no. 3 (Fall 1976), pp. 61-103; Gary G. Sick, 'Russia and the West in the Mediterranean: Perspectives for the 1970s,' in *Naval War College Review*, vol. 22, no. 10 (June 1970), pp. 49-69; and Frederick J. Cox, 'The Russian Presence in Egypt,' in *Naval War College Review*, vol. 22, no. 6 (February 1970), pp. 45-53.

15. Tai Sung An, 'Soviet Access to Cam Ranh Bay: Political and Military Implications,' in *Proceedings*, vol. 105, no. 9 (September 1979), pp. 111-13; and William H. Walls and Edwin R. McDaniel, 'Soviet Bases in Vietnam: Implications for the Seventh Fleet,' in *Proceedings*,

vol. 105, no. 9 (September 1979), pp. 113-16.

16. Peter Tsouras, 'Soviet Naval Tradition,' in *The Soviet Navy: Strengths and Liabilities*, edited by Bruce and Susan Watson (Boulder, CO: Westview Press/Arms & Armour Press, 1986), pp. 3-25.

17. 'Soviets More Aggressive on the Sea,' in *Proceedings*, vol. 95, no. 1 (January 1969), p. 147; Bruce W. Watson and Margurite A. Walton, '*Okean-75*,' in *Proceedings*, vol. 102, no. 7 (July 1976), pp. 93-7; and Charles G. Pritchard, 'The Soviet Marines,' in *Proceedings* vol. 98, no. 3 (March 1972), p. 28.

18. Bruce W. Watson, 'Comments on Gorshkov's *Sea Power of the State*,' in *Proceedings*, vol. 103, no. 4 (April 1977), pp. 41-7; 'Soviet Fleet Admirals Praise Russian Navy Striking Force,' in *Proceedings*, vol. 98, no. 1 (January 1972), p. 111; 'Chief of Soviet Navy Boasts of Its Global Nuclear Might,' in *Proceedings*, vol. 97, no. 10 (October 1971), p. 109; and 'Soviet Admiral Boasts Greatest Naval Power,' in *Proceedings*, vol. 96, no. 4 (April 1970), p. 133.

19. Peter Tsouras, 'Soviet Naval Strategy,' in *The Soviet Naval Threat to Europe: Military and Political Dimensions*, edited by Bruce W. Watson and Susan M. Watson (Boulder, CO: Westview Press, 1989), p. 18.

20. Labayle Couhat, pp. 583-4; *Conway's Part II*, p. 496; 'Soviet Y-class Submarines Patrol off US East Coast,' in *Proceedings*, vol. 98, no. 7 (July 1972), p. 126; and *Jane's Fighting Ships, 1986-1987*, p. 537. The submarine program was not without its mishaps. On 12 April 1970, a *November* SSN sank 400–600 nm north-west of Spain and, on 29 February 1972, a *Hotel* SSBN was disabled while on patrol in the North Atlantic 600 nm north-east of Newfoundland and was towed back to the Baltic.

21. Labayle Couhat, pp. 581-3; *Conway's Part II*, p. 497; and *Jane's Fighting Ships, 1986-1987*, pp. 535-6.

22. Labayle Couhat, pp. 585-6; *Conway's, Part II*, p. 497; and *Jane's Fighting Ships, 1986-1987*, pp. 540-1.

23. Labayle Couhat, pp. 589-90; and *Conway's, Part II*, pp. 497-8.

24. Labayle Couhat, pp. 592, 593-4; 'Strength of Soviet Navy, Naval Air Force Discussed,' in *Proceedings*, vol. 96, no. 6 (June 1970), pp. 129-30; and *Jane's Fighting Ships, 1986-1987*, p. 551.

25. Labayle Couhat, pp. 572-5; *Conway's, Part II*, pp. 479-80; Norman Polmar, 'The Soviet Aircraft Carrier,' in *Proceedings*, vol. 102, no. 10 (October 1976), pp. 138-41; *Jane's Fighting Ships, 1986-1987*, p. 558; J. W. Kehoe, Herbert A. Meier, Larry J. Kennedy, and Don C. Gast, 'US Observations of the *Kiev*,' in *Proceedings*, vol. 103, no. 7 (July 1977), pp. 105-11; and Ulrich Schulz-Torge, 'The *Kiev*: A German View,' in *Proceedings*, vol. 103, no. 7 (July 1977), pp. 112-15.

26. Labayle Couhat, pp. 595-8; and *Jane's Fighting Ships, 1986-1987*, p. 558.

27. Labayle Couhat, pp. 598-601.

28. Ibid., pp. 608-12.

29. Ibid., pp. 617-21.

30. Ibid., pp. 626-7; '*Nanuchka* Class Increases Soviet Offensive Capability,' in *Proceedings*, vol. 101, no. 4 (April 1975), pp. 106-7; and *Jane's Fighting Ships, 1986-1987*, p. 5.

31. Labayle Couhat, pp. 636-8.

32. Martin Streetly, 'Ocean Reconnaissance System Operations,' in Watson and Watson, *Soviet Naval Threat to Europe*, pp. 158-9; and 'Soviet Ocean Surveillance Effort Employs Two Types of Satellites,' in *Proceedings*, vol. 102, no. 8 (August 1976), p. 106.

33. William W. Kaufmann, *A Thoroughly Efficient Navy*, Studies in Defense Policy, (Washington, DC: Brookings Institution, 1987), pp. 6-8; and 'Navy to Trim Fleet Below 500,' in *Proceedings*, vol. 101, no. 1 (January 1975), p. 107. The amphibious ship reduction from 162 to 67 units, while higher than other types, was less significant, since many of these were no longer needed after the river operations in Vietnam were ended.

34. Labayle Couhat, pp. 718-19; *Conway's, Part I*, pp. 234-5; and *Jane's Fighting Ships, 1986-1987*, p. 699.

35. Labayle Couhat, pp. 717-18; *Conway's, Part I*, pp. 234-5; and 'Navy Seeks Faster Submarine,' in *Proceedings*, vol. 94, no. 10 (October 1968), p. 154.

36. US Government, Department of Defense, *Statement of Secretary of Defense Elliot L. Richardson Before the House Armed Services Committee on the Fiscal Year 1974 Defense Budget and FY 1974-78 Program, Tuesday, April 10, 1973* (Washington, DC: Department of the Defense, 1973), pp. 53-7; *Report of Secretary of Defense Harold Brown to the Congress on the Fiscal Year 1980 Budget, FY 1981 Authorization Request, and FY 1980-1984 Defense Programs, January 25, 1979*, p. 66; US Government, Department of the Navy, *CNO Report: A Report by Admiral James O. Holloway, III, US Navy, Chief of Naval Operations, Concerning the Fiscal Year 1979 Military Posture and Budget of the US Navy, March 1978* (Washington, DC: Department of the Navy, 1978), pp. 93-5; and *Jane's Fighting Ships, 1986-1987*, p. 694.

37. Labayle Couhat, pp. 698-9; *Conway's, Part I*, p. 207; and *Jane's Fighting Ships, 1986-1987*, pp. 706-7.

38. George, Quester, ed., *Sea Power in the 1970s* (New York: Dunellen, 1975), p. 48; Roy Beavers, 'The End of an Era,' in *Proceedings*, vol. 98, no. 7 (July 1972), pp. 23-4; and John Lehman, *Aircraft Carriers: The Real Choices*, The Washington Papers, no. 52, Center for Strategic and International Studies, Georgetown University (Beverly Hills, CA: SAGE Publications, 1978), pp. 5, 19-24, 29, 36-7, 40.

39. Elmo R. Zumwalt, Jr., *On Watch* (New York:

Quadrangle/The New York Times Book Company, 1976), p. 121.

40. Other Navy proponents were also concerned about the carriers' cost. Admiral Holloway took issue with Admiral Rickover and argued publicly for the need for a larger navy. (See: James A. Nathan and James K. Oliver, *The Future of United States Naval Power* (Bloomington: University of Indiana Press, 1979), pp. 6-8.) Sherman E. Wright and Robert H. Smith argued that ASW was being neglected. (See: Sherman E. Wright, Jr., 'ASW and the Modern Submarine,' in *Proceedings*, vol. 99, no. 4 (April 1973), pp. 65-8; and Robert H. Smith, 'ASW–The Crucial Naval Challenge,' in *Proceedings*, vol. 98, no. 5 (May 1972), pp. 126-31, 133-7.) In 1972, Admiral Thomas Moorer and others warned that the Navy might not be able to protect the sea lanes through the North Atlantic during wartime. (See: Frank B. Case, 'Time to Secure the Seas,' in *Proceedings*, vol. 99, no. 8 (August 1973), p. 26.)

41. Labayle Couhat, pp. 724-5; *Conway's, Part I*, p. 216; George W. Davis, Jr. 'USS *Virginia* (CGN-38),' in *Proceedings*, vol. 103, no. 8 (August 1977), pp. 85-9; George N. Maddox, 'The *Virginia*'s Combat System Department,' in *Proceedings*, vol. 103, no. 8 (August 1977), pp. 90-1; Vin Vinci, 'Mk 86 Gunfire Control System,' in *Proceedings*, vol. 103, no. 8 (August 1977), pp. 92-4; 'USS *Virginia* (CGN-38),' in *Proceedings*, vol. 103, no. 8 (August 1977), pp. 95-105; and *Jane's Fighting Ships, 1968-1969*, p. v; and *1986-1987*, pp. 716-17, 719.

42. Labayle Couhat, pp. 737-40; *Conway's, Part I*, p. 219; 'Plans to Build Two Frigates Are Dropped by Pentagon,' in *Proceedings*, vol. 97, no. 8 (August 1971), p. 109; 'Navy Designing Smaller Ships with Higher Speed, Lower Cost,' in *Proceedings*, vol 97, no. 8 (August 1971), p. 109; 'USS *Spruance* (DD-963), in *Proceedings*, vol. 102, no. 2 (February 1976), pp. 61-9; and A. M. Osborne, '*Kidd*-class Destroyers to Join the Fleet,' in *Proceedings*, vol. 106, no. 1 (August 1980), pp. 96-8. *Jane's* was critical of *Spruance*'s light armament, noting that she had only two 5in guns, ASROC, two triple torpedo tubes, and two LAMPS helicopters. See: *Jane's Fighting Ships, 1977-1978*, p. 119.

43. Labayle Couhat, pp. 744-6; *Jane's Fighting Ships, 1986-1987*, p. 739. *Jane's* was critical of *Knox*, noting that the original design had only one shaft that provided 23 knots, a 5in gun, an ASROC launcher, DASH, and an SQS-26 sonar. See: *Jane's Fighting Ships, 1973-1974*, p. 75.

44. Labayle Couhat, pp. 741-3; *Conway's, Part I*. pp. 226-8; John D. Beecher, 'FFG-7: The Concept and Design,' in *Proceedings*, vol. 104, no. 3 (March 1978), pp. 148-50; Stephen J. Durch, 'The Navy's Newest Ship: FFG-7,' in *Proceedings*, vol. 104, no. 3 (March 1978), pp. 150-3; R. E. Hammond and Pat Tierney, 'The LAMP ship Team,' in *Proceedings*, vol. 104, no. 3 (March 1978), pp. 154-8; Dan Manningham, 'LAMPS III,' in *Proceedings*. vol. 104, no. 3 (March 1978), pp. 159-61; and *Jane's Fighting Ships, 1986-1987*, p. 736.

45. Labayle Couhat, p. 753; *Conway's, Part I*, pp. 241, 242; 'First New Amphibious Ships Launched at Mississippi Yard,' in *Proceedings*, vol. 100, no. 2 (February 1974), pp. 116-17; and *Jane's Fighting Ships, 1986-1987*, p. 743-5.

46. This approach would be considered again in the 1980s. See: James L. George, 'Building Warships in Peacetime,' in *Proceedings*, vol. 106, no. 9 (September 1980), pp. 66-70.

47. *Annual Report for Fiscal Year 1967, Including the Reports of the Secretary of Defense, Secretary of the Army, Secretary of the Navy, and Secretary of the Air Force*, pp. 108-9; *Report of Secretary of Defense Donald H. Rumsfeld to the Congress on the Fiscal Year 1978 Budget, FY 1979 Authorization Request, and FY 1978-1982 Defense Programs, January 17, 1977*, pp. 183-4, 197; *Annual Report of the Secretary of the Navy, Fiscal Year 1970*, pp. 37-8; *Report of the Secretary of Defense James R. Schlesinger to the Congress on the Fiscal Year 1975 Defense Budget and FY 1975-1979 Defense Program, March 4, 1974*, p. 137; and *Report on the 1980 Budget*, p. 165.

48. P. G. Boxhall, 'The Strategic Use of Islands in a Troubled Ocean,' in *RUSI*, vol. cxi, no. 644 (November 1966), pp. 336-41; 'UK Defense Plans Announced,' in *Proceedings*, vol. 95, no. 8 (August 1968), pp. 156-7; Jonathan Trumbull Howe, *Multicrises; Sea Power and Global Politics in the Missile Age* (Cambridge, MA: The MIT Press, 1971), pp. 320-22; Quester, pp. 106, 142; and 'A Review of the Royal Navy's Future,' in *Proceedings*, vol. 95, no. 8 (August 1968), pp. 156-7.

49. *Conway's, Part I*, p. 143; and *Jane's Fighting Ships, 1970-1971*, pp. 81, 86; *1972-1973*, p. 76; *1973-1974*. p. 77; and *1975-1976*, p. 97.

50. Labayle Couhat, pp. 208-9; *Conway's, Part I*, p. 173; p. 208; 'British Polaris Submarines Have Nuclear Warheads,' in *Proceedings*, vol. 96, no. 6 (June 1970), p. 130; and *Jane's Fighting Ships, 1986-1987*, pp. 642-3.

51. *Conway's, Part I*, p. 145; and Howe, pp.320-2.

52. *Conway's, Part I*, p. 151.

53. Labayle Couhat, pp. 211-12, 216-17; *Conway's, Part I*, p. 156; 'HMS *Sheffield* Launched; First Type 42 Destroyer,' in *Proceedings*, vol. 97, no. 12 (December 1971), p. 112; and *Jane's Fighting Ships, 1986-1987*, pp. 648-9.

54. Labayle Couhat, pp. 216-17; *Conway's, Part I*, p. 167; and Norman L. Dodd, 'HMS *Sheffield*: A Ship for the 80s,' in *Proceedings*, vol. 102, no. 2 (February 1976), pp. 95-7.

55. Labayle Couhat, pp. 133-4; 'The French Navy: New *raison d'être*, in *Proceedings*, vol. 101, no. 3 (March 1975), pp. 32-42; 'French Nuclear Policy Stresses Submarines,' in *Proceedings*, vol. 102, no. 2 (February 1976), p. 109; 'French Navy to Modernize,' in *Proceedings*, vol. 95, no. 10 (October 1969), p. 157; Quester, p. 107; 'France Tests Submarine Missile,' in *Proceedings*, vol. 95, no. 10 (October 1969), p. 158; 'France Launches Second Nuclear Submarine,' in *Proceedings*, vol. 96, no. 6 (June 1970), p. 130; Middleton, p. 141; and *Jane's Fighting Ships, 1986-1987*, p. 166.

56. Labayle Couhat, p. 134; *Conway's, Part I*, p.

46; and *Jane's Fighting Ships, 1986-1987*, p. 167.

57. Labayle Couhat, pp. 143-4; *Conway's, Part I*, pp. 36-8, 41; 'French Navy Expanding Fleet with Carriers and Other Ships,' in *Proceedings*, vol. 99, no. 2 (February 1973), p. 117; and *Jane's Fighting Ships, 1977-1978*, p. 126; and *1986-1987*, pp. 172, 178, 736.

58. In 1972, Admiral Turner warned that one of the reasons behind the Soviet naval build-up was the ability to exert pressure on the flanks of NATO (Turkey and Norway/Scandinavia) by operating in the eastern Mediterranean and Norwegian Sea, respectively. (See: Stansfield Turner, 'The United States at a Strategic Crossroads,' in *Proceedings*, vol. 98, no. 10 (October 1972), p. 20. See also: Desmond Wettern, 'NATO's Northern Flank,' in *Proceedings*, vol. 95, no. 7 (July 1969), pp. 52-9; 'Mystery of the Northland–Norwegian Fjords Bugged?' in *Proceedings*, vol. 100, no. 7 (July 1974), p. 122; and Albert L. Romaneski, 'Nordic Balance in the 1970s,' in *Proceedings*, vol. 99, no. 8 (August 1973), pp. 32-41.

59. *Conway's, Part I*, pp. 97-8; 'Norwegian Navy Gets First of Six Fast Patrol Boats,' in *Proceedings*, vol. 96, no. 7 (October 1970), p. 103; and *Jane's Fighting Ships, 1986-1987*, pp. 386-8.

60. *Conway's, Part II*, pp. 382-4; and *Jane's Fighting Ships, 1986-1987*, pp. 475-7; *1975-1976*, p. 108; *1978-1979*, p. 137; and *1979-1980*, p. 147. In 1975, *Jane's* reported impressive new construction, but by 1978, it was obvious that continued defense cuts were preventing the replacement of older ships and that to solve the problem, Sweden was focusing on submarines and fast attack craft.

61. *Conway's, Part I*, pp. 261-8; and *Jane's Fighting Ships, 1975-1976*, pp. 97, 107; *1977-1978*, p. 126; and *1986-1987*, pp. 206-11.

62. *Conway's, Part I*, pp. 2, 84-9; Ezio Bonsignore, '*Kortenaer*/F-122: A Standard Frigate for NATO Navies,' in *Proceedings*, vol. 104, no. 11 (November 1978), pp. 154-8; 'Dutch Cruiser Retired,' in *Proceedings*, vol. 94, no. 12 (December 1968), p. 157; and *Jane's Fighting Ships, 1977-1978*, pp. 126, 127; *1979-1980*, pp. 139, 145; *1986-1987*, pp. 44-6, 369; and *1975-1976*, p. 107.

63. *Conway's, Part I*, pp. 101-6; and *Jane's Fighting Ships, 1975-1976*. p. 108; *1977-1978*, p. 119; and *1986-1987*, p. 430.

64. *Conway's, Part I*, pp. 112-14; *Annual Report Fiscal Year 1979*, p.112; 'US to Lend 16 Ships to Spanish Navy.' in *Proceedings*, vol. 97, no. 4 (April 1971), p. 112; and *Jane's Fighting Ships, 1973-1974*, p. 75; *1975-1976*, pp. 97, 108; *1978-1979*, p. 131; and *1986-1987*, pp. 458-61.

65. Labayle Couhat, pp. 306-8; *Conway's, Part I* pp. 71-4; and *Jane's Fighting Ships, 1975-1976*, pp. 97, 107; *1977-1978*, p. 126; *1978-1979*, p. 131; and *1986-1987*, pp. 279-80, 285-7.

66. *Conway's, Part I*, pp. 55-60, 119-23; G. Drossinos, 'The Royal Hellenic Navy,' in *Proceedings*, vol. 97, no. 3 (March 1971), pp. 32-7;

'Smaller Warships Sought by Greek Navy,' in *Proceedings*, vol. 96, no. 2 (February 1970), p. 124; 'Greek Navy Orders Four FPBs from French Shipbuilder,' in *Proceedings*, vol. 96, no. 6 (June 1970), p. 130; and *Jane's Fighting Ships, 1975-1976*, pp. 97, 107-8; *1977-1978*, p. 126; and *1979-1980*, p. 147.

67. *Conway's, Part II*, pp. 301-3, 447-8; 'Egyptian KOMAR Fleet Growing,' in *Proceedings*, vol. 95, no. 1 (January 1969), p. 159; Shlomo Slonim, 'Suez and the Soviets,' in *Proceedings*, vol. 101, no. 4 (April 1975), pp. 37-41; *Jane's Fighting Ships, 1971-1972*, pp. 92-4, 310; and *1979-1980*, p. 147; and Robert D. Colvin, 'Aftermath of Elath,' in *Proceedings*, vol. 95, no. 1 (January 1969), pp. 60-7.

68. *Conway's, Part II*, pp. 437-9, 447-8; Reuben Porath, 'The Israeli Navy,' in *Proceedings*, vol. 97, no. 9 (September 1971), pp. 33-9; Martin J. Miller, Jr., 'The Israeli Navy: 26 Years of Non-Peace,' in *Proceedings*, vol. 101, no. 2 (February 1975), pp. 48-54; and *Jane's Fighting Ships, 1975-1976*, p. 107; *1977-1978*, p. 126; and *1978-1979*, p. 137.

69. *Conway's, Part II*, pp. 299, 309-10, 320, 437-9, 447-8; 'South Africa to Get First of Three French Submarines,' in *Proceedings*, vol. 96, no. 10 (October 1970), p. 103; and *Jane's Fighting Ships, 1975-1976*. p. 107; *1977-1978*, p. 126; *1978-1979*, p. 137; *1979-1980*, pp. 146, 147; and *1985-1986*, p. 480-2.

70. *Conway's, Part I*, p. 10; W. G. Kinsman, 'Canada Must Face Reality,' in *Proceedings*, vol. 98, no. 8 (August 1972), pp. 32-7; 'Canadians Developing Frigates,' in *Proceedings*, vol. 95, no. 10 (October 1969), p. 158; and *Jane's Fighting Ships, 1975-1976*, p. 107; *1979-1980*. p. 145; and *1985-1986*, p. 74.

71. *Conway's, Part II*, pp. 404-6, 408, 410-12, 413-16, 422-4, 428-30; and *Jane's Fighting Ships, 1975-1976*, pp. 107, 108; *1977-1978*, p. 126; *1978-1979*, pp. 125, 137; and *1979-1980*, pp. 24, 145, 146, 147.

72. *Conway's, Part II*, pp. 339-41; A. P. S. Bindra, 'The Indian Ocean As Seen by an Indian,' in *Proceedings*, vol. 96, no. 5 (May 1970), pp. 178-203; 'New Delhi Buying Soviet Warships,' in *Proceedings*, vol. 95, no. 11 (November 1969), p. 158; 'India's Naval Role Takes Shape,' in *Proceedings*, vol. 94, no. 8 (August 1968), p. 158; 'Indian Navy Gets New Look,' in *Proceedings*, vol. 94, no. 11 (November 1968), p. 158; and *Jane's Fighting Ships, 1975-1976*, p. 107; *1977-1978*, p. 126; and *1979-1980*, p. 145.

73. *Conway's, Part II*, pp. 304, 323, 354, 434-6; *Jane's Fighting Ships, 1975-1976*, pp. 99, 107; *1977-1978*, pp. 126, 127; *1978-1979*, p. 133; and *1979-1980*, pp. 145-6; 'Iran Builds Indian Ocean Navy to Guard Oil Shipping Route,' in *Proceedings*, vol. 101, no. 1 (January 1975), p. 108; and 'Iran Agrees to Buy Four More Warships,' in *Proceedings*, vol. 101, no. 1 (January 1975), p 108.

74. *Jane's Fighting Ships, 1975-1976*, p. 107; and *1977-1978*, p. 126.

75. Hideo Sekino, 'Japan and Her Maritime Defense,' in *Proceedings*, vol. 97, no. 5 (May 1971), pp. 98-121; Drew Middleton, 'Japan Urged by United States to Bolster Submarine Defenses,' in *Proceedings*, vol. 100, no. 2 (February 1974), p. 119; *Jane's Fighting Ships, 1977-1978*, pp. 121, 127; *1978-1979*, p. 133; *1979-1980*, p. 145. For alternative views on this issue, see: J. E. Auer, 'Japanese Militarism,' in *Proceedings*, vol. 99, no. 9 (September 1973), pp. 54-5; H. E. McCracken, Jr., 'Japan's View of Korea,' in *Proceedings*, vol. 98, no. 2 (February 1972), p. 47; Richard A. Miller, 'Indonesia's Archipelago Doctrine and Japan's Jugular,' in *Proceedings*, vol. 98, no. 10 (October 1972), p. 27; and Turner, p. 20.

76. *Conway's, Part I*, pp. 292-6; *Conway's, Part II*, pp. 361-2; and *Jane's Fighting Ships, 1975-1976*, p. 108; and *1974-1975*, p. 217.

77. *Conway's, Part I*, p. 278; and *Jane's Fighting Ships, 1973-1974*, p. 77. For an alternative position, see T. B. Millar, 'The Australian Naval Situation,' in *Proceedings*, vol. 98, no. 5 (May 1972), pp. 216, 221.

5
The Reagan Years: The Maritime Strategy, the 600-Ship Navy, and the Third World War, 1980–8

THE EFFECTS OF THE INFLUENCING FACTORS

Political Events, Technological Progress, and Mahan's Theory

In many ways, the events from 1980 to 1989 were tantamount to a war between the superpowers. While not a shot was fired (in fact relations between the two improved over the period), the following aspects of the Soviet–American military competition made it seem as if a conflict had been fought and won.[1] First, such an intense competition had been waged between the two that the Soviet economy approached the brink of ruin because its military expenditures had sorely outstripped the economy's capacity. Second, the US ability to continue this competition in arms development seemed unlimited. Third, the Soviet military research and development community had been left so far behind that, given its current level of knowledge and expertise, it was relegated to a position of being able to produce only relatively obsolete military equipment compared to that of the United States. Fourth, this trend promised to continue – the technological gap between Soviet and American arms programs would continue to widen further – meaning that the nation's strategic position *vis-à-vis* the United States would not only continue to deteriorate, but also that the military equipment the Soviet Union produced would be increasingly obsolete. Fifth, if this military competition were continued, its negative effect on the economy would continue also, and would almost certainly lead to Soviet economic chaos. Sixth, the Soviet leadership, realizing this dilemma, sought to correct it through significant changes. Seventh, while the political and social changes that were undertaken were not done specifically to assuage the West, they were to the West's liking. Specifically, they promised to supplant the existing Soviet Marxist–Leninist ideology, one that strove for world revolution, and one that the West found to be the pernicious aspect of the Soviet political-social system. *If a war had actually been fought and the West had been victorious, then the resultant demands on the Soviet Union – the abrogation of communism, the recognition of human rights, and the agreement to delete world revolution and aggression from its agenda – were in fact very similar to* what the Soviet leadership conceded.

In essence then, what had occurred in Europe in the 1980s was tantamount to the Third World War. It was Reagan's war and it was won without firing a shot. Instead, the US research and development (R&D)

programs, hallmarked by Star Wars, so outspent the Soviet R&D community, so drove the Soviet economy down, and created a situation in which the new western technology so outpaced the Soviets that they recognized the resultant strategic danger and virtually capitulated. In 1990, this fact was not realized in the United States because it did not think strategically. However, the Soviet leadership did. Since Lenin, it had revered the military theorist Carl von Clausewitz, establishing a military strategy and a system that conformed to his theories. Assessing in Clausewitzian terms the situation in the 1980s and projecting it into the future, the Soviets realized that they were losing. This quasi-war had been waged totally in the realm of defense expenditures and had centered on the R&D abilities of both nations. The accession of President Reagan ushered in a period of intense defense spending which quickly re-established the Soviet–American balance of power. This spending was very effective, accomplishing such significant research and development that the Soviet Union was left far behind. It was hallmarked by the Star Wars program, which virtually assured a US strategic advantage for several decades. However, the Reagan program went far beyond this and encompassed all sectors of military technology. The events in the naval world were an important subset of this competition, pitting the world's strongest maritime nation against the world's strongest land power.

To backtrack a bit, the years of US introspection were reversed radically when Reagan became President in 1981. The result in maritime affairs was a period of significant US naval development which challenged recent Soviet advances, and was hallmarked by the goal of a 600-ship navy. In construction, the highlights were continuing the *Nimitz* carrier program, building *Ohio* SSBNs, and planning for *Sea Wolf* to replace the *Los Angeles* nuclear-powered attack submarines. These efforts were accompanied by a fresh maritime strategic formulation which called for the forward deployment of US naval forces and several naval reactions that showed that the United States was not afraid to use its maritime might. The responses in Soviet naval construction were significant – the *Typhoon*, *Oscar*, *Mike*, and *Sierra* submarine classes, and the *Tibilisi*-class aircraft carrier. In space, Moscow attempted to counter the US Strategic Defense Initiative (SDI), popularly known as the Star Wars program. These efforts not only were clearly inferior to America's, but were so burdensome economically that they sent the nation's economy to the brink of disaster. As such, they amounted to one of several factors that would prompt the Soviet Union to reconsider her foreign and defense policies, ushering in the unprecedented changes of 1989 that promised to reform the international order.

Because of these factors, the period from 1980 to 1989 was hallmarked by significant naval shipbuilding activity – one in which a great deal of construction but only moderate naval innovation occurred – and the possible conclusion of the Soviet–American arms race. If such a resolution had been reached, it could have ushered in a de-emphasis in naval development in the 1990s. In order to best understand these phenomena, it is helpful first to examine US and Soviet naval developments and their major operations.

THE UNITED STATES

Reagan's naval program began in 1981, with an articulation of a forward maritime strategy which argued that America needed a Navy that could sail northward into the Norwegian Sea and attack Soviet submarines in the Arctic bastion, their naval forces at sea, and their military facilities on the Kola Peninsula in wartime.[2] Although this was presented as a new strategy, much of it was a restatement of traditional Mahanian views concerning force projection. As such, it meshed ideally with traditional naval construction views and therefore meant continuing at a heightened pace the existing programs, rather than drastically reorienting US naval shipbuilding programs. Along with it came the goal of building a 600-ship navy. There was nothing magic about the figure of 600 ships; in fact, many argued that, based on analyses of Second World War German U-boat operations, 600 ships were inadequate to counter the existing Soviet threat. It served, however, as a target which could be presented publicly, providing the glitter behind which the Navy could proceed to re-establish its strength.

Submarines
The ballistic missile submarine (SSBN) construction program was continued. Since the new Trident missile's longer range meant that patrolling SSBNs no longer had to be forward deployed, the Navy began withdrawing its SSBNs from Guam in July 1980. The *Ohio* SSBN program was continued, the lead unit, *Ohio*, was commissioned on 11 November 1981, the first deployment to the Pacific occurred in 1982, and several more were commissioned subsequently. Missile technology also progressed, resulting in Trident II, and although the failure of its March 1989 test delayed its deployment, it would be deployed in the early 1990s. Likewise, the *Los Angeles* program was sustained, producing dozens of attack submarines. Meanwhile, planning commenced for a new class, *Sea Wolf*, to succeed *Los Angeles* in the 1990s. Construction of *Sea Wolf* was begun in 1988 and emphasized quieting and providing the latest sensors and weapons systems.[3]

Surface Combatants
An extremely ambitious shipbuilding program, begun shortly after the inception of the Reagan administration, was sustained throughout the decade, producing dozens of combatants. By the end of fiscal year 1982, the naval inventory was down to twelve deployable carriers. This began to change when *Carl Vinson* entered the fleet in 1982. Subsequently, three carriers, *Therodore Roosevelt*, *Abraham Lincoln*, and *George Washington*, were built, and in fiscal year 1989 funding was begun for two more carriers to replace older units.[4]

Regarding other surface combatants, the most notable developments were the deployment of Aegis and Tomahawk. Both were tantamount to minor revolutions in naval warfare and probably were among the factors that demonstrated to the Soviets that the state of their R&D lagged considerably behind the West. John Moore, called Aegis 'one of the most impressive advances in naval weaponry in 15 years'.[5] Tomahawk had a number of test flight problems in 1981 and 1982, and the program was reorganized in order to achieve the stated goals.[6] Its range, fire power, and accuracy allowed it to strike targets hundreds of miles away with either nuclear or conventional warheads, thereby posing a most serious threat to enemy combatants and shipping. It also reduced the distinction between land and sea warfare, as it could be used against land targets many miles inland. Tomahawk meant that significant damage could be incurred on enemy ground forces' rear echelons without resorting to nuclear weapons, thereby increasing significantly the relevance of naval power.

Most surface combatant construction amounted to continuing the existing programs, but upgrading the weapons and electronics that were installed aboard the new ships. The fourth and final *Virginia* guided-missile cruiser, *Arkansas*, was commissioned in 1980, USS *Hayler*, the 31st and last *Spruance* destroyer was commissioned in 1983, and a 51-ship *Oliver Hazard Perry* series of guided-missile frigates was completed in 1989.[7]

Two innovative classes, the 27-ship *Ticonderoga*-class Aegis-equipped cruiser, and the *Arleigh Burke* Aegis-equipped destroyer, an intended replacement for the *Adams* and *Coontz* guided missile destroyers, were built. The *Ticonderoga* was wrapped in controversy. She carried two LAMPS helicopters, and was armed with SAMs, Harpoon missiles, ASROC, 5in mounts, 20mm Phalanx systems, and Mark 32 torpedo tubes. The initial criticism ranged from her possibly being so top-heavy that she would capsize in heavy weather, to claims that she was not armed adequately. Her mixed performance in a series of tests in April 1983 only added to the controversy, which was not dispelled when she performed much more satisfactorily in September 1983. She performed admirably on her first deployment to the Mediterranean in 1984 and then went through an exhaustive series of tests upon her return. Again she performed admirably, and it appeared that her critics had been assuaged. However, controversy arose again on 3 July 1988, when the third unit of the class, USS *Vincennes*, in the midst of a battle with Irani gunboats in the Strait of Hormuz, shot down a civilian Irani airliner. The intense investigation following this incident tried to determine whether the cause was human or systems error. The results noted the confusion that could result in the ship's confined control spaces during intense combat. Construction of the class was continued while design refinements were considered and some changes were incorporated.[8]

Less notoriety accompanied the *Arleigh Burke* destroyer. This 466-foot, 8,300-ton ship was armed with Tomahawk and Harpoon missiles, a single 5in and two 20mm Phalanx guns, and Mark 32 torpedoes, and had facilities to refuel and rearm LAMPS helicopters. The program was delayed because of funding, but the lead unit was laid down in 1985. Intense shipyard competition for the program resulted in some criticism concerning its cost, but the government could retort that *Arleigh Burke* was the most powerful destroyer ever to put to sea.[9]

In amphibious ship construction, highlights included 15,746-ton *Whidbey Island* dock landing ships to replace the *Thomaston*-class, and 96 air cushion landing craft.[10]

Soviet construction of the *Kirov* battle cruiser and a need for an effective shore-bombardment capability prompted bringing back the old battleships. In their reactivation, they were given new electronic systems, Harpoon and Tomahawk missiles, and Phalanx 20mm CIWS mounts. Recommissioned in 1982, *New Jersey* was deployed to the Pacific, Central America, and Lebanon. *Iowa* was recommissioned in 1984 and saw duty off Lebanon, as the Navy refurbished *Missouri* and *Wisconsin* as well. The program appeared to be very successful and the ships provided valuable support, particularly during the Lebanon operations. In April 1989, however, a gun turret on *Iowa* exploded, killing 47 men. The resulting intensive investigation tentatively placed the blame on Gunner's Mate Second Class Clayton M. Hartwig. Critics were not assuaged, and it was to the Navy's credit that it admitted that it could not positively establish the explosion's cause. *Iowa* subsequently deployed and fired her guns, but did not use the turret involved in the explosion.[11]

Table 5.1
Order of Battle – US Navy, 1980–9

	Year								
	80	81	82	83	84	85	86	87	88	89
SSBNs	40	34	33	34	35	37	39	37	37	36
Submarines	82	87	96	98	98	100	101	102	100	99
Attack carriers	13	12	13	13	13	13	14	14	14	14
Battleships	0	0	0	1	2	2	3	3	3	4
Cruisers	26	27	27	28	29	30	32	36	38	40
Destroyers	94	91	89	71	69	69	69	69	69	68
Frigates	71	78	86	95	103	110	113	115	107	100
Mine Warfare	25	25	25	21	21	21	21	22	22	22
Patrol Vessels	3	1	4	6	6	6	6	6	6	6
Amphibious Units	66	65	65	63	61	62	62	63	63	65
Auxiliaries	110	101	117	103	120	121	123	127	114	137
Totals	530	521	555	533	557	571	583	594	573	592

Although the question of the cause was important, the resulting criticism focused on the age of the ships, alleging that they were no longer safe, regardless of the degree of rehabilitation. While they provided a valuable capability, they might not be retained in the budget conscious reductions anticipated in the early 1990s because of the *Iowa* incident.

Conclusions
Not all the Navy's goals were met. Between 1982 and 1986, Congress funded only 105 of the 150 major new ships that were requested. Navy Secretary John Lehman, a crucial figure in the program, resigned to return to private industry and was replaced by James Webb. In 1988 however, Webb had a dispute with Secretary of Defense Carlucci, in which Webb wanted to delete a Trident submarine from the naval construction program. Sixteen elderly frigates and destroyers were dropped instead and Webb resigned when it

became obvious that the goal of a 600-ship Navy would not be reached.[12] While not all the goals had been achieved, what was more important was what had been accomplished. Table 5.1 shows that the fleet was increased by 62 ships. The only major shrinkage, in frigates, would be offset partially by building the *Arleigh Burke*s. At the beginning of 1989, 97 new ships were under construction. The fiscal 1988-1992 building program included five SSBNs, fifteen SSNs, another aircraft carrier (with a second to follow), five Aegis cruisers, twenty Aegis destroyers, eight amphibious ships, fifteen mine warfare ships, and 28 auxiliaries, certainly reflective of a nation that had an accurate understanding of the value of sea power.[13] Its true significance lies in the way this power was used and the effect it had on progressive Soviet decision-making.

POLITICAL EVENTS

Reconstituting a strong navy was one thing; having the resolve to use it was quite another. Whereas US indecision in the 1970s precluded its active participation in crises, thereby providing opportunities for opposing forces and groups, in the 1980s the United States demonstrated repeatedly that it had made great progress in resolving its Vietnam experience and would again use its naval power when necessary. This provided clear lessons for both maintaining and using naval power.

Grenada

On 25 October 1983, US Marines from USS *Guam*, and US Army soldiers invaded the island of Grenada to protect US medical students and establish calm as Maurice Bishop's government fell. USS *Independence* provided air support in an operation that was politically successful. Order was established and when President Reagan visited the island a year later, more than 90 per cent of the Grenadians turned out to express their gratitude. Operation 'Urgent Fury' also reflected a US resolve to use its military power.[14] Conversely, this joint-service exercise was fraught with military problems. The scenario was suited ideally to the application of naval power, but the Army and Air Force insisted on taking part. The problems were significant and widespread. Communications were notoriously poor, command and control was confused, intelligence was incomplete, the Army performed marginally, and the complex logistics chain was often unresponsive. While the goal was accomplished, it would have been difficult not to achieve it, given that the United States enjoyed total air and naval superiority and had ground forces that simply overwhelmed Grenadian and Cuban forces. Subsequent analyses of 'Urgent Fury' would recommend quietly but resolutely that many changes be made in US joint operations procedures.

Lebanon

Concurrently, on 24 October, the US Marine headquarters in Beirut was blown up and hundreds of Marines were killed by a fanatic driving a truck loaded with explosives. The political and pyschological damage was so profound that the Marines subsequently were withdrawn. None the less, Lebanon is worthy of investigation because of the type of naval operations that were conducted.

A US Marine Corps presence in Beirut, Lebanon predated the use of US naval power by several months. As Israel prepared to withdraw its forces in August 1983, US Marine forces in Beirut became endangered as the fighting between the warring Lebanese factions escalated. This continued, and on 29 August, the Marines fought a pitched battle with Shiite Moslems near Beirut airport. Two Marines were killed and fourteen were wounded the following day as the fighting continued. The United States then moved a contingent of ships with 2,000 Marines to the Lebanese coast, and the Marine presence in Beirut was reinforced. As Israel began its withdrawal in early September, the fighting became more intense. The first US naval bombardment occurred on 8 September, when a US frigate shelled Druse positions in the hills of Beirut, and on 12 September, President Reagan authoriz d 'aggressive self-defense tactics' by US forces. This included allowing the Marines to call upon US naval and air power. The USS *New Jersey* was sent to the Lebanese coast, and additional shellings occurred later in September against Syrian-controlled positions deep inside Lebanon and against anti-government forces in the hills overlooking Beirut. The situation continued to deteriorate, and, when a suicide terrorist with a truckload of explosives blew up the US Marine headquarters on 24 October, fatal damage had occurred to the US plan and the troops were subsequently withdrawn. While the naval bombardment operations were conducted successfully and meant a new aspect in the application of US naval power in the 1980s, it seemed that there were limits to the utility of conventional naval power against terrorists in certain scenarios.[15]

Libya
Libyan territorial claims to the entire Gulf of Sirte and its support for terrorism were among the causes of US–Libyan tension. Intermittent US naval operations in the area prompted clashes, such as one in March 1986, when two Libyan missile craft were destroyed and two more were seriously damaged.[16] The United States responded with Operation 'El Dorado Canyon', a joint Navy–Air Force air operation against Libya. At midnight on 14 April, US Air Force F-111Fs left the British Royal Air Force Base, Lakenheath and EF-111s departed Heyford RAF Base for Libya. Since France refused to allow them to overfly her territory, four silent refuelings were required en route, as the aircraft flew their extended 2,800-mile journey. At 5.45 a.m., A-6Es were launched from *America* and *Coral Sea* to attack Benina air base and the Sidi Bilal training area, as the Air Force F-111Fs attacked Tripoli's Al Jumahiriya barracks and military airport. All Navy aircraft were recovered, while one Air Force F-111F was lost.[17]

Three aspects of the operation are relevant to this study. It was a political success in that Qadhafi said little for months afterward, and Libya's terrorist stance was tempered considerably. Second, like 'Urgent Fury', 'El Dorado

Canyon' was a joint US exercise, but it was far superior to the Grenada operation because it was essentially a combination of two service exercises conducted in semi-isolation, with the requirement that both forces hit their targets on schedule. Structured in this way, the chronic problems that occurred in joint US operations were minimized. Third, the reason given for participation of the Air Force was that if it were exclusively a Navy operation, carrier-borne aircraft would have had to make two strikes. That this was a superficial excuse covering the continued service rivalry was obvious.[18] What was less obvious was the effect of the Air Force participation which, to its chagrin, demonstrated the superiority of maritime power. This was true because maritime power would come from US ships at sea, not foreign bases, and Libyan post-attack reprisals could not be waged on America's allies. Many British understandably believed that Britain was a likely target for any reprisals, since the US aircraft had staged from British bases. Thus, by insisting on participating in the exercise, the Air Force had endangered the British and was unprepared to defend them from post-attack retaliation. No such post-exercise vulnerability would have existed had only US Navy aircraft been used.

Achille Lauro

The terrorist seizure of the passenger liner *Achille Lauro* also created a crisis. After killing a handicapped, defenseless passenger, Leon Klinghoffer, the terrorists released the other hostages in return for guarantees of safe passage. US intelligence was able to determine when the terrorists' aircraft left for Libya, and US naval aircraft intercepted it, forcing it to land in Italy. Italy refused to release the terrorists to US forces, but the operation was an example of the effective use of naval and naval air power.

Iranian Mining in the Persian Gulf

The US naval operations in the Persian Gulf were relevant for several reasons. While ultimately successful as a contributor to the eventual cessation of Irani–Iraqi hostilities, the US Navy was less than ideally equipped to fulfill the requisite minesweeping and escort duties.

The US naval role in the Persian Gulf was increased considerably after the USS *Stark* was hit by an Iraqi air-to-surface missile in May 1987. The United States agreed to escort Kuwaiti tankers through the Persian Gulf, and the first such convoy passed through the Gulf to Kuwait in July, but when Iran continued to mine the Gulf waters, and the Kuwaiti tanker *Bridgeton*, then under US naval escort, hit a mine on 24 July, the US expanded its role.

The difficulty was that the United States had concentrated on reacting to the Soviet Navy by building submarines and large combatants, and neglecting smaller combatants, including minesweepers. The division of responsibility among NATO members, in which the United States concentrated on the mission of keeping the SLOCs across the North Atlantic open – a mission that required submarines, aircraft carriers and large combatants – and the Netherlands, Belgium, and others emphasized the minesweeping mission in their navies, also contributed to the problem. None the less, the US response was innovative. To compensate for this weak minesweeping capability, the United States deployed minesweeping helicopters and equipment aboard the amphibious assault ship USS *Guadalcanal*, which arrived in Bahrain in mid August. Meanwhile, the Navy was ordered to activate eight reserve mine-sweepers and send them to the Gulf.[19]

The United States also responded by turning to its Allies for help, but Great Britain, France, Italy, West Germany, and the Netherlands all initially refused to provide assistance, fearful that the US policy would escalate hostilities. In spite of this, the US continued its policy and Great Britain and France reconsidered their decisions, opting to provide minesweepers on 11 August. Belgium, the Netherlands, and other allies would later follow suit, and the Soviet Union would also detail ships to the region.[20]

Tension continued to rise, and on 21 September, US forces attacked and captured an Iranian ship engaged in minelaying. On 8 October, three Iranian gunboats were destroyed.[21] The situation reached a climax when Iranian missiles struck a US–registered tanker in Kuwaiti waters on 15 October. The United States responded by shelling two off-shore platforms which Iran was using to base gunboats deployed to attack tankers transiting the Persian Gulf.[22]

Tension continued and, on 14 April 1988, *Samuel B. Roberts* was almost cut in two when she hit a mine. On 18 April, the Navy staged Operation 'Praying Mantis', achieving a lop-sided victory over Iran. *Wainwright* and *Simpson* sank the *Joshan*, one of Iran's *Combattante-II* patrol boats, while aircraft from *Enterprise* destroyed a Boghammar gunboat, as three others went aground. Meanwhile, the *Saam*-class frigate *Sahand* was sunk by A-6s, an Iranian F-4 aircraft was shot down, and US aircraft and surface ships hit but did not sink the frigate *Sabalan*, which was allowed to return to port. Finally, the Sirri, Rahkish, and Sassan oil platforms, which had Iranian observers aboard, were attacked. Tension remained high in the following months and, on 3 July, *Vincennes*, in the midst of combatting Iranian gunboats in the Strait of Hormuz, shot down a civilian Iranian Airbus, killing all 290 people aboard.[23] On 20 August, Iran and Iraq accepted a UN cease-fire, ending their eight-year war. In it, a total of 543 ships had been attacked within and 90 outside the Gulf.[24]

Conclusions

These uses of naval power provided several lessons. First, they demonstrated its utility and second, they showed the Western nations' determination to use their naval power, if necessary. Third, the Persian Gulf operations were initially waged by the United States alone. Although the Allies quickly reassessed their positions and provided sorely needed minesweeping support, the lesson of the liabilities of an unbalanced navy – in this case a US Navy with a weak minesweeping capability – was evident. Fourth, they revealed a factor that was very relevant to the discussions concerning curtailing sea power in the early 1990s. In all these confrontations, the opponent was not the Soviet Union and in those situations where Soviet clients were involved, Soviet responses were muted. In the scurrying of nations to divest themselves of sea power that would probably occur in the 1990s, it would help to remember that these major naval reactions had nothing to do with Soviet imperialism and that similar non-Soviet threats would probably exist into the 21st century. This point would be seen vividly in the 1991 Persian Gulf War. Finally, although the Soviet Navy was not directly involved, US resolve was a factor in shaping subsequent Soviet naval policy which, in turn, had significant effects on subsequent naval development and innovation.

THE SOVIET UNION

Political Influences
Western resolve was only one of several factors affecting Soviet naval policy. A critically deteriorating Soviet economy, caused in large part by the defense burden, was a major factor. *Perestroika*, the Soviet response espoused by Mikhail Gorbachev, was comprehensive and profound. It called for a de-escalation with the United States and implied that Soviet military forces were to be cut to the bone, providing a strategic defense against aggression, but little more. In a nation which for centuries, had relied on its Army for its security it seemed likely that the Navy would suffer if the cutbacks were drastic.

Foreign policy factors reinforced this. Perestroika called for the self-determination of all nations, clearly indicating that the USSR intended to back off from its policy of involvement in the Third World for at least the near term. This was logical. Moscow now faced a resolute Washington that would react, making further gains much less likely. Also, of the billions of roubles spent on establishing radical Third World governments – in Aden, Guinea, Somalia, Ethiopia, Mozambique, and elsewhere – only Cuba and Vietnam could be considered firmly in the Soviet camp. The remainder pursued independent courses which often diverged from Moscow's positions. These amounted to small returns for so high an investment, prompting an evaluation of its worth. And since the Navy's role in this policy was a major factor in its justification, when the policy was ended, this only weakened the Navy's *raison d'être*.

The restrictions concerning the Navy were not immediate, nor should they have been. Resources had been committed, were in the pipeline, and existing programs would be completed. Reductions in naval construction would not occur before 1994 or 1995 and would be influenced by events in the interim. Thus, while Gorshkov was forced to retract his statements in 1979 and was succeeded by the less independent Chernavin, his influence lingered on in naval construction, producing additional innovative naval combatants and submarines.

Submarine Construction
The submarine program continued to receive the top priority. Table 5.2 shows that, while there were decreases in SSBNs owing to compliance with SALT, there were increases in other submarine types. Additionally, while the SSBN inventory shrank slightly, newer classes replaced older ones, ac-

counting for a more serious threat. The *Delta III*, *Charlie II*, *Alfa*, *Victor III*, *Kilo*, and *Tango* submarine programs were all active in 1980. The Soviets continued developing their *Delta* submarines and in 1984 launched the first *Delta IV*, with sixteen SS-NX-23s that had greater throw weight, seven MIRV warheads, and greater accuracy than SS-N-18 missiles. The highlights of 1988 were the launching of the *Oscar* SSGN and the *Typhoon* SSBN in the spring and autumn, respectively. Both were significant contributions to naval technology. The 14,500-ton *Oscar* was the largest cruise missile submarine ever built. Carrying 24 SS-N-19 missiles, she was intended to operate in heavily protected waters. A longer version, *Oscar II*, was later built, with the additional length possibly related to efforts to quiet the submarine.[25]

The 25,000-ton *Typhoon*, armed with twenty SS-N-20, 4,800-mile solid fuel missiles with seven MIRV warheads, the largest submarine ever built, was a major contribution to the Soviet Union's strategic security. Having developed such missiles that could be launched from heavily defended Arctic sanctuaries against virtually all enemy targets, the Soviets could progress from smaller SSBNs to the mammoth *Typhoon*, which would patrol in very secure areas behind extremely powerful submarine, surface combat, and air screens. Having provided such safety, the Soviets felt that they could justify putting so many strategic assets on one platform. The first *Typhoon* entered service in 1983, with others following in the 1980s for a total of six before production ceased.[26]

In non-SSBN developments, the Soviets produced three classes of attack submarines: *Akula*, *Sierra*, and *Mike*. The 10,000-ton *Akula* was believed to be a successor to *Victor III*. She was capable of 35 knots, was armed with torpedoes and could also fire SS-NX-21 and SS-N-15 and -16 missiles. The first *Akula* was launched in 1983. The 7,550-ton, 35-knot *Sierra* was believed to be a possible successor to *Alfa* and was armed with six torpedo tubes.[27]

Table 5.2
Selected Force Levels – Soviet Navy, 1980–9

	Year									
	80	81	82	83	84	85	86	87	88	89
Ballistic Missile Nuclear Submarines	69	72	69	65	64	64	64	62	62	62
Ballistic Missile Diesel Submarines	15	14	14	14	14	14	14	14	12	8
Cruise Missile Nuclear Submarines	47	47	48	48	49	46	46	51	50	50
Cruise Missile Diesel Submarines	20	20	19	18	14	15	16	16	16	16
Nuclear Attack Submarines	51	57	60	61	66	67	69	80	77	81
Diesel Attack Submarines	162	164	165	152	151	147	147	129	125	120
Carriers	2	2	2	3	3	3	3	4	4	4
Helicopter Carriers	2	2	2	2	2	2	2	2	2	2
Nuclear Battle Cruisers	1	1	1	1	2	2	2	2	2	3
Cruisers	35	35	36	37	38	38	36	34	34	34
Guided Missile Destroyers	36	39	39	46	49	44	43	44	45	41
Gun-Armed Destroyers	30	30	25	25	25	25	22	15	15	10

Frigates	168	175	176	177	177	177	179	163	163	186
Coastal/Patrol	308	482	485	460	440	391	385	382	410	415
Mine Warfare	361	352	353	355	357	371	369	365	373	375
Amphibious Ships	93	84	82	80	78	77	81	84	80	80
Amphibious Craft	92	85	90	100	109	120	120	125	150	155

This program was not without its failures. A *Charlie* that was transferred to India had such significant reactor problems that the Indians dubbed it the 'Chernobyl-class.' In 1986, three crewmen died and several were injured when a fire occurred in one of the port missile tubes of a *Yankee* submarine patrolling off the US east coast. She sank in 6,000 metres of water, deep enough to prevent the recovery of any usable information. However, the most devastating loss may have been the only *Mike* nuclear-powered attack submarine. Believed to be based on the experience gained from *Alfa*, the single 6,400-ton *Mike* was launched in June 1983. She had a titanium hull and was powered by a pressurized water reactor. She was lost while conducting operations on 7 April 1989, after the crew had tried unsuccessfully to extinguish a raging fire. The loss was great; 42 of the 69-man crew perished and the submarine sank.[28]

Despite these setbacks, the program was continued, further assuring the nation's strategic security and posing an ever more dangerous submarine threat to Western forces on the high seas. The use of hull coatings and titanium hulls, building *Typhoon*, the world's largest submarine, continued ballistic missile developments, MIRVing, engineering improvements, quieting advances, and improved sensors, communications, and electronics highlighted this very impressive program.

Aircraft Carriers and Other Surface Combatants
While surface warships had a lower priority than submarines, the Soviets continued to produce such combatants, building additional *Kirov*s, *Slava*s, *Sovremennyy*s, and *Udaloy*s for naval use, and *Koni* frigates for export. The first *Udaloy* and *Sovremennyy* destroyers were completed in 1981, and the first *Slava* cruiser in 1983. *Kirov* was completed in 1980, and her sisters, *Frunze* and *Kalinin*, were subsequently completed. *Frunze* was given a new twin 130mm dual-purpose mount in place of the two 100mm mounts on *Kirov*, and *Kalinin* was given a new CIWS, meaning that the *Kirov* program was dynamic enough to incorporate changes in succeeding units of the same class.[29]

A new frigate that might replace *Krivak*, was reported under construction in the Baltic in 1989. Displacing about 4,000 tons, this ship had surface-to-surface missiles, dual-purpose and AA guns, ASW systems, and would probably carry a helicopter.[30] In amphibious warfare, the second *Ivan Rogov* LPD, *Aleksandr Nikolaev* was completed in 1982, and the third, in succession to *Ropucha*, was reportedly under construction in 1989.

The greatest progress was made in aircraft carriers. *Baku*, last of the four *Kiev* carriers, was launched in 1982 and had modifications in her design, including changes to her island superstructure to allow for new electronics and communications systems, and different weaponry. Also, when *Kiev* was refitted, she was given Ka-27 Helix-A helicopters and three steel barriers were added to the port side of her forcastle to reduce air turbulence on her flight deck.[31] (It had been predicted that turbulence would be a problem, given *Kiev*'s initial design, and this estimate had proven true.) The changes made to *Kiev* during her refit and the major changes observed in *Baku* reflected what one would expect, a flexible program that continually considered design problems and could provide corrections.

As significant as *Kiev* was, she was placed in perspective when the Soviets advanced to the new 64,000-ton *Tbilisi*.[32] *Tbilisi* was launched on 5 December 1985, and her sister, *Riga*, was laid down on 10 December, a procedure that was necessary because there was only one dock large enough to build *Tbilisis*, restricting production to one every four to five years. Her armament was expected to be lighter than *Kiev*'s and might include SA-N-9 missiles and 30mm Gatling guns. She had two deck-edge elevators and her propulsion plant was probably a combined nuclear and steam (CONAS) system similar to *Kirov*'s. She had a skijump ramp and arresting gear, but did not have catapults. The estimate that the embarked air wing would consist of 30 to 40 aircraft, including V/STOL and fixed-wing aircraft and helicopters (Ka-27 Helix As) appeared accurate when, on 21 November 1989, an Su-27 Flanker, a MiG-29 Fulcrum, and an Su-25 Frogfoot all conducted takeoffs and landings on *Tbilisi*. The possibility that the initial complement might also include Yak-38 Forgers that had been embarked on the *Kiev*s, could not be precluded. In 1989, as she conducted sea trials and *Riga* was fitting out, a third carrier, *Ulyanovsk*, was reported under construction. She was said to displace 75,000 tons, 10,000 more than *Tbilisi*, implying that she was a new class.[33] If so, this would be a return to the *Moskva* trend, when only two units were produced before shipbuilders went on to *Kiev*. Producing only two *Tbilisis* would therefore be unusual, since hardly enough time had passed to allow for a firm judgment concerning her ability to meet mission requirements. Conversely, given the scarcity of funds that might occur in the 1990s, the Navy might have wanted to proceed as rapidly as possible with its program and, since only one building way was available, it would have had to forego building more *Tbilisis* in favor of building the new class.

Conclusions

In view of the opposition to Gorshkov's *Sea Power of the State* and the natural orientation of the nation toward ground warfare, the Navy's performance in the 1980s was most noteworthy.[34] None the less, the US shipbuilding program restored the imbalance in naval forces and the new weapons that America produced affected further the US–Soviet balance of power in favor of the United States. Thus, the Navy was not immune in the Soviet leadership's evaluation that its military R&D effort was considerably behind the US effort and that it would lag further behind in the future. Additionally, a visit

by two of the Navy's newest warships to Norfolk, Virginia in July 1989 allowed Western observers a detailed look at two of the Soviet Navy's newest combatants, revealing the inferior quality of many aspects of Soviet warship construction.

The succession of Admiral Gorshkov by Admiral Vladimir Chernavin as the Navy's commander-in-chief in 1985 was further proof of the Navy's reorientation. Chernavin had a record of being a 'party man' who enjoyed an excellent relationship with Soviet Ground Forces leaders. If so, one would expect him to allow the Navy to assume a much more defensive, supportive role, rather than the assertive, world-wide role which Gorshkov had espoused. This was both good and bad news to the West. On the one hand, assertive naval reactions on the high seas such as the one of October 1973 might be a thing of the past. On the other hand, the highly capable *Tbilisi*s, *Kiev*s, *Kirov*s, *Slava*s, *Udaloy*s, and *Sovremennyy*s which had been intended for sustained operations on the high seas would now be used to protect Soviet submarines patrolling in the Artic sanctuaries, posing a most critical threat to Western submarines that might be detailed to penetrate the sanctuaries in wartime. Regardless of how the Soviet Navy might fare in any defense funding cutbacks in the 1990s, the ships built in the 1980s provided a potent force that would assure an effective defense into the 21st century.

GREAT BRITAIN

While the US and Soviet naval programs produced several noteworthy ships and submarines in the 1980s, the remainder of the world's navies were affected much more by the high cost of naval construction. As a result, the maritime nations fell into two classes: those that minimized naval development, preferring to rely on others for their defense, and those that continued their naval development. Great Britain should be addressed because she reconsidered her military expenditure after the Falklands War, but ultimately continued restricted funding.

The Falkland Islands War
In one sense, Britain's East of Suez policy was a failure of her leaders to see the importance of sea power. The policy was not clearcut because, instead of a total withdrawal, it was revised to allow for keeping some distant territories. British defense policy, however, was in accord with the original policy, producing a navy that was appropriate for London's regional NATO role, but not providing the force projection necessary to defend the distant territories. This left such possessions vulnerable to regional intrigues, and to attack by nations that never would have challenged the strong Britain of years past. Just such a set of events occurred in the Falklands.

Argentina's claim to the Falklands, or Malvinas, had been unresolved, as had Argentine incursions into Britain's Antarctic territory. Superimposed upon this were two other factors that prompted the conflict. Argentina had considerable domestic problems that spawned national discontent, leading to the assumption that British naval power had so declined that she could not project her power into the South Atlantic without great difficulty. The result was that Argentina tried to seize the Falklands in order to provide a foreign policy victory that would distract the population from its domestic difficulties. In doing so, it probably calculated that this was a relatively safe venture, believing that Britain would seek to resolve the issue in an international forum rather than to defend the islands militarily. However, Britain rallied to their defense and war occurred.

Several conclusions could be drawn from the war. First, in spite of recent great technological advances, the validity of the traditional views concerning good training and leadership were proven true. The speed with which the British task force moved showed a commendable base organization, and Britain's rapid conversion of 87 merchant ships was also noteworthy. Argentine pilots performed valiantly and heroically, even flying virtual suicide missions. The Argentine Navy, on the other hand, did not. The British sinking of the Argentine cruiser *General Belgrano* was so demoralizing that the Argentine aircraft carrier and other surface combatants were drawn back to port, thereby leaving the seas to the British.[35] The British response was prompt, innovative, and masterful. The regrouping of forces at Ascension Island was sound and the invasion of the Falklands was accomplished with great professionalism. The lack of an airborne early warning capability cost the British dearly, because they had to use surface combatants that had not been designed to operate in a hostile air environment for picket duty. On 4 May, the destroyer HMS *Sheffield* was struck by a single Exocet missile, filling her with toxic fumes, and she subsequently sank. Her sister, *Coventry*, was sunk by bombs on 25 May.[36]

Contemporary observers offered additional conclusions. If the planned cuts, including the sale of *Invincible* to Australia, had been effected, the operation could not have been carried out. Second, Argentine fleet movements had been inhibited by British SSNs, a testament to their value. Third, the British task force had suffered from an insufficient number of embarked fighter aircraft. Fourth, the *Sheffield*'s loss was due in part to a failure to provide protection against sea-skimming missiles despite warnings over the previous ten years that this was a weakness in the *Type 42*'s armament. But the most significant message was the hardest to perceive: having sea power provided several advantages. Actively, it allowed one to defend one's interests from aggression. On the passive side, it allowed one the reputation of being willing and able to defend one's interests if forced to do so. For decades, Great Britain had been able to maintain peace at relatively little expense and little conflict because she had such a reputation. The result was that she maintained peace based on a sophisticated potential application of maritime power – one in which opposing forces would not attempt aggression for fear of retaliation. When she forgot this, she became vulnerable to aggression. Unfortunately, she did not profit from this lesson. Rather, her response was short-lived attention to maritime defense, thereby only interrupting the current trend of curtailing the fleet, before returning to the policy of minimizing defense expenditures.

The Political Context
It is ironic that Great Britain, given her glorious naval history, could forget so completely the importance of sea power. She should have profited from the lessons of the Cod War and realized that when a great power forgets its defenses, lesser powers, like jackals on the hide of fallen prey, might take full advantage of the situation. Just such a nation was Argentina, which tried to seize the Falklands in order to reduce domestic discontent and to resolve a perennial dispute over the Islands. The British victory was a lot closer than many would have liked, and the courage and innovation of Admiral John Woodward, General Jeremy Moore and the British forces often accomplished the impossible, thereby compensating for obvious naval weaknesses. These weaknesses *had been identified* but had not been compensated for by an unknowing, apparently uncaring political leadership. The lesson was obvious – London could not have it both ways. Either she would have to pay the expense if she wished to retain her world power status or she would have to be content with relegation to the role of a more regional power. And yet this lesson was not recognized and the truth was not confronted. While the Falklands prompted short-term attention to defense, this quickly was supplanted with the more traditional cost-minimizing stance.

Submarines
A great deal of the Royal Navy's resources were devoted to maintaining a strategic capability. The Labour government's decision in the late 1970s to replace the Polaris fleet with four Trident-equipped submarines was upheld by the Conservatives, and the *Vanguard*-class was begun in 1986. A 15,850-ton submarine, she was equipped with sixteen Trident D5 missiles and was to be in service in 1994. While there was a degree of prestige resulting from such a program, many questioned the wisdom of the decision. One commentator noted that while its SSBN fleet let the Navy claim to be the world's third strongest, this was accomplished at the expense of the surface fleet.[37]

The cause of this British dilemma, a complex mix of factors that began in 1981, has been incisively examined by John Jordan. The Defence Review issued by then-Secretary of Defence John Nott argued against mid-life refits of British surface combatants. Nott's reasoning seemed sound in that British surface combatants had been ordered piecemeal and had been designed around specific weapon systems. The refitting of such ships was perceived as being very expensive, and Nott argued that it would be wiser to build new ships than to refit old ones. The Falklands War did little to change the trend in which Nott's argument for not refitting older ships was accepted but his preference for newer ships was not. As a result, the British surface fleet suffered accordingly.[38]

Jordan also addressed the subsequent national themes that muddied the waters even further. In late 1988, he questioned the wisdom of building Polaris and then Trident submarines, and subsequent events in the Soviet Union and Eastern Europe have confirmed his belief that these systems not only are practically useless, but also tie British policy positions to those of the United States. These systems have little utility in anything but an all-out nuclear war, and their construction has been at the expense of the general-purpose British surface forces which proved so valuable in the Falklands.

Likewise the second theme – that the British Army forces in Germany are costing so much that they prevent British surface ship contruction – merely muddles the basic misappropriation of funds to the nuclear-powered ballistic missile-equipped submarine programs. The British commitment of forces to Germany is a valid one and cannot be disregarded.[39]

Jordan concludes that the situation is extremely critical and that if significant investment is not made in surface ships, British shipyards will close, with a consequent and permanent loss in indigenous shipbuilding capability. He calls for nothing less than the termination of the entire Trident program and the immediate reallocation of resources to surface combatant construction.[40]

Greater justification could be found for the nuclear-powered attack submarines, as these could be used in a conventional war. The *Swiftsure* program, completed when the sixth and final unit, *Splendid*, was commissioned on 21 March 1981, was succeeded by the *Trafalgar*-class. The first of the seven *Trafalgars* was commissioned on 27 May 1983. She was a very good design and had a pressurized water-cooled reactor which allowed her to sustain 30 knots when submerged. The diesel-powered submarine program was also continued, producing the *Upholder*-class, the first of which was commissioned in June 1990.[41]

Surface Combatants

While Table 5.3 shows that there was only a slight shrinkage in the fleet's size, it does not reflect the preparedness of the ships, the capabilities of the replacements, or the fleet's sea projection capability. For the most part, existing designs were continued. The Type 42 *Sheffield* destroyer and Type 22 *Broadsword* frigate programs were sustained, and each eventually produced twelve ships.[42] Changes were made to the later batches of each class, based on the Falklands experience. Beyond this, little was done to compensate for deficiencies in early warning, air cover, and AAW that were observed during the war.

The *Leander* conversion programs went ahead and, on 19 December 1985, *Norfolk*, the first of the new Type 23 *Duke* general-purpose frigates, was laid down. She was completed and began trials in 1989. This ship was armed with Harpoon and Sea Wolf missiles, guns, and a helicopter. Political indecision and cost overruns plagued the *Duke* program.[43].

These measures, while noteworthy, were not sufficient to reverse the Navy's decline. In 1984, one expert correctly noted that the Navy's role should be as a member of NATO, implying that the nation's foreign policy should be tailored accordingly. In the same year, the decision to refit *Hermes* was rescinded because of manpower shortages, and it was decided to make her a harbour training ship. In 1985, the Navy was still running down in spite of the Falklands War and one commentator, Desmond Wettern, noted that the government's policy was still confused. It was obvious that the Navy would soon have to face the carrier issue, since *Fearless* and *Intrepid*, held over after Falklands, were nearing the end of their useful lives. In 1986, it was revealed that there were plans to replace them, but in 1987, for the first time in the Thatcher government, there was no defence growth and there would be zero defence growth henceforth. The situation deteriorated further when *Hermes* was sold to India. In 1988, it was estimated that replacing *Invincible* would cost 2.5 per cent of the total defense budget, but without a carrier replacement, the Navy might be reduced to an escort role in NATO. The situation was almost as critical in the remainder of the surface fleet. The Navy's size continued to diminish and Richard Sharpe said that the Navy would have only 30 frigates/destroyers in the future, not the 50 that the government claimed. Additionally, in order to cut costs, no close-in weapon system, needed to combat anti-ship missiles, would be provided on the *Duke*-class, thereby reducing the ships' capabilities.[44]

Table 5.3
Selected Force Levels – Royal Navy, 1980–9

	Year									
	80	81	82	83	84	85	86	87	88	89
Ballistic Missile Submarines	4	4	4	4	4	4	4	4	4	4
Nuclear Attack Submarines	11	11	11	12	13	13	14	15	16	16
Diesel Submarines	16	16	16	15	15	15	15	14	11	11
Carriers – Light	1	2	3	3	3	3	3	3	3	3
Assault Ships	2	2	2	2	2	2	1	1	1	1
Cruisers	1	0	0	0	0	0	0	0	0	0
Destroyers	12	14	12	12	12	15	15	14	13	13
Frigates	54	46	45	44	43	41	39	35	34	33
Mine Warfare	37	38	35	36	38	42	43	42	41	35

Summary

In 1989, the Navy was plagued with the same problems that it had faced in 1980: there were too few modern warships to protect Britain's interests and, while she refused to provide adequately for her defense, she also refused to reduce her foreign policy commitments and tailor her role to a regional nation. The result was a perilous situation that could come home to haunt her.

FRANCE

While Table 5.4 shows a slight decline in the French Navy, of greater import was the types of ships that were added. The ballistic-missile submarine fleet was increased from five to six units, and a nuclear-powered attack submarine fleet was created, offsetting a decline in diesel submarines. The destroyer inventory shrank from 19 to 16 ships, but there was an increase in frigates. Also of significance was that most shrinkage occurred in the ship types that were not directly related to force projection. In essence, quantitatively, the evolution of the French fleet reflected money wisely spent to produce a slightly smaller but much more modern fleet, one more capable of projecting power outward on to the high seas. This view was reflected by John Moore, who in 1980 said:

Despite its interests in the Atlantic and Mediterranean it deploys a world-wide presence, the major ships of which include a flagship and five destroyers/

frigates in the Indian Ocean, two frigates in the West Indies and three frigates in the Pacific. At home this leaves two carriers, a cruiser, nineteen submarines, and 31 destroyer/frigates to deal with major operations . . . The French navy has many problems: political, administrative, and man-power. If these could be solved the result could be a strong and first-class fleet.[45]

In 1980 France decided to retain two attack carriers and one helicopter carrier into the 1990s. In that year, *Le Tonnant*, last of the *Le Redoubtable* SSBN class, was commissioned. The lead unit of a succeeding class, *L'Inflexible*, had already been laid down in 1979 and was operational in 1985. She had sixteen tubes for the new M4 ballistic missile which could deliver six 150-kiloton MIRV warheads. The M4 was launched successfully in September 1987, as French SSBNs patrolled in the North Atlantic, the Mediterranean, and the Norwegian Sea. Finally, *Le Triomphant*, the first of a new class of SSBNs was begun. After delays, *Rubis*, France's first nuclear-powered attack submarine, was commissioned in 1983. Three more were built in the 1980s and, when restricted funding was imposed, the Navy simply delayed delivery of these units rather than cancel the program. *Amethyste*, the lead unit of a four-unit SSN series, was laid down in October 1983 and is operational.[46]

Similar moderation and intelligence was reflected in the rest of the French program. The *Georges Leygues*, destroyer program was continued, with a total of seven units planned. The AAW variant, the *Cassard* (Type C 70) AAW destroyer, was begun in 1982 and was completed in 1988. A new frigate class, *FL 3000*, was to begin in 1986, but funding restrictions forced a delay. These 3,000-ton, 371-foot ships were to be armed with Exocets, Crotale SAMs, a CIWS, 100 and 20mm guns, torpedo tubes, and a torpedo-armed helicopter, and were scheduled to begin fitting out in early 1991.[47] In amphibious ships, *Foudre*, a new class of 11,000-ton dock landing ships, was laid down in 1986. Two sister ships were cancelled. A smaller, 4,800-ton ship was laid down in the same year.

The greatest wisdom was displayed in the carrier program. The Mitterand government committed itself to replacing one of the two carriers with the nuclear-powered carrier, *Charles de Gaulle*, which would carry 40 aircraft and would be completed in 1998, and to a second carrier for later in the decade. The 36,800-ton, 858-foot ship was laid down in 1989. She would have a nuclear plant, would carry 40 aircraft, would have catapults, and would be armed with SAMs and CIWS. Such reasoned planning meant that, when France had to restrict her defense spending for three years beginning in 1989, the delayed completion of the carrier from 1996 to 1998 would have less of an adverse impact on naval operations.[48]

Table 5.4
Selected Force Levels – French Navy, 1980–9

	Year									
	80	81	82	83	84	85	86	87	88	89
Ballistic Missile Nuclear Submarines	5	5	5	5	5	6	6	6	6	6
Nuclear Attack Submarines	0	0	1	2	2	2	2	3	4	6
Diesel Submarines	21	21	20	18	15	15	15	14	14	14
Carriers	2	2	2	2	3	3	3	3	2	2
Cruisers	1	1	1	2	1	1	1	1	2	2
Destroyers	20	20	19	19	19	19	17	16	15	15
Frigates	24	20	23	24	25	25	25	25	24	24

| Mine Warfare | 32 | 32 | 31 | 25 | 19 | 25 | 25 | 25 | 29 | 30 |
| Coastal Craft | 20 | 14 | 15 | 12 | 10 | 11 | 12 | 30 | 22 | 21 |

The French naval program was more successful than the British, because both the left and right accepted their responsibilities for France's defense and acted accordingly. This allowed for timely planning and, when funds caused building delays, the impact was less critical. More importantly, Paris never took an 'all or nothing' approach of either totally accepting or deleting a program, preferring to accept programs but to modify or delay their completion if finances became a problem. The result was that France fielded an impressive naval force in 1989 which would be sustained into the 21st century.

JAPAN

The Japanese naval program of the 1980s was surrounded in controversy. Part of this was due to Japan's maritime needs which were not met by her program. However, resentment over her economic success and her military spending of under 1 per cent of her GNP did much to cloud such naval development as did occur. To begin, while 1 per cent was not a sizeable portion of a nation's GNP, in a great economy such as Japan's it meant a considerable investment. Also, not sufficiently publicized was the fact that Japanese politicians did not want to go above 1 per cent for fear of acceding to defense advocates.[49] Second, the United States pursued an inconsistent policy. It enjoyed the use of Japanese bases for its ships, allowing it to maintain sea control in the Western Pacific, while it continued to call for Japan to assume a greater portion of her defense. However, as Japan rearmed, Washington cautioned Tokyo against producing systems that could be perceived as offensive.

In the midst of all of this, Japan did develop her maritime power and, as Table 5.5 reflects, expanded her fleet modestly so that by 1989, she had an impressive, balanced naval force with a respectable regional projection capability. The Yuushio submarine, Shirane and Hatsuyuki destroyer programs, and a single Ishikari-class frigate were completed, and several new programs were begun. An Improved Yushio submarine was begun, and the first of two 5,600-ton Hatakaze destroyers was commissioned in 1986. With armament that included SAMs, Harpoon SSMs, CIWS, ASROC, and torpedo tubes, Hakakaze was a very well-armed, versatile ship. An area defense destroyer, well designed and smart in appearance, she was a radically different design, representing the innovation of Japanese shipbuilding. Likewise the 3,700-ton Hatsuyuki, armed with Harpoon and Sea Sparrow missiles, Phalanx CIWS, a 76mm gun, ASROC, torpedoes, and a helicopter, was heavily armed and versatile, taking full advantage of existing domestic and foreign technology. The Asagiri, an improvement on the Hatsuyuki design and begun in 1985, was slightly larger and longer and had better electronics and communications. Similarly, the Yubari, and Ishikari frigates were very successful designs. The single 1,290-ton Ishikari, although it was considered cramped, provided valuable input for the design of the larger, 1,760-ton Yubari, which was provided with a versatile weapon suit, including Harpoon missiles, provision for Phalanx CIWS, torpedo tubes, and ASW weapons. A subsequent class, the Abukuma, was begun, with the first units commissioned in December 1989. She represented a continuation of existing technology.[50]

These ships provided Japan with a good regional capability. However, in the contexts of US–Japanese relations and Japanese domestic politics, the fleet elicited reactions. In the US–Japanese context, the force, while developing, was clearly inferior to expanding Soviet naval power in the Pacific. This was used to support the US argument that Japan should assume more responsibility for her defense.

The domestic reaction was equally significant. In 1985, Tokyo curtailed the Japanese Maritime Self-Defense Force's (JMSDF) naval building program because of finances, but still signified its intention to develop a force of 60 escorts. It was realized that the 1 per cent of the GNP limit would have to be exceeded if Japan were to increase her naval strength. The JMSDF still hoped to have a force of sixteen submarines by 1988, and expressed its interest in the British *Invincible* carrier design. A political storm was created when the JMSDF considered buying a helicopter carrier, and its suggestion that it might include a new 16,000-ton light carrier in its construction program was rejected by the government. The fiscal year 1987 defense budget was 1.004 per cent, surpassing the controversial 1 per cent limit. This in itself created an uproar, with opponents stating that Japan should not become militaristic, while defense proponents called for a more capable defense. In 1988, naval development continued as the four *Improved Yubari* frigates were laid down, and in 1989, Japan was easily the world's third largest spender on defense after the United States and the Soviet Union, although her investment was only slightly over 1 per cent of her GNP. In that year, the US Senate approved a burden-sharing package that directed the President to develop a plan for the 'complete offset by Japan of the costs of deploying US forces in defense of Japan'.[51] Meanwhile, Tokyo approved the 1990 defense budget. It contained a 6.1 per cent increase, enough to allow her almost to complete her current mid-term defense program.[52] The situation remained unchanged when President Bush and the Japanese Prime Minister concluded their meetings on 3 March 1990.

Table 5.5
Selected Force Levels – Japanese Navy, 1980–9

	Year									
	80	81	82	83	84	85	86	87	88	89
Submarines	14	14	14	14	14	15	15	15	14	14
Destroyers	33	34	33	31	34	34	34	35	36	37
Frigates	15	16	16	17	18	18	18	18	25	25
Fast Torpedo Boats	5	5	5	5	5	5	5	5	5	5
Mine Warfare	42	42	42	43	43	43	44	44	45	45
Coastal Ships/Craft	9	16	14	14	14	11	11	10	14	14

Japanese shipbuilding in the 1980s produced a force with a modest regional capability, consisting of ships that were heavily armed and were of successful designs. Greater development had been precluded by governmental limits on defense spending. Whether Tokyo would permit the JMSDF to develop more rapidly in the 1990s remained problematic in 1990.

NORTHERN EUROPE

While politics and expense precluded other navies from developing as significantly, there was noteworthy regional development. In Europe, many nations deferred or minimized defense spending, believing that the United States would provide for their national security. As others attempted to maintain their defenses, feeling obliged to honor their duties to NATO, dissention resulted within NATO as to each nation's obligation to contribute. Such differences were carried over into other NATO ventures, such as building a NATO frigate replacement, NFR 90. It was fraught with such delays and cost overruns that London withdrew from the multi-national venture in 1989, France and Italy soon followed suit, and the project failed.[53] US frustration became more pronounced and public and in 1988, it stated that the 3 per cent increase per year in defense spending that had been agreed upon in 1979 was not too much to ask of NATO members. The Danish government's response was definite: in November, it voted for zero growth in its 1989 budget.[54] This reflected an atmosphere in Europe that was not conducive to naval development and maritime innovation would suffer accordingly.

Scandinavia

Norway's record was above average, since as a front line nation bordering on the USSR, it was sensitive to Soviet naval expansion. None the less, it did not provide adequately for its defense. In 1980, the last of six *Hauk* missile craft was completed, but in the next few years naval appropriations were low. In 1986, it set about rejuvenating its fleet and, by 1988, the building of six 1,300-ton *Type 210* submarines was under way to correct for a declining submarine inventory (see Table 5.6).[55]

Table 5.6
Selected Force Levels – Norwegian Navy, 1980–9

	Year									
	80	81	82	83	84	85	86	87	88	89
Submarines	15	15	15	14	14	14	14	14	12	11
Frigates	5	5	5	5	5	5	5	5	5	5
Corvettes	3	2	2	2	2	2	2	2	2	2
Mine Warfare	11	11	10	10	11	12	14	16	10	10
Coastal Craft	45	49	51	48	39	38	38	38	40	42

Table 5.7
Selected Force Levels – Swedish Navy, 1980–9

	Year									
	80	81	82	83	84	85	86	87	88	89
Submarines	14	12	12	12	12	12	13	13	14	14
Destroyers	6	3	2	2	2	1	0	0	0	0
Missile Attack Craft	12	16	17	24	28	28	30	30	30	30
Torpedo Attack Craft	22	18	18	6	6	6	6	6	6	6
Mine Warfare	40	47	49	56	30	30	28	28	32	30
Coastal Craft	36	33	33	35	34	32	33	22	21	23
Amphibious Craft	79	144	144	146	141	123	128	133	135	130

Sweden's situation was even more critical. Not only was it not in NATO, but it suffered from Soviet submarine intrusions. Usually, the intruders quickly withdrew when detected, but from 1980 onward, they became bolder and remained in Swedish waters. Sweden also photographed what were interpreted as mini-submarine tracks on the ocean floor in its territorial waters. This became a crisis when a *Whiskey* submarine was grounded in Sweden's waters. The Soviet captain's determination and Moscow's resolute support created a situation in which the tide quickly turned as Sweden seemed to grovel for concessions from the intruder. These were minimal and the boat was finally freed and left Swedish waters. In later discussions, Sweden came to believe that the USSR would no longer violate its integrity. To Sweden's chagrin, however, Moscow then denied such an agreement, and the intrusions continued.[56] There were two lessons to be drawn from the incidents. They upheld Mahan's principles to the extent that when a nation did not provide for its defense, it might be prey to aggression. Simply put, some nations did not respect weakness and would take advantage when they sensed it in others. The second lesson could be gleaned from Swedish politics. Throughout the prolonged situation the government did not fall and there was no widespread reaction. In fact the government's clearly inadequate response – minimally increasing defense expenditures and devoting slightly more support to the Navy – was considered appropriate. The lesson then was that there were limits to the influence and impact of naval power in that when a nation chose to ignore its defense and was willing to suffer national disgrace, the political utility of an opposing nation's naval power was restricted.

The Swedish Navy made the best of a bad situation and widely touted the improvements that were made. These efforts had some effect, since reporting by observers was mixed. In 1982, Milan Vego said that, due to funding problems, Sweden had lost much of its ASW and offensive capabilities. A year later, stressing the new units that were commissioned, an observer claimed that the Navy was rebuilding and, in 1986, another observer claimed that Sweden's defenses were a wild card that the Soviet Union had to consider in its military planning. The reality was that the Navy barely maintained its size in the 1980s (see Table 5.7), although the force was modernized considerably. This became a political issue in 1988, as the government pondered a 3 per cent defense spending increase. Even this was grossly inadequate, causing Richard Sharpe to caution that 'some urgent decisions on defense expenditure are required if the drift to passive neutrality is to be checked'.[57]

Denmark's situation was not as critical, but its actions verged on the irresponsible. As the harbourmaster of the Baltic – it restricted egress from that sea – its strategic location was so vital that NATO would have to defend Denmark if she refused to defend herself. This was precisely what transpired. Criticism of Copenhagen was answered by loudly touting the naval progress that had occurred and by claims that Denmark's weakness could be compensated by training and early fielding of forces. In 1986, because of low funding, manning on the largest Danish ships, *Herluf Tolle* and *Peder Skram*, was reduced to nucleus crews, to be fully manned only in emergencies. In April 1988, the Social Democrats and left wing opposition adopted a resolution that

Table 5.8
Selected Force Levels – Danish Navy, 1980–9

	Year								
	80	81	82	83	84	85	86	87	88	89
Submarines	6	6	5	5	5	4	4	4	4	4
Frigates	6	10	10	10	10	10	10	10	3	3
Corvettes	2	0	0	0	0	0	0	0	0	0
Missile Attack Boats	10	10	10	10	10	10	10	10	10	10

Torpedo Attack Boats	6	6	6	6	6	6	6	6	6	6
Patrol Craft		46	50	27	27	27	27	27	28	33	33
Mine Warfare		15	13	13	13	13	13	13	9	9	9

required notifying ships calling in Denmark of a 30-year ban on nuclear weapons. The British promptly cancelled a scheduled visit. This and a Danish decision in 1988 to retire the frigates that were still seaworthy prompted a US response in July, when William Taft said, 'The Danes want the benefit of nuclear deterrence without making any contribution whatsoever to it, even in the form of passive cooperation.' Tempers cooled, but the situation did not change. In 1989, in a compromise between the Social Democrats and the conservative-liberal government, it was determined that thirteen 300-ton Standard flex patrol boats would be built, but that the two frigates would be retired and Copenhagen naval yard would be closed. Also, there would be no growth in defense spending.[58] This prompted one NATO naval officer to comment that 'Denmark was still providing enough in defense to insure that in wartime the coffee would be hot for the Allies when they arrived to defend the nation.'

On a more serious note, Table 5.8 shows that there was shrinkage in the Danish Navy, and it appeared that the Social Democratic opposition had acted irresponsibly. Conversely, all of this should also be viewed in light of a sustained and proud Danish tradition of neutrality. Thus, while it compromised its traditional position by joining NATO in order to provide for its defense, it, like Sweden, was traditionally wary of defense spending. From this perspective, the other NATO nations could find satisfaction in Denmark's continued membership in NATO and should not have expected stronger Danish defense spending.

Federal Republic of Germany

Table 5.9 shows that there was a slight decline in the West German Navy's size, with the greatest losses in torpedo-boats and mine warfare ships. What it does not reveal is the significant modernization that occurred. This was partially in response to East German naval developments (see Table 5.10),

Table 5.9
Selected Force Levels – West German Navy, 1980–9

| | *Year* | | | | | | | | | |
	80	*81*	*82*	*83*	*84*	*85*	*86*	*87*	*88*	*89*
Submarines	24	24	24	24	24	24	24	24	24	24
Missile Destroyers	11	9	7	7	7	7	7	7	7	7
Frigates	6	6	7	7	8	9	9	9	9	8
Corvettes	6	6	6	6	5	5	5	5	5	5
Missile Boats	30	30	30	34	38	40	40	40	40	40
Mine Warfare	57	70	75	75	75	65	57	56	55	55
Torpedo Boats	10	10	10	5	0	0	0	0	0	0

Table 5.10
Selected Force Levels – East German Navy, 1980–9

| | *Year* | | | | | | | | | |
	80	*81*	*82*	*83*	*84*	*85*	*86*	*87*	*88*	*89*
Frigates	2	2	2	2	2	2	3	3	3	3
Corvettes	0	1	5	9	13	15	20	18	17	16
Missile Attack Boats	12	15	15	15	15	15	11	12	12	12

Torpedo Attack Boats	60	49	49	49	49	49	46	36	27	20
Mine Warfare	60	50	47	46	46	51	48	47	47	42
Landing Ships/Craft	22	18	12	12	12	13	12	12	12	12
Coastal Craft	32	32	28	27	26	26	20	20	20	20

and receipt of three *Koni* frigates and *Parchim* and *Tarantul* corvettes, and the growing power of the Soviet Baltic Fleet. Given the need to field an air force and an army as a frontline NATO nation, and the Greens coalition opposition, this progress was even more impressive. By 1980, the *Lindau* minehunter conversions had been completed, the eight-unit *Bremen* frigate program was under way, and *Type 143A* missile craft had been ordered. The remaining two *Fletcher* destroyers were sent to Greece, as the Navy continued its construction programs. Bonn admitted that it was under some financial strain in 1985, but continued its naval program. By the end of the year, all ten *Type 143 A* fast attack craft were in service. Although the *Type 211* submarine program was cancelled in 1988, the last two *Bremen*s were launched in 1987, and planning for four *Type 123* air defense frigates was begun. The Navy also began planning for more minesweepers/hunters to compensate for a future shrinkage in its fleet of these ships.[59] Thus while the German program did not meet the NATO security needs for the Baltic's entire defense and elicited occasional US concern for regional security, it was a considerable contribution considering the nation's other defense needs and the political opposition.

Belgium and the Netherlands
Belgium concentrated on mine warfare, building *Tripartite* minehunters (see Table 5.11). The Netherlands' earnest attempt to maintain her fleet included adding a *Walrus* submarine (1990), *Kortenaer* frigates, *Alkmaar* minehunters, and modernizing *Van Speijk* frigates. As funding became a problem the government was forced to re-examine its defense needs, announcing in 1988 that two *Van Speijk* frigates would be sold to Indonesia and that there would be no modernization for the *Tromp* frigates.[60] The Dutch Navy had suffered a significant shrinkage, although it had replaced its destroyer force with frigates (see Table 5.12).

Table 5.11
Selected Force Levels – Belgian Navy, 1980–9

	Year									
	80	81	82	83	84	85	86	87	88	89
Frigates	4	4	4	4	4	4	4	4	4	4
Fleet Minesweepers/Hunters	7	7	7	7	7	6	6	6	6	6
Coastal/Inshore Minesweepers	20	19	20	20	20	17	14	21	21	21

Table 5.12
Selected Force Levels – Netherlands Navy, 1980–9

	Year									
	80	81	82	83	84	85	86	87	88	89
Submarines	6	6	6	6	6	5	5	5	5	5
Destroyers	7	5	2	2	2	2	2	2	2	2
Frigates	9	10	12	16	18	17	17	16	16	16
Corvettes	6	6	6	4	4	0	0	0	0	0
Mine Warfare	34	34	34	19	11	10	20	24	25	25

SOUTHERN EUROPE

Spain and Portugal

Portugal was unable to do more than maintain the size of its fleet in the 1980s (see Table 5.13). In 1988, plans for buying three *Meko 200* frigates were permitted to proceed. The Spanish program, however, was significant. Establishing a goal of building two carrier task forces, in 1987 Spain commissioned the first carrier, *Principe de Asturias*, a 14,700-ton, 574-foot ship built to the design of the US sea control ship. Given a skijump, it could carry a mixed complement of V/STOL aircraft and helicopters, but could sustain only 26 knots. Elsewhere, the focus was on modernizing an ageing navy. While Table 5.14 shows that there was a slight shrinkage in the fleet, this was offset by the superior capabilities of the new ships. Meanwhile, with US assistance, Spain began building six *Perry*-class frigates, commissioning the first, *Santa Maria*, in 1986, with the others following suit. As Spain joined NATO and reduced the US presence on her territory, she entered the 1990s with a small but modern naval force that contributed to security on NATO's south-western sector.[61]

Table 5.13
Selected Force Levels – Portguese Navy, 1980–9

	\multicolumn{10}{c}{Year}
	80	*81*	*82*	*83*	*84*	*85*	*86*	*87*	*88*	*89*
Submarines	3	3	3	3	3	3	3	3	3	3
Frigates	17	17	17	17	17	17	17	16	15	15
Amphibious Craft	15	14	14	13	13	13	13	12	12	12
Coastal Craft	27	27	18	23	23	19	19	19	20	20

Table 5.14
Selected Force Levels – Spanish Navy, 1980–9

	\multicolumn{10}{c}{Year}
	80	*81*	*82*	*83*	*84*	*85*	*86*	*87*	*88*	*89*
Submarines	8	8	8	8	9	8	8	8	8	8
Helicopter Carriers	1	1	1	1	1	1	1	2	2	2
Destroyers	11	12	12	11	11	11	11	9	8	7
Frigates	16	16	20	11	15	11	11	12	13	14
Corvettes	0	0	0	4	5	9	4	4	0	0
Mine Warfare	15	9	9	12	12	12	12	12	12	12
Coastal Craft	82	91	84	94	90	88	85	91	77	63
Amphibious	88	91	91	93	90	88	82	84	85	86

Italy

Italian naval development, while imaginative and original, suffered from two problems that precluded its contributing more significantly to world naval development. The first was that Italy could not decide on the type of navy she wanted. On the one hand, she built large combatants, such as cruisers and the aircraft carrier *Giuseppe Garibaldi*, that were suited to a navy intended for projection on to the world's oceans; while on the other hand she built lighter forces that were ideal for operations in the central Mediterranean. The second problem was the complexity of Italian politics, which often delayed decisions and inhibited naval development.

By 1980, there had been a sharp decline in the number of Italy's small combatants, including frigates and patrol escorts.[62] The Navy's low point was reached in 1982, when its total tonnage fell to 81,000 tons. Italy then set a goal of 105,000 tons that was to be reached in the 1990s. In submarines, four *Sauro* units were commissioned by 1983 and two *Salvatore Pelosi* (Improved-*Sauro*) boats were built from 1983 onward. Although moderately innovative, they were successful designs, were well suited for operations in the central Mediterranean, and updated the ageing submarine fleet. The carrier *Giuseppi Garibaldi* was surrounded in controversy. Opponents questioned the wisdom of spending the money necessary for such a ship that did not seem ideally suited for Italy's role as a regional Mediterranean power. Additionally, the Italian Air Force was adamant concerning its right to fly aircraft from the carrier. Extended governmental discussions resulted in legislation in February 1989 allowing the Navy to operate fixed-wing aircraft from the ship.[63] The 13,240-ton, 591-foot ship was capable of about 30 knots and could carry twelve helicopters or V/STOL aircraft.

Table 5.15
Selected Force Levels – Italian Navy, 1980–9

	Year									
	80	81	82	83	84	85	86	87	88	89
Submarines	9	9	9	10	10	10	9	9	10	10
Carriers (Light)	1	1	1	1	1	2	2	2	1	1
Cruisers	2	2	2	2	2	2	2	2	3	3
Guided Missile Destroyers	6	4	4	4	4	4	4	4	4	4
Gun-Armed Destroyers	2	1	1	0	0	0	0	0	0	0
Frigates	14	12	11	13	15	16	16	14	22	22
Corvettes	8	8	8	8	8	8	8	11	3	3
Fast Attack Craft	4	4	4	2	2	4	5	6	7	7
Mine Warfare	42	32	32	24	21	23	24	23	22	22
Amphibious Ships	21	21	21	21	21	22	28	23	2	2

In related developments, the Navy ordered two *Animoso* destroyers in 1986 to replace its ageing destroyer force, and commissioned the last of four *Lupo* frigates in 1980 and eight *Maestrale* frigates from 1982 to 1985 (see Table 5.15). *Animoso* was launched on 29 October 1989. The last *Maestrale* frigate was in service in 1985 and the first of the new *Minerva* SAM-equipped corvettes was laid down in 1985, with four operative in 1988. The mine-sweeping force was modernized with *Lerici* minesweepers.[64]

In sum, in the midst of confused Italian politics, there was a consistent respect for adequate naval power and a commitment to honor her NATO obligations. For example, between September 1987 and August 1988, eleven frigates, six minehunters, and three support ships were deployed in reaction to the Persian Gulf crisis. Italy entered the 1990s with a program that was rebuilding her naval power and provided considerably to the central Mediterranean's defense.[65]

Greece and Turkey

The Greek and Turkish Navies, relevant as contributions to eastern Mediterranean defense, were more important in terms of the deteriorating relationship between the two nations. In 1980, there was continued expansion of Greek shipyards that would provide more significant indigenous support, and

Greece received the last of eight *Type 209* submarines. In 1981, the last six of ten *La Combattante III* missile-equipped fast attack craft were in hand (see Table 5.16). *Gearing* and *Fletcher* destroyers were obtained, thus sustaining the ageing destroyer force. Two Dutch-built *Kortenaer* frigates were in service in 1981 and 1982 and, by 1986, the Greek shipyard capability had been so expanded that it could now build ships up to the size of frigates. As its relations with the United States and Turkey soured Greece closed the US Air Force base at Hellenikon when the existing agreement expired at the end of 1988.[66]

Table 5.16
Selected Force Levels – Greek Navy, 1980–9

	Year									
	80	81	82	83	84	85	86	87	88	89
Submarines	10	10	10	10	10	10	10	10	10	10
Destroyers	12	16	16	14	14	14	14	14	14	12
Frigates	4	6	6	7	6	6	7	7	7	6
Missile Attack Craft	11	15	14	18	14	15	16	16	14	14
Torpedo Attack Craft	16	12	11	11	10	8	6	6	6	6
Mine Warfare Units	14	16	15	16	17	16	16	16	16	16
Coastal Craft	3	2	9	11	11	10	9	10	12	15
Amphibious Units	83	84	84	91	91	87	83	89	89	89

Table 5.17
Selected Force Levels – Turkish Navy, 1980–9

	Year									
	80	81	82	83	84	85	86	87	88	89
Submarines	14	14	16	16	16	16	17	17	17	17
Destroyers	12	14	15	13	13	13	13	12	12	12
Frigates	2	2	2	2	2	4	4	4	6	7
Missile Fast Attack Craft	12	13	13	13	14	15	15	15	14	14
Torpedo/Gun Fast Attack Craft	7	8	8	6	4	8	11	5	5	4
Mine Warfare Units	31	36	36	32	28	30	33	35	32	33
Coastal Craft	54	49	49	36	29	28	28	28	28	28
Amphibious Units	74	77	75	75	75	75	80	80	80	80

In spite of a powerful Greek lobby that continued to influence US Greco-Turkish policy in favor of Greece, Ankara was able to secure aid from the United States and substantial West German assistance to modernize its fleet and maintain its size with only minor shrinkage (see Table 5.17). The last four German *Type 209* submarines and three US *Gearing* and two *Carpenter* destroyers were received in the early 1980s and Germany transferred two *Köln* frigates in 1983. In lighter forces, four additional attack craft were commissioned, the first *Cakabey* and two *Sarucabey* minelayer/landing ships were built, and other units were refurbished. In spite of this and of the fact that it could build all but the biggest warships, in 1986, Turkey still had a great deal of obsolete naval equipment and needed assistance. It built and acquired four *Meko* guided-missile frigates, began building its own frigates, and received a *Koln* frigate on 6 June 1989.[67]

As this program evolved, the problems with Athens continued. In 1986 and 1987, there were near confrontations over territorial rights at sea.[68] Greece protested to Turkey concerning air space violations in 1986 and, on

17 September, Turkish warships fired shots close to the bow of the Greek patrol boat *E Panagopoulos I* which was operating in international waters near the island of Lesbos. In 1988, there were further Greek protests concerning Turkish violations. Both nations entered the 1990s in an atmosphere of mutual distrust.[69]

THE MIDDLE EAST AND NORTH AFRICA

Arab-Israeli tension prompted continued naval development in the Arab nations and Israel. Extensive Soviet assistance to Syria included *Romeo* submarines, *Osa II* fast attack craft, and *Yevgenya* and *Sonya* minesweepers (see Table 5.18). In return, it allowed the Soviet Navy to establish a facility in Tartus that was described inaccurately as the largest 'Soviet naval forward deployment base outside the USSR'.[70] In 1989, Syria had a sizeable naval force, a factor influencing Israeli naval development.

Although Israel considered the land and air threats to be the most critical, its attention to its navy was highlighted by the *Saar* series of corvettes and missile-armed fast attack craft (*Saar 4*, *Saar 4.5*, and *Saar 5*), impressive mixtures of foreign technology and Israeli innovation. Table 5.19 shows that the Navy shrank only slightly in the 1980s and amounted to a potent force that had to be considered in Arab defense planning.[71]

Table 5.18
Selected Force Levels – Syrian Navy, 1980–9

	Year									
	80	81	82	83	84	85	86	87	88	89
Submarines	0	0	0	0	0	0	2	3	3	3
Frigates	2	2	2	2	2	2	2	2	2	2
Missile Patrol Boats	18	18	18	19	20	22	24	24	16	16
Torpedo/Gun Patrol Boats	9	9	9	10	12	13	15	15	10	6
Mine Warfare	3	3	3	3	4	6	9	9	9	9

Egypt's break with the Soviet Union caused critical problems for its navy, because, in the aftermath, it found itself with large amounts of ageing Soviet equipment for which spare parts were restricted. Cairo eased this problem by procuring foreign naval ships, including many from Communist China. Table 5.20 shows a slight shrinkage in the fleet, which in 1989, had Chinese *Romeo* submarines, *Jianghu* frigates, *Hainan* LPCs, *Hoku* guided missile patrol boats, Spanish *Descubierta* frigates, and British *Ramadan* missile craft. These were supplemented with domestically built *October* and *Timsah* craft that were successful designs but sported little technological innovation. While the procurement of spare parts for this multinational inventory might drive the Egyptian logistics staff insane, it showed what a nation could do in attempting to overcome a critical block obsolescence problem.[72]

Table 5.21 shows substantial Libyan naval expansion. Much of this was Soviet aid that included *Koni* frigates, *Foxtrot* submarines, *Nanuchka II* missile corvettes, *Osa II* fast attack craft, *Natya* minesweepers, and *Polnocny* LSMs. These were supplemented with ships from other nations, including

Table 5.19

Selected Force Levels – Israeli Navy, 1980–9

	Year									
	80	81	82	83	84	85	86	87	88	89
Submarines	3	3	3	3	3	3	3	3	3	3
Corvettes	0	2	2	3	4	5	6	4	3	3
Missile Attack Boats	22	22	22	22	22	22	23	22	28	28
Amphibious Craft	9	9	7	10	12	12	12	12	10	9
Coastal Craft	38	40	43	44	45	43	41	36	34	31

Table 5.20

Selected Force Levels – Egyptian Navy, 1980–9

	Year									
	80	81	82	83	84	85	86	87	88	89
Submarines	10	9	12	12	12	12	12	12	12	12
Destroyers	5	5	5	5	5	3	3	3	2	1
Frigates	3	3	3	4	5	6	6	6	5	5
Missile Patrol Boats	18	20	19	24	24	30	32	30	25	23
Torpedo/Gun Patrol Boats	36	36	42	46	50	60	73	63	40	18
Mine Warfare	14	14	14	12	12	12	12	15	12	9
Amphibious Ships	17	17	17	17	16	16	16	17	10	3

Table 5.21

Selected Force Levels – Libyan Navy, 1980–9

	Year									
	80	81	82	83	84	85	86	87	88	89
Submarines	3	4	5	6	6	6	6	6	6	6
Frigates	1	1	1	1	1	1	1	2	3	3
Corvettes	1	4	6	8	8	8	7	7	7	7
Missile Attack Boats	14	16	18	25	25	25	24	24	24	24
Mine Warfare	0	0	2	6	6	7	7	8	8	8
Amphibious Warfare Craft	5	8	8	9	25	25	25	22	21	21
Coastal Craft	11	10	10	8	8	8	8	15	20	24

nine French *Combattante II* attack craft, British Thornycroft craft, and some ships from Turkey. While this force was significant, two factors made its future problematic. First, Qadhafi's outrageous actions, such as declaring the entire Gulf of Sirte Libyan territorial water, mining two areas in the Red Sea in 1984, and his support for terrorism could bring Libya into conflict with other nations and did lead to the US Operation 'El Dorado Canyon' in 1986.[73] Second, the Soviets were increasingly concerned over the equipment that had been provided, because the Libyans clearly were not maintaining the ships they had received. This and the Soviet foreign policy reassessment of the 1980s made further Soviet aid uncertain.

The Soviet Union also provided Algeria with ships including *Koni* frigates, *Nanuchka II* corvettes, *Osa I* and *II* and *Zhuk* craft, and *Polnocny* LSMs.[74]

SUB-SAHARAN AFRICA

The UN arms embargo had a great effect on South African naval development in the 1980s, as it was forced to expand an indigenous shipbuilding
capability in order to field a coastal defense force. Table 5.22 shows that this
was fairly successful, as the Navy grew over the years into a good coastal
defense force, although it had little force projection capability. Funding
became a problem and, in 1988, although the defense budget was increased
by 22.6 per cent, this was actually only a 1.1 per cent increase after inflation.
Within it, the Navy's share was reduced from 7.2 to 6.9 per cent.[75] None the
less, South Africa demonstrated what imagination, resourcefulness, and
planning could accomplish when funding and access to foreign arms were
restricted critically.

Table 5.22
Selected Force Levels – South African Navy, 1980–9

	Year									
	80	81	82	83	84	85	86	87	88	89
Submarines	3	3	3	3	3	3	3	3	3	3
Frigates	3	3	1	1	1	1	1	1	1	1
Missile Attack Boats	12	9	6	8	9	9	9	9	9	9
Mine Warfare Units	10	6	6	6	6	6	6	6	9	9

Except for South Africa and Zimbabwe, none of the African nations was
rich enough to afford a navy of its own and had to rely on outside largess for
their development. In the 1980s, the USSR provided naval aid to several
African nations. In return for access to Angolan facilities, it provided Luanda
with *Osa* and *Shershen* attack craft. The Beninian Navy was given four Soviet
Zhuk boats, while Cape Verde received Soviet *Shershen* and *Zhuk* craft.[76]

CANADA

In spite of its proud maritime history during the Second World War, in the
1970s Canada let its navy wither and by 1980, it seemed that it had chosen the
Danish defense formula. Its coasts were so important to US security that if
Canada would not provide for its protection, the United States would.
Despite claims that Canadian concern for its national security had replaced its
reliance on the United States, in 1980 its defenses were so weak that it could
not even meet its reduced NATO commitments (see Table 5.23). No naval
ships had been built since the *Iroquois* frigates were completed in 1973 and
the situation went from bad to worse. By 1982, inadequate spending and
organization had combined to create a critical defense problem and, in 1983,
the Canadian Senate's Subcommittee on National Defence study concluded
that the Navy could neither defend the nation's coasts nor fulfil its obligations
to NATO. It called for an immediate rearmament and reorganization. However, as a program to build six new *City* patrol frigates was begun, it
immediately encountered delays. In 1985, most believed that the Navy
needed an immediate, massive infusion of funds, far above the level of
appropriations.

Table 5.23
Selected Force Levels – Royal Canadian Navy, 1980–9

	Year									
	80	81	82	83	84	85	86	87	88	89
Submarines	3	3	3	3	3	3	3	3	3	3
Destroyers	4	4	4	4	4	4	4	4	4	4
Frigates	19	16	16	16	16	16	16	16	15	15
Coastal Craft	12	12	12	12	12	12	11	12	12	12

An incident occurred in August 1985, when the US Coast Guard ice-breaker *Polar Sea* sailed the North-west Passage after notifying Canadian authorities but without asking permission. While the United States does not recognize Canadian sovereignty over the passage and the ship therefore had conformed to the tradition of not notifying the Canadians, it is unclear if the voyage was a deliberate attempt to incite Ottawa in hopes of prompting it to face its defense needs more responsibly. If this were the purpose, it had the desired effect in the short-term. By 1987, however, it was evident that Canada's naval program, which included building from ten to twelve nuclear-powered attack submarines (SSNs) and twelve *Halifax* frigates, was proceeding more slowly than was expected.

Building SSNs required a transfer of nuclear technology from Great Britain and this, in turn, required US permission, as it had provided the technology to London. This was finally granted, but in 1989, the SSN program was considerably behind schedule. Subsequently, in May, Ottawa cancelled the SSNs in a significant defense cutback and considered building conventional submarines instead.[77] In such an adverse and poorly thought out situation, naval innovation was impossible to accomplish.

THE CARIBBEAN AND CENTRAL AMERICA

As Table 5.24 shows, the Cuban Navy maintained its size. This was done with Soviet assistance.[78] But as Moscow reassessed its foreign policy commitments in the late-1980s with an eye to cutting cost, additional support to Havana in the 1990s was less certain.

Although Soviet naval assistance to Nicaragua paled when compared to its other military assistance, some units, including *Zhuk* craft and *Yevgenya*

Table 5.24
Selected Force Levels – Cuban Navy, 1980–9

	Year									
	80	81	82	83	84	85	86	87	88	89
Submarines	1	3	1	1	2	2	2	3	3	3
Frigates	0	0	1	1	1	2	2	2	2	3
Missile Attack Boats	24	24	26	28	32	23	23	23	18	18
Torpedo Attack Boats	22	24	24	20	18	13	6	0	0	0
Mine Warfare Units	3	9	9	12	12	12	11	14	14	14
Coastal Craft	33	34	28	22	13	42	42	37	42	42

minesweepers, and North Korean *Sin Hung* patrol craft, were given.[79] The result could hardly be considered a threat to Managua's neighbors.

Table 5.25
Selected Force Levels – Mexican Navy, 1980–9

					Year					
	80	81	82	83	84	85	86	87	88	89
Destroyers	2	2	4	3	3	3	3	3	3	3
Frigates	6	6	6	6	6	6	6	6	6	6
Corvettes	38	38	34	41	41	41	43	40	37	36
Amphibious Warfare	3	3	3	3	2	2	2	1	0	0
Coastal Craft	40	45	45	49	49	49	55	54	54	51

In Mexico, as the drug problem became more critical, the Navy's importance as a coastal patrol force increased. Although there was some growth in the 1980s including *Azteca* boats and transfer of two *Fletcher* and two *Gearing* destroyers, an *Edsall*-class frigate, some US minesweepers, and six Spanish *Halcon* boats (see Table 5.25), the fleet remained rather dated.[80]

SOUTH AMERICA

Several South American navies updated their forces in the 1980s. Colombia procured four West German *FS 1500* frigates that sustained its Navy's size (see Table 5.26). If the drug war spread to the seas, it would require external assistance to fulfil greater coastal defense and surveillance duties. Ecuador received the last of its six Italian corvettes and Venezuela the last of its Italian *Lupo* frigates. The Peruvian Navy received the rest of its four Italian *Modified Lupo* frigates, French *PR-72P* missile craft, and German *Type 1200* submarines, and acquired seven Dutch *Friesland* destroyers (see Table 5.27).[81]

Table 5.26
Selected Force Levels – Colombian Navy, 1980–9

					Year					
	80	81	82	83	84	85	86	87	88	89
Submarines	4	4	4	4	4	4	4	4	4	4
Destroyers	3	3	3	3	2	1	1	0	0	0
Frigates	2	1	1	4	4	4	4	4	4	4
Corvettes	3	3	3	4	4	4	4	0	0	0
Gun-Armed Attack Boats	0	0	0	0	4	4	4	3	3	0
Coastal Craft	23	23	23	23	16	16	14	14	14	14

Table 5.27
Selected Force Levels – Peruvian Navy, 1980–9

					Year					
	80	81	82	83	84	85	86	87	88	89
Submarines	8	9	10	12	12	12	12	12	12	11
Cruisers	3	3	3	2	2	2	2	2	2	2
Destroyers	7	9	9	10	10	10	8	8	8	8

(see Table 5.31) was a disaster – the Indian Navy subsequently dubbed it the 'Chernobyl-class'.[85] None the less, this did not detract from the fact that the Soviet Union had given India the most modern equipment that it had provided to any foreign nation in quantities that were unprecedented.

Table 5.28
Selected Force Levels – Brazilian Navy, 1980–9

	Year									
	80	81	82	83	84	85	86	87	88	89
Submarines	8	8	8	8	7	7	7	7	7	7
Carrier (Light)	1	1	1	1	1	1	1	1	1	1
Destroyers	12	12	12	12	10	12	10	10	10	10
Frigates	6	6	6	6	6	6	6	6	6	6
Corvettes	10	10	10	16	16	16	9	9	9	9
Mine Warfare	6	6	6	6	6	6	6	6	6	6
Amphibious Ships	6	9	9	9	9	6	5	5	5	2
Coastal Craft	22	22	22	22	21	12	12	12	12	12

Table 5.29
Selected Force Levels – Argentine Navy, 1980–9

	Year									
	80	81	82	83	84	85	86	87	88	89
Submarines	4	4	3	3	3	3	4	4	4	4
Carrier (Light)	1	1	1	1	1	1	1	1	1	1
Cruisers	1	1	0	0	0	0	0	0	0	0
Destroyers	8	9	8	7	7	7	6	6	6	6
Corvettes	2	2	3	5	6	6	5	6	6	6
Mine Warfare	6	6	6	6	6	6	6	6	6	6
Coastal Craft	15	18	15	15	14	14	14	12	67	69

The size of the Brazilian Navy shrank in the 1980s (see Table 5.28). All six Vosper-Thornycroft Mk 10 frigates were in service as the *Niteroi* class in 1980. By 1984, it appeared that Brazil had decided to build a 25,000-ton carrier to replace the *Minas Gerais* and to buy nuclear submarines. However, a final decision was delayed due to the nation's economic problems and a general climate of regional peace. It became evident that the carrier would not be seen in this century.[82]

Finally, Chilean and Argentine naval developments were relevant because of the recent animosity between the two nations over sovereignty in the Beagle Channel and continued Argentine claims to the Falkland Islands (Malvinas). After the sinking of the cruiser *Belgrano* and the beaching of the submarine *Santa Fe* during the Falkland Islands War, the Argentine Navy was updated. Future units, based on orders placed both before and after the war, included five German *Type TR 1700* submarines, four *Meko 360* destroyers, and six *Meko 140* frigates.[83] As Table 5.29 shows, the Argentine naval order of battle was sizeable in 1989, which would be of great concern to Great Britain if there were further disputes concerning the Falklands.

There was some modernization in the Chilean Navy in the 1980s (see

Table 5.30). Acquisitions included four British *County* destroyers, two *Type 1300* submarines, and Israeli *Saar 4* attack craft.[84]

Table 5.30
Selected Force Levels – Chilean Navy, 180–9

	Year									
	80	81	82	83	84	85	86	87	88	89
Submarines	3	3	3	3	3	4	4	4	4	4
Cruisers	3	3	3	2	2	2	2	0	1	1
Destroyers	6	6	6	6	4	4	4	7	8	8
Frigates	5	5	5	5	2	2	2	2	2	2
Corvettes	3	3	2	0	0	0	0	0	0	0
Missile Attack Boats	0	2	2	2	2	2	2	2	2	2
Torpedo Attack Boats	4	4	4	4	4	4	4	4	4	4
Amphibious Ships/Craft	12	16	15	15	9	4	5	5	3	3
Coastal Craft	15	20	22	24	26	15	10	10	4	4

THE INDIAN OCEAN

India

The evolving Indian Navy and Pakistan's response dominated regional naval affairs in the 1980s. India began the decade with such a close relationship with the Soviet Union that many questioned whether India was becoming a client, thereby bringing into question its non-aligned status. However, the program was subsequently broadened to include Western ships as well. Among the deliveries were the British carrier *Hermes* in 1986, German *Type 1500* submarines, Soviet *Kilo* submarines, *Kashin* destroyers, and *Yevgenya* and *Natya* minesweepers. Indian building included *Godavari* frigates and changes to the carrier *Vikrant*. In the late 1980s, additional Indian orders included *Kresta* cruisers, *Kilo* submarines, and *Kashin* destroyers. The transfer of the first Soviet *Charlie* nuclear-powered cruise-missile submarine

Table 5.31
Selected Force Levels – Indian Navy, 1980–9

	Year									
	80	81	82	83	84	85	86	87	88	89
Nuclear Attack Submarine	0	0	0	0	0	0	0	0	1	1
Submarines	8	8	8	8	8	8	8	11	13	14
Carriers	1	1	1	1	1	1	1	2	2	2
Cruisers	1	1	1	1	1	1	0	0	0	0
Destroyers	3	2	2	3	3	3	3	4	5	5
Frigates	26	24	21	22	23	24	23	23	24	24
Corvettes	4	3	3	3	3	3	4	4	5	6
Missile Attack Craft	16	16	16	16	16	14	14	14	13	12
Frigates	2	2	2	2	2	3	3	4	4	4
Missile Attack Boats	0	3	6	6	6	6	6	6	6	6
Amphibious Warfare	4	5	5	5	4	4	5	5	4	4
Coastal Craft	8	11	11	9	9	11	10	10	10	10

Mine Warfare	11	14	14	14	16	16	18	18	17	17
Coastal Craft	6	4	4	5	7	8	11	9	14	14
Amphibious	7	7	11	11	10	12	12	13	10	10

The Navy had proceeded responsibly and had developed a force of modern units. The purchase of *Hermes* allowed the time that was needed for India seriously to consider the type of carrier it wanted in the future. In 1989, it was reported that an Indian-built carrier was in the planning stage, and that it might be a 30 to 35,000-ton ship of the French design, and might be capable of carrying 40 aircraft. These plans may have been delayed when India's fiscal 1989-90 budget was cut slightly and the Navy's reductions were taken from its modernization program. In the autumn of 1989, India and the United States both made efforts to improve their relations, which might portend increased Indian arms procurements from the West.[86] One thing was certain – the Indian Navy had grown to the extent that in 1989 it was the major regional naval force, a factor that had to be considered in the planning of all nations concerned with the Indian Ocean.

Pakistan

Given the 1971 Indo-Pakistani War, Indian naval development concerned Pakistan, which attempted unsuccessfully to balance rising Indian naval power with naval development of its own. There were some significant additions – two French *Agosta* submarines, a British *County* destroyer, additional US *Gearing* destroyers, and Chinese *Huangfen* and *Hegu* fast attack craft. In 1986, the naval program was slowed, an order for two more *Agosta* submarines and a frigate order with Great Britain were never placed. The situation improved and in 1989, Karachi purchased two British *Leander* frigates and leased eight US *Garcia* and *Brooke* frigates (see Table 5.32). A US commentator argued that Washington should encourage Pakistan to become a regional naval presence in the Indian Ocean. The wisdom of this view was questionable, since Pakistan did not have the resources to compete with India, and major Pakistani arms purchases would probably prompt India to pursue an arms race.[87]

Table 5.32
Selected Force Levels – Pakistani Navy, 1980–9

	Year									
	80	81	82	83	84	85	86	87	88	89
Submarines	9	9	9	9	9	9	9	9	6	6
Cruisers	1	1	1	1	1	1	1	0	0	0
Destroyers	6	8	10	7	8	8	8	8	8	8
Frigates	1	0	0	0	0	0	0	0	6	8
Missile Attack Boats	0	0	0	4	4	8	8	8	8	8
Torpedo Attack Boats	4	4	4	4	4	4	4	4	4	4
Gun-Armed Attack Boats	15	12	12	12	12	12	12	12	15	17
Mine Warfare	7	6	6	6	3	3	3	3	3	3

Other Regional Development

Both Sri Lanka and Bangladesh accomplished some naval modernization. Sri Lanka acquired Chinese *Shanghai II* patrol craft, while Bangladesh received Chinese *Shanghai II*, *Hainan*, *Hegu*, and *P4* craft. Saudi Arabia's naval problem was significant, given its shipment of vast amounts of oil. In the 1980s there was some modernization and an increase in size as shown in Table 5.33. Significant additions included French-built *Al Madinah* frigates and nine large guided missile patrol boats from the United States. Elsewhere in the Red Sea and Gulf of Aden there were minor deliveries. South Yemen and Ethiopia each received *Osa* missile craft, while Ethiopia received a *Turya* hydrofoil, two *Zhuk* patrol craft, two *Petya II* frigates, and two *Polnocny* LSMs.[88]

THE PERSIAN GULF

Persian Gulf naval development was disrupted drastically due to Iran's break with the United States and the embargo of arms exports during the Iran-Iraq War. By 1980, the Iranian Navy's condition was poor due to the withdrawal of US and British maintenance teams. The result was a serious shortage of spares that kept the ships in port. The Iraqi Navy also suffered because, although it had ordered ships, these were not to be delivered due to the wartime arms embargo. While Tables 5.34 and 5.35 show only minor changes in Iranian and Iraqi naval strengths, more relevant was that, in addition to the ships actually damaged or destroyed in the war, the condition of both navies deteriorated considerably. In 1989, both were only beginning to recover from the war's effects.[89]

Table 5.33
Selected Force Levels – Saudi Arabian Navy, 1980–9

	Year									
	80	*81*	*82*	*83*	*84*	*85*	*86*	*87*	*88*	*89*
Frigates	0	0	0	0	0	0	2	4	4	4
Corvettes	0	4	4	4	4	4	4	4	4	4
Missile Attack Boats	2	7	9	9	9	9	9	9	9	9
Torpedo Attack Boats	3	3	3	3	3	3	3	3	3	3
Mine Warfare	4	4	4	4	4	4	4	4	4	4
Amphibious Craft	4	12	12	16	16	16	16	16	16	12

Table 5.34
Selected Force Levels – Iranian Navy, 1980–9

	Year									
	80	*81*	*82*	*83*	*84*	*85*	*86*	*87*	*88*	*89*
Destroyers	3	3	3	3	3	3	3	3	3	3
Frigates	4	4	4	4	4	4	4	4	4	3
Corvettes	4	4	4	4	4	4	4	4	4	2
Missile Attack Boats	9	9	9	9	10	11	12	12	11	10
Torpedo Attack Boats	3	0	0	0	0	0	0	0	0	0
Mine Warfare Units	5	5	5	5	5	5	5	5	3	3
Amphibious Units	3	3	3	3	4	5	6	6	10	21
Coastal Craft	31	47	47	47	43	38	35	33	22	22

Table 5.35
Selected Force Levels – Iraqi Navy, 1980–9

	Year									
	80	*81*	*82*	*83*	*84*	*85*	*86*	*87*	*88*	*89*
Frigates	1	1	1	1	1	1	1	1	1	1
Missile Attack Boats	12	12	12	12	12	12	12	12	8	9
Torpedo Attack Boats	12	12	12	12	10	8	0	0	0	0
Mine Warfare	5	5	5	8	8	8	8	8	8	8
Amphibious	3	3	4	4	5	5	6	6	6	6
Coastal Craft	31	31	31	32	33	33	33	33	33	20

THE PACIFIC OCEAN

North-east Asian maritime naval development was in reaction to Soviet and North Korean naval affairs. Within this context, besides the significant Japanese program, North and South Korean, Chinese, and Taiwanese developments were noteworthy. The North Korean Navy was expanded with additions of frigates, missile fast attack craft, assault craft, and amphibious ships.[90] Table 5.36 shows its growth in the 1980s. The South Korean naval program appeared not only to be in response to North Korean naval growth, but also to the possibility that US military forces in Korea might be reduced in the future. In 1981, John Moore said that, 'In their turn the South Koreans have designed and are building a bewildering array of . . . small vessels of 500 tons and below. . . .' One of the most innovative additions was the *Ulsan* frigate, an impressive ship armed with Harpoon, guns, and torpedo tubes. In 1989, Korea stated its intention to have an independent naval capability by the end of the century, and placed orders for at least three *Type 209* submarines from Germany. The technology would then be transferred and as many as twelve units would be built in Korea. The Navy also indicated a desire to acquire new destroyers.[91]

The Taiwanese Navy also grew as it bolstered its missile attack boat force. Additional US destroyers were delivered, as the Navy built many 50-ton *Hai Ou* missile-equipped fast attack craft (see Table 5.38). In 1989, Taiwan announced that it would build eight modified-*Oliver Perry* frigates locally.[92] It entered the 1990s with a navy that presented a respectable regional combat capability.

Table 5.36
Selected Force Levels – North Korean Navy, 1980–9

	Year									
	80	*81*	*82*	*83*	*84*	*85*	*86*	*87*	*88*	*89*
Submarines	16	19	17	19	19	19	22	19	20	21
Frigates	4	4	4	4	2	2	2	2	2	3
Missile Attack Boats	18	18	18	19	34	32	32	32	30	30
Torpedo Attack Boats	165	177	175	155	142	146	136	163	168	173
Gun-Armed Attack Boats	134	141	151	155	163	164	167	162	158	158
Amphibious Warfare Craft	80	94	107	107	113	118	128	128	126	126
Coastal Craft	70	63	58	65	65	65	65	62	62	60

Table 5.37
Selected Force Levels – South Korean Navy, 1980–9

Year

	80	81	82	83	84	85	86	87	88	89
Submarines	0	0	0	0	0	1	1	1	1	1
Destroyers	10	10	11	11	11	11	11	9	8	8
Frigates	7	7	7	8	8	6	6	12	18	31
Corvettes	6	3	3	3	3	4	16	16	11	11
Missile Attack Boats	8	8	8	9	9	11	11	11	11	11
Mine Warfare	9	9	9	9	8	8	8	9	9	9
Amphibious Ships/Craft	21	24	28	30	33	36	35	46	52	52
Coastal Craft	43	38	36	36	35	64	64	80	94	94

Table 5.38
Selected Force Levels – Taiwanese Navy, 1980–9

Year

	80	81	82	83	84	85	86	87	88	89
Submarines	2	2	2	2	2	2	2	3	4	4
Destroyers	22	23	23	24	26	26	26	25	24	24
Frigates	11	10	10	10	10	10	10	10	10	10
Corvettes	3	3	3	3	4	4	3	3	3	3
Missile Attack Boats	1	2	2	33	33	52	52	52	52	52
Torpedo Attack Boats	9	9	9	0	0	0	0	0	0	0
Mine Warfare	22	22	22	22	22	22	22	22	22	22
Amphibious Ships/Craft	51	50	50	50	50	50	50	49	49	49
Coastal Craft	14	14	14	28	28	28	28	28	28	43

The People's Republic of China

The Soviet military response to the Sino-Vietnamese War of 1979 and subsequent Soviet naval operations from Cam Ranh Bay were among the factors spurring Chinese naval development. This program was very uneven, producing impressive results on the one hand while displaying significant weaknesses on the other. All this was accomplished by a nation that correctly

Table 5.39
Selected Force Levels – PRC Navy, 1980–9

Year

	80	81	82	83	84	85	86	87	88	89
SSBNs	0	0	0	1	1	1	1	1	1	1
SSBs	1	1	1	1	1	1	1	1	1	1
Attack/Cruise Missile Submarines	85	104	104	110	103	107	110	120	126	135
Destroyers	11	15	12	18	18	19	19	19	18	18
Frigates	16	17	16	23	26	30	30	33	34	33
Corvettes	8	9	12	14	14	14	13	13	10	8
Missile Attack Boats	181	195	207	215	222	232	232	233	228	200
Torpedo Attack Boats	220	230	255	250	240	220	204	190	185	185
Gun-Armed Attack Boats	336	345	372	407	375	365	360	355	343	340

Mine Warfare	20	20	21	22	24	25	27	27	28	28
Amphibious Ships/Craft	514	516	507	503	574	582	595	615	615	615
Coastal Craft	140	169	166	164	205	182	182	182	183	183

viewed the Soviet ground and strategic threats as more critical than the maritime threat and by a regime that hoped to minimize defense spending as part of its Four Modernizations Program. In 1980, it was obvious that the PLA Navy needed much modernization, which it began in 1981. Later, China successfully fired its first SLBM. The subsequent years witnessed the construction of submarines and surface combatants, including *Han* nuclear-and *Ming* diesel-powered submarines, *Luda* destroyers and *Jianghu* frigates (see Table 5.39). In 1986, however, the program was curtailed considerably, as military spending was reduced to 0.5 per cent of the GNP in 1987, a \$5 billion decrease. In the next years, there were reports that questioned the reliability of Chinese naval systems such as shipboard air conditioning and ships' fin stabilizers.[93] In 1989, PLA naval development was characterized by uneven development growth, producing a fleet that was believed to have serious equipment problems.

SOUTH-EAST ASIA

As the Soviet Union developed the facilities at Cam Ranh Bay in the 1980s, it provided greater naval assistance to the region's nations. Vietnam received five *Petya II* and *III* frigates, *Osa*, *Turya* and *Shershen* attack craft, patrol boats, *Yurka* and *Yevgenya* minesweepers and *Polnocny* LSMs. Kampuchea received a *Turya* hydrofoil, four *Schmel* and a *Stenka* craft, and landing craft.[94]

Malaysia, which has two coasts and Sarawak to protect, developed its naval power in the 1980s. Acquisitions included two German *Type 1500* frigates, corvettes, and Swedish *Spica M* attack craft. Indonesia also developed its navy, and acquired two German *Type 209* submarines, five Dutch *Van Speijk* frigates, three Dutch-built *Fatahilah* frigates, two more British *Tribal* frigates (for a total of three), patrol craft, mine countermeasures ships, and amphibious ships.[95]

AUSTRALASIA

The Australian naval program was disrupted considerably when Britain decided to keep its aircraft carrier *Invincible* after the Falklands War. She had been intended to replace *Melbourne*, and was not equipped to handle aircraft more modern than the A-4. This fact, political opposition, and no perceived maritime threat stifled considerably Australian naval development, resulting in no naval innovation during the 1980s. The acquisition of *Perry*-class frigates was continued, but, in 1983, the Labour government's decision not to obtain an aircraft carrier meant disbanding the Navy's fleet air arm and the assumption of maritime duties by the Australian Air Force (see Table 5.40).[96] By 1989, the Navy clearly did not have the capability to defend the nation from a serious naval threat.

Table 5.40
Selected Force Levels – Royal Australian Navy, 1980–9

	Year									
	80	81	82	83	84	85	86	87	88	89
Submarines	6	6	6	6	6	6	6	6	6	6
Carriers (Light)	1	1	0	0	0	0	0	0	0	0
Missile Destroyers	4	4	3	3	3	3	3	3	3	3
Frigates	6	8	8	9	10	10	10	9	9	9
Mine Warfare	3	3	3	3	1	1	2	2	5	5
Coastal Craft	13	14	16	20	21	21	21	21	22	22
Amphibious Craft	6	6	6	7	5	5	6	6	4	4

New Zealand's Navy suffered similarly from a lack of a threat, and by 1982 it was too small to counter any determined submarine or mining campaign. In October 1982 the *Leander*-class HMS *Bacchante* was transferred as HMNZS *Wellington* and HMS *Dido* was transferred in July 1983 as HMNZS *Southland*. The decision to break with ANZUS in 1988 further compounded the defense problem, and it faced the future with an uncertain naval program and a very weak force.[97]

CONCLUSIONS

In January 1989, as the end of another decade neared, the world could look back on the 1980s as a period in which there had been significant US and Soviet naval growth. This competition was a part of the greater Soviet–American defense competition that had been so sustained and so significant financially that it drove the Soviet economy to the brink of ruin. The result was such a dramatic and comprehensive reassessment of the nation's purpose and goals that it was tantamount to a social revolution. The resulting program, as codified in President Mikhail Gorbachev's perestroika program, seemed to promise change in the 1990s, with the possibility of a peaceful world, but, no one imagined the effects that his policies would have, and that 1989 was to be a most remarkable year.

NOTES

1. This argument concerning the peaceful execution of the Third World War and the argument concerning the possibility of a Fourth World War were developed jointly with Professor Raimondo Luraghi, University of Genoa. Italy. Professor Luraghi is developing the concepts farther in books that he is writing on the history of the US Navy.

2. Stanley J. Heginbotham, 'The Forward Maritime Strategy and Nordic Europe,' in *Naval War College Review*, vol. 38, no. 6 (November–December 1985), p. 22.

3. Labayle Couhat, p. 715; 'Polaris Subs Will Leave Guam,' in *Proceedings*, vol. 106, no. 6 (June 1980), p. 125; US Government, Department of the Navy, *Fiscal Year 1984 Report to Congress*

(Washington, DC: Department of the Navy, 1983), p. 7; 'Test Failure Forces SLBM Delay,' in *Jane's*, vol. 11, no. 19 (13 May 1989), p. 851; Joint Chiefs of Staff, *United States Military Posture for 1989* (Washington, DC: Organization of the Joint Chiefs of Staff, 1988), pp. 51-2; and *Jane's Fighting Ships, 1983-1984*, p. 146; *1984-1985*, p. 140; *1985-1986*, p. 149; *1986-1987*, p. 137; *1987-1988*, p. 133; *1988-1989*, p. 123; and *1989-1990*, p. 97.

4. US Government, Joint Chiefs of Staff, *United States Military Posture for 1982* (Washington, DC: Organization of the Joint Chiefs of Staff, 1981), p. 87; *for 1981*, p. 57; US Government, Department of the Navy, *Fiscal Year 1985 Report to Congress* (Washington, DC: Department of the Navy, 1984), p. 10; *Fiscal Year 1986*, p. 15;

Fiscal Year 1987, p. 7; *Fiscal Year 1988*, pp. 38-9; *Fiscal Year 1989*, p. 30; and *Jane's Fighting Ships, 1980-1981*, p. 139, and *1981-1982*, p. 141.

5. *Jane's Fighting Ships, 1987-1988*, p. 111.

6. *Fiscal Year 1984, Report to Congress*, p. 28.

7. Labayle Couhat, pp. 723-4; *Conway's, Part 1*, pp. 216, 219, 228; and *Jane's Fighting Ships, 1980-1981*, p. 139; *1983-1984*, p. 146; and *1984-1985*, p. 140.

8. Labayle Couhat, pp. 727-9; Ronald O'Rourke, 'Gulf Ops,' in *Proceedings*, vol. 115, no. 5 (May 1988), p. 42; and *Jane's Fighting Ships, 1984-1985*, p. 140; *1985-1986*, p. 149; *1986-1987*, pp. 137, 724; and *1987-1988*, p. 133. For alternative positions on *Ticonderoga*, see: R. G. Guibault, '*Ticonderoga*: First and Formidable,' in *Proceedings*, vol. 108, no. 11 (November 1982), pp. 113-15; and Strafford Morss, '*Ticonderoga*: Another *Hood*?' in *Proceedings*, vol. 108, no. 8 (August 1982), pp. 116-17.

9. Labayle Couhat, p. 732-3; *Jane's Fighting Ships, 1986-1987*, p. 728; and U.S. Government, Department of the Navy, *Fiscal Years 90-91 Report to Congress* (Washington, DC: Department of the Navy, 1983), pp. 50-51.

10. Labayle Couhat, p. 757; and *Jane's Fighting Ships 1985-1986*, p. 149; and *1986-1987*, p. 137.

11. US Government, Joint Chiefs of Staff, *United States Military Posture for 1983* (Washington, DC: Organization of the Joint Chiefs of Staff, 1982), p. 89; *for 1986*, pp. 51-2; *for 1987*, pp. 20-1; '47 Die in *Iowa* Gun Turret Explosion, Inquiry Begins,' in *Jane's*, vol. 11, no. 17 (29 April 1989), p. 724; Len Famiglietti, '"Loner" Caused *Iowa* Explosion, Says Report,' in *Jane's*, vol. 12, no. 11 (16 September 1989), p. 494; and '*Iowa* Fires Salvo from Two Turrets,' in *Jane's*, vol. 12, no. 7 (19 August 1989), p. 286.

12. 'Webb Resigns as US Navy Secretary after Clash over 600 Ships, in *Jane's*, (5 March 1988), p. 382.

13. *Jane's Fighting Ships, 1987-1988*, p. 133; and *1989-1990*, p. 97.

14. Peter M. Dunn and Bruce W. Watson, eds., *American Intervention in Grenada: The Implications of Operation 'Urgent Fury'* (Boulder, CO: Westview Press, 1985); Robert Scheina, 'Latin American Navies,' in *Proceedings*, vol. 110, no. 3 (March 1984), p. 31; and US Government, Joint Chiefs of Staff, *United States Military Posture for 1985* (Washington, DC: Organization of the Joint Chiefs of Staff, 1984), p. 93.

15. *New York Times*: 11 August 1983, p. 1; 29 August 1983, p. 1; 2 September 1983, p. 1; 4 September 1983, p. 1; 9 September 1983, p. 1; 13 September 1983, p. 1; 14 September 1983, p. 1; 18 September 1983, p. 1; 29 September 1983; 24 October 1983, p. 1; 25 October 1983, p. 1.

16. *Jane's Fighting Ships, 1986-1987*, p. 125.

17. 'Countdown to Operation "El Dorado Canyon",' in *Jane's*, vol. 5, no. 16 (26 April 1986), p. 736; Bob Raggett, 'Admiral Praises C³I in US Raid on Libya,' in *Jane's*, vol. 5, no. 23 (14 June 1986), p. 1083; *Jane's Fighting Ships, 1986-1987*, p. 111; 'Libyan SAM Missiles Hit Civilian Areas, Says USA,' in *Jane's*, vol. 5, no. 16 (26 April 1986), p. 737; 'UK-Based F-111Fs the Best for Strike,' in *Jane's*, vol. 5, no. 16 (26 April 1986), p. 737; 'Basis for UK's Decision over Use of Air Bases,' in *Jane's*, vol. 5, no. 16 (26 April 1986), p. 740; 'Effect on Alliance Co-operation,' in *Jane's*, vol. 5, no. 16 (26 April 1986), p. 740; 'Libyan Scud B Attack on Lampedusa Island,' in *Jane's*, vol. 5, no,. 16 (26 April 1986), p. 739; and '"Measured" Soviet Reaction to Crisis,' in *Jane's*, vol. 5, no. 16 (26 April 1986), p. 739.

18. The US Navy was more than capable of accomplishing the operation on its own. A first strike could have suppressed Libyan defenses, and the second could have hit the targets.

19. *New York Times*: 22 July 1987, p. 1; 23 July 1987, p. 14; 30 July 1987, p. 1; 1 August 1987, p. 1; 5 August 1987, p. 1.

20. *New York Times*: 12 August 1987, p. 1; 17 August 1987, p. 1; 20 August 1987, p. 1; 9 October 1987, p. 1; 6 December 1987, p. 26; 14 January 1988, p. 11.

21. *New York Times*, 9 October 1987, p. 1.

22. *New York Times*: 16 October 1987, p. 1; 19 October 1987, p. 1.

23. Norman Friedman, 'The Attack on the Stark,' in *Proceedings*, vol. 113, no. 7 (July 1987), pp. 96-7; Ronald O'Rourke, 'Gulf Ops,' in *Proceedings*, vol. 115, no. 5 (May 1988), p. 42; Howard M. Hensel, 'Superpower Interests and Missions in the Indian Ocean,' in *Naval War College Review*, vol. 38, no. 1 (Jan-Feb 1985), pp. 53-74; Bud Langston, 'Operation "Praying Mantis": The Air View,' in *Proceedings*, vol. 115, no. 5 (May 1988), p. 57; J. B. Perkins, III, 'Operation "Praying Mantis": The Surface View,' in *Proceedings*, vol. 115, no. 5 (May 1988), pp. 66-70; and Norman Friedman, 'The *Vincennes* Incident,' in *Proceedings*, vol. 115, no. 5 (May 1988), p. 72.

24. O'Rourke, p. 43. The Fiscal Year 1987 cost to the United States Navy, $69 million, was absorbed by the Navy by deferring maintenance projects. Similarly, in Fiscal Year 1988, $16 million of a total of $116 million was absorbed by the Navy's Operations and Maintenance account. In terms of lives, 53 Americans died in 1987 and 1988, most of these were on the *Stark* (O'Rourke, pp. 49-50).

25. Labayle Couhat, pp. 582-3; 'Exclusive: First Picture of "Oscar II",' in *Jane's*, vol. 9, no. 13 (24 September 1988), p. 733; John Jordan, '"Oscar": A Change in Soviet Naval Policy,' in *Jane's*, vol. 5, no. 20 (24 May 1986), pp. 942-7; John Jordan, 'Soviet Submarines from "Yankee" to "Delta",' *Jane's*, vol. 8, no. 6 (15 August 1987), pp. 277, 279-80; '"Delta I" and "Charlie I" in View,' in *Jane's*, vol. 9, no. 14 (1 October 1988), p. 821; and *Jane's Fighting Ships, 1980-1981*, p. 139; *1981-1982*, p. 141, *1982-1983*, p. 133; *1983-1984*, p. 146; and *1986-1987*, p. 535.

26. John Jordan, 'Leviathan of the Deep,' in *Jane's*, vol. 5, no. 8 (1 March 1986), pp. 376-9; and *Jane's Fighting Ships, 1986-1987*, p. 534.

27. Labayle Couhat, pp. 587-98; 'Soviet "Akula" Submarine in Close-up,' in *Jane's*, vol. 7, no. 7 (21 February 1987), pp. 256-7; 'More Launches of "Akula" and "Sierra", in *Jane's*, vol. 5, no. 13 (5 April 1986), p. 596; and *Jane's Fighting Ships, 1984-1985*, p. 140; *1985-1986*, p. 149; *1986-1987*, pp. 544-5; and *1989-1990*, p. 83.

28. Labayle Couhat, pp. 588-9; Antony Preston, 'Political Consequences of the Soviet "Yankee" SSBN Sinking,' in *Jane's*, vol. 6, no. 15 (18 October 1986), pp. 876-7; 'Soviet SSBN Sinks After Explosion off US Coast,' in *Jane's*, vol. 6, no. 14 (11 October 1986), p. 759; 'First Views of "Mike" Submarine,' in *Jane's*, vol. 7, no. 11 (21 March 1987), pp. 468-9; 'Soviets Count Cost of "Mike" Loss,' in *Jane's*, vol. 11, no. 16 (22 April 1989), p. 705; and '42 Die as "Mike" Submarine Sinks,' in *Jane's*, vol. 11, no. 15 (15 April 1989), p. 629.

29. Labayle Couhat, pp. 595-8; *Conway's Part II*, pp. 484-6; 'Frunze and Kirov Compared,' in *Jane's*, vol. 3, no. 11 (16 March 1985), pp. 445-7; and Barbara Starr, 'Soviets Building New Cruiser,' in *Jane's*, vol. 12, no. 2 (15 July 1989), p. 57.

30. 'Krivak Class Replacement in Progress,' in *Jane's*, vol. 11, no. 11 (18 March 1989), p. 428; *Jane's Fighting Ships, 1980-1981*, p. 139.

31. 'Analysis of Changes to *Baku*,' in *Jane's*, vol. 9, no. 6 (6 August 1988), p. 225; 'First Picture of *Baku*'s Layout,' in *Jane's*, vol. 10, no. 14 (8 October 1988), p. 893; 'Closeup on *Baku*'s Defences,' in *Jane's*, vol. 11, no. 3 (21 January 1989), pp. 74-5; '*Baku* View Analysed,' in *Jane's*, vol. 11, no. 7 (18 February 1989), p. 279; '*Kiev* After Refit,' in *Jane's*, vol. 4, no. 8 (24 August 1985), pp. 352-3; and '*Kiev* Refit Gives Insight into Soviet Naval Air Developments,' in *Jane's*, vol. 4, no. 7 (17 August 1985), pp. 308-9.

32. The class name appeared to be a kiss of death. For a short time it was rumored that the lead unit would be named *Kremlin*. However, if this name was considered, it was changed to *Brezhnev*. But when Brezhnev was reduced in prestige, the name was changed to *Tbilisi*. In February 1990, demonstrations and riots that included the storming of the steps of the town square by two trucks as demonstrators attempted to pull down the city's statue of Lenin, made one pause to consider the wisdom of naming the nation's most prestigious ship after the city. The correctness of the choice of *Riga*, as the name of the second unit was also questionable.

33. Richard Gross, 'New Soviet Carrier Challenge to US Navy,' in *Jane's*, vol. 5, no. 3 (25 January 1986), p. 87; 'Carrier *Tbilisi*: STOL or V/STOL?' in *Jane's*, vol. 9, no. 9 (27 August 1988), p. 388; '*Tbilisi* to Carry Only 10 Aircraft' in *Jane's*, vol. 12, no. 2 (15 July 1989), p. 86; *Jane's Fighting Ships, 1986-1987*, p. 137; Norman Polmar, 'The

Soviet Navy: The New Carrier,' in *Proceedings*, vol. 114, no. 8 (August 1988), pp. 66-7; '*Tbilisi* STOL Tests Successful,' in *Jane's*, vol. 12, no. 23 (9 December 1989), p. 1261; '*Tbilisi* CTOL Tests,' in *Jane's*, vol. 12, no. 24 (16 December 1989), p. 1317; and 'First Picture of *Tbilisi*,' in *Jane's*, vol. 12, no. 18 (4 November 1989), p. 94.

34. This progress was not without its difficulties. On 13 May 1984, the missile storage facility at Severomorsk Naval Base on Kola peninsula blew up in a series of huge explosions, causing extensive damage. It was estimated that so many of the surface-to-surface and surface-to-air missiles had been destroyed that it inhibited Northern Fleet operations for six months, and that it took two years to restore the facility. None the less, the Navy recovered from this disaster and conducted its largest naval exercise to date in the summer of 1985. Dubbed 'SUMMEREX 85', the evolution included 275 sorties by naval aircraft. (See: Derek Wood, 'Soviets' Northern Fleet disabled . . . "Not Viable" for Six Months,' in *Jane's*, vol. 2, no. 1 (14 July 1984), p. 3; Derek Wood, 'Six Explosions in Past Seven Months,' in *Jane's*, vol. 2, no. 1 (14 July 1984), p. 3; 'Who Takes the Blame for Severomorsk?' in *Jane's*, vol. 2, no. 1 (14 July 1984), p. 4; Antony Preston, 'Blast May Have Started in Ready-use Magazine,' in *Jane's*, vol. 2, no. 1 (14 July 1984), p. 4; and Mark Daly, 'Soviets' "SUMMEREX 85" Their Largest Exercise,' in *Jane's*, vol. 4, no. 5 (3 August 1985), p. 198.

35. The choice of an old torpedo to sink *Belgrano* rather than a modern one reflected the Captain's lack of confidence in modern British torpedoes.

36. Lawrence Germaine, 'A Diary of the Falklands Conflict,' in *Military Lessons of the Falkland Islands War*, edited by Bruce W. Watson and Peter M. Dunn (London: Arms & Armour Press, and Boulder, CO: Westview Press, 1984), p. 151. The intense investigations following her sinking resulted in modifications to later *Type 42*s built for the Royal Navy.

37. Labayle Couhat, pp. 207, 208; *Jane's Fighting Ships, 1985-1986*, p. 135; Eric J. Grove, 'After the Falklands,' in *Proceedings*, vol. 112, no. 3 (March 1986), pp. 127, 129; Norman Friedman, 'Western European and NATO Navies,' in *Proceedings*, vol. 112, no. 3 (March 1986), pp. 38-9; Stephen S. Roberts, 'Western European and NATO Navies,' in *Proceedings*, vol. 108, no. 3 (March 1982), pp. 41-2; and John E. Woods, 'The Royal Navy Since World War II,' in *Proceedings*, vol. 108, no. 2 (March 1982), pp. 89-91.

38. John Jordan, 'Loosening the Stranglehold on the Royal Navy,' in *Proceedings* (March 1989), p. 34.

39. Ibid., pp. 36-8.

40. Ibid., pp. 38-9.

41. Labayle Couhat, p. 208; *Jane's Fighting Ships, 1986-1987*, pp. 641-2, 645; Simon Elliott, 'SSN Delay Risks RN Force Strength,' in *Jane's*, vol.

11, no. 16 (22 April 1989), p. 675; 'SSN Cuts for RN,' in *Jane's*, vol. 12, no. 2 (15 July 1989), p. 59; 'RN: Dip in SSN Numbers Ahead,' in *Jane's*, vol. 12, no. 12 (23 September 1989), p. 557; Tony Banks, 'RN Facing Big Problems in Submarine Manning,' in *Jane's*, vol. 8, no. 17 (31 October 1987), p. 983; 'UK Reveals Next Generation Nuclear-Powered Submarine,' in *Jane's*, vol. 11, no. 5 (4 February 1989), p. 170; Mark Daly, 'Royal Navy Set to Order SSN 20 Systems,' in *Jane's*, vol. 13, no. 1 (6 January 1990), p. 11; and 'UK Reveals Next Generation Nuclear-Powered Submarine,' in *Jane's*, vol. 11, no. 5 (4 February 1989), p. 170.

42. Labayle Couhat, pp. 210-12; and Stephen S. Roberts, 'Western European and NATO Navies,' in *Proceedings*, vol. 107, no. 3 (March 1981), p. 30; and *Jane's Fighting Ships, 1986-1987*, pp. 648-9.

43. Labayle Couhat, pp. 213-14, 218-21; Norman Friedman, 'Western European and NATO Navies,' in *Proceedings*, vol. 116, no. 3 (March 1990), p. 118; J. V. P. Goldrick, 'Britain Builds New Castles,' in *Proceedings*, vol. 107, no. 3 (March 1981), p. 133; and *Jane's Fighting Ships, 1986-1987*, p. 649.

44. Labayle Couhat, pp. 213-14; Sir Peter Stanford, 'The Current Position of the Royal Navy,' in *Proceedings*, vol. 110, no. 3 (March 1984), pp. 100-07; Norman Friedman, 'Western European and NATO Navies,' in *Proceedings*, vol. 111, no. 3 (March 1984), pp. 39, 41-3; Desmond Wettern, 'Britain's Forgotten Lessons,' in *Proceedings*, vol. 113, no. 3 (March 1987), pp. 112-20; Anthony Wells, 'A New Defense Strategy for Britain,' in *Proceedings*, vol. 113, no. 3 (March 1987), p. 114; 'Three Bid to Replace Fearless and Intrepid,' in *Jane's*, vol. 10, no. 14 (8 October 1988), p. 853; Robin Knox-Johnston, 'RN Considers Future Aircraft Carrier,' in *Jane's*, vol. 11, no. 22 (3 June 1989), p. 1075; *Jane's Fighting Ships, 1989-1990*, p. 87; 'No CIWS for RN's Latest Type 23s,' in *Jane's*, vol. 11, no. 23 (10 June 1989), p. 1137; 'UK Confirms Type 23s to Sail Without SSCS,' in *Jane's*, vol. 12, no. 8 (26 August 1989), p. 332; and 'Three More Type 23 Frigates Ordered,' in *Jane's*, vol. 13, no. 1 (6 January 1990), p. 11.

45. *Jane's Fighting Ships, 1980-1981*, p. 129.

46. Labayle Couhat, pp. 133-4; Norman Friedman, 'Western European and NATO Navies,' in *Proceedings*, vol. 116, no. 3 (March 1990), p. 118; Stephen S. Roberts, 'Western European and NATO Navies,' in *Proceedings*, vol. 107, no. 3 (March 1981), p. 31; *Jane's Fighting Ships, 1985-1986*, p. 147; and *1988-1989*, p. 122; and Jacques Isnard, 'France Claims SSBN Advantage,' in *Jane's* (1 October 1988), p. 746.

47. Labayle Couhat, pp. 136-9; Jacques Isnard, 'France Details Defense Budget Cuts,' in *Jane's*, vol. 11, no. 22 (3 June 1989), p. 1035; and '*Rivière* Replacement Set for 1991 Delivery Date,' in *Jane's*, vol. 11, no. 26 (1 July 1989), p.

1371. By 1985, the results of this well-reasoned program were evident. One commentator expounded on the French Navy's global reach, while a second stated that although France now had a limited nuclear capability, this must be considered by the Soviets in their strategic planning. (See: Robert L. Cogne, 'France's Global Reach,' in *Proceedings*, vol. 113, no. 3 (March 1987), pp. 76-82; and John J. Hyland, III, 'France's Nuclear Reach,' in *Proceedings*, vol. 113, no. 3 (March 1987), pp. 83-7.)

48. Labayle Couhat, p. 128; John A. Burgess, 'La Marine,' in *Proceedings*, vol. 111, no. 3 (March 1985), p. 99; Norman Friedman, 'Western European and NATO Navies,' in *Proceedings*, vol. 112, no. 3 (March 1986), pp. 36-48 and vol. 113, no. 3 (March 1987), p. 45; John A. Burgess, 'Into the 21st Century,' in *Proceedings*, vol. 111, no. 3 (March 1985), p. 98; 'Carrier Work Begins,' in *Jane's*, vol. 11, no. 16 (29 April 1989), p. 737; Jacques Isnard, 'SSBN Reactors Give de Gaulle Slow Speed,' in *Jane's*, vol. 12, no. 12 (23 September 1989), p. 548; 'Aircraft Carrier Contracts Awarded,' in *Jane's* (21 May 1988), p. 1007; Paul Beaver, 'The Long Arm of the French Navy,' in *Jane's*, vol. 6, no. 5 (18 October 1986), pp. 899-901; Jacques Isnard, 'French Budget Splits Government,' in *Jane's*, vol. 11, no. 18 (6 May 1989), p. 786; and Jacques Isnard, 'France Details Defense Budget Cuts,' in *Jane's*, vol. 11, no. 22 (3 June 1989), p. 1035.

49. Joseph F. Bouchard, 'The Japanese Maritime Self-Defense Force,' in *Proceedings*, vol. 107, no. 3 (March 1981), pp. 60-8; J. V. P. Goldrick and P. D. Jones, 'Far-Eastern Navies,' in *Proceedings*, vol. 108, no. 3 (March 1982), pp. 60-1. For insights into this complex issue see: Joseph F. Bouchard and Douglas J. Hess, 'The Japanese Navy and Sea Lanes Defense,' in *Proceedings*, vol. 110, no. 3 (March 1984), pp. 94-6. The authors argue that Japan, if she does expand her naval sphere, will defend her sea lanes, but will not be the regional guarantor that the US wants. See also: Otto Lehrack III, 'Search for a New Consensus,' in *Proceedings*, vol. 110, no. 3 (March 1984), pp. 96-9, in which the author examines the complexities of Japan's rearming.

50. Labayle Couhat, pp. 328-36; *Jane's Fighting Ships, 1986-1987*, pp. 302, 304, 306; J. V. P. Goldrick, and P. D. Jones, 'Far-Eastern Navies,' in *Proceedings*, vol. 116, no. 3 (March 1990), p. 150; John Jordan, 'New Destroyers for Japan, Part 2: The *Hatakaze* Class,' in *Jane's*, vol. 4, no. 11 (14 September 1985), pp. 551, 553, 555; 'Japan Demonstrates Its Maritime Capabilities,' in *Jane's*, vol. 4, no. 6 (24 August 1985), p. 349; John Jordan, 'New Destroyers for Japan Will Deter Soviet Threat; Part 1: The *Hatsuyuki* and Improved *Hatsuyuki* Classes,' in *Jane's*, vol. 4, no. 4 (27 July 1985), pp. 175-8; and 'Japan Completes Sea Trials of the Destroyer *Asagiri*,' in *Jane's*, (29 February 1988), p. 326.

51. J. V. P. Goldrick and P. D. Jones, 'The Far-

Eastern Navies,' in *Proceedings*, vol. 111, no. 3 (March 1985), pp. 60-1; vol. 112, no. 3 (March 1986), pp. 64-5; and vol. 113, no. 3 (March 1987), p. 65; Kensuke Ebata, 'Japan Defence Budget to Exceed 1% of GNP,' in *Jane's*, vol. 7, no. 1 (10 January 1987), p. 3; 'Japanese Increase Defence Spending Levels,' vol. 4, no. 15 (12 October 1985), p. 79; and Japan Urged to Take Greater Share of Costs,' vol. 12, no. 6 (12 August 1989), p. 236; Hiroshi Doi, 'Self-Defense Is Enough,' in *Proceedings*, vol. 113, no. 3 (March 1987), pp. 94-8; Kensuke Ebata, 'Ocean Air Defense Japanese Style,' in *Proceedings*, vol. 113, no. 3 (March 1987), pp. 98-101; *Jane's Fighting Ships, 1986-1987*, p. 131; *1988-1989*, p. 122; and *1989-1990*, p. 93.

52. 'Japanese Defence Budget to Rise by 6.35% Next Year,' in *Jane's*, vol. 12, no. 3 (22 July 1989), p. 105; Kensuke Ebata, 'Japan Approves 6.1% for FY91,' in *Jane's*, vol. 13, no. 2 (13 January 1990), p. 51.

53. 'UK Pulls Out of NFR 90 over Timetable,' in Jane's, vol. 12, no. 14 (7 October 1989), p. 726; 'NFR 90: The Pains of Collaboration,' in *Jane's*, vol. 12, no. 15 (14 October 1989), p. 783; and Barbara Starr, 'NFR 90: USN "Had No Official Interest,"' in *Jane's*, vol. 12, no. 15 (14 October 1989), p. 762.

54. 'Taft Hits Out over Burden Sharing,' in *Jane's*, vol. 10, no. 15 (15 October 1988), p. 908; 'Allies Must Take Bigger Share of Burden,' in *Jane's*, vol. 12, no. 2 (15 July 1989), p. 78; and 'Liberals Put Freeze on Danish Budget,' in *Jane's*, vol. 10, no. 18 (5 November 1988), p. 1120.

55. *Conway's, Part I*, p. 98; Bjarne Grimsvedt, 'Norwegian Maritime Operations,' in *Proceedings*, vol. 112, no. 3 (March 1986), pp. 147-9; Stephen S. Roberts, 'Western European and NATO Navies,' in *Proceedings*, vol. 107, no. 3 (March 1981), p. 34; and *Jane's Fighting Ships, 1980-1981*, p. 137; *1986-1987*, p. 119; and *1987-1988*, p. 131.

56. M. G. M. W. Ellis, 'Sweden's Ghosts?' in *Proceedings*, vol. 112, no. 3 (March 1986), pp. 94-100; Norman Friedman, 'Western European and NATO Navies 1984,' pp. 44-5; 'Shallow Water ASW: Sweden's Problems,' in *Jane's*, vol. 5, no. 2 (18 January 1986), p. 66; '"Whiskey" on the Rocks,' in *Proceedings*, vol. 108, no. 4 (April 1982), pp. 112-15; and 'Submarine Incursions into Swedish Waters Continue,' in *Jane's*, vol. 8, no. 17 (31 October 1987), p. 979.

57. Claes Tornberg, 'Sweden Rethinks Its Strategy,' in *Proceedings*, vol. 116, no. 3 (March 1990), pp. 80-4; Milan Vego, 'The Royal Swedish Navy,' in *Proceedings*, vol. 108, no. 3 (March 1982), p. 131; Lars Wedin, 'The Royal Swedish Navy in Transition,' in *Proceedings*, vol. 111, no. 3 (March 1985), pp. 182-3; 'Swedish Missile Corvette *Göteborg* Launched,' in *Jane's*, vol. 11, no. 16 (29 April 1989), p. 729; Michael N. Pocalyko, 'Neutral Sweden Toughens NATO's Northern Tier,' in *Proceedings*, vol. 113, no. 3

(March 1987), pp. 128-30; Gison Rapp, '"Vulnerable" Sweden to Boost Defence Budget,' in *Jane's*, vol. 10, no. 10 (19 November 1988), p. 1269; 'Sweden Needs 3% Higher Defence Budget,' in *Jane's*, vol. 10, no. 6 (22 October 1988), p. 985; and *Jane's Fighting Ships, 1989-1990*, p. 85.

58. Jorgen F. Bork, 'Crisis Management in Denmark,' in *Proceedings*, vol. 108, no. 3 (March 1982), p. 109; David Foquet, 'Denmark Sets Tough Nuclear Test,' in *Jane's* (7 May 1988), p. 887; 'New Move in Danish Row with NATO,' in *Jane's* (30 April 1988), p. 819; Friedman, 'Western European and NATO Navies, 1986,' p. 47; 'Denmark "Indifferent" to NATO Defense, Says Taft,' in *Jane's* (30 July 1988), p. 156; Nils Boesgaard, 'Danish Navy Mothballs Major Surface Warships,' in *Jane's* (23 January 1988), p. 115; 'Denmark Agrees Zero Growth Defense Budget,' in *Jane's*, vol. 11, no. 11 (18 March 1989), p. 428; and 'Liberals Put Freeze on Danish Budget,' in *Jane's*, vol. 10, no. 18 (5 November 1988), p. 1120.

59. *Conway's, Part I*, pp. 261-9; Milan Vego, 'East European Navies,' in *Proceedings*, vol. 108, no. 3 (March 1982), pp. 43-7; vol. 108, no. 3 (March 1983), pp. 43-6; vol. 110, no. 3 (March 1984), p. 44; vol. 111, No. 3 (March 1985), pp. 46-7; Milan Vego, vol. 112, no. 3 (March 1986), p. 49; vol. 116, no. 3 (March 1990), pp. 130-5; and *Jane's Fighting Ships, 1980-1981*, p. 137; *1981-1982*, p. 139; *1982-1983*, p. 131; *1983-1984*, p. 145; *1984-1985*, p. 139; *1985-1986*, pp. 137, 139, 147; *1986-1987*, p. 135; and *1988-1989*, p. 122.

60. J. D. Doorman, 'Upgrading the Royal Netherlands Navy,' in *Proceedings*, vol. 110, no. 3 (March 1984), pp. 184-5; Roy L. Leverich, 'Inside the Royal Netherlands Navy,' in *Proceedings*, vol. 107, no. 3 (March 1981), pp. 90-6; 'Dutch Central Front Force Gets Priority,' in *Jane's* (24 September 1988), p. 688; 'Last Van Speijk Frigate Sold to Indonesia,' in *Jane's*, vol. 11, no. 21 (27 May 1989), p. 987; 'M Class Frigate "Vulnerable",' in *Jane's*, vol. 12, no. 12 (23 September 1989), p. 555; 'Third M Class Frigate Launched,' in *Jane's*, vol. 13, no. 1 (6 January 1990), p. 15; and *Jane's Fighting Ships, 1980-1981*, p. 137; *1981-1982*, p. 141; *1982-1983*, p. 133; *1983-1984*, p. 146; *1984-1985*, p. 140; and *1986-1987*, pp. 135, 137.

61. *Conway's, Part I*, pp. 101-6; Labayle Couhat, p. 484; Richard H. Purnell, 'New Carrier for Tomorrow's Spanish Armada,' in *Proceedings*, vol. 110, no. 3 (March 1984), pp. 177-9; Richard H. Purnell, 'An Armada for the 1990s,' in *Proceedings*, vol. 111, no. 3 (March 1985), pp. 172-4; 'Aboard *Santa Maria*: Spain's Newest Frigate,' in *Jane's* (12 September 1987), pp. 537, 539, 541; Scott C. Truver, 'Naval Dimensions of Spain in NATO,' in *Proceedings*, vol. 112, no. 3 (March 1986), pp. 154-7; and *Jane's Fighting Ships, 1980-1981*, p. 139; *1981-1982*, p. 141; *1982-1983*, p. 133; *1984-1985*, p. 140; *1986-1987*, p.

214 1980 — 1988

137; and *1987-1988*, p. 131.

62. Michele Cosentino, 'Keeper of NATO's Southern Flank,' in *Proceedings*, vol. 116, no. 3 (March 1990), pp. 96-8; and Stephen S. Roberts, 'Western European and NATO Navies,' in *Proceedings*, vol. 107, no. 3 (March 1981), p. 33.

63. Labayle Couhat, pp. 300-02; Alfredo Brauzzi, 'The Fall and Rise of the Italian Navy,' in *Proceedings*, vol. 113, no. 3 (March 1987), pp. 156-7; Ezio Bonsignore, '*Giuseppe Garibaldi*: The Italian Navy's TDC,' in *Proceedings*, vol. 108, no. 3 (March 1982), pp. 134-5; and Norman Friedman, 'Western European and NATO Navies,' in *Proceedings*, vol. 113, no. 3 (March 1987), pp. 44-5.

64. Labayle Couhat, pp. 302-8; Norman Friedman, 'Western European and NATO Navies,' in *Proceedings*, vol. 116, no. 3 (March 1990), p. 123; and vol. 112, no. 3 (March 1986), pp. 36-48; and *Jane's Fighting Ships, 1980-1981*, p. 137; *1982-1983*, p. 131; *1983-1984*, p. 145; *1984-1985*, p. 139; *1985-1986*, p. 147; and *1988-1989*, p. 122.

65. *Jane's Fighting Ships, 1989-1990*, p. 89.

66. Labayle Couhat, pp. 249-52; *Jane's Fighting Ships, 1980-1981*, pp. 131, 137; *1981-1982*, p. 139; *1982-1983*, p. 131; *1983-1984*, p. 145; and *1987-1988*, p. 131; and Gillian Whittaker, 'Greece Confirms US Base Closure,' in *Jane's* (13 August 1988), p. 241.

67. Stephen Chadwick, 'Eastern Anchor of NATO,' in *Proceedings*, vol. 111, no. 3 (March 1985), pp. 131-2; 'Turkey Steps Up Naval Force with Latest Koln Frigate,' in *Jane's*, vol. 11, no. 24 (17 June 1989), p. 1219; Gillian Whittaker, 'Greece Confirms US Base Closure,' in *Jane's* (13 August 1988), p. 251; 'Greek Protest Over US Frigates for Turkey,' in *Jane's*, vol. 11, no. 15 (15 April 1989), p. 632; and *Jane's Fighting Ships, 1980-1981*, p. 139; *1981-1982*, p. 141; *1982-1983*, p. 133; *1983-1984*, p. 146; *1984-1985*, p. 140; *1986-1987*, pp. 515-23; *1987-1988*, p. 133; and *1988-1989*, p. 123.

68. *Jane's Fighting Ships, 1988-1989*, p. 109.

69. Bruce George MP and Mark Stenhouse, 'Turkey Comes to Terms with Its Vulnerability,' in *Jane's* (2 July 1988), pp. 1374-6, 1379; 'Greece Protests to Turkey over Shots,' in *Jane's*, vol. 6, no. 12 (27 September 1986), p. 655; and Gillian Whittaker, 'Greek Protest over Airspace Violation,' in *Jane's* (5 March 1988), p. 388.

70. Labayle Couhat, pp. 491-520; Michael Vlahos, 'Middle Eastern, North African, and South Asian Navies,' in *Proceedings*, vol. 112, no. 3 (March 1986), p. 55; 'Soviets to Expand Tartus Base,' in *Jane's* (21 May 1988), p. 1035; and *Jane's Fighting Ships, 1981-1982*, p. 141; *1983-1984*, p. 146; *1985-1986*, p. 149; and *1986-1987*, p. 137. The facility consisted of one fixed and two floating piers, logistical supply dumps, and a C³ facility, and could service ships as large as Soviet *Kara* cruisers. (See: Simon Elliott, 'Syrian Base Boosts Soviet Power,' in *Jane's*, vol. 12, no. 4 (29 July 1989), p. 154.)

71. Labayle Couhat, pp. 294-6; Michael Vlahos, 'Middle Eastern, North African, and South Asian Navies,' in *Proceedings*, vol. 116, no. 3 (March 1990), p. 139; Eli Rahav, 'Missile Boat Warfare: Israeli Style,' in *Proceedings*, vol. 112, no. 3 (March 1986), pp. 107-13; Clyde Owan, 'The Arab-Israeli Naval Imbalance,' in *Proceedings*, vol. 108, no. 3 (March 1983), p. 109; and *Jane's Fighting Ships, 1980-1981*, p. 137; *1981-1982*, p. 139; *1982-1983*, p. 131; *1983-1984*, p. 145; and *1988-1989*, p. 122.

72. Labayle Couhat, pp. 109-11; William L. Dowdy III, 'Middle Eastern, North African, and South Asian Navies,' in *Proceedings*, vol. 108, no. 3 (March 1982), p. 48; Simon Elliott, 'Egypt Set to Buy Walrus, Oberon,' in *Jane's*, vol. 11, no. 18 (6 May 1989), p. 801; 'Egyptian Navy to Buy ex-RN Submarines,' in *Jane's*, vol. 12, no. 14 (7 October 1989), p. 701; and *Jane's Fighting Ships, 1980-1981*, p. 137; *1981-1982*, p. 139; *1983-1984*, p. 145; *1984-1985*, p. 139; *1985-1986*, p. 147; and *1989-1990*, p. 89.

73. Labayle Couhat, pp. 375-9; Dowdy, p. 49; Selcuk Emre and Antony Preston, 'Soviet Frigate New Naval Reinforcement for Libya,' in *Jane's*, vol. 5, no. 26 (5 July 1986), p. 1275; Raphael Danziger, 'Mediterranean: Qadhafi's Choke Point?' in *Proceedings*, vol. 108, no. 3 (March 1982), p. 139; and *Jane's Fighting Ships, 1985-1986*, p. 133; *1986-1987*, pp. 137, 340-5; *1987-1988*, p. 131; and *1989-1990*, p. 89.

74. Labayle Couhat, pp. 1–4; and *Jane's Fighting Ships, 1986-1987, pp.* 4-6; *1988-1989*, p. 122; and *1989-1990*, p. 89.

75. Norman L. Dodd, 'African Navies South of the Sahara,' in *Proceedings*, vol. 108, no. 3 (March 1982), pp. 53-7; vol. 110, no. 3 (March 1984), pp. 56-7; and vol. 112, no. 3 (March 1986), p. 60; Robert L. Scheina, 'African Navies South of the Sahara,' in *Proceedings*, vol. 108, no. 3 (March 1982), p. 58; James E. Meason, 'African Navies South of the Sahara,' in *Proceedings*, vol. 113, no. 3 (March 1987), pp. 62-3; and 'South African Defence Budget Rises by 22.6%,' in *Jane's*, vol. 9, no. 12 (26 March 1988), p. 567.

76. Labayle Couhat, pp. 4, 32-3, 64; A. K. du Toit, 'African Navies South of the Sahara,' in *Proceedings*, vol. 116, no. 3 (March 1990), pp. 144-9; O. A. Oladijeji, 'Where Are the African Navies Going?' in *Proceedings*, vol. 116, no. 3 (March 1990), pp. 101-3; Norman L. Dodd, 'African Navies South of the Sahara,' in *Proceedings*, vol. 107, no. 3 (March 1981), pp. 47-9; vol. 111, no. 3 (March 1985), p. 56; and *Jane's Fighting Ships, 1980-1981*, pp. 131, 137; *1983-1987*, p. 145; and *1984-1985*, p. 139.

77. Robert L. Scheina, 'Latin American Navies,' in *Proceedings*, vol. 107, no. 3 (March 1981), pp. 22-3; Jeffrey G. Gilmore, 'Canada's Defense Débâcle,' in *Proceedings*, vol. 108, no. 3 (March 1982), pp. 110-16; Norman Friedman, 'Western European and NATO Navies,' in *Proceedings*, vol. 113, no. 3 (March 1986), pp. 46-7; and vol.

113, no. 3 (March 1987), pp. 44-5; Sharon Hobson, 'Canadian Senate Salvo,' in *Proceedings*, vol. 110, no. 3 (March 1984), pp. 147-8; P. J. Taggert, 'Canada's Blind Spot,' in *Proceedings*, vol. 113, no. 3 (March 1987), pp. 144-9; John G. H. Halstead, 'Canada's Navy is Coming Back,' in *Proceedings*, vol. 112, no. 3 (March 1986), pp. 79, 82-3; Sharon Hobson, 'Canadian Naval Modernization Programmes,' in *Jane's*, vol. 4, no. 3 (20 July 1985), pp. 133-5; Sharon Hobson, 'Canada Cancels Submarine Plans,' in *Jane's*, vol. 11, no. 18 (6 May 1989), p. 788; and 'Canada Reconsidering SSKs After SSN Cancellation,' in *Jane's*, vol. 11, no. 20 (20 May 1989), p. 907.

78. *Conway's, Part II*, pp. 413-14; Robert L. Scheina, 'Latin American Navies,' in *Proceedings*, vol. 108, no. 3 (March 1982), pp. 31-2; and *Jane's Fighting Ships, 1989-1990*, p. 95.

79. *Jane's Fighting Ships, 1984-1985*, p. 140; and *1986–1987*, p. 137.

80. *Conway's, Part II*, pp. 419-20; *Jane's Fighting Ships, 1983-1984*, p. 145.

81. *Conway's, Part II*, pp. 412, 416, 422-4, 428; and *Jane's Fighting Ships, 1980-1981*, pp. 137, 139; *1981-1982*, p. 141; *1982-1983*, p. 133; *1983-1984*, pp. 145, 146; and *1985-1986*, p. 147.

82. *Conway's, Part II*, pp. 404; Eduardo Italo Pesce: 'The Brazilian Naval Modernization Program,' in *Proceedings*, vol. 108, no. 3 (March 1982), pp. 145-8; 'The Brazilian Mark-10 Frigates,' vol. 107, no. 3 (March 1981), p. 127; 'A Case for a V/STOL Brazilian Air Arm,' vol. 108, no. 3 (March 1983), pp. 127-31; 'Brazilian Navy Progress Report,' vol. 110, no. 3 (March 1984), pp. 157-60; 'Brazilian Navy Update,' vol. 110, no. 3 (March 1984), pp. 185-7' 'Brazil's Navy Must Wait,' vol. 113, no. 3 (March 1987), pp. 134-8; Robert Scheina: 'Latin American Navies,' in *Proceedings*, vol. 112, no. 3 (March 1986), pp. 34-5; vol. 113, no. 3 (March 1987), p. 37; vol. 116, no. 3 (March 1990), p. 112.

83. Labayle Couhat, pp. 5-7; E. J. Kurzanski, 'The Armada Argentina,' in *Proceedings*, vol. 107, no. 3 (March 1981), p. 135; Robert L. Sheina, 'Latin American Navies,' in *Proceedings* vol. 111, no. 3 (March 1985), pp. 34-5; and *Jane's Fighting Ships, 1980-1981*, p. 137; *1981-1982*, p. 139; *1982-1983*, p. 131; *1983-1984*, p. 145; *1984-1985*, p. 139; *1985-1986*, p. 147; and *1988-1989*, p. 122.

84. Labayle Couhat, pp. 64-7; and *Jane's Fighting Ships, 1982-1983*, p. 131; *1984-1985*, p. 139; *1985-1986*, p. 147; and *1986-1987*, p. 135.

85. Labayle Couhat, pp. 267-73; Charles Sills, 'Middle Eastern Navies,' in *Proceedings*, vol. 107, no. 3 (March 1981), p. 46; Joel Larus, 'India: The Neglected Service Faces the Future,' in *Proceedings*, vol. 107, no. 3 (March 1981), p. 77; William L. Dowdy, III, 'Middle Eastern, North African, and South Asian Navies,' in *Proceedings*, vol. 108, no. 3 (March 1982), pp. 48-55; Michael Vlahos, 'Middle Eastern, North African, and South Asian Navies,' in *Proceed-*

ings, vol. 112, no. 3 (March 1986), pp. 57-8; vol. 113, no. 3 (March 1987), pp. 55-6; C. U. Bhaskar, 'Indian NavAir,' in *Proceedings*, vol. 113, no. 3 (March 1987), p. 108; 'Indian Navy Greets First Nuclear-Powered Submarine,' in *Jane's* (13 February 1988), p. 241; 'India's SSGN Identified,' in *Jane's* (6 February 1988), p. 199; and *Jane's Fighting Ships, 1980-1981*, p. 137; *1981-1982*, p. 139; *1983-1984*, p. 145; *1984-1985*, p. 139; *1985-1986*, p. 147; *1986-1987*, pp. 127, 135; and *1987-1988*, p. 131.

86. 'Second "Charlie I" Set for Indian Navy,' in *Jane's*, vol. 12, no. 17 (28 October 1989), p. 893; Sadananda Mukherjee, 'India Sets Date for New Aircraft Carrier,' in *Jane's*, vol. 11, no. 23 (10 June 1989), p. 1124; 'Army and Navy Bear Brunt of Indian Budget Cuts,' vol. 11, no. 10 (11 March 1989), p. 386; 'India's New Relationship with USA,' vol. 12, no. 17 (28 October 1989): p. 912; *Jane's Fighting Ships, 1989-1990*, p. 91; and M. K. Roy, 'The Indian Navy from the Bridge,' in *Proceedings*, vol. 116, no. 3 (March 1990), pp. 66-8, 70, 72-4.

87. Labayle Couhat, pp. 432-4; Keith Jacobs, 'Pakistan's Navy,' in *Proceedings*, vol. 110, no. 3 (March 1984), p. 150; Michael Vlahos, 'Middle Eastern, North African, and South Asian Navies,' in *Proceedings*, vol. 113, no. 3 (March 1987), p. 55; 'Pakistan Buys Weapons for Ex-US Frigates,' in *Jane's*, vol. 11, no. 24 (17 June 1989), p. 1223; Desmond Wettern, 'Pakistan and UK in Navy Talks,' in *Jane's*, vol. 9, no. 16 (23 April 1988), p. 780; Mark Montgomery, 'The US–Pakistani Connection,' in *Proceedings*, vol. 116, no. 7 (July 1989), pp. 67-73; 'Major Modernization for Pakistan Navy,' in *Jane's* (9 April 1988), p. 673; 'India Accuses Pakistan Over Arms,' in *Jane's* (30 April 1988), p. 831; and *Jane's Fighting Ships, 1980-1981*, p. 139; *1981-1982*, p. 141; *1982-1983*, p. 133; *1983-1984*, p. 146; *1984-1985*, p. 140; and *1989-1990*, p. 91.

88. Labayle Couhat, pp. 114-15, 469-71, 498, 626-7; *Jane's Fighting Ships, 1980-1981*, p. 139; *1981-1982*, pp. 139, 141; *1983-1984*, p. 145; *1984-1985*, pp. 139-40, and *1985-1986*, p. 147.

89. Labayle Couhat, pp. 290-2; Michael Vlahos, 'Middle Eastern, North African, and South Asian Navies,' in *Proceedings*, vol. 111, no. 3 (March 1985), pp. 53-4; and *Jane's Fighting Ships, 1980-1981*, pp. 133, 137; *1981-1982*, p. 139; *1983-1984*, p. 145; *1984-1985*, p. 139; *1985-1986*, p. 147; *1986-1987*, p. 135; and *1989-1990*, p. 91. For good summaries of the war's events, see: Raphael Danziger, 'The Naval Race in the Persian Gulf,' in *Proceedings*, vol. 108, no. 3 (March 1982), p. 98; 'Naval Line-up in the Persian Gulf,' in *Jane's*, vol. 8, no. 12 (26 September 1987), pp. 671-3; Tony Banks, 'Running the Gauntlet in the Gulf,' in *Jane's*, vol. 8, no. 4 (1 August 1987), p. 182; James Bruce, 'Unprecedented Iranian Naval Build-up,' in *Jane's*, vol. 8, no. 1 (11 July 1987), p. 15; '*Stark* Locked on to Mirage Seconds Before Impact,' in

Jane's, vol. 7, no. 25 (13 June 1987), pp. 1164-5; and '*Stark* Design Questioned After Iraqi Attack,' in *Jane's*, vol. 7, no. 21 (30 May 1987), p. 1040.

90. *Jane's Fighting Ships, 1984-1985*, p. 139; and *1986-1987*, p. 135.

91. Labayle Couhat, pp. 366-70; Hideo Sekino, 'Asian Navies,' in *Proceedings*, vol. 107, no. 3 (March 1981), pp. 52-9; Robert Karniol, 'South Korea: Preparing to Fill the Arms Gap?' in *Jane's*, vol. 11, no. 7 (18 February 1989), pp. 270-1; J. V. P. Goldrick and P. D. Jones, 'The Far Eastern Navies,' in *Proceedings*, vol. 112, no. 3 (March 1986), p. 66; vol. 113, no. 3 (March 1987), p. 67; and *Jane's Fighting Ships, 1981-1982*, p. 133; *1982-1983*, p. 131; *1983-1984*, p. 145; and *1989-1990*, p. 93. An excellent analysis of the North Korean and insight into South Korean fears concerning the same are contained in Kim Hyun-ki, 'North Korea Aims South,' in *Proceedings*, vol. 116, no. 3 (March 1990), pp. 40-1, 43.

92. Labayle Couhat, pp. 521-9; 'Taiwan Confirms Frigate Plans, But Numbers Drop to Eight,' in *Jane's*, vol. 10, no. 10 (19 November 1988), p. 1252; Jaques Isnard, 'Taiwan in $1.8bn Frigate Deal,' in *Jane's*, vol. 13, no. 2 (13 January 1990), p. 46; and *Jane's Fighting Ships, 1981-1982*, p. 141; *1982-1983*, p. 133; *1983-1984*, p. 146; *1985-1986*, p. 147; *1986-1987*, p. 135; *1987-1988*, p. 131; and *1988-1989*, p. 123.

93. Burrell H. Landes, Jr., 'Sino-Soviet Relations Since the Death of Mao Zedong,' in *Naval War College Review*, vol. 32, no. 5 (Sept-Oct 1979), pp. 29-47; Desmond Wettern, ' P. R. C. Navy Close-Up,' in *Proceedings*, vol. 107, no. 3 (March 1981), pp. 126-7; J. V. P. Goldrick and P. D. Jones, 'Far Eastern Navies,' in *Proceedings*, vol. 108, no. 3 (March 1982), pp. 61-3; vol. 108, no. 3 (March 1983), p. 59; vol. 112, no. 3 (March 1986), p. 65; David G. Muller, 'China's SSBN in Perspective,' in *Proceedings*, vol. 108, no. 3 (March 1983), p. 125; 'Record-Breaking Trial for China's "Xia",' *Jane's*, vol. 7, no. 2 (17 January 1987), p. 54; Bradley Hahn, 'China: Emerging Sea Power,' in *Proceedings*, vol. 111, no. 3 (March 1985), pp. 102-7; 'Hai Fang,' vol. 112, no. 3 (March 1986), pp. 119-20; Andrew Li, 'The "Luta" Fleet,' in *Proceedings*, vol. 108, no. 3 (March 1982), pp. 131-2; 'Two New Warship Types for PLA Navy,' in *Jane's*, vol. 6, no. 4 (2 August 1986), p. 146; Gordon Jacobs and Raymond Cheung, 'China's "Jianghu" Frigate Program,' in *Jane's*, vol. 7, no. 11 (21 March 1987), pp. 507, 509; 'China's Drastic Cut in Defense Budget,' in *Jane's*, vol. 8, no. 9 (5 September 1987), p. 412; G. Jacobs, 'China's

Coastal Forces,' in *Jane's*, vol. 3, no. 11 (16 March 1985), pp. 450, 452, 454, 456-7; 'Chinese Navy Shows Its Defects,' in *Jane's*, vol. 8, no. 30 (20 August 1988), p. 295; and *Jane's Fighting Ships, 1980-1981*, p. 137; *1982-1983*, p. 131; *1983-1984*, p. 145; *1985-1986*, p. 147; *1986-1987*, p. 135; *1987-1988*, p. 131 and *1989-1990*, pp. 83, 93.

94. Labayle Couhat, pp. 363, 847-9; *Jane's Fighting Ships, 1981-1982*, p. 141; *1984-1985*, p. 140; *1985-1986*, p. 147; and *1986-1987*, pp. 135, 808-9.

95. Labayle Couhat, pp. 276-82, 379-383; J. V. P. Goldrick and P. D. Jones, 'The Far Eastern Navies,' in *Proceedings*, vol. 112, no. 3 (March 1986), pp. 68-9; vol. 113, no. 3 (March 1987), pp. 68-9; Joseph Morgan, 'Enough Navy for the Job?' in *Proceedings*, vol. 110, no. 3 (March 1984), pp. 112-13; and *Jane's Fighting Ships, 1980-1981*, p. 137; and *1983-1984*, p. 139.

96. Robert E. Stumpf, 'A Look at the Future of Australia's Fleet Air Arm,' in *Proceedings*, vol. 107, no. 3 (March 1981), p. 130; Geoffrey Evans, 'America's Ally "Down Under",' in *Proceedings*, vol. 107, no. 3 (March 1981), p. 87; J. V. P. Goldrick and P. D. Jones, 'Far Eastern Navies,' in *Proceedings*, vol. 108, no. 3 (March 1982), pp. 62-3, 65; vol. 10, no. 3 (March 1984), p. 65; vol. 112, no. 3 (March 1986), p. 69; vol. 113, no. 3 (March 1987), p. 70; Stephen S. Roberts, 'Western European and NATO Navies,' in *Proceedings*, vol. 108, no. 3 (March 1983), p. 41; Cort D. Wagner, 'Australia,' in *Proceedings*, vol. 108, no. 3 (March 1983), pp. 85-6, 88-90; and Thomas-Durell Young, '"Self-Reliance" and Force Development in the RAN,' in *Proceedings*, vol. 112, no. 3 (March 1986), pp. 159-62. For an excellent discussion of Australian defense problems and its failure to develop a coherent strategy, see: John Kenny, 'Still in Need of a Defense Strategy,' in *Proceedings*, vol. 116, no. 3 (March 1990), pp. 50-5. An excellent discussion on the duties of the Royal Australian Air Force is found in Peter B. Layton, 'The RAAF in Maritime Operations,' in *Proceedings*, vol. 116, no. 3 (March 1990), pp. 56-9. The article does present what appears to be an unrealistically optimistic picture of co-operation between the Air Force and Navy, however.

97. 'Defending New Zealand After ANZUS,' in *Jane's*, vol. 9, no. 6 (13 February 1988), pp. 263-5; Roger Foley and Frank Cranston, 'Consortia Tighten ANZAC Costs,' in *Jane's*, vol. 11, no. 23 (10 June 1989), p. 1113; Roger Foley: ' N. Zealand Forces Set for Major Shake-Up,' in *Jane's*, vol. 11, no. 23 (10 June 1989), p. 1113; 'NZ Forces Face Major Crisis,' vol. 11, no. 11 (18 March 1989), p. 1113; and *Jane's Fighting Ships, 1983-1984*, pp. 139, 146.

6
Toward a Kinder, Gentler, More Peaceful World? The 1990s and Beyond

THE EFFECTS OF THE INFLUENCING FACTORS

The events of 1989 were so dramatic and unprecedented that together they made that year one of the three or four most important thus far in this century, on a level with those two dreadful days in August 1945 when atomic weapons were exploded over Japan to bring the Second World War to an end. In one sense the year meant the conclusion of a virtually non-violent war and therefore signalled the end of an era. The Iraqi invasion of Kuwait in August 1990 meant the birth of another period, marked by the importance of several naval powers instead of only two, as had been the case for several decades. Thus we may come to call the period from 1945 to 1989 the 'Soviet-American Period', 'the Superpower Period', 'the NATO-Soviet Bloc Period', or by some equally catchy phrase that historians coin and which do more to cloud and gloss over the complexities of an era than they do to explain them.

The Significance of 1989 – An End to the Third World War?

In Chapter 5, it was noted that the intense US–Soviet military R&D competition was a non-violent type of quasi-war, one which both nations had made massive efforts to win.[1] And just as so often happens in a violent war, the effects of this competition were such that the economy of one was virtually ruined. Realizing that this was the case, the Soviet Union under President Gorbachev took actions dramatically to alter the tenor of the East–West relationship. While the United States did not realize it, it had emerged victorious and was in a very strong position, able to influence very significantly subsequent affairs. In essence, if the Third World War had in fact occurred, what could we expect of the peace that would follow? In most peace treaties, the loser is willing to make the requisite political and social changes and territorial concessions that are demanded by the victor. The question, then, was how far was the Soviet Union willing to go in respect of revising the world order? The answer was given and it made 1989 a most exceptional year.

To summarize the situation in January 1989, the United States saw George Bush inaugurated as President, thereby ending the eight-year Reagan era. During that period, the US Navy had experienced a revival, as scores of new ships and submarines were built. But this had cost a great deal and, to a large extent, it was the doing of the 'great communicator,' who had convinced the public that minimizing spending in the civilian sector was necessary in order to provide for the nation's defenses. Even before President Reagan left office, there were signs that this might be nearing an end. John Lehman's departure was an omen and James Webb's was proof that there were harder times ahead for the Navy. George Bush's accession provided further uncertainty, because capable and experienced though he was, it would be difficult for anyone to match his predecessor's communicative skill and charismatic relationship with the US public. Thus, the Navy faced 1989 with uncertainty.

By January 1989, much of NATO had had just about enough of the cold war. Canada, after seriously considering a fleet of nuclear-powered attack submarines, had decided against incurring such an expense. Scandinavia had become more and more neutral, defense spending in Norway and Sweden was inadequate for their defense needs, and Denmark's actions were tantamount to a rebellion by the Danish Social Democrats. West Germany had become increasingly dissatisfied with the foreign, particularly US, troops on its territory and its defense spending was less than adequate from the US perspective.[2] Great Britain, after considering the Falklands War, decided against significantly increasing her naval appropriations, while France had worked more closely with NATO in recent years, but had maintained her independence. Everyone in Europe looked forward to the new Union in the 1990s, hoping that it would create an economic power that could compete more effectively on the international market. On the southern European flank, Spanish and Italian naval developments, although their pace had slowed, none the less were continued. Greece and Turkey continued their development, but possibly more with the intention of winning a Greco-Turkish war than one against the Soviet Union.

The Soviet Navy also faced an uncertain future. On the one hand, Moscow had invested heavily in naval development. The new generation of ships – *Kirov*s, *Kiev*s, *Slava*s, *Sovremennyy*s, and *Udaloy*s – were impressive modern combatants, built with more space than the earlier *Kresta*s and *Kara*s, and provided with ample weapons reloads. They were designed for sustained operations in areas distant from the Soviet Union. Moreover, the Soviet program was continuing, with the new *Tbilisi* working up, *Riga* fitting out, and a new carrier on the building ways. These were products of the navy that Admiral Gorshkov had envisioned; ships that could defend the state's interests on the high seas, far from the homeland. Conversely, President Gorbachev's perestroika program called for the right of self-determination of all nations, implying that the Soviet Union would no longer as actively support insurgent movements in the Third World. Such a renunciation of the earlier, more active foreign policy had direct implications for the Navy, because one of its missions had been to support and protect just such a policy, and without it, there would be little need for the protection. Also, there were clear indications that Moscow would reduce defense spending radically, intending to invest the savings in R&D. The residual force would be enough to assure the nation's security, but little more. Given that the USSR was a land power that had relied traditionally on her Army for protection, the Navy would be hit heavily in such reductions. Finally, Chernavin did not appear as feisty as Gorshkov and might fight far less strongly against future cutbacks in naval appropriations. Thus the

Navy, while it had made tremendous strides in the past three decades, could be less sure of its continuing success.

In 1989, naval development in the Middle East and Africa was at a low level. Likewise in Latin America, while the Cuban Navy was strong and Nicaragua had received naval aid, neither posed a particularly serious problem to regional maritime peace. Further southward, Brazil's program had been slowed, largely because Brazil did not perceive a serious naval threat to its interests. The Argentine Navy continued to develop, with possible designs on the Falklands and Antarctica. In the Indian Ocean, India was in the midst of a significant naval development program and had already amassed such power that it made its neighbors uneasy. The Iran-Iraq War had ended, bringing peace after many years of bloody conflict. Iraq garnered its forces and planned for a sudden attack on Kuwait in August 1990. In the Far East, Japan had built an impressive regional naval force and appeared to be approaching a crossroads where she would have to decide whether to remilitarize seriously. US dissatisfaction with defending Japan was increasing and it was uncertain how much longer Washington would be willing to guarantee the maritime security of the North-west Pacific. Meanwhile, the Republic of Korea supported a strong naval program with the goal of achieving a self-sufficient defense in the early 21st century. Its feud with North Korea continued, a festering sore in regional politics and defense. The People's Republic of China's Navy remained the PLA Navy, a constant reminder of the Navy's second place to the Army in Chinese defense priorities. None the less, it was developing, but unevenly, and its combat capability was uncertain. Finally in the South Pacific, Malaysia and Indonesia had invested in defense, but their navies remained inadequate for their defense needs. Largely because they did not perceive a threat, Australia and New Zealand minimized defense spending and had weak navies.

THE EVENTS OF 1989

Although naval power was not involved directly, the events of 1989 had the most significant implications for the future of world naval development and it is of value to examine and assess them. The year's significance lies in the changes in the Soviet Union and the Warsaw Pact because these reduced significantly the threat posed against NATO.

The Soviet Union

The year began in the Soviet Union with food and consumer goods shortages that seemed to grow more acute daily. On 5 January, Georgi Markov, a traditionalist hard-liner, retired as chairman of the Soviet Writers' Union, paving the way for a more liberal chairman. On the 6th, the Communist Party called for the mass rehabilitation of Soviet citizens convicted in the Stalin courts. Throughout January, Boris Yeltsin, who had been demoted from his Politburo post in 1988, openly continued his criticism of the Party and called for more rapid change. On 19 January, Gorbachev announced that the USSR would reduce its military budget by 14.2 per cent and weapons and hardware production by 19.5 per cent. The rehabilitation of Leon Trotsky and condemnation of Josef Stalin's wartime policies occurred when Marshal Georgi Zhukov's memoirs, which contained discussions of both, were released.[3]

In February, Estonia moved to sever ties with the Soviet Union, a Moscow election district revamped the means of selecting its legislators, creating a model on which future political selection should be based, the deaths of thousands of Soviet citizens killed by the Stalinists and buried in Bykovnya forest was investigated, and Jewish emigration to the West exploded in response to the new more liberal emigration laws. The Party accepted Gorbachev's sweeping agricultural reforms on 16 March, but the most stunning event in March pertained to the elections for the new national congress. The reformed voting procedures, which included secret ballots, resulted in a stunning upset, in which the mayor and second-ranking communist official of Moscow, the top five communists in Leningrad, the president and premier of Lithuania, the Estonian KGB chief, and other incumbents were defeated by candidates promising more rapid change. Two of the losers in Leningrad had even run unopposed, but still lost as voters scratched their names off the secret ballots. Boris Yeltsin won by a landslide.[4]

In April, Khruschev's famous secret speech, delivered before the Twentieth Party Congress in 1956 and never officially released in the Soviet Union, was disseminated. On 7 April, troops and armored personnel carriers were sent into the streets of Tbilisi to quell demonstrations by 100,000 people. In the following days, tanks and toxic tear-gas were used and, on 9 April, nineteen people were killed as demonstrators refused to disperse. Soviet Foreign Minister Shevardnadze was sent to investigate, the head of the Communist Party in Georgia resigned, and blame was placed on the precipitous actions of the troops. On 15 April, Moscow relaxed its policy on religion, returning hundreds of old churches to their congregations. In the coming days, so many people were baptized that the priests became exhausted, requiring them to limit baptisms to specific but lengthy periods daily. On the same day, news was released that the bodies of Tsar Nicholas II, his wife Alexandra, and their children had been unearthed in the graves where they had been placed after they were murdered on Bolshevik orders in July 1918. On 20 April, Andrei D. Sakharov, dissident Soviet physicist, was elected to the Soviet Union's new parliament. On 25 April, the Communist Party approved a sweeping purge of top-ranking political conservatives, including Andrei Gromyko, Nikolai Tikhonov, and nine generals and marshals.[5]

In May, faced with a mass of wildcat strikes, the Party passed a law giving the workers the right to strike. On 15 May, Latvian, Lithuanian, and Estonian representatives asked the United Nations to help their nations gain freedom, and on the 19th, Lithuania's legislature adopted an independence resolution. In June, the dialogue at the new National Congress of People's Deputies was unprecedented in its attacks on the Party, and included speeches by Sakharov. On 13 June, Gorbachev called for much closer economic co-operation between the USSR and West Germany, stating that the current level of trade between the two was ridiculously low. He implied that he wanted West Germany to play a much greater role in the Soviet Union's future.[6]

Ethnic violence continued in Kazakhstan and Uzbekistan and spread to Tadzhikistan. In July, two were killed and twenty people were injured in Armenian-Azerbaijani violence, while eleven were killed and 127 were injured in ethnic violence in Georgia. On 22 July, Soviet Marshal Sergei F. Akhromeyev, testifying before the US House Armed Services Committee, said that the USSR would cut tank production by 40 per cent, but that the chances for arms control were dim unless the United States took a more conciliatory approach. In July, there was a Soviet naval visit to Norfolk, Virginia, and on 25 July, 200,000 people marched on the Georgian capital, Tbilisi, demanding independence.[7]

In August, Latvia, Lithuania, and Estonia continued their drive for independence. On 20 September, three of twelve voting and two of eight non-voting members of the Politburo were ousted in a Gorbachev purge.[8] On 25 September, an Azerbaijani rail blockade of trains going to Armenia had railroad cars backed up all the way to the Baltic and ships were unable to unload goods because of the lack of cars to carry the goods away from the ports. In November, thousands marched in an alternative parade to the one commemorating the Revolution, carrying banners with inscriptions such as 'Workers of the world, please forgive us', and 'the CPSU – 72 years of aimless wandering'.

The Warsaw Pact

Events within the Warsaw Pact were equally remarkable. While the year began with promise, few anticipated the pace with which such promise would be fulfilled. In the early months, popular demonstrations were met with force. For example, in January, police used truncheons and tear-gas to disperse 5,000 demonstrators in Prague. But in almost all such cases, such official opposition soon yielded to popular demands.

In April, Solidarity was legalized in Poland, opening the way to free elections. In May, more than 100,000 people turned out for an opposition parade against the annual communist May Day festivities in Budapest. In June, Solidarity swept the elections in Poland, and in Hungary, Imre Nagy was given a hero's funeral. In August, Solidarity took power in Poland, in September, Hungary opened its borders with the West, allowing thousands of East Germans to cross the frontier, and in October, the Hungarian Communist Party changed its name to the Hungarian Socialist Party. In Germany, Honecker's hard line approach failed, he resigned on 18 October, and was soon followed by the Politburo and then the entire government. Finally, on 9 November, East Germany opened its borders as people flooded through to West Berlin. The wall subsequently was dismantled. The communist government in Czechoslovakia fell in December.[9] In sum, except in Albania, like dominoes, one after another, the communist governments fell. The last to go, Ceausescu's Romania, was also the bloodiest transition. It too finally fell, however, and Ceausescu and his wife, arrested while trying to flee the country, were summarily tried and executed.

Accompanying these changes were demands from the new eastern European leaders to revise the Soviet military occupation of their nations. Moscow's response was measured, assuring the nations that their forces would be withdrawn, but gradually.

AN ASSESSMENT OF THE SIGNIFICANCE OF THE EVENTS

Many commentators on these events believed that conditions had gotten out of hand, that they had progressed in both time and intensity at rates that far exceeded what the Soviet leadership had anticipated. There is both fiction and truth in this view.

The fiction lies in the fact that history has witnessed recent examples of similar reform and that it would have been myopic for the Soviet leadership not to have been aware of them. The first example could be found in 19th-century Russian history, when, having lost the Crimean War, the tsardom realized that, technologically, the nation was significantly behind the West. Serfdom was identified as a major factor in Russian backwardness, the serfs were freed, and the throne instituted a series of military, educational, and social reforms that were tantamount to a revolution from above. Concurrently, Russia sought and received a tremendous infusion of European financial aid and technology, as European banks invested and French, German, and English technicians went to Russia to assist in the nation's development. All of this was done to maintain Russia's strategic position among the European powers. It was believed that if such changes did not occur, Russia would slide farther downward and become a secondary European power. But, once initiated, the reforms unleashed social currents that had different ends and carried the reform in other directions that were far beyond the tsardom's strategic goals. The bombings and terrorist acts of the 1880s and the revolutionary discontent of the early 20th century were among the undesired results of a program that had been initiated by the throne. And when the Russian defeat in the Russo-Japanese War proved that Russia still had not achieved her strategic purposes, even greater reform resulted. In the wake of the Revolution of 1905. the October Manifesto, the Dumas, and additional land reforms were approved. The First World War interrupted the progression of events, prompting the revolutions of 1917 and the installation of a tyrannical communist system that was even more oppressive than the despotic tsarist system that it replaced. In some ways the throne had assured its eventual demise when it emancipated the serfs, because this unleashed social forces that eventually brought it down.

The second example was Iran. The throne had identified the national backwardness and had set about to modernize. Education was stressed, students were taught to read and the older ones were sent abroad to study in universities. The goals were similar to those of Russian tsardom: to rid the country of the backwardness that was perceived to be a strategic threat to its existence. The progression was similar in that these actions, virtually a revolution from above, unleashed undesirable and unanticipated social forces. But in Iran, it was conservative forces that eventually prevailed, deposing the Shah and establishing a despotic Islamic fundamentalist system that was far more tyrannical than the one it replaced.

Thus, these examples pertained to the phenomenon concerning the enlightened despot, and in virtually all cases of enlightened despotism in history, the despot has failed to achieve his goals. These examples were there for the Soviet leadership to consider, and we should assume that they were pondered. What then compelled them to embark on such a risky course and what did they envisage as its outcome? The answer to the first appears to be that the leadership saw no alternative. Soviet communism had proven itself to be a grossly inefficient system. Decision-making was centered in the highest levels, a phenomenon that Stalin had deliberately established and that persisted decades after his death, and this system, with its lack of incentives, had produced technological backwardness and economic stagnation. It was true that the Soviet system could garner its resources in one or two sectors, such as arms production or space exploration, and excel, but the same system was incapable of sustaining a vital economy across the board. The situation was critical. For more than two decades, 'The Soviets have been depriving themselves of a technological future by diverting up to 90 per cent of their basic science resources to one-time, short-term, 'crash project' military technologies and products to preclude continued, comparative obsolescence.'[10] This policy had not only failed to meet the technological goals, but also had produced adverse politico returns, prompting the United States to accomplish 'its largest peacetime military build-up in history'.[11] The result was that the Soviet Union had been left with a vast but inefficient military force structure, an arsenal of weapons that were fast becoming obsolete, and a scientific-technical base that could not meet the demands of re-equipping the armed forces with quality weapons in sufficient quantities.[12] Adverse effects were evident in the civilian sector as well, because the 'primacy of the military-technical sphere over the politico-social one had produced a severely distorted economy that had led to an increasing gap in the living standards between East and West, a gap that must be closed if the Soviet Union as we know it is to survive'.[13] Stated another way, Soviet defense spending had caused a responding US military build-up and subsequently the Soviet Union had been outspent, creating critical economic and strategic dilemmas in the process.

Attempting to cope with this problem, the leaders deliberately chose two aged successors who were approaching death, Andropov and Chernenko, to serve as interim leaders, in order to allow the leadership the time to select a 'younger' leader who would lead the nation into the 21st century. Their choice was Mikhail Gorbachev and a group of reformers.

It is absurd to think that a man of Gorbachev's brilliance and political acumen could not foresee the dangers of reform. However, like the Tsar and the Shah before him, he had no alternative. Thus, the decision was made to proceed with reform, with the full awareness that once it was begun, it would spawn unexpected currents and changes, some of which would be desirable, while others would not. A reasonable approach was to set the goal of enhancing the strategic power and position of the nation so that it would remain strong and to realize that all else was negotiable. Here the leadership should have realized that it might not be able to determine the type of political and social systems that would result from reform, but that the goal would be to produce a modern state that could defend the nation's interests in the world of the early 21st century. Certainly efforts would be made to influence the course of events and the outcome, but these had to be considered negotiable in the transformation that was to occur, because to attempt to overdirect the development would probably result in failure – a failure similar to the failed attempts of the enlightened despots of the past.

And what of the Russian–Soviet empire? Western commentators assumed that Moscow wanted to retain its possessions and borders. Soviet leaders may have been more realistic and may have realized that (a) the current Warsaw Pact bloc was not sufficient to assure the victory or even the survival of Russia in a war, and (b) the expense of administering and controlling the vast empire, spread across eleven time zones, was in fact, retarding Russian development. In one sense, since its earliest days in the 9th century, Russian policy had been to move out from a stronger power base on to weaker peoples, defeating and then assimilating them into the empire. Albeit with occasional setbacks, the Russian record was one of eventual victory until the débâcle in Afghanistan. The approach, then, may have been one that realized that the nationalities issue would arise very early in the reform and would be a major problem. The leadership, if it were wise, should have anticipated the possibility of having to cut some of these national areas loose to fend for themselves. The net result – the worst case situation in bureaucratic parlance – would be to lose all the national regions, leaving a federation of Slavic states. However, even this could be an acceptable result because, short of its imperialistic possessions, such a confederation would be able to define a root Slavic national identification on which, exploiting the resources of Siberia, many of which had not even been tapped, a modern, strong nation could be built that could maintain the strategic position previously enjoyed by the Soviet Union. In essence, Halford Mackinder's heartland would be free of the political distractions and financial drain that the national regions imposed and, under a new economic system, would be able to develop the region's full potential.

And what of communism? This should have been identified as another major factor in Russia's backwardness. Not only did it perpetuate mediocrity and stifle incentive, spawning cynicism (hallmarked by comments from the rank and file such as 'they pretend to pay us and we pretend to work'), but it also prompted a rather permanent alienation from the West, because Marxism–Leninism demanded that an atmosphere of hostility be maintained until the eventual victory of communism. This had to go, to be replaced it was to be hoped by a very liberal capitalist or a socialist system in which the state would exert considerable influence over economic development. Such a nation, divorced of its aura of threatening communism, might be welcomed into the great power community and assume a role similar to the great role that Russia had played through the 19th century – a leading European power that was an important factor as a leader in regional affairs. Along with this role would come economic benefits, such as access to Western technology.

Was this outcome reasonable to expect? The answer was yes, and one did not have to look backward too far into Soviet political writings to find its justification. In Chapter 1, we noted that in his secret speech to the leaders of the Bolshevik cadres in Moscow on 6 December 1920, Lenin had surveyed the international scene.[14] He stated his belief that the new Soviet Union was too weak to make a frontal assault on capitalism and would not be strong

63. A *Spruance*-class guided-missile destroyer seen while launching a Harpoon surface-to-surface missile. Harpoon is an all-weather cruise missile that can be launched by aircraft, submarines, or surface ships. The shipboard version can be launched from SAM and ASROC launchers. With inertial guidance and active homing, the surface-launched Harpoon travels at Mach 0.85 to ranges in excess of 60 nautical miles.

64. The *Virginia*-class nuclear-powered guided-missile cruiser USS *Mississippi* (CGN 40) seen operating at sea. The weapons systems are upgraded continually and all of them now are equipped with eight Tomahawk cruise missiles and are receiving the 'New Threat Upgrade' combat systems improvements.

65. The USS *Los Angeles* (SSN 688), lead ship of a multi-unit nuclear-powered attack submarine class. In service in 1976, *Los Angeles* combined the speed of the earlier *Skipjacks* with the sonar and weapon capability of the *Permit* class. Initially equipped with torpedoes, later ships were provided with twelve vertical tubes for Tomahawk, which supplements their torpedo tubes that can also fire Harpoon.

66. Three *Perry*-class guided-missiles frigates: USS *Oliver Hazard Perry* (FFG 7), USS *Antrim* (FFG 20) and USS *Jack Williams* (FFG 24), under way in formation. 51 *Perrys* were authorized in a large shipbuilding program. On 17 May 1987, USS *Stark* (FFG 31) was hit by two Iraqi-fired Exocet missiles, one of which did not explode. There were many deaths, but the ship survived and was repaired.

66

67. The USS *Alabama* (SSBN 731), which entered service in 1985, is the fifth of the *Ohio*-class nuclear-powered ballistic missile submarines. Twenty units are planned in an ongoing program, but this may be curtailed due to budget constraints. Each submarine, armed with 24 Trident C-4 or D-5 missiles, can submerge to 300 metres.

68. A Tomahawk cruise missile in flight after its test launch from an A-6 Intruder. The strategic version has a 1,400 nautical mile range, operates at an altitude from 15 to 100 metres, and at a speed of Mach 0.7. When fired from submarines, it is fired from torpedo tubes in a special container that is jettisoned when the missile leaves the water. The conventional version has a 250 nautical mile range and therefore requires external target designation.

67

68

69. The *Ticonderoga*-class guided-missile cruiser *Vincennes* (CG 49). This 27-ship class elicited considerable controversy, with differences focusing on whether it was top heavy, whether its weapons range was adequate, and whether it could accomplish the many missions that had been assigned. As such controversy subsided, *Vincennes* shot down a civilian Irani airliner in the Strait of Hormuz on 3 July 1988 while in action against Irani gunboats. An intense investigation followed and some changes were made to the ship's design.

70. Members of the 32nd Marine Amphibious Unit aboard a utility landing craft are preparing to go ashore to participate in the multi-national peacekeeping force in Beirut, Lebanon.

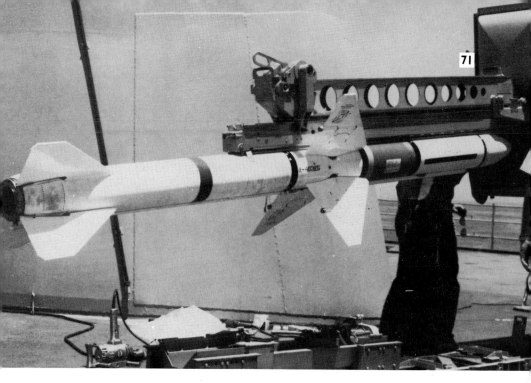

71. This photograph shows a Rim 7 Sea Sparrow missile being loaded into an eight-cell Mk-29 launcher aboard the replenishment oiler USS *Kansas City* (AOR 3). Known as the first basic point defense missile system (BPDMS), it is 3.6 metres long, weighs 204 kilograms, and has a range of eight nautical miles. The warhead of the earlier RIM 7H, consisting of expanding rods, has been replaced by one that has a blast fragmentation warhead.

72. A Phalanx Mk 15 close-in weapons system (CIWS) on board USS *Kitty Hawk* (CV 63) is shown with its barrels elevated. *Kitty Hawk*'s sister, *America* (CV 66), was the first ship to receive the system in April 1980. The Mk 15 system, designed to destroy missiles, consists of a multi-barrel gun capable of firing 3,000 rounds per minute, and two co-mounted radars that follow the target and the stream of rounds that the system fires. An improved version, which has an even greater rate of fire, entered service in 1988.

72

73. This *Oscar*-class nuclear-powered cruise missile submarine (SSGN), seen at sea in 1984, is equipped with 24 SS-N-19 SSMs that have a maximum range of 300 nautical miles. It is a major improvement over earlier Soviet SSGN classes.

74. This *Mike* titanium-hulled nuclear-powered attack submarine (SSN) was an experimental design that was launched in June 1983. She is seen here in 1986. Subsequently, she had an accident in the Norwegian Sea and sank.

75. The two *Ivan Rogov*-class landing ships, *Ivan Rogov* and *Aleksandr Nikolaev*, entered service in 1978 and 1982, respectively. *Rogov* has bow doors and an articulating cargo ramp which leads to a vehicle cargo deck forward, a stern door that provides access to a floodable well deck aft, and a helicopter hanger for four Helix helicopters. The ability to launch air-cushion vehicles, to beach, and to deploy helicopters was a vast improvement over the existing Soviet naval amphibious capability. *Rogov* deployed initially to the Pacific Fleet in 1979, and subsequently returned to the Baltic. Both she and *Nikolaev* are currently attached to the Pacific Fleet.

76. This *Sovremennyy*-class guided-missile destroyer (DDG) is seen at sea in February 1986. Using the same hull form and propulsion, *Sovremennyy*'s design is derived from that of *Kresta I* and *II*, although she is significantly larger than either of them. Primarily intended for anti-surface warfare missions, including anti-ship, shore bombardment and anti-air defense, she complements well the capabilities of the *Udaloy* DDG, Seven *Sovremennyy*s were in service in 1987.

77. Eight *Udaloy*-class guided-missile destroyers were in service by 1988. The *Admiral Spiridov* is seen at sea in this photograph. Note the two helo hangars aft that house two Helix helicopters. *Udaloy* is intended largely for ASW, but is equipped with SA-N-9 vertical SAM launchers and anti-aircraft and dual-purpose guns, which enhance her capability. At 6,500 tons, she is larger than the earlier *Kresta* and *Kynda* cruisers, reflecting the growth in Soviet surface combatants as they were provided with greater sustainability and more sophisticated weapons and electronics suites.

77

78. A *Slava*-class cruiser is seen at sea. The lead ship, *Slava*, entered service in 1982, while a second ship, *Admiral Ustinov*, participated in a Soviet port visit to Norfolk, Virginia in the summer of 1989. At 10,000 tons, the *Slava* is a smart-looking ship, but has many systems that are not of the latest type in the Soviet system. None the less, her SSM and SAM systems and ASW rocket-launchers provide her with a considerable multi-purpose capability.

79. The *Kirov*-class nuclear-powered guided-missile cruiser *Frunze* is seen at sea. The world's largest cruisers, the *Kirov*s might more accurately be classified as battlecruisers or pocket battleships. *Frunze* is deployed to the Pacific Fleet and *Kirov* to the Northern Fleet. A third unit, *Kalinin*, has been built, and a fourth unit is under construction. Because of her size, *Kirov* is a dramatic departure from Western naval trends away from such large ships. The *Kirov*s are certainly capable of operating independently, but would also make excellent escorts for *Tbilisi*, the new aircraft carrier, or for the *Kiev*-class V/STOL carriers.

80. Type 21 *Amazon*-class frigate HMS *Antelope* (F 170), second of a class of eight ships, entered service in July 1975. The class was the result of shipbuilders' lobbying against MOD design requirements and was their solution to the need for a more reasonable ship design. The cost was still high, the ship lacked sufficient space to accept newer systems, and the aluminium superstructure was considered a liability in combat. Two units, *Ardent* (F 184) and *Antelope* (F 170), were lost in the Falkland Islands War. Because of their design problems the ships were not modernized.

81. This Type 22 ASW frigate, HMS *Broadsword* (F 88), the lead ship of a four-unit class, entered service in May 1979. She is armed with Exocet and Sea Wolf missiles, AA guns, ASW torpedoes and one or two Lynx helicopters. She was succeeded by the Type 22 Batch 2 *Boxer*-class ASW frigates, which had a lengthened hull to improve seaworthiness, endurance and habitability, and to provide space for a towed linear passive hydrophone array.

82. The Type 22 Batch 3 frigate HMS *Chatham* (F 87) is the last of a four-unit general-purpose *Cornwall* class, the third series in the Type 22/*Broadsword* design. The world's largest 'frigate' design, she is armed with Sea Wolf and Harpoon missiles, a Goalkeeper AA gun system, AA guns, torpedo tubes, and a Sea King or two Lynx helicopters.

83. This Type 23 class frigate, *Norfolk* (F 230), the lead ship of a projected class of eight, was launched in July 1987. The ships have the first bow-mounted sonars in the Royal Navy, and the ship's design was modified considerably as a result of the lessons learned from the Falkland Islands War. Meant as lineal replacements for the remainder of the *Leander*-class frigates, these 3,700-ton (fl) ships carry Harpoon SSMs, Sea Wolf, and either Goalkeeper or CIWS.

84. The torpedo attack submarine *Upholder* (S 40) (Type 2400) was launched on 2 December 1986 and entered service in March 1988. Twelve were initially projected for this class, which was meant to replace *Oberon*. At 2,400 tons (submerged), and a diving depth of more than 250 metres, *Upholder* can sustain 20 knots and is armed with six torpedo tubes that can fire Harpoon.

85. The 1 C 65-class guided missile destroyer *Aconit* (F 703) entered service in March 1973. This 3,840-ton (fl) ship can sustain 27 knots and was to have been the first of a class of five ships, but the remaining ships were redesigned to the C 67 class. The fact that only one unit was built may indicate French dissatisfaction with the propulsion plant, the single screw, or the lack of a helicopter. In 1975, her pennant number was changed to D 609, and during a 1984–5 refit, her weapons suite was improved, to include the addition of Exocet.

86. The guided-missile destroyer *Tourville* (D 610), lead unit of a three-ship class, entered service in June 1974. These ships have a very high standard of habitability and excellent sea keeping qualities. Crotale SAMs were added and the ships are also armed with Exocet, dual-purpose guns, ASW weapons and torpedoes, and carry two Lynx helicopters.

86

87. *D'Estienne D'Orves-* (Type A-69) class frigate *Jean Moulin* (F 785) entered service in November 1977, the fifth in a seventeen-ship class. These are very seaworthy ships, designed for coastal ASW operations. Armed with Exocet, AA and dual-purpose guns, an ASW rocket-launcher and ASW torpedoes, they are very economical to run. Three have been sold to Argentina.

88. The *Le Redoubtable-*class nuclear submarine *Le Terrible* (S 12), second of a five-unit class, entered service in January 1973. Armed with sixteen M 20 or M 4 ballistic missiles and torpedo tubes, the class is a principal element in the French sea-based strategic deterrent. With the exception of *Le Redoubtable*, all were retro-fitted to carry the M 4 missile. All units were modernized in the latter 1980s.

89. This Type 103B-class guided-missile destroyer, *Lutjens* (D 185), is the lead ship of a three-ship class. All were built in the United States, were Tartar-missile-equipped and of a modified *Charles F. Adams* class. The boilers were subsequently modified and the electronics and weapons were updated.

90. The Type 143/143B-class guided-missile patrol boat *Albatros* (S 61) (P 6111) was launched in October 1973 as the lead ship of a ten-ship class. Designed to replace the Type 141, she has a wood-planked hull on a steel frame and carries Exocet missiles, 76mm guns, and aft-launching torpedoes.

91. The guided-missile frigate *Lupo* (F 564), the lead ship of a four-unit class, was completed in September 1977. Additionally, Venezuela received six, Peru received four, and Iraq received four units. Her armament includes Ottomat and Sea Sparrow missile systems.

92. The guided-missile frigate *Maestrale* (F570) entered service in March 1982 as the lead ship of a class of eight units. Capable of 33 knots, these ships are enlarged versions of the *Lupo*s and are armed with Ottomat SSMs, Albatross SAMs, anti-aircraft guns, torpedo tubes, ASW weapons and two helicopters.

93. The helicopter carrier *Giuseppe Garibaldi* entered service in September 1985 as the pride of the Italian Navy. Essentially an ASW ship for up to twelve Sea King helicopters, she can also handle V/STOL aircraft. The bow has a small ski-jump, purportedly for dryness. Her armament suite includes Ottomat-Teseo SSMs, Albatros SAMs, anti-aircraft guns, torpedoes and helicopters. The ship elicited much controversy with critics such as Raimondo Luraghi arguing that the available funds would be better spent on submarines.

93

94. The corvette *Minerva* (F 551), the lead ship of a planned class of eight ships, entered service in 1987. Intended for surveillance, coastal escort, fisheries protection, training and search and rescue, these ships are armed with an Albatros SAM system, 76mm rapid-fire guns, and torpedoes.

95. The inshore minesweeper *MSB 711*, in service since 1975, is seen under way. These wooden-built boats have no radar. Six were built at two Japanese yards from 1973 to 1975.

96. *Nagatsuki* (DD 167), the fourth and last of the *Takatsuki* class of guided-missile destroyers, was completed in 1970. Originally designed as DASH-equipped destroyers, the DASH was removed in 1977 after it proved unsuccessful. The first two units, *Takatsuki* (DD 164) and *Kikizuki* (DD 165), were modernized in the 1980s, being given Sea Sparrow, Harpoon, a Mk 15 CIWS, and other improvements. The final two units, *Mochizuki* (DD 166) and *Nagatsuki*, were not modernized, and the latter now serves as a naval cadet training ship.

enough to do so in the near future. In the interim, Moscow would conduct her foreign policy in the pose of a traditional nation, but would take advantage of adversary relationships, animosities that were to be exploited for her benefit. In the long-range context, the Soviet Union should identify long-range adversary relationships, animosities that were so complex and so difficult to resolve that they would endure, to be major themes in 20th-century international relations. Lenin identified five such animosities, three in detail, and two by inference. The first was Germany versus Europe, owing to the fact that the Treaty of Versailles was so pro-French that Germany could not continue under it over the long-term and would work for its revision. Lenin believed that France would not permit this and war would result. In the interim, Germany would not be reintegrated into Europe, but rather would remain the orphan of the continent.

The second and third relationships involved the United States. The second was the United States versus Europe, because the United States had superior potential economic power while Europe's political power was excessive, particularly as it pertained to the European nations' colonial empires. The third was the United States versus Japan. Japan was imperialistic and militarily aggressive, while the United States was expanding economically into the Pacific basin. The two would eventually conflict and a Pacific war would result. The fourth and fifth conflicts were inferred. The fourth was an antagonism between the European colonial empires and their colonies, as the colonies sought independence and the imperialist nations tried to retain them in their colonial empires. The final one was capitalism versus communism and here the inference was the Soviet Union, then the only communist nation, versus the United States, which had the economic potential to be a capitalist superpower.

One does not have to like Lenin to appreciate the brilliance of his postulations. His first three themes identified accurately the major issues of the inter-war period and actually predicted the Second World War, both in Europe and in the Pacific. Likewise, in the final two themes, he had predicted post-war international developments; no other issues so dominated post-war international affairs as the Soviet–American superpower rivalry, and the emerging nations of the Third World. Finally, in 1990, 70 years after his speech, neither had other long-range conflicts arisen to supplant them, nor had the themes been resolved. Rather, each had been influenced by the events of the 20th century. The first three themes had reached temporary resolution at the end of the Second World War, as the final two – Soviet–American competition and Third World affairs – dominated events. And this had been one of the factors that had gotten the Soviet Union into its present predicament. Thus, perestroika aimed at nothing less than changing history by resolving one of the long-term conflicts – the US–Soviet or capitalist – communist rivalry.

This should not be considered to be a ploy, and to deem it as such demeans Gorbachev's brilliance. The policy, by its mere inception, unleashed political forces and international themes that had been inhibited or even frozen for decades. Indeed, Moscow had to do nothing more than to allow reform to assure their resurgence. Believing correctly that it was the communist system and not Soviet military power *per se* that upset the West, renouncing this system, the same system that was responsible for the nation's economic woes, should remove suspicion as the new Russia assumed the position of the old pre-Soviet Russia as a major power. While the new system might exploit Lenin's animosities for its own benefit, these latent conflicts would be operative and very important even if Moscow did nothing. This was true because the Soviet–American superpower rivalry that had existed since the war's end in 1945 had been a world-wide superpower conflict which acted as a blanket smothering or stifling the other animosities. They continued to exist none the less and, if Moscow resolved the Soviet-American animosity, the others would be free to reassert themselves. In 1985, if one had said that Germany still had not been integrated into post-war Europe, he would have been criticized immediately. And yet, in 1989, as the Berlin wall came down, what was often thought but seldom said was unsettling: would the new Germany resume its glorious 19th-century place as the intellectual center of Europe or would it be the problem Germany that had waged the two most devastating wars of the 20th? This was perhaps best summarized by one wag who, when told in 1990 that the combined military forces of East and West Germany totalled about 700,000 men, asked if anyone had bothered to check the satellite photography to see which way these forces were facing. Indeed, Germany still had not been integrated fully into Europe in 1990, the issue of its border with Poland was unresolved and the German theme still required attention in international politics. Likewise, the Japanese theme remained unresolved. Post-war Japan had emerged as an economic giant and the rearmament that she had accomplished before 1989 should have been re-examined in a different light. Certainly, the underlying causes of US–Japanese competition in the Pacific had not been resolved and were alive as factors that would play a part in the international affairs of the 21st century. This truth was reflected in the words of one Japanese representative at US–Japanese trade negotiations who, when Japan was criticized concerning the lack of greater Japanese defense expenditures, replied that since the United States had found Japan's economic competition to be so disconcerting, did it really want to face serious Japanese military competition?

ANTICIPATED SOVIET MILITARY DEVELOPMENTS

While all of this was unprecedented and interesting, it remains to determine the effect that it had on the Soviet-American military balance. On the one hand, the events in eastern Europe had definitely affected the Soviet–Warsaw Pact military posture in that, given the disruptive effects of the disintegration of the Pact's communist systems on the military, the bloc did not pose as great a threat against NATO. Conversely, in the spring of 1990, Western intelligence agencies were correct in still noting that there had been little change in the orders of battle. Thus, it appeared that much of what Gorbachev was saying was rhetoric and that the threat remained. This was reflected in the US reaction. In January 1989, for example, National Security Advisor Brent

Scocroft downplayed the changes in the Soviet Union, saying that their purpose was to foster further discord within NATO. The US position remained unchanged in the following months and the administration appeared to question the sincerity of Gorbachev's offers. In May, it was reported that the Bush administration was annoyed with the press response to Gorbachev, claiming that he was more style than substance. However, this view began to change. When Secretary of Defense Richard Cheney predicted the eventual defeat of Gorbachev, he seemed to imply that Gorbachev was sincere, but that he probably would not succeed and would fall in the process. President Bush quickly dissociated himself from Cheney's remarks, saying that he expected Gorbachev to remain in control. Evidence that this period – one in which the United States tried to decide if Gorbachev 'was for real' – had ended was given on 13 May, when President Bush said that the United States was ready to welcome the USSR 'back into the world order'. Elsewhere, the President said that he wanted the economic and political changes initiated by Gorbachev to succeed.[15]

Given that the changes in the Soviet Union and eastern Europe were so significant, why had it taken the Bush administration so long to respond? Part of the explanation could be attributed to traditional distrust. The United States had been taken advantage of in Soviet ploys in the past and Bush did not want to be a party to another. This was prudent and reflected the heartbeat of America, which, based on the polls, gave high marks to Bush's policy. But an even more important factor was that the Soviet military remained largely unchanged. True the Soviet position in eastern Europe was less strong, but real, substantive reductions in the military orders of battle had not occurred. This was reported consistently by Western intelligence and was reinforced by US allies. For example, while reporting by the Japanese was somewhat contradictory in 1989, in January 1990, Japanese analysts were adamant when they said that in spite of the Soviet announcement in December 1989 that it would reduce its Far East presence by 120,000 men and restructure its forces to a defensive posture, Soviet power remained as potent in the Far East as it had been in the past.[16] Thus, rather than leg-dragging, Bush's response had been prudent politics. A third factor was that the Bush administration may have realized the results of Reagan's defense build-up – forcing the Soviet Union to reform – and intended to keep the pressure on so that such reform was as comprehensive as possible.

Thus, the problem lay in the inconsistency between Gorbachev's statements and Soviet military preparedness. The reasons for this divergence were identified by the analysts of the US Army Intelligence and Threat Analysis Center (ITAC), who conducted an intense analysis of contemporary Soviet literature to ascertain the effects of perestroika on Soviet military strategy.[17] They concluded that the Soviet military had probably been told that to continue the current military programs would accomplish two things. It would perpetuate the obsolescence of Soviet military equipment, because the level of Soviet technology on which it was based was behind the West, separated by a gap that could not be closed without a substantial R&D effort that would have to include infusions of Western technology. Second, continued defense spending had not only created the gap but also would prevent its closing because it used the same funds that were spent on R&D and because it had convinced the West that the USSR was hostile, thereby preventing the needed infusion of Western technology. However, if military spending were minimized to the extent that only the amount necessary to assure the strategic defense of the nation were spent, the Soviet Union could devote funds to R&D and, by reducing its arms levels, convince the West that it posed less of a threat (ideally no threat at all), thereby easing the way for the provision of Western technology. This strategic defense should be a defense in depth, a layered defense that conformed to the combined armed strategy and consisted of layers of defense staged by all branches of the armed forces to insure that a foe would be defeated. Here the argument stressed the Battle of Kursk, that great Second World War battle in which a layered defense in depth held against a German offensive and which, with the Battle of Stalingrad, broke the back of the German Army and ultimately assured a Russian victory on the eastern front. Finally, the argument stated that the Soviet military was being asked to wait for that period of time when the new technological position could be achieved, the gap could be closed, and the new technology could be applied to arms, producing equipment that equalled that of the West.[18]

ITAC concluded that there were three major reactions to this strategic postulation. The first was from the hard-liners, Admiral Sergei Gorshkov and others, who would have none of this. Most of them had either died of old age or had been retired. The second group were the moderates or reformists, who agreed with the new formulations, but called for balanced reductions at the bargaining table with the West, thereby assuring an even de-escalation on both sides. Finally, there were the academics, who advised applying pressure to the West to get it to disarm, but called for immediate unilateral Soviet disarmament in order to hasten the application of resources to R&D, the reduction of tension with the West, and the infusion of Western technology.

The Alternative Futures of the Soviet Navy
All of this had obvious implications for the Soviet Navy, and in a larger context, for future world naval development. In considering the future of the Soviet Navy, however, it cannot be overemphasized that in the spring of 1990, the Navy was alive and well and that no serious cutbacks had occurred. Indeed, there had been changes in the fleet's operations, resulting in a lower out-of-area presence, but this merely meant that ships' crews were getting less training on the high seas. Much of this could be compensated by exercise activity in areas closer to home ports. Further, while there had been a great deal of discussion about naval reductions, none had occurred and there had been no reduction in current naval construction. The first conclusion, then, is that the Soviet–American naval rivalry could continue into the 21st century. In that case, we could expect a continuation of the past, in which future Soviet and US naval development would be governed by responding to the perceived threat that each posed against the other. In such an event, the current naval themes would continue. The United States would remain focused on antisubmarine warfare in order to guarantee the safety of the sea lanes to

Europe in wartime, and would continue to develop those forces necessary to penetrate the Soviet Arctic SSBN bastions in order to deny the USSR this strategic capability. For its part, the Soviet Navy could be expected to work toward further securing the Arctic bastions, concentrating on further SSBN, SSGN, and SSN development. Additionally, the aircraft carrier program would continue with even more capable classes than *Tbilisi*. One should not immediately dismiss this option, as all indications in the spring of 1991 indicated that the US–Soviet naval competition had been relatively unaffected by the changes discussed above and was still continuing, producing those remarkable naval systems discussed in Chapter 5.

Having said this, one must immediately follow the statement by noting that the potential for change was great in 1990. In this respect, the importance of the location of the Bush–Gorbachev Malta meetings in December 1989 – in the Mediterranean aboard naval combatants – cannot be overstated. Not since Nikita Khrushchev's use of the *Sverdlov* cruiser *Ordzhonikidze* to visit Portsmouth, England, had the diplomatic use of the Navy by the highest Soviet leader been so symbolic. Gorbachev's purposes were to highlight the issue of sea power and to accentuate the problem it created in the Soviet–American dialogue. And when the weather in Malta worsened, Gorbachev had the opportunity to reiterate his point by noting the uselessness of such ships.

In this context, it is helpful to remember that the Soviet Union is a land power. When Soviet naval leaders met their contemporaries, they were a few blue-suiters in a sea of Army green. Arguments and positions that British and Americans, with their maritime traditions, might accept as fact had to be argued and fought for by the Soviet naval leaders. Indeed, it was a rough road and could get rougher. Peter Tsouras has probably expressed it best. He believed that very early in its existence, a nation defined its defense needs and identified itself as a land or a sea power. If it made the wrong decision, it probably did not survive. If it made the right decision, it came to rely on this chosen type of power as the guarantor of its security. It is true that land powers experimented occasionally in sea power, the most prominent examples possibly being the Romans during the Roman Empire and, much later, the Germans in the Second World War. However, when a crisis occurred and the national security was at stake, such experiments were quickly abandoned as the nation again relied on the type of military power that had proven so successful in the past.[19] The pronouncements that were made almost daily in Moscow in 1989 and 1990 were ample evidence that the Soviet leadership saw itself at just such a crossroads, and if the cuts were going to be deep, the Navy would have to accept its share of them. But how much would the Navy suffer?

The theoretical battle that the Soviet Navy had waged had been lost by 1979, when Admiral Gorshkov had been forced to issue a revision to his *Sea Power of the State*. Subsequently, the foreign policy justification for the Navy has ceased to exist, since in perestroika Gorbachev had indicated that the Soviet Union, at least for the immediate future, stood for the right of self-determination of all nations. And with the loss of its foreign policy role, the Navy's justification as a major sea projection force had become tenuous. Thus, there was only one gambit yet to be played, the US Navy card. Admiral

Chernavin could reasonably argue that the threat posed by the US Navy still existed and had to be countered. However, if he pursued this approach, it could easily backfire for the following reason. It was true that unilateral Soviet naval cutbacks could create a naval imbalance, with a preponderance of US naval power. But there also existed a NATO–Warsaw Pact imbalance concerning the ground forces in Europe that was so pronounced that if the West abandoned its nuclear umbrella, it could be overwhelmed in wartime. In the cost-conscious Kremlin, the policy might be to trade reductions in Soviet land-based power in Europe for reductions in US naval strength.

In any sweeping reduction in the Soviet military, the Navy probably would experience profound cutbacks. It was doubtful if such curtailments would equal those of the 1950s, when ships on the building ways were scrapped as the USSR drastically altered its fleet's composition. Rather, the resources that had been allocated to existing programs would remain committed and the ships then being built would be completed. Additionally, the initial cutbacks involved retiring older ships. Thus, while the ITAC analysts believed that the academics were dominant in the reduction discussions that were taking place because they had Gorbachev's ear, Soviet actions into 1990 reflected the dominance of the moderates who favored the second approach, working for balanced East-West reductions, with only a minor influence by the academics. This was in spite of Soviet publicity that portrayed the Soviet Union as disarming unilaterally, and accounted for the inconsistency in Western reporting. For example, the USSR touted the fact that it had scrapped four cruisers and sixteen destroyers since 1987. However, these were older ships, inferior to newer ones that had vastly more firepower. Likewise, in December 1989, when the Soviets committed themselves to unilateral reductions staged over the next two years, these involved twelve diesel submarines (including three ageing *Golf II* SSBs) and 28 old surface ships, and amounted to only a slight reduction in the Navy's capability. For example, the *Golf*s had been assigned to patrol in the Baltic and when the USSR announced that they would be removed from the Baltic in 1990, many in the West interpreted this as a substantive strategic reduction. In reality, their retirement meant that their targets probably were reassigned to *Yankee*s patrolling in the Norwegian Sea. In sum, in 1990, NATO intelligence spokesmen stated that all the announced Soviet reductions would amount to no more than a 10 per cent reduction.[20]

Conversely, the Soviet Navy's capabilities might easily decline in the future because it had a block-obsolescence problem; much of the fleet had been built in the 1960s and early 1970s, meaning that a disproportionately large portion of the fleet would reach retirement age in the 1990s.[21] If the Navy were forced to conform to the academic's dictum of abandoning today for a technologically modern navy that could begin construction in the latter part of the first decade of the 21st century, there could, indeed, be a period of serious decline in Soviet naval power from the 1990s to as late as 2015. If Soviet policy remained defensive throughout this period, these concessions could appear acceptable to the leadership.

The second conclusion, then, is that while Soviet naval reductions had not taken place in the spring of 1990, the potential for such reductions was great none the less. If they did occur, this would have obvious implications for the world's other great maritime power – the United States.

The Effects of Possible Soviet Naval Reductions on the US Navy

We should expect that the Soviet academics will experience opposition in their program of unilaterally reducing Soviet arms levels. This had already prompted the Kremlin's attempt to gain the greatest concessions possible from the West in 1989, so that there would be some reduction on both sides. This was especially true in relation to the Soviet Pacific Fleet. The fleet had been the backwater of the Navy in the 1950s and 1960s, but beginning with the transfer of the carrier *Minsk* in 1979, the Navy laid emphasis on the fleet, providing it with the newest warships and submarines. By 1989, the fleet comprised 30 per cent of Soviet naval power. While this amounted to a quantitative decrease in the threat, the threat had actually increased because of the vastly greater capabilities of the new ships that had been provided. None the less, the Soviet approach was to call for a reduction in the US naval presence in the Western Pacific, justifying their request by noting the defensive nature of Soviet naval exercises and widely publicizing the scrapping of ships that were actually obsolete, in an attempt to convey a lesser naval threat to the West. In March, for example, Andrei Kokoshin, Deputy Director of the Institute of the USA and Canada, said that a 40-ship reduction in the Pacific Fleet had taken place over the last five years and that Soviet naval exercise activity had changed from offensive scenarios to defending the Soviet coasts. In this dialogue, Cam Ranh Bay, Vietnam figured prominently. The United States had used this, one of the best port facilities along the Asian coast, during the Vietnam War, developing the shore-line and constructing two piers. After the Soviet Union supported Vietnam in the Sino-Vietnamese War of 1979, it was granted use of the Bay for its naval needs. The Soviet improvements were significant, and included adding five piers and developing a nearby airfield, effectively quadrupling the facilities available there. Soviet use of Cam Ranh Bay was heavy, amounting to a presence of more than fifteen units per day, including surface combatants and submarines that could sortie for operations in the region. The airfield also was heavily used to stage flights by Tu-95 Bear D long-range reconnaissance aicraft and attack and maritime aircraft as well. Access to the bay had effectively countered the regional US naval hegemony that had previously existed and meant that Soviet naval reactions to Indian Ocean crises could now be much more prompt, because Cam Ranh Bay and the US naval facility at Subic Bay from which US naval ships would sortie for crisis response were on roughly the same latitude. Gorbachev had mentioned Cam Ranh Bay publicly several times, stating that the Soviets would give up their presence there, if the United States would vacate its facilities in the Philippines. In 1988, however, the Japanese Defense Agency reported that the Soviets had reduced their presence in Cam Ranh Bay considerably, including deploying fewer aircraft and possibly withdrawing Naval Infantry forces.[22]

It seemed logical that the Soviet Union would focus on US naval reductions, because the United States enjoyed such an advantage with its

Navy. For its part, the US Navy was vulnerable to such pressure. Not even considering the US national debt in 1990, which screamed for financial temperance in Federal expenditures, a reduction in Soviet power could prompt many US legislators to consider arms reductions as a means of easing the economic crunch. Admiral Thomas Brooks astutely observed that the Soviet Union was not the only problem looming over the horizon. Indeed, in the 1980s, low-intensity conflict, Arab fundamentalism, and periodic regional troubles had prompted considerable US naval responses, but not once did the Navy react to deployed Soviet naval power during a crisis.

The US Navy should have prepared for the eventuality of Soviet naval reductions, anticipating that this would prompt a stampede for reducing US military appropriations. Indeed, just such a phenomenon had occurred in the 1940s, following the Second World War, when America reduced its forces to unacceptably low levels. Furthermore, the Navy was unprepared to cope with such pressure. For years, Soviet naval expansion had been more than sufficient to justify US naval development and the Navy therefore had not fully informed the public of the nature and the demands of its other missions. Likewise, even though it experienced moments of brilliance in John Lehman's maritime strategy, and there have been some very encouraging changes during Admiral Kurth's tenure at the Naval War College in Newport, the Navy had let matters slide in terms of naval strategy, and year after year, the US Naval Institute *Proceedings* and *Naval War College Review* had relied on Steve Kime, William Manthorpe, Robert Herrick, Norman Polmar and a few others to provide strategic direction. Although these people had offered excellent guidance over the years, they had developed their strategic expertise on their own. The fact that the Navy did little officially to spawn such activity did not speak well for the Navy's efforts to foster strategic thinking in its ranks. Thus, while possible future Soviet naval cutbacks would almost certainly result in US naval reductions, their severity could be tempered with a little prudent homework in strategy and a program that educated the US public concerning the other maritime problems confronting America.

THE FUTURE OF NAVAL DEVELOPMENT WORLD-WIDE

Continuation of the Past?

The first possibility then, when one considers world-wide naval development into the 21st century, was that the changes within the Soviet Union and the Warsaw Pact that occurred in 1989 and 1990 would have no effect and that the Soviet-American naval competition would continue. This would mean that the future would be much like the past, in which maritime innovation would largely occur in the US and Soviet navies, and that it would be governed by the threat that each perceived from the other. While the above factors implied that there would be a Soviet naval reduction, this had not occurred by the summer of 1990, and a continuation of US–Soviet naval competition was a distinct possibility.

Or a New Direction?

Because of the factors discussed above, however, it seemed far more likely that the Soviet Union would reduce its naval expenditures, thereby decreasing the naval threat that it posed. If this occurred, a complimentary reduction in US naval development might occur and might result in a period in which there would be only minor innovation and advancement in the world's naval technology. Such a period could last into the first decade of the 21st century.

Returning to Lenin's long-range animosities, those pertaining to Europe, the United States, and Japan had been suppressed as the greater US–Soviet competition was waged. These dissensions had persisted none the less and could easily re-emerge if the Soviet–American rivalry were resolved. To add to this pessimism was the fact that 1990 offered the possibility of forming a new world order, one in which the Soviet Union might evolve into a modern-day federation of Slavic states, as the possessions gained through Russian and Soviet imperialism were freed. This new Russia might play a role very similar to the one played by the Russia before 1917 – a strong, land-based European power which saw its interests as well as threats to its existence firmly based in Europe and north-east Asia. But there appeared to be no one with the brilliance of Disraeli or Bismark to grasp the implications of all this, and the possibility that the discordant themes of the past might emerge to prominence in the future. France still pursued a semi-independent course in 1990; the reunification of Germany brought into being a nation that initially would probably create a liberal, left-of-center government, and the United Kingdom was still trying to adjust to her new role as a regional European power. The new Russia reasonably could be expected to want to maintain some influence over eastern Europe so that she had a buffer insulating her from any future Western aggression. This had been her traditional policy in the past, and would be prudent in the realpolitik of the early 21st century. But this influence would not necessarily mean control, and the old Balkan animosities of the past would be free to emerge. Hungary's allowing East German citizens to pass through its territory and assisting them to go westward in 1989 was merely one example that the old feelings remained.

It could be expected that such a change would prompt a responding change in the West, in that the political effect of NATO as a body that moderated regional western European disputes would decline. Much has been written about the discord in NATO concerning its responses to the Soviet threat and there has been much criticism of it as a viable regional military body. Much less attention has been paid to NATO's role as a mediating body among the Western nations, and the fact that in this capacity, it has served a valuable purpose. In those situations, such as the Cod War between Iceland and Great Britain, or the Greco–Turkish difficulties, when hostilities did occur, NATO acted as a mediating influence which encouraged the belligerents to seek a resolution. NATO's evolution in the 1990s might mean that such a calming influence would decline, unless it were specifically maintained or unless its mediating role were assumed by another organization.

The situation in the Far East also gave one reason to pause. Japanese economic expansion and aggressive trade policies had prompted US reactions and in 1990, 'Japan-bashing' was popular in some US circles. It would be prudent to review the causes of the Second World War in the Pacific and remember that *both* the United States and Japan *had* made contributions to a situation that prompted the Japanese to attack Pearl Harbor. In 1990, a latent anti-Asian racism seemed to be emerging in the United States, one that increasingly focused on Japan. The failure of US–Japanese talks in March 1990 indicated that little was being done by either side to reverse this situation. In this light, recent Japanese military developments were noteworthy. Although Japan had noted a lesser Soviet presence in Cam Ranh Bay in 1989, it also reported that the Soviet Pacific Fleet was expanding, was becoming more modern, and was posing an ever greater threat.[23] The inconsistent US policy toward Japan that wanted her to rearm on the one hand but feared Japanese remilitarization on the other matured into one of misgivings, prompting Deputy Assistant Defense Secretary Carl Jackson to warn Japan in 1988 that there 'are limits beyond which it should not go in terms of its military build-up,' because 'such a move would be viewed apprehensively by all the powers in the area'.[24]

Russian possession of the Japanese islands that she had occupied toward the end of the Second World War had still not been resolved, adding an additional element of uncertainty. The islands were integral to Russian defense, since they sat on the entrance to the Soviet submarine sanctuary in the Sea of Okhotsk. Conversely, the Japanese had never accepted the loss of the islands, calling continually for their return. This problem would persist, standing in the way of future peace. If the reader thinks that this point is overstressed, the words of the Soviet Foreign Minister in 1951, who said that the San Francisco Peace Treaty which included Japan's renunciation of the Northern Territories, was a blueprint for the next world war, should be considered.[25]

Further southward, the intransigence of the Chinese ruling hierarchy, so vividly demonstrated in the brutal repression of the demonstrators in Tiananmen Square in 1989, inferred that China would be content to remain in semi-isolation if that is what the world imposed. This might continue to complicate its relations with Russia. Similarly, its relations with Vietnam, highlighted by such incidents as the Sino-Vietnamese War of 1979 and a massive 30,000-shell Chinese bombardment of northern Vietnam in September 1985, while Chinese soldiers advanced into Vietnamese territory with the loss of 200 Chinese soldiers, remained a problem.[26]

The Role and Future Uses of Sea Power
One would like to believe that the future would provide an extended period of peace, in which the world would be free to spend its wealth on programs other than those related to defense. However, centuries of violent world history in which the wars had been waged largely by the European powers, the United States, and Japan argued against such unfounded optimism. The Soviet–American superpower rivalry had acted as a controlling blanket, in which lesser conflicts and animosities had been suppressed, lest they endanger

the larger superpower defenses. In this respect, *it may seem ironic, but the type of military force that the Soviet Union and America had developed had actually worked to keep the peace.*[27] This was due to the rapid pace of technology. In the early 1950s, both the USSR and the United States could think in terms of nuclear war because the early nuclear weapons were of limited yield and both nations were large enough geographically to be able to absorb the damage of a nuclear war of the early 1950s' dimensions. In essence, at this time, while nuclear war was feasible it was highly undesirable, and the results were bomb shelters and civilian drills to prepare for such an eventuality. Technology progressed rapidly, however, and soon the dimensions of a potential Soviet–American conflict became so devastating that such wars were no longer feasible. Thus, a nuclear stalemate occurred and peace was maintained.

If the strategic center of power had remained in Europe after the Second World War and had not slipped to the eastern-western, Soviet-American wings as it had, military technology might have progressed quite differently, because the nations of Europe are much smaller than either the United States or the Soviet Union. Weapons with the radiation and destructive power of today's nuclear weapons have minimal applicability in a European war, where their use would mean damage to one's own nation as well as devastation to one's opponent. In essence, there cannot be thought of a future nuclear war among Europe's nations, because to use such weapons would be so devastating that they could destroy the entire continent. Hence, it is feasible to consider war without nuclear weapons in Europe – a taboo such as existed in the Second World War in which both sides were capable of producing chemical and biological warfare weapons but did not use them for fear of retaliation. Thus as in that war, future European wars could be fought on this lower level and future weapons R&D programs could seek to develop surgical weapons that could destroy specific targets or cities without affecting the adjacent countries. In such a milieu, naval power would be at least as important as it had been in the past.

One might still wish to write off the importance of sea power in the future. To do this would be wrong, since the world's oceans are becoming continually more important. Indeed, Gorshkov was quite correct when he said in *Sea Power of the State* that the seas were of great importance in terms of tidal energy, as sources of food, minerals, and oil, and as a means of transportation and communication. Competition for these resources would increase in the future and the need for sea power to protect a nation's interests would continue.[28] Thus, at a minimum, we should expect that naval forces and naval development would continue, although this might be on a reduced scale over the near term.

Land-Based Versus Sea-Based Power

In this consideration of the future of sea power, it is prudent to remember the past. In this book's introduction, the theories of Alfred Mahan and Halfred MacKinder were mentioned, and this work opened by addressing the period immediately after the land-based German coalition had been defeated by a sea-based Atlantic coalition for the second time in this century. In a very real sense, the Soviet–American superpower rivalry was yet a third iteration of this theme, this time with a land-based Warsaw Pact facing a NATO that relied heavily on US naval power for its protection.

The recent events in the Soviet Union and Warsaw Pact, prompted by a critical economic situation that had been brought about by inordinately excessive defense spending in an economy that could not afford it, provided two messages that are relevant to the future. The first was that, although war had been averted during the period from 1945 to 1989, the Atlantic coalition had emerged the victor none the less, to the extent that it had the resources that provided for its defense, outstripping the Warsaw Pact economies in the process.

The second message was that there was an enduring theme, an animosity between land-based European power and maritime Atlantic power. This was a theme that was so persistent that it had resulted in war twice in this century and a 40-year period of intense military competition. Lenin had hit upon this in his theme of Europe versus the United States. However, we should expand upon it by noting that the theme reached maturity only in the 20th century, because it was at this time that the United States fully developed its potential, emerging as a world power that could not only challenge but affect significantly the affairs of Europe. Thus a competitor to traditional European power had emerged, creating a competition or animosity that few appreciated and which remained unresolved. While MacKinder's heartland might undergo a radical economic and political transformation in the early 1990s, the power inherent in this region, coupled with continental Europe's intentions to unify economically into an economic superpower, indicated that this competitive theme remained unresolved. Just how this power base would finally look was undetermined in 1990. For example, would Russia be a part of it or would she remain an independent player? Likewise, would France and Germany reconcile themselves to the extent that integrated economies were possible, or would they continue to compete for influence on the continent and elsewhere? While such an integration was possible, France's departure from NATO, her independent defense policy, and her traditional competition with Germany argued against this. Further, Germany would emerge to assume its traditional place as a major central European power, one that had to consider the security of both its eastern and western borders. Would it accept the territorial adjustments that had been made after the war or would it again seek to reclaim the lost territory? Finally, one should consider Great Britain. Her interests were primarily oceanic and her ties with Canada and the United States should have been considered of the greatest importance. Yet, she had turned toward the Common Market in the 1970s and was avid concerning participating in the European economic program of the 1990s. Would she be able to settle her traditional competition with France and Germany and was it in her interests to participate in the European plan?

The Influence of Sea Power on Other Nations
In Chapter 5, we presented a detailed survey of the world's most significant navies in order to offer a comprehensive view of the loci of naval power in

1990. For technological and political reasons, naval developments would continue to have an impact on many of the world's nations. Technologically. naval development would continue to produce economical systems such as missile-armed fast attack boats and cruise missiles that the world's developing nations could afford and could find useful. This trend would continue the dispersion of the world's naval power among more and more nations.

In respect to political influences, it was quite possible in 1990 that there would be a reduction in Western naval strength as these nations pared down their navies to meet perceived peacetime needs. If the trend that followed the Second World War was repeated, many ships from these navies would be transferred to the navies of less affluent nations. Additionally, political trends in the developing world would make sea power more important, as the seas' importance continued to rise. The trends of extending territorial boundaries outward into the seas, establishing sovereignty over straits areas, and claims to the seas' resources would continue, requiring naval power to protect such claims. From here, one merely had to look for potential crises in which sea power would be relevant to determine those nations that would wish to invest in naval power. Here, Canada in North America, Peru, Argentina, Chile, and Brazil in South America, South Africa and Nigeria in sub-Saharan Africa, Algeria, Libya, Tunisia, Egypt, and Syria in the Mediterranean, Iraq and Iran in the Persian Gulf, Pakistan, and India in the Indian Ocean, and Australia, New Zealand, and Taiwan in the Pacific, would be among the nations likely to increase their naval power. The fact that some of these nations' interests conflicted with those of the European nations, coupled with the European nations' failing adequately to defend their sea lanes in the 1990s, could lead to some dangerous confrontations on the high seas before the end of the century. Indeed, there is justification for concern over possible naval confrontations in the future.

Future Naval Development

Future naval innovation, while it might suffer from a period of stagnation in the 1990s and into the early years of the 21st century, would occur because advancements in technology will have application to naval warfare. Such innovation would be spawned primarily by the world's economic powers and here the United States, Russia, Japan, Italy, France, Germany, and possibly Korea would be the most likely contributors.

One should not expect too much from such innovation. Rather, it would be far wiser to use the progression of the last 45 years as a yard-stick. In this context, one would expect a continuation of current trends. The aircraft carrier and the submarine will remain the pre-eminent systems. While submersible aircraft carriers and other dramatic systems that had been proposed in the past were possible, these were not probable due to the expense that they would incur. Rather there probably would be only minor improvements in the carrier's construction. Conversely, significant advances in the aircraft's speed, payload, and combat capabilities were much more likely.

Advances in submarine technology were inevitable. German experiments in fuel cells had already progressed to the point that an operational platform was envisioned in the 1990s. If successful, these would reduce vastly the noise that submarines made, making then even less vulnerable to detection. Improvements in the submarine's weapons – long-range missiles and the like – would certainly continue.

Amphibious warfare forces would certainly continue to develop. In spite of 45 years of post-war advances in military technology, no one had found a suitable replacement for the Marine who landed on and secured the enemy beach. His value would continue and the means of protecting him and making him an even greater threat would be developed.

Finally, the greatest advances would occur in electronics, the realm in which the most significant advances had occurred in the past. Further progress in C^3, electronic warfare, and in defensive systems would make the navies of the future even more powerful than those of the past.

Expense would continue to be a problem and only the richest or most dedicated nations would be able to participate in the naval research and development programs of the future. The world's remaining nations would be expected to draw on these innovations, maintaining fleets as prudent responses to perceived threats. Here the western European nations, Great Britain, Brazil, Chile, Argentina, South Africa, Egypt, Israel, Saudi Arabia, Iran, Iraq, India, and Australia would be the major purchasers.

CONCLUSIONS

In closing, while it would be nice to have a world free of military forces and to be writing an epitaph to naval power in this book, such an approach is wishful thinking. Rather, sea power and maritime advancement are assured in the future, as the world trudges on into the next century. Indeed, we may someday look back on the Soviet-American naval competition from 1945 to 1990 as the good old days, when by the grace of God, Washington and Moscow had assured a kinder, gentler, more peaceful world.

NOTES

1. This argument concerning the peaceful execution of the Third World War and the argument concerning the possibility of the Fourth World War were developed jointly with Professor Raimondo Luraghi, University of Genoa, Italy. Professor Luraghi is developing the concepts further in a book that he is writing on the history of the US Navy.

2. *Jane's Fighting Ships, 1989-1990*, p. 85.

3. *New York Times*: 1 January 1989, sect. I, p. 1; 5 January 1989, sect. I, p. 10; 6 January 1989, sect. I, p. 1; 15 January 1989, sect. I, p. 1; 19 January 1989, sect. I, p. 4; 5 January 1989, sect. I, p. 6; and 21 January 1989, sect. I, p. 3.

4. *New York Times*: 5 February 1989, sect. IV, p. 5; 12 February 1989, sect. I, p. 1; 6 February 1989, sect. I, p. 1; 14 February 1989, sect. I, p. 16; 21 March 1989, sect. II, p. 3; 17 March 1989, sect. I, p. 1; 27 March 1989, sect. I, p. 1; 28 March 1989, sect. I, p. 1; 29 March 1989, sect. I, p. 22; and 30 March 1989, sect. I, p. 10.

5. *New York Times*: 6 April 1989, sect. I, p. 12; 9 April 1989, sect. I, p. 1; 14 April 1989, sect. I, p. 13; 15 April 1989, sect. I, p. 3; 16 April 1989, sect. I, p. 19; 17 April 1989, sect. I, p. 7; 21 April 1989, sect. I, p. 11; and 26 April 1989, sect. I, p. 1.

6. *New York Times*: 4 May 1989, sect. I, p. 1; 15 May 1989, sect. I, p. 3; 17 May 1989, sect. I, p. 1; 19 May 1989, sect. I, p. 1; 26 May 1989, sect. I, p. 1; 10 June 1989, sect. I, p. 1; and 14 June 1989, sect. I, p. 1.

7. *New York Times*: 25 June 1989, sect. I, p. 16; 11 July 1989, sect. I, p. 1; 17 June 1989, sect. I, p. 1; and 25 July 1989, sect. I, p. 1.

8. *New York Times*, 20 September 1989, sect. I, p. 1.

9. *Newsweek* (25 December 1989), pp. 26, 33.

10. James T. Westwood, 'The New Soviet Defensive Strategy,' in *Jane's Soviet Intelligence Review* (June 1989), p. 279.

11. Ibid.

12. Richard Gasparre, '*Perestroika* and Soviet

Military Power–Does Reform Equal Peace?' in *Jane's Soviet Intelligence Review* (December 1989), p. 550.

13. Christopher N. Donnelly, 'Future Soviet Military Policy; Part 1: Doctrine and Economics,' in *International Defense Review*, no. 1/1989, p. 21.

14. V. I. Lenin, 'Speech Delivered at a Meeting of Activists of the Moscow Organisation of the R.C.P.(B.), 6 December 1920,' *Lenin: Collected Works*, vol. 31: April-December 1920 (Moscow: Progress Publishers, 1966), pp. 427-59.

15. *New York Times*: 23 January 1989, sect. I, p. 1; 18 May 1989, sect. I, p. 10; 2 May 1989, sect. I, p. 1; 13 May 1989, sect. I, p. 1; and 25 May 1989, sect. I, p. 1.

16. 'The Bear in the East,' in *Jane's*, vol. 13, no. 1 (6 January 1990), p. 23.

17. Department of the Army, US Army Intelligence Threat and Analysis Center, US Army Intelligence Agency, *The Soviet Strategic Debate: Striving for Reasonable Sufficiency* (Washington, DC: US Army Intelligence Threat and Analysis Center, 1988).

18. Ibid.

19. Peter Tsouras, 'Soviet Naval Tradition,' in *The Soviet Navy: Strengths and Liabilities*, edited by Bruce and Susan Watson (Boulder, CO: Westview Press, 1986), pp. 3-4.

20. Arthur K. Cebrowski, 'A Matter of Timing?' in *Proceedings* (Naval Review 1989), pp. 138-9; 'Soviet Navy More Capable Despite Losing 20 Ships,' in *Jane's*, vol. 12, no. 14 (7 October 1989), p. 683; '"Golf" Cuts Highlight Renewed Push for Naval Reductions,' in *Jane's*, vol. 12, no. 22 (2 December 1989), p. 1233; 'All "Golf IIs" to Leave Baltic by Next Year,' in *Jane's*, vol. 11, no. 19 (13 May 1989), p. 174; and J. A. C. Lewis, 'Soviet Arms Cuts "Will Not Top 10%",' in *Jane's*, vol. 13, no. 3 (20 January 1990), p. 92.

21. Cebrowski, pp. 138-9.

22. G. Jacobs, 'Growth in Strength of Soviet Pacific Fleet,' in *Jane's*, vol. 12, no. 1 (8 July 1989), pp. 34-5; 'Chinese Scepticism over Soviet Cuts,' in *Jane's*, vol. 11, no. 21 (27 May 1989), p. 980; 'Growing Interest in Asian Sea Areas,' in *Jane's*. vol. 11, no. 2 (14 January 1989), p. 851; 'US Presence in Pacific "Intolerable",' in *Jane's*, vol. 12, no. 17 (28 October 1989), p. 901; 'New Defensive Stance for Naval Deployment,' in *Jane's*, vol. 10, no. 17 (29 October 1988), p. 1084; 'Soviet Analyst Details 40-Ship Pacific Fleet Cuts to Congress,' in *Jane's*, vol. 11, no. 12 (25 March 1989), p. 496; 'Cam Ranh Bay: USA Shows Evidence,' in *Jane's*, vol. 7, no. 7 (21 February 1987), p. 269; Kensuke Ebata, 'Soviets "Cutting Cam Ranh Base",' in *Jane's*, vol. 13, no. 3 (20 January 1990), p. 89; and 'Cam Ranh Bay "Is Not A Soviet Base",' in *Jane's*, vol. 10, no. 17 (29 October 1988), p. 1044.

23. In September 1985, for example, it reported that a Soviet exercise held in August and September was a simulated attack on Hokkaido. (See: Kensuke Ebata, 'Soviets Simulate Attack on Japan,' in *Jane's*, vol. 4, no. 13 (28 September 1985), p. 664.) In 1988, Japan reported that Soviet bomber aircraft flights in the region had increased. See: 'Pacific Backfire Sightings Increase,' in *Jane's*, vol. 10, no. 17 (29 October 1988), p. 1082.

24. 'Pentagon Tells Japan: Limit Arms Build-up,' in *Jane's*, vol. 8, no. 33 (10 September 1988), p. 516. A complete discussion of the complexities of the US-Japanese relationship and some excellent advice concerning future US policy are contained in Paul G. Johnson, 'Japan: A True Partner in Defense,' in *Proceedings*, vol. 116, no. 3 (March 1990), pp. 34-8.

25. Brian Cloughley, 'Japanese-Soviet Territorial Dispute,' in *Jane's*, vol. 6, no. 2 (19 July 1986), p. 62.

26. 'Heavy Casualties in China-Vietnam Clash,' in *Jane's*, vol. 4, no. 14 (5 October 1985), p. 719.

27. This argument concerning the possibility of the Fourth World War and the earlier argument concerning the peaceful execution of the Third World War were developed jointly with Professor Raimondo Luraghi, University of Genoa, Italy. Professor Luraghi is developing the concepts further in books that he is writing on the history of the US Navy.

28. There were a host of examples of nations staking out and expanding their claims to the world's oceans. The extension of Icelandic coastal waters that prompted the Cod War has already been mentioned, as has the Greco-Turkish conflict over Limnos Island, the Argentine–Chilean dispute over the Beagle Channel and Canadian claims to the North-west Passage. Another claim was Indonesia's concerning its territorial waters, an issue of territorial rights over the Straits. In September 1988, it closed the Sundra, Malacca, Makassar, and Lombar Straits in order to conduct live firing exercises. Among the implications of the closing was a clear intention to demonstrate Indonesia's sovereignty over the waterways. (See: *Jane's Fighting Ships, 1989-1990*, p. 93 and Joseph R. Morgan and Abu Bakar Jaafar, 'Strait Talk,' in *Proceedings*, vol. 111, no. 3 (March 1985), pp. 120-7.)

Postscript

Given the tremendous importance of two dramatic events of 1990 and 1991 – the Soviet repression in Latvia and Lithuania and the Persian Gulf War – it is of value to consider the conclusions of this book in light of what has transpired. Before beginning, it should be noted that as these words were being written in February 1991, the Persian Gulf War was raging. It was in its air phase, and the Allies were preparing for a ground war. As in any war, the Persian Gulf conflict is somewhat unpredictable and will have its unexpected surprises that will influence subsequent events. Alternatively, themes that are currently observable will continue to progress, thereby providing a degree of predictability. Having provided this word of caution, it is of value to consider the two events and assess their significance to future naval development.

Soviet Action Against the Baltic Republics

Although the Soviet repression in the Baltic Republics did not involve the use of naval power, it would have a significant effect on the future of naval development worldwide. As the Allied response occurred in reaction to the 2 August 1990 Iraqi invasion of Kuwait, the Soviet Union continued to experience the most severe problems, including intense national unrest, low morale, and an economic crisis. In the summer and autumn of 1990, public confidence in the rouble fell to the extent that packs of cigarettes were accepted as an alternate standard of currency, and, given the shortage of coal, the nation braced itself for a very difficult winter. The spring and autumn 1990 call-ups of conscripts for military service had yielded very poor results, with overwhelming numbers of young men refusing to register, thereby breaking the law. The number of these offenders was so great that Moscow opted to arrest only a few of them in hopes of setting an example. For its part, faced with its portion of the manpower shortage, the Soviet Navy tried an innovative approach: it sought to develop an all-volunteer force.

Amidst this turmoil, the independence movements in Latvia, Lithuania, and Estonia became ever greater challenges to Moscow's authority. It was noted earlier in this book that the nationalities problem was becoming more serious and that the day could come when Moscow might consider permitting some of the republics – those remote, strategically less important republics in Asia, to leave the Union. However, the Baltic republics' critical importance to Soviet defense precluded their leaving, since they bordered strategically on the Baltic Sea, and they contained some of Russia's most significant defence complexes. This, and their general proximity to Moscow and some of Russia's largest industrial centers made their retention within the Union mandatory.

The situation reached a climax in January 1991 when, in response to continually greater Lithuanian demands, Soviet troops stormed Lithuania's broadcasting center in Vilnius, killing thirteen people. A week later, Soviet forces stormed Latvia's interior ministry in Riga, killing four people. The West's response was relatively muted. Washington's reaction was to delay a Bush-Gorbachev summit that had been scheduled for 11–13 February 1991 to sometime later in the spring, stating publicly that the ongoing Persian Gulf War made such a delay necessary.

The Persian Gulf War

The title of the concluding chapter of the book, *Toward a Kinder More Gentle World? The 1990s and Beyond*, implied satirically that international strife would reappear in the future and that naval power would therefore remain relevant. The decade had barely begun when, on 2 August 1990, Iraq's Saddam Hussein ordered his forces to invade Kuwait, thereby fulfilling the prophesy implied in that chapter title. In the months that followed, a multi-national alliance was formed, UN resolutions calling for the withdrawal of Iraqi forces from Kuwait were passed, and a blockade of Iraq was established in order to compel such a withdrawal.

Concurrently, a multi-national force consisting of air, ground and naval power was deployed to Saudi Arabia. The UN resolutions called for an Iraqi withdrawal by 15 January 1991. As the world waited to see if the blockade would be sufficient to compel Iraq to moderate its stance by withdrawing from Kuwait, the Allied forces deployed to Saudi Arabia trained and Iraqi forces in Kuwait dug in as both prepared for the impending hostilities.

The nature of the conflict – operations against a nation that possessed a small navy but the world's fourth largest army – meant that naval power would be used primarily against ground rather than naval forces. Table 5.35 shows that, in 1989, the Iraqi Navy, composed of five frigates, six missile corvettes, seven missile attack boats, eight torpedo attack boats, eight mine warfare ships, six amphibious units, and about twenty coastal craft, was hardly a world naval power. Rather, its navy could be defeated easily by a moderately sized contingent of modern warships deployed from any one of a number of nations. Likewise, the Iraqi Air Force, while large and modern, was not that noteworthy, having performed inconsistently in the Iran–Iraq War. Alternatively, Iraq had a very strong well-trained, combat-experienced army, equipped with significant numbers of some of the world's most modern weapon systems. This, coupled with a missile capability that included Scud missiles, a chemical warfare capability that had been used in the Iran–Iraq War, and a developing nuclear capability, meant that the war would first be waged in the air to establish air supremacy, followed by continued air strikes to destroy strategic targets, and air, ground and naval missile strikes to soften up Iraqi ground forces, and then, if necessary, a possible ground assault to reclaim Kuwait.

Naval power played a significant role even before the war began. A multi-national naval force consisting of ships from seventeen nations was assembled, and by February 1991 it amounted to at least 176 ships. For the United States, this meant a worldwide projection of naval power that focused on the region. Ships and Marine forces were deployed from US east coast bases and proceeded to the Mediterranean or the Persian Gulf. Ships in the Mediterranean transited the Suez Canal to assume stations in the Red Sea, Arabian

Table 6.1

**Ships Deployed* on 15 February 1991
as the Allied Naval Response to the Persian Gulf War****

Nation	Number (Types) of Ships
United States	over 100 (including 6 CVA/CVANs, SSNs, 2 BBs, 10 CGs, 7 DDGs, 13 amphibious and 4 mine warfare and 16 supply ships)
Great Britain	20 (DDGs, other surface combatants and supply ships)
France	14 (frigates, other combatants and support ships)
Italy	5 (1 DDG, 2 FFGs, 1 oiler, 1 supply)
Belgium	5 (1 FFG, 3MSF, 1 command ship)
Germany	5 mine warfare ships
Spain	4
Soviet Union***	4
Australia	3 (1 DDG, 1 FFG, 1 oiler)
Canada	3 (1 DDH, 1DD, 1 oiler)
The Netherlands	3 (2 FFG, 1 supply)
Argentina	2 (1 DD, 1 corvette)
Turkey	2
Egypt	at least 1
Denmark	1 (1 corvette)
Greece	1 (1 frigate)
Norway	1 (1 patrol vessel)
Portugal	1 (1 frigate)

* Includes ships deployed to the Mediterranean, Red and Arabian Seas, Gulf of Oman, and Persian Gulf in response to the war. While not all were warships contributing to the combat potential, all contributed to the naval force projection into the region in response to the war.

** Information on the numbers of ships, their locations and their operations was very tightly controlled during the war. This table was prepared through liaison with US Department of Defense public relations offices and foreign naval attachés in Washington, DC, and was based on the best information available. If the war were a lengthy one, these figures would change as some ships were relieved of their duties, and others were added to or removed from the force to reflect increases or decreases in the tempo of naval operations.

*** The four Soviet ships were probably meant to monitor Allied naval operations. While they would probably assist should casualties to Allied forces occur and would fight in self-defence, they actually should not be counted as part of the Allied armada, since the USSR stated that it would not participate in the war.

Sea, Gulf of Oman, or the Persian Gulf. Meanwhile, ships and Marines from US west coast bases and Hawaii were deployed westward. Some of them, as well as Seventh Fleet ships on station in the Far East, were sent into the Indian Ocean and onward to the Persian Gulf region. For Great Britain and France, it meant sending ships from home ports and the Mediterranean to augment their Navies' Indian Ocean presence. For the other nations in the Alliance, it meant deploying ships to participate in an extremely large and impressive multi-national armada that was unprecedented in many respects. In the period from August 1990 to 16 January 1991, many of these ships were involved in enforcing the blockade, and by 8 January 1991, 6,566 ships had been intercepted, 785 had actually been boarded, and 34 diverted.[1]

When Allied combat operations were begun on 16 January 1991, there was little concern for the threat posed by the Iraqi Navy. Many of its units, including a minelayer and several minesweepers, had been sunk by 27 January, and by 4 February, Iraq was attempting to send its remaining ships to safe haven in Iranian ports.[2] This precluded any type of traditional battle for control of the seas. Rather, such control was established almost immediately after the US decision to react to the Iraqi invasion of Kuwait.

Having established sea control meant that future naval missions would primarily involve projecting power ashore. Here naval operations were significant and were highlighted by massive numbers of sea-based air strikes against Iraqi targets from the carriers *Theodore Roosevelt, America, Saratoga, John F. Kennedy, Midway*, and *Ranger*, positioned in the Persian Gulf and Red Sea and by British and French aircraft deployed to the region, Tomahawk strikes from seaborne platforms, including the battleships *Wisconsin* and *Missouri*, on station in the Persian Gulf, and shore bombardment by the USS *Missouri*'s and *Wisconsin*'s 16-inch guns. In all, more than 80,000 naval personnel were deployed to the theater. Additionally, the US Marines deployed 90,000 men, the largest force to deploy since the Second World War.[3] Those on land were assigned that sector of the battlefront on the Kuwaiti-Saudi Arabian border that faced the Persian Gulf coast and had seen action in and near the town of Khafji. An additional major Marine force was deployed on amphibious ships in the Persian Gulf and was prepared to conduct an amphibious landing on Kuwait, if required to do so.

The use of naval power was most impressive. For the United States Navy, it was the greatest amassing of naval power since at least the Vietnam War, and by 10 January 1991, included, in addition to the six carriers and two battleships mentioned above, deploying the following ships to the theater: two command ships (*La Salle* and *Blue Ridge*), two cruisers, two destroyers, two frigates, four mine warfare ships, ten amphibious ships, and two auxiliaries to the Persian Gulf; a cruiser, two destroyers, a frigate, and eight auxiliary ships to the Gulf of Oman; four cruisers, one destroyer, two frigates, and three auxiliaries to the Red Sea; and three cruisers, two destroyers, one frigate, three auxiliary ships, and three amphibious ships to the Mediterranean.[4]

The Significance of these Two Events
The importance of the Soviet intervention and the Persian Gulf War is that

they demonstrated that the conclusions stated earlier in this book are valid. Mainly, the Soviet-American superpower rivalry is over, and the world is entering a new era of sea power, in which rather than two nations – America and the Soviet Union – vying for control of the seas, many nations would contribute to the further development of sea power. Several aspects of both the Baltic and Persian Gulf situations support this view.

The Baltics It was a conclusion of this book that Gorbachev would have difficulty retaining power as an enlightened despot in that 'in virtually all cases of enlightened despotism in history, the despot has failed to achieve his goals'. In light of the Baltics repression, it would appear that in Gorbachev's case, this generality may again be valid and that the Soviet Union was moving away from democracy. Unable to control the forces that had been unleashed, Gorbachev could not stem the movement of the nation toward anarchy. In this setting, it was likely that the military became more and more concerned, and in February 1991 many observers were unsure of how much power Gorbachev retained and whether the military had acted independently in the Baltics. Foreign Minister Eduard Shevardnadze, a Georgian and the last high-ranking representative of the Soviet minorities in the Soviet national government, had resigned, stating the the Soviet movement toward democracy was being stifled. In this respect, his views were similar to Boris Yeltsin's, in that both strongly opposed the Baltic strategy. In respect to the military, it would appear that moderate, middle of the road military leaders were in charge, since the Baltic states were retained through repression, but with a minimum amount of violence, and that after control was established, the troops were removed as quickly as possible. While Soviet naval power was not involved, the repression none the less was of the greatest importance to the future development of naval power for the following reasons.

First, the repression was a major incident in the history of periodic Soviet anti-democratic interventions and its suppression of human rights. It was certainly more violent than the Prague intervention of 1968 and, while it was much less violent than the repression of Hungary in 1956, it bore many of the brutal characteristics of that invasion. None the less, while the White House announced the delay of the Bush-Gorbachev summit meeting that was to be held in February, it stated immediately its intention to hold the meeting before 30 June 1991. This indicated that while the meeting was delayed to signal American displeasure, the Baltic repression would not affect permanently US–Soviet relations.

Second, while the motive for Washington's cancellation was the Baltic repression, the official reason given was the ongoing Persian Gulf War. This further reflected the fact that the reaction in Washington was quite mild, indicating America's acceptance of a new reality in Europe, in which Russia, while she would probably evolve into a dictatorship, was expected to act reasonably in those situations that affected her strategic defence. Retention of the Baltic states was one of those situations and while Soviet actions were considered repressive, they were seen as amounting to a moderate rather than a brutal application of military power to achieve Soviet goals. The Bush administration reflected this view in February 1991, when it stated unofficially that the Cold War was over and Russian actions in the Baltic in no way signified that such a war was beginning once more.

Third, Soviet naval power had not played a role in the Baltic intervention, possibly reinforcing the belief concerning the limited utility of naval power to Soviet goals. This, coupled with the aforementioned refusal of Soviet conscripts to report for duty in 1990 and the nation's severe economic problems, seemed to imply that this book's earlier conclusion that the Soviet Navy would be curtailed remained valid. However, in February 1991, it was still too early to state conclusively, since those ships and systems in the Soviet naval construction and production pipelines would still be built, thereby delaying a halt in production until the mid-1990s. Additionally, currently unforeseen events in the early 1990s could influence future naval development.

Thus the significance of the Baltic repression to future naval development lay in the way it was viewed in the West. While unwelcomed, it was anticipated and was interpreted as Moscow's protection of her perceived strategic interests rather than a resurgence of the Cold War. To naval development, this meant that the West would not return to that time when the Soviet Navy was seen as the only threat, one that triggered the restrictive designing of ships that were built exclusively to combat a Soviet Navy in wartime. Rather, in the future, naval architects would be freer to predicate their designs on the perceived global needs for naval power, of which Soviet naval power would merely be one factor, rather than the *raison d'être*.

The Persian Gulf War

Equally significant to naval development was the Persian Gulf War, which, for several reasons, might well be the opening incident in a new era of world sea power.

First, while America's stated goal in the war was to force Iraq to relinquish its control over Kuwait, President Bush referred repeatedly to establishing a new order in both the region and the world. This implied a greater, long-term role for the United States in the Middle East and probably less attention to Europe.

Second, in responding to the war, the United States so reduced its defences in Europe, involving the movement of more than 40,000 US troops and their weapons and equipment to Saudi Arabia, that it was not too much of an exaggeration to say that, when it came to a possible Soviet threat, Europe had been abandoned. The fact that the major preoccupation of those US troops who remained in Europe was to defend against possible Arab terrorism rather than to be prepared for a Russian advance only reinforced the belief that the Cold War was over.

Third, while the naval war was greatly weighted in favour of the Alliance, some Iraqi actions, such as mining, reflected an imbalance in US naval forces that had been built primarily to defend against a Soviet threat. Although this was not significant in the Persian Gulf War since the mines were removed by an expert Anglo-American naval mine warfare force, this and other operations would spawn innovation in future US naval development, as America built its navy of the twenty-first century.[5]

Fourth, the war demonstrated that Lenin's views on the international order were still valid. In one sense, the Persian Gulf War was between the Third World – the poor Arab nations, and the First World – Europe and the rich Arab nations. Because of Russia's virtual renunciation of Communism, the issue of Communism versus capitalism did not play a role. However, other traditional themes did. The Soviet Union stated almost immediately that it would not react to the Iraqi aggression militarily. This was accepted in Washington, London, and elsewhere on the basis that Russia's immediate interests were not involved. However, it was a different matter in respect to Germany and Japan. In the past, both had adopted laws with American blessing and possible pressure that restricted the use of their military and prohibited such actions as deploying forces to remote areas such as the Middle East. Intending to comply with these restrictions, both nations provided assistance and financial support to the Alliance, and Germany eventually sent five mine warfare ships to the region as a response. One can debate whether this support was adequate in view of the nations' abilities to pay. However, what was more relevant was that, at least in America up to January 1991, there was a consistent belief that neither Germany nor Japan was paying its fair share. With respect to Japan, this feeling certainly coincided with the 'Japan-bashing' that was popular in some circles and harked back to Lenin's belief in the enduring animosity between Japan and the United States. Concerning Germany, the feeling might prompt one to consider the extent to which Germany had been integrated into Europe.

Fifth, in this book's concluding chapter, it was noted that Great Britain was throwing her lot in with Europe, while her immediate interests were possibly better served through closer ties with the United States and Canada. This remains an issue. On the one hand, a reason for Prime Minister Margaret Thatcher's fall from power was her pro-American policy, and after her fall, Great Britain pursued a pro-European policy. On the other hand, Great Britain made a far greater commitment to the war, given her relative resources, than any other European nation. And in terms of men and equipment, this was so significant that in many respects, on the battlefield the Alliance meant Anglo-American with significant help from the Saudis and other allies. How London would interpret the significance of her wartime policy was problematic in February 1991. Some would argue correctly that she had acted in the national interest. However, there would be others who would see the concord of Anglo-American interests in the war and would again question whether the nation would be better served through continuing a close relationship with Washington.

Sixth, very early in the war, an anti-war effort began in the United States. This was not a novel occurrence – there had been calls for peace on 8 December 1941, one day after Pearl Harbor, and the anti-war effort had figured prominently in the Vietnam War. More significant was the continual observation that America and Great Britain had made a larger military commitment than the other nations in the Alliance. This reflected profound change, and the world was entering a new era. In the previous period, other international themes and animosities either were subjugated to or were played out in the context of an overriding Soviet-American superpower rivalry. Now, one superpower remained – the United States – and other nations and regions, freer of both Soviet and American restraints than in the past, would require greater attention from Washington, as America faced the much more complex world of the future.

Conclusions

The Baltic repression and the Persian Gulf War provided the following messages. First, the Cold War had ended and would not be resumed. With its termination ended the tremendous influence that the US–Soviet superpower rivalry had had on international affairs. What remained was a single superpower, the United States, which, in 1991, was attempting to define and determine how to influence the new world order.

Second, a host of high-technology weapons – Patriot and Tomahawk missiles and laser-guided bombs, to name a few – that had been criticized because of their cost and previously had not been tested in combat were used in the war. The preliminary estimates concluded that these systems had performed superbly in combat, which meant that there would be greater investment in such systems in the future. Naval power would certainly share in the benefits of this new investment.

Third, the Persian Gulf War provided the US Navy with the ammunition it needed to justify continued naval development. In 1989, the Soviet naval threat was perceived as diminishing, and US naval leaders, most notably Admiral Thomas Brooks, were noting that the Soviet Union was not the only threat to US interests. However, Brooks suffered under the same liability that had plagued US naval leaders in the past: the US Navy was performing its missions so well that it was difficult to convince others of the importance of continued investment, based on abstract arguments of a perceived naval threat. Now, the Persian Gulf War proved the validity of Brook's argument – there were forces that threatened US interests abroad and US defenses must be preserved. Whether the argument would prove successful in the 1990s in light of the huge US budget deficit was problematic. However, the US Navy's position was certainly much stronger in 1991 than it had been a year before.

Fourth, the location of the war – outside the European-Atlantic theater – was important. It re-emphasized the importance of versatility in naval forces. No longer were the Soviet Navy and the European theater the yardsticks by which to design ships. Now one should consider other theaters of potential conflict and other likely missions. This should have a positive effect on the creativity in future naval design and development.

Finally, the invasion of Kuwait had occurred suddenly. Iraq had been a recent friend of the United States, and much of its power came directly from US and European arms sales. The fact that its aggression was so unexpected should have highlighted the reality that there were other potential conflict areas in the world. In this respect, writing in *Jane's Defense Weekly* in February 1991, Paul Beaver provided the following list of flashpoints that would exist in the world in the 1990s: Cuba, El Salvador, Nicaragua, and Colombia in the Caribbean Basin and Latin America; the Soviet Union, the

Balkans, and Hungary/Romania in Europe; Yugoslavia, the Aegean Basin, Lebanon, and Cyprus in the Mediterranean; Somalia/Kenya, Nigeria/ Cameroon, and Zaire in Africa; Kuwait and Iraq/Iran in the Persian Gulf, Pakistan/India, and the Malacca Straits in the Indian Ocean; and the Soviet Union, Korea, Taiwan/China, Indo-China, South China, Sea Islands, East Timor, Papua New Guinea, and Bougainville in the Pacific Ocean.[6] To this pessimistic but accurate list we might add Chile/Argentina and the Falklands in Latin America, Antarctica, the Sudan and South Africa in Africa, Israel in the Middle East, Sri Lanka in the Indian Ocean, and China/Vietnam in the Pacific Ocean. Hostilities could erupt in any of these flashpoints and sea power would be quite effective in influencing several of them.

Finally, if one adds to this list the uncertain effects that the aggressive defence programs that several nations, including the United States, Soviet Union, South Korea, Japan, India, Pakistan, and Germany are financing, the future appears even more uncertain. It is a certainty that the present instability in the world will require further innovative naval development. Additionally, Saddam Hussein's use of ecological terror and the threatened use of chemical warfare might presage a meaner type of international violence in the future and that this book's earlier conclusion that 'we may someday look back on the Soviet-American naval competition from 1945 to 1990 as the good old days, when by the grace of God, Washington and Moscow had assured a kinder, gentler, more peaceful world' might be valid.

NOTES

1. *Pentagon News Briefing*, 12.00 p.m., 8 January 1991.

2. *Pentagon News Briefing*, 3.30 p.m. (EST), 31 January 1991; and *Reuter's News Report*, 2 February 1991.

3. *Pentagon News Briefing*, 3.30 p.m., 10 January 1991; and *Pentagon News Briefing*, 31 January 1991.

4. *Pentagon News Briefing*, 10 January 1991.

5. *Pentagon News Briefing*, 3.30 p.m. (EST), 24 January 1991.

6. Paul Beaver, 'In the Shadows of Conflict,' in *Jane's Defence Weekly*, 5 January 1991, pp. 17–18.

Bibliography

BOOKS AND ARTICLES

Alford, Jonathan, ed. *Sea Power and Influence: Old Issues and New Challenges.* The Adelphi Library 2, International Institute for Strategic Studies. Westmead, Farnborough, Hampshire, England: Gower Publishing, 1980.

Anderson, Bern. 'Russia's New Kind of War,' in US Naval Institute *Proceedings* (hereinafter referred to as *Proceedings*), vol. 76, no. 11 (November 1950), pp. 1171–81.

Anderton, David A. 'Terrier-Armed Cruiser to Defend Navy's Atlantic Fleet Task Forces,' in *Aviation Week*, 7 November 1955.

An, Tai Sung. 'Soviet Access to Cam Ranh Bay: Political and Military Implications,' in *Proceedings,* vol. 105, no. 9 (September 1979), pp. 111–13.

Araldsen, O. P. 'Norway and Soviet Psychological Warfare,' in *Journal of the Royal United Services Institute for Defence Studies* (hereinafter referred to as *RUSI*), vol. cvi, no 624 (November 1961), pp. 582–8.

Ashburn, E. H. *'Pegasus* (PHM-1): The Patrol Hydrofoil Ship,' in *Proceedings*, vol. 103, no. 1 (January 1977), pp. 101–7.

Aston, W. J. 'Jet Age Carrier,' in *Proceedings*, vol. 82, no. 5 (May 1956), pp. 529–32.

Auer, J. E. 'Japanese Militarism,' in *Proceedings*, vol. 99, no. 9 (September 1973), pp. 46-55.

Baldwin, Hanson W. 'Soviet Submarine Lag,' in *New York Times*, 18 April 1963.

Banks, Tony. 'RN Facing Big Problems in Submarine Manning,' in *Jane's Defence Weekly* (hereinafter referred to as *Jane's*), vol. 8, no. 17 (31 October 1987), p. 983.

'Running the Gauntlet in the Gulf.' in *Jane's*, vol. 8, no. 4 (1 August 1987), p. 182.

Barker, Edward L. 'The Helicopter in Combat,' in *Proceedings*, vol. 77, no. 11 (November 1951), pp. 1207–10.

Barry, Donald. 'The British Navy in the Nuclear Age,' in *Proceedings*, vol. 83, no. 10 (October 1957), pp. 1069–77.

Beach, Edward L. *The United States Navy: A 200-Year History.* New York: Houghton, Mifflin, 1986.

— 'US Nuclear-Powered Submarines.' in *Proceedings*, vol. 93, no. 8 (August 1967), pp. 88–101.

Beecher, John D. 'FFG-7: The Concept and Design,' in *Proceedings*, vol. 104, no. 3 (March 1978), pp. 148–50.

Beaver, Paul. 'The Long Arm of the French Navy,' in *Jane's*, vol. 6, no. 5 (18 October 1986), pp. 899–901.

Beavers, Roy. 'The End of an Era,' in *Proceedings*, vol. 98, no. 7 (July 1972), pp. 18–25.

Berger, P.E.C. 'The Royal Navy: A Concept of Maritime Operations,' in *RUSI*, vol. 119, no. 3 (September 1974), pp. 9–17.

Bhaskar, C.U. 'Indian NavAir,' in *Proceedings*, vol. 113, no. 3 (March 1987), pp. 106-8.

Bidlingmaier, T. Gerhardt. 'The Strategic Importance of the Baltic Sea,' in *Proceedings*, vol. 84, no. 9 (September 1958), pp. 23–31.

Bindra, A.P.S. 'The Indian Ocean As Seen by an Indian,' in *Proceedings*, vol. 96, no. 5 (May 1970), pp. 178–203.

Blair, Leon B. 'A Historical Examination of Soviet Foreign Policy,' in *Proceedings*, vol. 75, no. 9 (September 1949), pp. 973–81.

— 'Mediterranean Geopolitics,' in *Pro-*

ceedings, vol. 77, no. 2 (February 1951), pp. 135–9.

Boesgaard, Nils. 'Danish Navy Mothballs Major Surface Warships,' in *Jane's*, vol. 9, no. 3 (23 January 1988), p. 115.

Bolt, A. S. 'HMS *Theseus* in the Korean War, and some Special Problems of Naval Aviation in that Theatre,' in *RUSI*, vol. xcvi, no. 584 (November 1951), pp. 545–61.

Bonsignore, Ezio. '*Giuseppe Garibaldi*: The Italian Navy's TDC.' in *Proceedings*, vol. 108, no. 3 (March 1982), pp. 133–6.

— '*Kortenaer*/F-122: A Standard Frigate for NATO Navies,' in *Proceedings*, vol. 104, no. 11 (November 1978), pp. 154–8.

Bork, Jorgen F. 'Crisis Management in Denmark,' in *Proceedings*, vol. 108, no. 3 (March 1982), pp. 104–9.

Bouchard, Joseph F. 'The Japanese Maritime Self-Defense Force,' in *Proceedings*, vol. 107, no. 3 (March 1981), pp. 60–8.

Bouchard, Joseph F., and Hess, Douglas J. 'The Japanese Navy and Sea Lanes Defense,' in *Proceedings*, vol. 110, no. 3 (March 1984), pp. 88–96.

Bowen, Harold G. Jr. 'Naval Aspects of the Mission to Turkey,' in *Proceedings*, vol. 77, no. 10 (October 1951), pp. 1041–49.

Boxhall, P. G. 'The Strategic Use of Islands in a Troubled Ocean,' in *RUSI*, vol. cxi, no. 644 (November 1966), pp. 336–41.

Brauzzi, Alfredo. 'The Fall and Rise of the Italian Navy,' in *Proceedings*, vol. 113, no. 3 (March 1987), pp. 153–7.

Breyer, Siegfried. *Guide to the Soviet Navy*. Annapolis, MD: US Naval Institute, 1970.

Brickloe, W. D. 'A Page from the New Navy: The *Forrestal*-Class Attack Carrier,' in *Proceedings*, vol. 84, no. 7 (July 1958), pp. 144–50.

Brown, Charles R. 'American National Strategy,' in *Proceedings*, vol. 76, no. 4 (April 1950), pp. 353–63.

Brown, David. *The Royal Navy and the Falklands War*. London: Leo Cooper, 1987.

Bruce, James. 'Unprecedented Iranian Naval Build-up,' in *Jane's*, vol. 8, no. 1 (11 July 1987), p. 15.

Buchan, Alastair. 'Britain East of Suez: Part One – The Problem of Power,' in *RUSI*, vol. cxii, no. 647 (August 1967), pp. 209–15.

Bunker, John. 'US Navy Outgrows "Jeep" Escort Carrier.' in *Christian Science Monitor*, 2 March 1956.

Burgess, John A. 'Into the 21st Century,' in *Proceedings*, vol. III, no. 3 (March 1985), pp. 98–100.

— 'La Marine.' in *Proceedings*, vol. 111, no. 3 (March 1985), pp. 94–101.

Bustard, M. E. 'A Page from the New Navy: USS *King* (DDG-10),' in *Proceedings*, vol. 87, no. 3 (March 1961), pp. 161–6.

Cable, James. *Gunboat Diplomacy 1919–1979: Political Applications of Limited Naval Force*. New York: St. Martin's Press, 1971.

Cagle, Malcolm W. 'The Jets Are Coming,' in *Proceedings*, vol. 74, no. 11 (November 1948), pp. 1343–9.

— 'Sea Power and Limited War,' in *Proceedings*, vol. 84, no. 7 (July 1958), pp. 23–7.

Carey, L. D. 'A Page from the New Navy: The USS *Henry B. Wilson* (DDG-7),' in *Proceedings*, vol. 87, no. 7 (July 1961), pp. 152, 154.

Carrington, Lord. 'British Defence Policy,' in *RUSI*, vol. cxviii, no. 3 (September 1973), pp. 3–10.

Case, Frank B. 'Time to Secure the Seas,' in *Proceedings*, vol. 99, no. 8 (August 1973), pp. 24–31.

Chadwick, Stephen. 'Eastern Anchor of NATO,' in *Proceedings*, vol. 111, no. 3 (March 1985), pp. 128–31.

Chesterton, A. K. 'The International Situation,' in *RUSI*: vol. xcviii, no. 589 (February 1953), pp. 122–3; vol. xcviii, no. 590 (May 1953), pp. 288–9; vol. xcviii, no. 591 (August 1953), pp. 457–61; vol. xcviii, no. 592 (November 1953), pp. 616–19; vol. xcix, no. 593 (February 1954), pp. 120–2; vol. xcix, no. 594 (May 1954), pp. 276–81; vol. xcix, no. 595 (August 1954), pp. 449–54; vol. xcix, no. 596 (November 1954), pp. 600–4; vol. c, no. 597 (February 1955), pp. 110–14; vol. c, no. 598 (May 1955), pp. 286–9; vol. c, no. 599 (August 1955), pp. 458–63; vol. c, no. 600 (November 1955), pp. 618–21; vol. ci, no. 601 (February 1956), pp. 99–104; vol. ci, no. 602 (May 1956); pp. 271-5; vol. cii, no. 605 (February 1957), p. 87.

Clark, Ellery H. 'New Ships and Conversions – 1945–1955.' in *Proceedings*, vol. 82, no. 3 (March 1956), pp. 303–25.

Clark, William. 'Britain East of Suez: Part II – The Problem of Influence,' in *RUSI*, vol. cxii, no. 647 (August 1967), pp. 216–20.

Clarkson, R. A. 'The Naval Heresy,' in *RUSI*, vol. cx, no. 640 (November 1965), pp. 316–20.

Cloughley, Brian. 'Japanese-Soviet Territorial Dispute,' in *Jane's*, vol. 6, no. 2 (19 July 1986), p. 62.

Cogne, Robert L. 'France's Global Reach,' in *Proceedings*, vol. 113, no. 3 (March 1987), pp. 76–82.

Colvin, Robert D. 'Aftermath of Elath,' in *Proceedings*, vol. 95, no. 1 (January 1969), pp. 60–7.

Conway's All the World's Fighting Ships, 1947–1982, Part I: The Western Powers; Part II: The Warsaw Pact and Non-Aligned Nations. Gardiner, Robert, ed. Annapolis, MD: Naval Institute Press, 1985.

Corville, R. F. 'Russia's Foreign Policy: The Lessons of History,' in *RUSI*, vol. xcv, no. 579 (August 1950), pp. 477–8.

Cosentino, Michele. 'Keeper of NATO's Southern Flank,' in *Proceedings*, vol. 116, no. 3 (March 1990), pp. 96–8.

Cottrell, Alvin, J., and Dougherty, James E. 'Algeria: A Case Study in the Evolution of a Colonial Problem,' in *Proceedings*, vol. 83, no. 7 (July 1957), pp. 723–33.

Cowie, J. S. 'Minelayers,' in *RUSI*, vol. c, no. 600 (November 1955), 601–10.

Cox, Frederick J. 'The Russian Presence in Egypt,' in *Naval War College Review*, vol. 22, no. 6 (February 1970), pp. 45–53.

Cranwell, John Philips. 'Sea Power and the Atomic Bomb,' in *Proceedings*, vol. 72, no. 10 (October 1946), pp. 1267–75.

Creecy, Richard B. 'Military Applications of Atomic Energy,' in *Proceedings*, vol. 76, no. 7 (July 1950), pp. 743–51.

Cushman, Robert E. 'Amphibious Warfare: Naval Weapon of the Future,' in *Proceedings*, vol. 74, no. 3 (March 1948), pp. 301–7.

Daly, Mark. 'Royal Navy Set to Order SSN 20 Systems,' in *Jane's*, vol. 13, no. 1 (6 January 1990), p. 11.

— 'Soviets' SUMMEREX 85 Their Largest Exercise,' in *Jane's*, vol. 4, no. 5 (3 August 1985), p. 198.

Danziger, Raphael. 'Mediterranean: Qaddafi's Choke Point?' in *Proceedings*, vol. 108, no. 3 (March 1983), pp. 138–40.

— 'The Naval Race in the Persian Gulf.' in *Proceedings*, vol. 108, no. 3 (March 1982), pp. 92–8.

Davidson-Houston, J. V. 'The Political Strategy of Russia,' in *RUSI*, vol. xcii, no. 565 (February 1947), pp. 118–22.

Davies, David. 'The Royal New Zealand Navy: Life Begins at 40,' in *Proceedings*, vol. 108, no. 3 (March 1982), pp. 139–41.

Davis, George W., Jr. 'USS *Virginia* (CGN-38),' in *Proceedings*, vol. 103, no. 8 (August 1977), pp. 85–9.

Deyo, M. L. 'How Far Can the Bear Walk?' in *Proceedings*, vol. 76, no. 11 (November 1951), pp. 1203–5.

Dickens, Gerald. 'Sea Power in a War with Russia,' in *Proceedings*, vol. 76, no. 10 (October 1950), pp. 1069–72.

Din, Hayaud. 'The Pakistan Navy,' in *Proceedings*, vol. 84, no. 9 (September 1958), pp. 59–63.

Dodd, Norman L. 'African Navies – South of the Sahara,' in *Proceedings*: vol. 107, no. 3, (March 1981), pp. 47–52; vol. 110, no. 3 (March 1984), pp. 55–9; vol. 111, no. 3 (March 1985), pp. 56–60; vol. 112, no. 3 (March 1986), pp. 58–64.

Doi, Hiroshi. 'Self-Defense Is Enough,' in *Proceedings*, vol. 113, no. 3 (March 1987), pp. 94–8.

Donnelly, Christopher N. 'Future Soviet Military Policy; Part 1: Doctrine and Economics,' in *International Defense Review*, No. 1/1989, pp. 19–22.

Dowdy, William L. III. 'Middle Eastern, North African, and South Asian Navies,' in *Proceedings*: vol. 108, no. 3 (March 1983), pp.53–6; vol. 108, no. 3 (March 1982), pp. 48–55.

Drossinos, G. 'The Royal Hellenic Navy,' in *Proceedings*, vol. 97, no. 3 (March 1971), pp. 32–7.

Dunn, Peter M., and Watson, Bruce W., eds. *American Intervention in Grenada: The Implications of Operation 'Urgent Fury.'* Boulder, Colorado: Westview Press, 1985.

Durch, Stephen J. 'The Navy's Newest Ship: FFG-7,' in *Proceedings*, vol. 104, no. 3 (March 1978), pp. 150–3.

Du Toit, A. K. 'African Navies South of the Sahara,' in *Proceedings*, vol. 116, no. 3 (March 1990), pp. 144–9.

Ebata, Kensuke. 'Japan Approves 6.1% for FY91,' in *Jane's*, vol. 13, no. 1 (13 January 1990), p. 51.

—'Japan Defence Budget to Exceed 1% of GNP,' in *Jane's*, vol. 7, no. 1 (10 January 1987), p. 3.

—'Japanese Increase Defence Spending Levels,' in *Jane's*, vol. 4, no. 15 (12 October 1985), p. 779.

—'Ocean Air Defense Japanese Style,' in *Proceedings*, vol. 113, no. 3 (March 1987), pp. 98–101.

—'Soviets Cutting Cam Ranh Base,' in *Jane's*, vol. 13, no. 3 (20 January 1990), p. 89.

—'Soviets Simulate Attack on Japan,' in *Jane's*, vol. 4, no. 13 (28 September 1985), p. 664.

Eller, Ernest M. 'Sea Power and Peace,' in *Proceedings*, vol. 73, no. 10 (October 1947), pp. 1161–74.

—'U.S. Destiny in the Middle East,' in *Proceedings*, vol. 82, no. 11 (November 1956), pp. 1161–9.

—'Will We Need a Navy to Win?' in *Proceedings*, vol. 76, no. 3 (March 1950), pp. 237–47.

Elliott, Simon. 'Egypt Set to Buy Walrus, Oberon,' in *Jane's*, vol. 11, no. 18 (6 May 1989), p. 801.

—'SSN Delay Risks RN Force Strength,' in *Jane's*, vol. 11, no. 16 (22 April 1989), p. 675.

—'Syrian Base Boosts Soviet Power,' in *Jane's*, vol. 12, no. 4 (29 July 1989), p. 154.

Ellis, M. G. M. W. 'Sweden's Ghosts?' in *Proceedings*, vol. 112, no. 3 (March 1986), pp. 94–100.

Eliot, George Fielding. 'How to Lose a War,' in *Proceedings*, vol. 76, no. 7 (July 1950), pp. 707–14.

Erickson, John. 'The Soviet Naval High Command,' in *Proceedings*, vol. 99, no. 5 (May 1973), pp. 66–87.

Evans, Geoffrey. 'America's Ally "Down Under",' in *Proceedings*, vol. 107, no. 3 (March 1981), pp. 84–9.

Eyre, James K. 'Naval Power and the American Destiny,' in *Proceedings*, vol. 77, no. 3 (March 1951), pp. 297–307.

Famiglietti, Len. '"Loner" Caused Iowa Explosion, Says Report,' in *Jane's*, vol. 12, no. 11 (16 September 1989), p. 494.

Foley, Roger. 'N. Zealand Forces Set for Major Shake-up,' in *Jane's*, vol. 11, no. 23 (10 June 1989), p. 1113.

—'NZ Forces Face Major Crisis,' in *Jane's*, vol. 11, no. 11 (18 March 1989), p. 1113.

—'US Presence in Pacific "Intolerable",' in *Jane's*, vol. 12, no. 17 (28 October 1989), p. 901.

Foley, Roger, and Cranston, Frank. 'Consortia Tighten ANZAC Costs,' in *Jane's*, vol. 11, no. 23 (10 June 1989), p. 1113.

Foquet, David. 'Denmark Sets Tough Nuclear Test,' in *Jane's* (7 May 1988), p. 887.

Freedman, Robert O. 'Soviet Policy Toward Sadat's Egypt from the Death of Nasser to the Fall of General Sadek,' in *Naval War College Review*, vol. 26, no. 3 (Nov–Dec 1973), pp. 63–79.

—'Soviet Policy Toward the Middle East from the Exodus of 1972 to the Yom Kippur War,' in *Naval War College Review*, vol. 27, no. 4 (Jan–Feb 1975), pp. 32–53.

—'Soviet Policy Toward the Middle East Since the October 1973 Arab-Israeli War,' in *Naval War College Review*, vol. 28, no. 3 (Fall 1976), pp. 61–103.

—'The Soviet Union and the Middle East: The High Cost of Influence,' in *Naval War College Review*, vol. 24, no. 5 (January 1972), pp. 15–34.

Friedman, Norman. 'The Attack on the Stark,' in *Proceedings*, vol. 113, no. 7 (July 1987), pp. 96–7.

—*U.S. Aircraft Carriers*. Annapolis, MD: Naval Institute Press, 1983.

—'The *Vincennes* Incident,' in *Proceedings*, vol. 115, no. 5 (May 1988), pp. 72–6.

—'Western European and NATO Navies,' in *Proceedings*: vol. 110, no. 3 (March 1984), pp. 35–43; vol. 111, no. 3 (March 1985), pp. 37–46; vol. 112, no. 3 (March 1986), pp. 36–48; vol. 113, no. 3 (March 1987), pp. 39–46; vol. 116, no. 3 (March 1990), pp. 116, 120, 123, 124, 127–9.

Gallimore, C. P. 'The Development of Propulsive Machinery for Surface and Submarine Warships,' in *RUSI*, vol. xcvi, no. 583 (August 1951), pp. 385–400.

Garthoff, Raymond L. 'Sea Power in Soviet Strategy,' in *Proceedings*, vol. 84, no. 27 (February 1958), pp. 85–93.

Gascoigne, Alvary. 'Russian Policy Since 1945,' in *RUSI*, vol. c, no. 597 (February 1955), pp. 24–31.

Gasparre, Richard. '*Perestroika* and Soviet Military Power – Does Reform Equal Peace?' in *Jane's Soviet Intelligence Review*, December 1989, pp. 549–51.

George, Bruce, MP, and Stenhouse, Mark. 'Turkey Comes to Terms with Its Vulnerability,' in *Jane's* (2 July 1988), pp. 1374–6, 1379.

George, James L. 'Building Warships in Peacetime,' in *Proceedings*, vol. 106, no. 9 (September 1980), pp. 66–70.

—ed. *The Soviet and Other Communist Navies: The View from the Mid 1980s*. Annapolis, MD: Naval Institute Press, 1986.

—ed. *The U.S. Navy: The View from the Mid-1980s*. Boulder, CO: Westview Press, 1985.

Gilmore, Jeffrey G. 'Canada's Defense Debacle,' in *Proceedings*, vol. 108, no. 3 (March 1982), pp. 110–16.

Given, Dean W., and Cashman, William. '"Whiskey" on the Rocks,' in *Proceedings*, vol. 108, no. 4 (April 1982), pp. 112–15.

Goldrick, J. V. P. 'Britain Builds New Castles,' in *Proceedings*, vol. 107, no. 3 (March 1981), pp. 132–3.

Goldrick, J. V. P., and Jones, P. D. 'Far-Eastern Navies,' in *Proceedings*: vol. 108, no. 3 (March 1982), pp. 60–5; vol. 110, no. 3 (March 1984), pp. 60–6; vol. 111, no. 3 (March 1985), pp. 60–5; vol. 112, no. 3 (March 1986), pp. 64–9; vol. 113, no. 3 (March 1987), pp. 64–70; vol. 116, no. 3 (March 1990), pp. 150–5.

— 'HMS *Sheffield*: A Ship for the 80s,' in *Proceedings*, vol. 102, no. 2 (February 1976), p. 95–7.

Goodwin, Hugh H. 'The Significance of Japan's Collapse As a World Power,' in *Proceedings*, vol. 73, no. 12 (December 1947), pp. 1425–43.

Green, Laurence B. 'A Case for the Attack Carrier in the Missile Age,' in *Proceedings*, vol. 84, no. 7 (July 1958), pp. 46–134.

Gretton, Peter. 'The Defence White Paper, 1966,' in *RUSI*, vol. cxi, no. 642 (May 1966), pp. 117–23.

Grimsvedt, Bjarne. 'Norwegian Maritime

Operations,' in *Proceedings*, vol. 112, no. 3 (March 1986), 144–9.

Grove, Eric J. 'After the Falklands,' in *Proceedings*, vol. 112, no. 3 (March 1986), pp. 121–9.

Guibault, R. G. '*Ticonderoga*: First and Formidable,' in *Proceedings*, vol. 108, no. 11 (November 1982), pp. 113–15.

Hadeler, Wilhelm. 'The Ships of the Soviet Navy,' in *The Soviet Navy*, ed. M. G. Saunders. New York: Frederick A. Praeger, 1958.

Haffner, Sebastian. 'The International Situation in Europe,' in *RUSI*, vol. xcvi, no. 581 (February 1951), pp. 1–14.

Hahn, Bradley. 'China: Emerging Sea Power,' in *Proceedings*, vol. 111, no. 3 (March 1985), pp. 102–7; 'Hai Fang,' in *Proceedings*, vol. 112, no. 3 (March 1986), p, 114–20.

Hallett, C. C. Hughes. 'Naval Logistics in a Future War,' in *RUSI*, vol. xcv, no. 578 (May 1950), pp. 232–45.

Halstead, John G. H. 'Canada's Navy is Coming Back,' in *Proceedings*, vol. 112, no. 3 (March 1986), pp. 79–83.

Hammond, R. E. and Tierney, Pat. 'The LAMP ship Team,' in *Proceedings*, vol. 104, no. 3 (March 1978), pp. 154–8.

Heath, Maurice. 'The Balance in Britain's Air Power: Land-Based or Carrier-Borne?' in *RUSI*, vol. cxi, no. 642 (May 1966), pp. 124–7.

Heginbotham, Stanley J. 'The Forward Maritime Strategy and Nordic Europe,' in *Naval War College Review*, vol. 38, no. 6 (Nov–Dec 1985), pp. 19–27.

Hellner, Maurice H. 'Sea Power and the Struggle for Asia,' in *Proceedings*, vol. 82, no. 4 (April 1956), pp. 353–61.

Hensel, Howard M. 'Superpower Interests and Missions in the Indian Ocean,' in *Naval War College Review*, vol. 38, no. 1 (Jan–Feb 1985), pp. 53–74.

Hessler, William H. 'Air-Sea Power on the Asian Perimeter,' in *Proceedings*, vol. 77, no. 10 (October 1951), pp. 1019–27.

—'Sixth Fleet: Beefed Up for a Bigger Job,' in *Proceedings*, vol. 84, no. 8 (August 1958), pp. 23–30.

Hewish, Mark. 'Weapon System: Exocet,' in *Proceedings*, vol. 102, no. 6 (June 1976), p. 102.

Hezlet, Vice-Admiral Sir Arthur. *Elec-*

tronics and Sea Power. New York: Stein and Day, 1975.

—*The Submarine and Sea Power*. New York: Stein and Day, 1967.

Hilton, Richard. 'The Soviet Armed Forces,' in *RUSI*, vol. xciv, no. 576 (November 1949), pp. 552–66.

Hittle, J. D. 'Korea – Back to the Facts of Life,' in *Proceedings*, vol. 76, no. 12 (December 1950), 1289–97.

—'Sea Power and a National General Staff,' in *Proceedings*, vol. 75, no. 10 (October 1949), pp. 1091–1103.

Hobson, Sharon. 'Canada Cancels Submarine Plans,' in *Jane's* vol. 11, no. 18 (6 May 1989), p. 788.

—'Canadian Naval Modernization Programmes,' in *Jane's*, vol. 4, no. 3 (20 July 1985), pp. 133–5.

—'Canadian Senate Salvo,' in *Proceedings*, vol. 110, no. 3 (March 1984), pp. 147–8.

Holbrook, Martin E. 'A Review of Post-War Construction,' in *Proceedings*, vol. 76, no. 11 (November 1950), pp. 1231–5.

—'The Rocket Firing Submarine,' in *Proceedings*, vol. 77, no. 1 (January 1951), pp. 47–51.

Houck, James W. 'The Chinese Navy's Prospects for Growth,' in *Proceedings*, vol. 107, no. 3 (March 1981), pp. 69–75.

Howard, Joseph L. 'The Navy and National Security,' in *Proceedings*, vol. 77, no. 7 (July 1951), pp. 749–53.

Howe, Jonathan Trumbull. *Multicrises: Sea Power and Global Politics in the Missile Age*. Cambridge, MA: The MIT Press, 1971.

Huan, Claude. 'The French Submarine Force,' in *Proceedings*, vol. 92, no. 2 (February 1966), pp. 42–53.

—'The Soviet Union and Its Submarine Forces,' in *Proceedings*, vol. 83, no. 7 (July 1957), pp. 734–41.

Humble, Richard, ed. *Naval Warfare: An Illustrated History*. New York: St. Martin's Press, 1983.

Hutton, R. M. J. 'The Future of Maritime Power,' in *RUSI*, vol. xcvi, no. 582 (May 1951), pp. 222–33.

Hyland, John J. III. 'France's Nuclear Reach,' in *Proceedings*, vol. 113, no. 3 (March 1987), pp. 83–7.

Isnard, Jacques. 'France Claims SSBN Advantage,' in *Jane's* (1 October 1988),

p. 746.

—'France Details Defense Budget Cuts,' in *Jane's*, vol. 11, no. 22 (3 June 1989), p. 1035.

—'French Budget Splits Government,' in *Jane's*, vol. 11, no. 18 (6 May 1989), p. 786.

—'SSBN Reactors Give de Gaulle Slow Speed,' in *Jane's*, vol. 12, no. 12 (23 September 1989), p. 548.

—'Taiwan in $1.8bn Frigate Deal,' in *Jane's* vol. 13, no. 2 (13 January 1990), p. 46.

Jacobs, Gordon. 'China's Coastal Forces,' in *Jane's* vol. 3, no. 11 (16 March 1985), pp. 450, 452, 454, 456–7.

Jacobs, Gordon, and Cheung, Raymond. 'China's "Jianghu" Frigate Program,' in *Jane's*, vol. 7, no. 11 (21 March 1987), pp. 507, 509.

Jacobs, Keith. 'Pakistan's Navy,' in *Proceedings*, vol. 110, no. 3 (March 1984), pp. 148–50.

Janes's Fighting Ships, 1946–1990, pubd annually. London: Sampson, Low, Marston & Co., Ltd.; New York: McGraw-Hill. Ed. variously: McMurtrie, F. E; Blackman, R. V. B.; Moore, J. E.

Johnson, Nicholas L. 'Soviet Space: 12 New Missions,' in *Jane's* vol. 9, no. 16 (23 April 1988), p. 808.

Johnson, Paul G. 'Japan: A True Partner in Defense,' in *Proceedings*, vol. 116, no. 3 (March 1990), pp. 34–8.

Jones, P. D., and Goldrick, J. V. P. 'Far-Eastern Navies,' in *Proceedings*, vol. 108, no. 3 (March 1983), pp. 57–63.

Jordan, John. 'Leviathan of the Deep,' in *Jane's*, vol. 5, no. 81 (1 March 1986), pp. 376–9.

—'New Destroyers for Japan, Part 2: The *Hatakaze* Class,' in *Jane's*, vol. 4, no. 11 (14 September 1985), pp. 551, 553, 555.

—'New Destroyers for Japan Will Deter Soviet Threat; Part 1: The *Hatsuyuki* and Improved *Hatsuyuki* Classes,' in *Jane's*, vol. 4, no. 4 (27 July 1985), 175–8.

—'"Oscar": A Change in Soviet Naval Policy,' in *Jane's*, vol. 5, no. 20 (24 May 1986), pp. 942–7.

—'Soviet Submarines from "Yankee" to "Delta",' in *Jane's*, vol. 8, no. 6 (15 August 1987), pp. 277, 279–80.

—*Soviet Submarines: 1945 to Present*,

London: Arms & Armour Press, 1988.

Kampe, Helmut. 'Defending the Baltic Approaches,' in *Proceedings*, vol. 112, no. 3 (March 1986), pp. 88–93.

Karniol, Robert. 'South Korea: Preparing to Fill the Arms Gap?' in *Jane's*, vol. 11, no. 7 (18 February 1989), pp. 270–1.

Kaufmann, William W. *A Thoroughly Efficient Navy*. Studies in Defense Policy. Washington, DC: Brookings Institution, 1987.

Kaul, Ravi. 'The Indo-Pakistani War and the Changing Balance of Power in the Indian Ocean,' in *Proceedings*, vol. 99, no. 5 (May 1973), pp. 172–95.

Kehoe, J. W.; Meier, Herbert A.; Kennedy, Larry J.; and Gast, Don C. 'U.S. Observations of the *Kiev*,' in *Proceedings*, vol. 103, no. 7 (July 1977), pp. 105–11.

Kennedy, Paul M. 'British Defence Policy Part II: An Historian's View,' in *RUSI*, vol. 122, no. 4 (December 1977), pp. 14–20.

Kenny, John. 'Still in Need of a Defense Strategy,' in *Proceedings*, vol. 116, no. 3 (March 1990), pp. 50–5.

Kidd, Isaac C., Jr. 'View from the Bridge of a Sixth Fleet Flagship,' in *Proceedings*, vol. 98, no. 2 (February 1972), pp. 18–29.

Kim Hyun-ki. 'North Korea Aims South,' in *Proceedings*, vol. 116, no. 3 (March 1990), pp. 40–1, 43.

Kinsman, W. G. 'Canada Must Face Reality,' in *Proceedings*, vol. 98, no. 8 (August 1972), pp. 32–7.

Kintner, William R. 'American Responsibilities in the Nuclear Age,' in *Proceedings*, vol. 82, no. 3 (March 1956), pp. 243–54.

—'Political Limitations of Air Power,' in *Proceedings*, vol. 76, no. 3 (March 1950), pp. 249–55.

Klessig, Lowell L., and Strite, Victor L. *The ELF Odyssey: National Security Versus Environmental Protection*. Boulder, CO: Westview Press, 1980.

Knox-Johnston, Robin. 'RN Considers Future Aircraft Carrier,' in *Jane's*, vol. 11 no. 22 (3 June 1989), p. 1075.

Koburger, Jr., Charles W. 'The Legal Background to the Suez Crisis,' in *Proceedings*, vol. 83, no. 3 (March 1957), p. 315–20.

Kurzanski, E. J. 'The Armada Argentina,' in *Proceedings*, vol. 107, no. 3 (March 1981), pp. 135–7.

Labayle-Couhat, Jean, and Baker, A. D. III (eds.) with Bernard Prézelin. *Combat Fleets of the World 1988–89: Their Ships, Aircraft and Armament*, Annapolis, MD: Naval Institute Press, 1988.

Landes, Burrell H. Jr. 'Sino-Soviet Relations Since the Death of Mao Zedong,' in *Naval War College Review*, vol. 32, no. 5 (Sept– Oct 1979), pp. 29–47.

Langston, Bud. 'Operation Praying Mantis: The Air View,' in *Proceedings*, vol. 115, no. 5 (May 1988), pp. 54–65.

Larus, Joel. 'India: The Neglected Service Faces the Future,' in *Proceedings*, vol. 107, no. 3 (March 1981), pp. 76–83.

Layton, Peter B. 'The RAAF in Maritime Operations,' in *Proceedings*, vol. 116, no. 3 (March 1990), pp. 56–9.

Le Bailly, L.E.S.H. 'The Royal Navy's Role in the Defence Service of the 1980s,' in *RUSI*, vol. cxi, no. 646 (May 1967), pp. 137–42.

Lehman, John. *Aircraft Carriers: The Real Choices*. The Washington Papers, no. 52, Center for Strategic and International Studies, Georgetown University. Beverly Hills, CA: SAGE Publications, 1978.

Lehrack, Otto III. 'Search for a New Consensus,' in *Proceedings*, vol. 110, no. 3 (March 1984), pp. 96–9.

Lenin, V.I. 'Speech Delivered at a Meeting of Activists of the Moscow Organization of the R.C.P.(B.), 6 December 1920.' In *Lenin: Collected Works*, vol. 31: April–Dec 1920. Moscow: Progress Publishers, 1966.

Leverich, Roy L. 'Inside the Royal Netherlands Navy,' in *Proceedings*, vol. 107, no. 3 (March 1981), pp. 90–6.

Lewin, Terance T. 'The Royal Navy in the Next Decade,' in *RUSI*, vol. cxiii, no. 651 (August 1968), pp. 202–9.

—'The Royal Navy – Its Contribution to National and Western Defence,' in *RUSI*, vol. 121, no. 3 (September 1976), pp. 3–10.

Lewis, J. A. C. 'Soviet Arms Cuts "Will Not Top 10%",' in *Jane's*, vol. 13, no. 3 (20 January 1990), p. 92.

Li, Andrew. 'The "Luta" Fleet,' in *Proceedings*, vol. 108, no. 3 (March 1982), pp. 131–2.

Lombard-Hobson, S. Le H. 'Communism and Cold War Policies.' in *RUSI*, vol. xcvi, no. 584 (November 1951), pp. 620–8.

Lovejoy, Charles D., Jr., and Watson, Bruce W., eds. *Chinese Military Modernization: Its Systemic Implications.* Boulder, Colorado: Westview Press, 1986.

Luce, William. 'Britain's Withdrawal from the Middle East and Persian Gulf,' in *RUSI*, vol. 114, no. 653 (March 1969), pp. 4–10.

Maddox, George N. 'The *Virginia's* Combat System Department,' in *Proceedings*, vol. 103, no. 8 (August 1977), pp. 90–1.

Manesergh, M. J. 'Naval Aviation,' in *RUSI*, vol. xcv, no. 580 (November 1950), pp. 571–9.

Mangold, Peter. 'Britain and the Defence of Kuwait, 1956–1971,' in *RUSI*, vol. 120, no. 3 (September 1975), pp. 44–8.

Manningham, Dan. 'LAMPS III,' in *Proceedings*, vol. 104, no. 3 (March 1978), pp. 159–61.

Marriott, John. 'The 1975–6 Cod War.' in *RUSI*, vol. 121, no. 3 (September 1976), pp. 45–51.

Martin, L. W. 'Sea Power and Modern Strategy,' in *RUSI*, vol. cxiii, no. 651 (August 1968), pp. 193–201.

Martin, Paul W. 'The Russian Navy – Past, Present, and Future,' in *Proceedings*, vol. 73, no. 6 (June 1947), pp. 657–61.

Matthews, Herbert L. 'U.S. Speeds Work on Spanish Bases,' in New York *Times*, 9 August 1956.

McAuley, John E. 'The Navy's Role in International Affairs,' in *Proceedings*, vol. 77, no. 1 (January 1951), pp. 15–19.

McClintock, Robert. 'The Atlantic Alliance,' in *Proceedings*, vol. 75, no. 8 (August 1949), pp. 857–63.

McCracken, H. E., Jr. 'Japan's View of Korea,' in *Proceedings*, vol. 98, no. 2 (February 1972), pp. 41–7.

McGeoch, J. L. M. 'Submarine Developments,' in *RUSI*, vol. cxi, no. 643 (August 1966), pp. 199–207.

Meason, James E. 'African Navies South of the Sahara,' in *Proceedings*, vol. 113, no. 3 (March 1987), pp. 56–64.

Middleton, Drew. 'Japan Urged by United States to Bolster Submarine Defenses,' in *Proceedings*, vol. 100, no. 2 (February 1974), p. 119.

—*Submarine: The Ultimate Naval Weapon – Its Past, Present and Future.* Chicago: Playboy Press, 1976.

Millar, T. B. 'The Australian Naval Situation,' in *Proceedings*, vol. 98, no. 5 (May 1972), pp. 208–21.

—'Developments in the Far East and South-East Asia Following the British Withdrawal,' in *RUSI*, vol. 114, no. 653 (March 1969), pp. 11–18.

Miller, Martin J., Jr. 'The Israeli Navy: 26 Years of Non-Peace,' in *Proceedings*, vol. 101, no. 2 (February 1975), pp. 48–54.

Miller, Richard A. 'Indonesia's Archipelago Doctrine and Japan's Jugular,' in *Proceedings*, vol. 98, no. 10 (October 1972), pp. 26–33.

Mitchell, Donald. 'Russian Mine Warfare: The Historical Record,' in *RUSI*, vol. cix, no. 633 (February 1964), pp. 32–9.

Moineville, Hubert. *Naval Warfare Today and Tomorrow.* Translated by P. R. Compton-Hall. Oxford: Basil Blackwell, 1983.

Montgomery, Mark. 'The U.S.–Pakistani Connection,' in *Proceedings*, vol. 116, no. 7 (July 1989), pp. 67–73.

Montgomery of Alamein, Field Marshal the Viscount. 'A Look Through a Window at World War III,' in *RUSI*, vol. xcix, no. 596 (November 1954), pp. 507–20.

Morgan, Joseph. 'Enough Navy for the Job?' in *Proceedings*, vol. 110, no. 3 (March 1984), pp. 108–13.

Morgan, Joseph R., and Jaafar, Abu Bakar. 'Strait Talk,' in *Proceedings*, vol. 111, no. 3 (March 1985), pp. 120–7.

Morris, James. 'The Royal Navy,' in *Proceedings*, vol. 98, no. 3 (March 1972), pp. 62–73.

Morss, Strafford, '*Ticonderoga*: Another *Hood*?' in *Proceedings*, vol. 108. no. 8 (August 1982), pp. 116–17.

Mountbatten of Burma, Admiral the Earl. 'Allied Naval and Air Commands in the Mediterranean,' in *RUSI*, vol. c, no. 598 (May 1955), pp. 171–83.

Mukherjee, Sadananda. 'Army and Navy

Bear Brunt of Indian Budget Cuts,' in *Jane's*, vol. 11, no. 10 (11 March 1989), p. 386.

—'India Sets Date for New Aircraft Carrier,' in *Jane's*, vol. 11, no. 23 (10 June 1989), p. 1124.

—'India's New Relationship with USA,' in *Jane's*, vol. 12, no. 17 (28 October 1989), p. 912.

Muller, David G. 'China's SSBN in Perspective,' in *Proceedings*, vol. 108, no. 3 (March 1983), pp. 125–7.

Murphy, F. M. 'The Soviet Navy in the Mediterranean,' in *Proceedings*, vol. xciii, no. 3 (March 1967), p. 41.

Murphy, Paul J. *Naval Power in Soviet Policy*. U.S. Air Force Studies in Communist Affairs, vol. 2. Washington, DC: GPO, 1978.

Nathan, James A. and Oliver, James K. *The Future of United States Naval Power*. Bloomington: University of Indiana Press, 1979.

Nitze, Paul; Sullivan, Leonard, Jr.; and the Atlantic Council Working Group on Securing the Seas. *Securing the Seas: The Soviet Naval Challenge and Western Alliance Options*. Boulder, CO: Westview Press, 1979.

Norris, John G. 'Navy Missile, Talos, Unveiled,' in *Washington Post*, 18 June 1957.

Oladijeji, O. A.. 'Where Are the African Navies Going?' in *Proceedings*, vol. 116, no. 3 (March 1990), pp. 101–3.

O'Neill, Robert J. 'Australian Defence Policy Under Labour,' in *RUSI*, vol. cxviii, no. 3 (September 1973), pp. 30–6.

O'Rourke, Ronald. 'Gulf Ops,' in *Proceedings*, vol. 115, no. 5 (May 1988), pp. 42–50.

Osborne, A. M. '*Kidd*-class Destroyers to Join the Fleet,' in *Proceedings*, vol. 106, no. 1 (August 1980), pp. 96–8.

Owan, Clyde. 'The Arab-Israeli Naval Imbalance,' in *Proceedings*, vol. 108, no. 3 (March 1983), pp. 101–9.

Paine, H. E. Felser. 'An Indian Ocean Pact,' in *RUSI*, vol. xcv, no. 577 (February 1950), pp. 70–4.

Parsons, W. S. 'Atomic Energy – Whither Bound?' in *Proceedings*, vol. 73, no. 8 (August 1947), pp. 895–905.

Peart, T. F. 'The Opposition View on Defence.' in *RUSI*, vol. 119, no. 2 (June 1974), pp. 9–14.

Pelly, P. D. H. R. 'The Pattern of a Future War,' in *RUSI*, vol. xcv, no. 578 (May 1950), pp. 221–4.

Perkins, J. B., III. 'Operation Praying Mantis: The Surface View,' in *Proceedings*, vol. 115, no. 5 (May 1988), pp. 66–70.

Pesce, Eduardo Italo. 'The Brazilian Mark-10 Frigates,' in *Proceedings*, vol. 107, no. 3 (March 1981), pp. 127–9.

—'The Brazilian Naval Modernization Program,' in *Proceedings*, vol. 108, no. 3 (March 1982), pp. 145–8.

—'Brazilian Navy Progress Report,' in *Proceedings*, vol. 110, no. 3 (March 1984), pp. 157–60.

—'Brazilian Navy Update,' in *Proceedings*, vol. 110, no. 3 (March 1984), pp. 185–7.

—'Brazil's Navy Must Wait,' in *Proceedings*, vol. 113, no. 3 (March 1987), pp. 134–8.

—'A Case for a V/STOL Brazilian Air Arm,' in *Proceedings*, vol. 108, no. 3 (March 1983), pp. 127–31.

Pocalyko, Michael N. 'Neutral Sweden Toughens NATO's Northern Tier,' in *Proceedings*, vol. 113, no. 3 (March 1987), pp. 128–30.

Pocock, Tom. 'We Must Go Down to the Sea Again: A Plea for a Return to a Maritime Strategy,' in *RUSI*, vol. cix, no. 633 (February 1964), pp. 23–6.

Polmar, Norman. 'The Soviet Aircraft Carrier,' in *Proceedings*, vol. 102, no. 10 (October 1976), pp. 138–41.

—*Soviet Naval Power: Challenge for the 1970s*. New York: National Strategy Information Center, 1972.

—'The Soviet Navy: The New Carrier,' in *Proceedings*, vol. 114, no. 8 (August 1988), pp. 66–7.

—'Soviet Shipbuilding and Shipyards,' in *Proceedings*, vol. 98, no. 5 (May 1972), pp. 272–80.

Porath, Reuben. 'The Israeli Navy,' in *Proceedings*, vol. 97, no. 9 (September 1971), pp. 33–9.

Pratt, Fletcher. 'World War II and the Changing Conception of Sea Power,' in *Proceedings*, vol. 72, no. 1 (January 1946), pp. 1–11.

Preston, Antony. 'Blast May Have Started in Ready-use Magazine,' in

Jane's, vol. 2, no. 1 (14 July 1984), p. 4.

—'Political Consequences of the Soviet "Yankee" SSBN Sinking,' in *Jane's*, vol. 6, no. 15 (18 October 1986), pp. 876–7.

Pritchard, Charles G. 'The Soviet Marines,' in *Proceedings*, vol. 98, no. 3 (March 1972), pp. 18–30.

Puleston, W. D. 'Dimensions and Characteristics of a Future War,' in *Proceedings*, vol. 76, no. 6 (June 1950), pp. 591–605.

Purnell, Richard H. 'An Armada for the 1990s,' in *Proceedings*, vol. 111, no. 3 (March 1985), pp. 172–4.

—'New Carrier for Tomorrow's Spanish Armada,' in *Proceedings*, vol. 110, no. 3 (March 1984), pp. 177–9.

Quester, George, ed. *Sea Power in the 1970s*. New York: Dunellen, 1975.

Raggett, Bob. 'Admiral Praises C³I in US Raid on Libya,' in *Jane's*, vol. 5, no. 23 (14 June 1986), p. 1083.

Rahav, Eli. 'Missile Boat Warfare: Israeli Style,' in *Proceedings*, vol. 112, no. 3 (March 1986), pp. 107–13.

Rairden, P. W., Jr. 'Soviet Sea Power,' in *Proceedings*, vol. 74, no. 1 (January 1948), pp. 61–7.

Rapp, Gison. '"Vulnerable" Sweden to Boost Defence Budget,' in *Jane's*, vol. 10, no. 10 (19 November 1988), p. 1269.

Raw, S. M. 'The Fleet Train,' in *RUSI*, vol. xcix, no. 593 (February 1954), pp. 31–3.

Rawson, Geoffrey. 'Problems of Australian Defence,' in *Proceedings*, vol. 84, no. 6 (June 1958), 51–65.

Reynolds, Clark G. 'Sea Power in the Twentieth Century,' in *RUSI*, vol. cxi, no. 642 (May 1966), pp. 132–9.

Richards, Guy. 'The Riddle of Combined Arms: 1949,' in *Proceedings*, vol. 75, no. 8 (August 1949), pp. 881–9.

Roberts, Stephen S. 'Western European and NATO Navies,' in *Proceedings*: vol. 107, no. 3 (March 1981), pp. 28–34; vol. 108, no. 3 (March 1982), pp. 35–42; vol. 109, no. 3 (March 1983), pp. 34–41.

Romaneski, Albert L. 'Nordic Balance in the 1970s,' in *Proceedings*, vol. 99, no. 8 (August 1973), pp. 32–41.

Roy, M. K. 'The Indian Navy from the Bridge,' in *Proceedings*, vol. 116, no. 3 (March 1990), pp. 66–8, 70, 72–4.

Ruge, Friedrich. 'The Postwar German Navy and Its Mission,' in *Proceedings*, vol. 83, no. 10 (October 1957), pp. 1035–43.

Ryan, Paul B. *First Line of Defense: The U.S. Navy Since 1945*. Stanford, CA: Hoover Institution Press, 1981.

Scheina, Robert L. 'African Navies South of the Sahara.' in *Proceedings*, vol. 108, no. 3 (March 1982), pp. 56–9.

—'Latin-American Navies,' in *Proceedings*: vol. 108. no. 3 (March 1982), pp. 30–4; vol. 107, no. 3 (March 1981), pp. 22–7; vol. 109, no. 3 (March 1983), pp. 30–4; vol. 110, no. 3 (March 1984), pp. 30–5; vol. 111, no. 3 (March 1985), pp. 32–7; vol. 112, no 3 (March 1986), pp. 32–6; vol. 113, no. 3 (March 1987), pp. 34–8; vol. 116, no. 3 (March 1990), pp. 110–15.

Schofield, B. B. 'Britain's Postwar Naval Policy,' in *Proceedings*, vol. 84, no. 5 (May 1958).

Schulz-Torge, Ulrich. 'The *Kiev*: A German View,' in *Proceedings*, vol. 103, no. 7 (July 1977), pp. 112–15.

Scott, Harriet Fast, and Scott, William F. *The Armed Forces of the USSR*. 3rd edn, rev. Boulder, CO and London, UK: Westview Press and Arms & Armour Press, 1984.

Scott-Moncrieff, A. K. 'Naval Operations in Korean Waters,' in *RUSI*, vol. xcviii, no. 590 (May 1953), pp. 218–26.

Seim, H. B. 'Atomic Bomb, The X-Factor of Military Policy,' in *Proceedings*, vol. 75, no. 4 (April 1949), 387–93.

—'The Navy and the "Fringe" War,' in *Proceedings*, vol. 77, no. 8 (August 1951), pp. 835–41.

Sekino, Hideo. 'Asian Navies,' in *Proceedings*, vol. 107, no. 3 (March 1981), pp. 52–9.

—'Japan and Her Maritime Defence,' in *Proceedings*, vol. 97, no. 5 (May 1971), pp. 98–121.

Sharpe, Richard, ed. *Jane's Fighting Ships 1988–1989*. New York: McGraw-Hill: 1988; 1989–90, 1989.

Sheehan, Neil. 'Admiral Says Soviet Shadowing Often Imperils Ships in Sixth Fleet,' in *New York Times*, 1 June, 1967, p. 18.

Sick, Gary G. 'Russia and the West in the Mediterranean: Perspectives for the 1970s,' in *Naval War College Review*, vol. 22, no. 10 (June 1970), pp. 49–69.

Sills, Charles. 'Middle-Eastern Navies,' in *Proceedings*, vol. 107, no. 3 (March 1981), pp. 39–46.

Simons, Roger L. 'Sweden's Defense Problem,' in *Proceedings*, vol. 84, no. 11 (November 1958), pp. 63–70.

Slonim, Shlomo. 'Suez and the Soviets,' in *Proceedings*, vol. 101, no. 4 (April 1975), pp. 37–41.

Smith, Robert H. 'ASW – The Crucial Naval Challenge,' in *Proceedings*, vol. 98, no. 5 (May 1972), pp. 126–41.

Smith, Russell H. 'Notes on Our Naval Future,' in *Proceedings*, vol. 72, no. 4 (April 1946), pp. 489–503.

Spaight, J. M. 'Pax Atlantica,' in *RUSI*, vol. xcvi, no. 583 (August 1951), pp. 434–9.

Stanbury, R. 'Some Naval Aspects of an Assault Landing,' in *RUSI*, vol. xcvi, no. 581 (February 1951), pp. 117–20.

Stanford, Sir Peter. 'The Current Position of the Royal Navy,' in *Proceedings*, vol. 110, no. 3 (March 1984), pp. 100–07.

Starr, Barbara. 'NFR 90: USN "Had No Official Interest",' in *Jane's*, vol. 12, no. 15 (14 October 1989), p. 762.

—'Soviets Building New Cruiser,' in *Jane's*, vol. 12, no. 2 (15 July 1989), p. 57.

—'Soviets "May Be Ahead" in Submarine Technology,' in *Jane's*, vol. 11, no. 13 (1 April 1989), p. 540.

Stead, Ronald. 'British Reassess Singapore,' in *Christian Science Monitor*, 17 April 1956, pp. 3–4.

Stevens, T. M. P. 'A Joint Operation in Tanganyka,' in *RUSI*, vol. cx, no. 637 (February 1965), pp. 48–55.

Stock, Ernest. *Israel on the Road to Sinai, 1949–1956*. Ithaca, NY: Cornell University Press, 1967.

Strope, Walmer Elton. 'The Navy and the Atomic Bomb,' in *Proceedings*, vol. 73, no. 10 (October 1947), pp. 1221–7.

Stumpf, Robert E. 'A Look at the Future of Australia's Fleet Air Arm,' in *Proceedings*, vol. 107, no. 3 (March 1981), pp. 130–2.

Sweetman, Jack. *American Naval History: An Illustrated Chronology*. Annapolis, MD: Naval Institute Press, 1984.

Taggert, P. J. 'Canada's Blind Spot,' in *Proceedings*, vol. 113, no. 3 (March 1987), pp. 144–9.

Talerico, Anthony. 'Sea of Decision,' in *Proceedings*, vol. 76, no. 9 (September 1950), pp. 941–9.

Thomas, Vincent C., Jr., ed. *The Almanac of Seapower 1987*. Washington, DC: Navy League of the United States, 1987.

Tornberg, Claes. 'Sweden Rethinks Its Strategy,' in *Proceedings*, vol. 116, no. 3 (March 1990), pp. 80–4.

Treadgold, Donald W. *Twentieth Century Russia*. 6th edn., Boulder, CO: Westview Press, 1987.

Trimingham, D. 'The Composition and Design of Our Post-War Fleet,' in *RUSI*, vol. xci, no. 561 (February 1946), pp. 73–6.

Truver, Scott C. 'Naval Dimensions of Spain in NATO,' in *Proceedings*, vol. 112, no. 3 (March 1986), pp. 154–7.

Tsouras, Peter G. 'Soviet Naval Strategy,' in *The Soviet Naval Threat to Europe: Military and Political Dimensions*. Edited by Bruce W. Watson and Susan M. Watson. Boulder, CO: Westview Press, 1989.

Tuleja, Thaddeus V. 'The Historic Pattern of Russian Naval Policy,' in *Proceedings*, vol. 77, no. 9 (September 1951), pp. 966–7.

Turner, Stansfield. 'The United States at a Strategic Crossroads,' in *Proceedings*, vol. 98, no. 10 (October 1972), pp. 18–25.

Uhlig, Frank R., Jr. 'The New Battle Cruisers,' in *Proceedings*, vol. 75, no. 1 (January 1949), pp. 33–7.

Vego, Milan. 'East European Navies,' in *Proceedings*: vol. 108, no. 3 (March 1982), 43–7; vol. 109, no. 3 (March 1983), pp. 42–6; vol. 110, no. 3 (March 1984), pp. 44–7; vol. 111, no. 3 (March 1985), pp. 46–9; vol. 112, no. 3 (March 1986), pp. 49–53; vol. 113, no. 3 (March 1987), pp. 47–51; vol. 116, no. 3 (March 1990), pp. 130–5.

—'The Royal Swedish Navy,' in *Proceedings*, vol. 108, no. 3 (March 1982), pp. 128–31.

Vinci, Vin. 'Mk 86 Gunfire Control System,' in *Proceedings*, vol. 103, no. 8 (August 1977), pp. 92–4.

Vlahos, Michael. 'Middle Eastern, North African, and South Asian Navies,' in *Proceedings*: vol. 111, no. 3 (March

1985), pp. 50–5; vol. 112, no. 3 (March 1986), pp. 53–8; vol. 113, no. 3 (March 1987), pp. 52–6; vol. 116, no. 3 (March 1990), pp. 138–40, 142.

Vyunenko, N. P., Makeyev, B. N., and Skugarev, V. D. *The Navy: Its Role, Prospects for Development and Employment*. Moscow: Voyenizdat, 1988.

Wagner, Cort D. 'Australia,' in *Proceedings*, vol. 108, no. 3 (March 1983), pp. 82–90.

Wainwright, R. C. P. 'Changes in Naval Warfare Owing to New and Modern Weapons,' in *RUSI*, vol. xciii, no. 570 (May 1948), pp. 187–94.

Walker, Peter. 'The Opposition's View of British Defence Policy,' in *RUSI*, vol. 120, no. 2 (June 1975), pp. 3–8.

Walls, William H., and McDaniel, Edwin R. 'Soviet Bases in Vietnam: Implications for the Seventh Fleet,' in *Proceedings*, vol. 105, no. 9 (September 1979), pp. 113–16.

Walters, Robert E. *Sea Power and the Nuclear Fallacy: A Re-evaluation of Global Strategy*. New York: Holmes and Meier, 1975.

—'The Submersible Fleet of the Future,' in *RUSI*, vol. cxi, no. 644 (November 1966), pp. 317–22.

Watson, Bruce W. 'The Caribbean Theater of Operations,' in *The U.S. Navy: The View from the Mid-1980s*. Edited by James L. George. Boulder, Colorado: Westview Press, 1985, pp. 345–63.

—'Comments on Gorshkov's *Sea Power of the State*,' in *Proceedings*, vol. 103, no. 4 (April 1977), pp. 41–7.

—'Gorshkov's Views on A Unified Military Strategy and Its Implications for the Soviet Navy,' in *Soviet Union/Union Soviétique*, vol. 9, Pt. 2 (1982), pp. 225–31.

—'Problems of Sea Power in the Mediterranean As We Approach the Twenty-First Century.' Chapter in *Problems of Sea Power As We Approach the Twenty-First Century*. Edited by James L. George. Washington, DC: American Enterprise Institute for Public Policy Research, 1978, pp. 97–122.

—*Red Navy at Sea: Soviet Naval Operations on the High Seas, 1956–1980*. Boulder, CO and London: Westview Press

and Arms & Armour Press, 1982.

—'The Soviet Navy in the Third World,' in *The Soviet and Other Communist Navies*. Edited by James L. George. Annapolis, Maryland: Naval Institute Press, 1986, pp. 251–82.

—'The Soviet Submarine Threat,' in *The Submarine Review*, vol. 1, no. 1 (April 1983), pp. 17–35.

Watson, Bruce W., and Dunn, Peter M., eds. *The Military Lessons of the Falkland Islands War: Views from the United States*. Boulder, Colorado: Westview Press, 1984.

—*The Soviet Navy As We Approach the Year 2000*. Boulder, Colorado: Westview Press, 1985.

Watson, Bruce W., and Walton, Marguerite A. 'Okean-75,' in *Proceedings*, vol. 102, no. 7 (July 1976), pp. 93–7.

Watson, Bruce W., and Watson, Susan M., eds. *An Encyclopedia of Naval Terms*. New York: Garland Press, 1991 (forthcoming).

—*The Soviet Naval Threat to Europe: Military and Political Dimensions*. Boulder, CO: Westview Press, 1989.

—*The Soviet Navy: Strengths and Liabilities*. Boulder, CO and London: Westview Press and Arms & Armour Press, 1986.

Watt, D. C. 'The Role of the Aircraft Carrier in Some Recent British Military Operations,' in *RUSI*, vol. cxi, no. 642 (May 1966), pp. 128–31.

Wedin, Lars. 'The Royal Swedish Navy in Transition,' in *Proceedings*, vol. 111, no. 3 (March 1985), pp. 182–3.

Wegener, Edward. 'Theory of Naval Strategy in a Nuclear Age,' in *Proceedings*, vol. 98, no. 5 (May 1972), pp. 190–207.

Wells, Anthony. 'A New Defence Strategy for Britain,' in *Proceedings*, vol. 113, no. 3 (March 1987), pp. 114–17.

Westwood, James T. 'The New Soviet Defensive Strategy,' in *Jane's Soviet Intelligence Review*, (June 1989), pp. 278–80.

Wettern, Desmond. 'Britain's Forgotten Lessons,' in *Proceedings*, vol. 113, no. 3 (March 1987), pp. 110–20.

—'Britain's New Frigates,' in *The Nautical Magazine* (September 1956).

—'Britain's New Frigates,' in *Proceed-*

ings, vol. 83, no. 8 (August 1957), pp. 906–7.

—'NATO'S Northern Flank,' in *Proceedings*, vol. 95, no. 7 (July 1969), pp. 52–9.

—'Pakistan and UK in Navy Talks.' in *Jane's*, vol. 9, no. 16 (23 April 1988), p. 780.

—'P.R.C. Navy Close-Up,' in *Proceedings*, vol. 107, no. 3 (March 1981), pp. 122–7.

Wheeler, Gerald E. 'Naval Aviation in the Jet Age,' in *Proceedings*, vol. 83, no. 11 (November 1957), pp. 1214–31.

Whiteley, E. A. 'Allied Defence Co-operation in the Far East,' in *RUSI*, vol. c, no. 600 (November 1955), pp. 532–49.

Whittaker, Gillian. 'Greece Confirms US Base Closure,' in *Jane's*, vol. 10, no. 5 (13 August 1988), p. 241.

—'Greek Protest over Airspace Violation,' in *Jane's*, vol. 9, no. 10 (5 March 1988), p. 388.

Wilcox, Edward E. 'Back Door in the Pacific,' in *Proceedings*, vol. 76, no. 2 (February 1950), pp. 187–9.

Wilkenson, J. Burke. 'The Big Bear Wets His Paws,' in *Proceedings*, vol. 74, no. 10 (October 1948), pp. 1225–32.

Williams, Robert Hugh. 'Amphibious Warfare – Two Concepts,' in *Proceedings*, vol. 77, no. 5 (May 1951), pp. 467–71.

Wilson, Eugene E. 'Sea Power in Competitive Coexistence,' in *Proceedings*, vol. 82, no. 11 (November 1956), pp. 1170–73.

Wood, Derek. 'Six Explosions in Past Seven Months,' in *Jane's*, vol. 2, no. 1 (14 July 1984), p. 3.

—'Soviets' Northern Fleet disabled . . . "Not Viable" for Six Months,' in *Jane's*, vol. 2, no. 1 (14 July 1984), p. 3.

Woods, John E. 'The Royal Navy Since World War II,' in *Proceedings*, vol. 108, no. 2 (March 1982), pp. 82–91.

Wright, Sherman E., Jr. 'ASW and the Modern Submarine,' in *Proceedings*, vol. 99, no. 4 (April 1973), pp. 62–8.

Wylie, J. C. 'The Sixth Fleet and American Diplomacy,' in *Soviet-American Rivalry in the Middle East*, ed. by J. C. Hurewitz, pp. 55–60. New York: Frederick A. Praeger, 1969.

Xydis, Stephen G. 'The Genesis of the Sixth Fleet,' in *Proceedings*, vol. 84, no. 8 (August 1958), pp. 41–50.

Young, Peter. 'The Arab-Israeli War–I,' in *RUSI*, vol. cxii, no. 648 (November 1967), pp. 324–31; 'The Arab-Israeli War–II.', vol. cxii, no. 648 (November 1967), pp. 332–9.

Young, Thomas-Durell. '"Self-Reliance" and Force Development in the RAN,' in *Proceedings*, vol. 112, no. 3 (March 1986), pp. 157–62.

Zumwalt, Elmo R., Jr. *On Watch: A Memoir*. New York: Quadrangle/The New York Times Book Co., 1976.

International Institute for Strategic Studies. *The Communist Bloc and the Western Alliances: The Military Balance.* Pubd. annually 1961–1969; *The Soviet Union and the Nato Powers: The Military Balance*, 1969–1970; *The Military Balance*, 1790–1989.

ARTICLES

US Naval Institute *Proceedings*

'United States – Navy Plans for 1949.', vol. 74, no. 9 (September 1948), pp. 1170–3.

'The Principles of War.', vol. 75, no. 6 (June 1949), pp. 621–35.

'France – Ship Traits.', vol. 75, no. 7 (July 1949), p. 840.

'Great Britain – Review of Carrier Strength.', vol. 75, no. 9 (September 1949), pp. 1071–3.

'USSR – *Cochino* Accused of Spying.', vol. 75, no. 11 (November 1949), pp. 1309–10.

'China.', vol. 75, no. 11 (November 1949), p. 1310.

'Ceylon.' vol. 76, no. 1 (January 1950), p. 106.

'Belgium.', vol. 76, no. 2 (February 1950), p. 225.

'France – Naval Reductions.', vol. 76, no. 3 (March 1950), p. 342.

'USSR – Conflicting Reports on Soviet Navy.', vol. 76, no. 3 (March 1950), pp. 342–3.

'USSR – Soviets Commission a New Battleship.', vol. 76, no. 3 (March 1950); p. 343.

'Norway.', vol. 76, no. 3 (March 1950), p. 344.

'Sweden.', vol. 76, no. 3 (March 1950), pp. 344–5.

'Italy.', vol. 76, no. 3 (March 1950), p. 344; vol. 77, no. 2 (February 1951), p. 217; vol. 77, no. 10 (October 1951), p. 1125.

'Oriskany.', vol. 76, no. 5 (May 1950), p. 573–4.

'Twelve DEs to Pact Countries.', vol. 76, no. 5 (May 1950), p. 574.

'Destroyer for South Africa.', vol. 76, no. 5 (May 1950), p. 576.

'USSR – Sea Power Increasing.', vol. 76, no. 5 (May 1950), pp. 576–8.

'USSR – Baltic Navy.', vol. 76, no. 5 (May 1950), pp. 576–8.

'Netherlands.', vol. 76, no. 5 (May 1950), p. 579.

'Great Britain – Carrier Launching.', vol. 76, no. 6 (June 1950), p. 690.

'United States – Experimental Destroyer Turbine.', vol. 76, no. 6 (June 1950), p. 688.

'United States – Atomic Sub Planned.', vol. 76, no. 6 (June 1950), p. 688.

'France – Maneuvers in Mediterranean.', vol. 76, no. 7 (July 1950), p. 688.

'United States – Mediterranean Fleet Missions.', vol. 76, no. 7 (July 1950), pp. 804–5.

'Australian Destroyer Trials.', vol. 76, no. 7 (July 1950), p. 809.

'Destroyers for Australia.', vol. 76, no. 8 (August 1950), p. 927.

'H.M. Aircraft Carrier Ark Royal.', vol. 76, no. 8 (August 1950), pp. 927–8.

'Brazil.', vol. 76, no. 8 (August 1950), p. 929.

'Netherlands.', vol. 76, no. 8 (August 1950). p. 929.

'Sweden.', vol. 76, no. 8 (August 1950), pp. 930–1.

'Belgium – The Belgian Navy.', vol. 76, no. 9 (September 1950), p. 1042.

'USSR – International Rights in the Baltic.', vol. 76, no. 9 (September 1950), p. 1043.

'Sweden – Admiral Stromback and the Baltic Situation.', vol. 76, no. 9 (September 1950), p. 1043.

'Britain's Fleet.', vol. 76, no. 10 (October 1950), p. 1155.

'USSR – Soviet Navy Eyes Arctic and Pacific.', vol. 76, no. 10 (October 1950), pp. 1156–7.

'Australia.', vol. 76, no. 10 (October 1950), pp. 1160.

'Aviation – Britain's Sub Killers.', vol. 76, no. 10 (October 1950), p. 1160.

'Navy's European Base.', vol. 76, no. 11 (November 1950), pp. 1268–9.

'Great Britain – New Destroyer.', vol. 76, no. 11 (November 1950), p. 1270.

'Spain.', vol. 76, no. 11 (November 1950), p. 1274.

'France – French Five-Year Plàn.', vol. 76, no. 12 (December 1950), p. 1387.

'USSR – Red Gibraltar.', vol. 76, no. 12 (December 1950), p. 1388.

'USSR – Territorial Waters.', vol. 76, no. 12 (December 1950), pp. 1388–9.

'USSR – Soviet Navy.', vol. 76, no. 12 (December 1950), pp. 1389–90.

'Holland.': vol. 76, no. 12 (December 1950), p. 1390; vol. 77, no. 4 (April 1951), pp. 443–4.

'Spain.', vol. 76, no. 12 (December 1950), p. 1391.

'Naval Program.', vol. 77, no. 1 (January 1951), p. 97.

'Missiles Super-Agency.', vol. 77, no. 1 (January 1951), p. 97.

'AA Cruiser.', vol. 77, no. 1 (January 1951): p. 98.

'Great Britain – Naval Program.': vol. 77, no. 1 (January 1951), p. 99; vol. 77, no. 5 (May 1951), pp. 555–6.

'Far East Base.', vol. 77, no. 2 (February 1951), p. 213.

'Great Britain – Britain's Revitalized Navy.': vol. 77, no. 2 (February 1951), pp. 214–15; vol. 77, no. 3 (March 1951), p. 330.

'USSR – Soviet Navy.', vol. 77, no. 3 (March 1951), pp. 333–5.

'USSR – Undersea Fleet.', vol. 77, no. 3 (March 1951), p. 335.

'Great Britain: Naval Exercises.', vol. 77, no. 4 (April 1951), p. 439.

'Great Britain: Royal Navy 1950.', vol. 77, no. 4 (April 1951), pp. 439–40.

'USSR: Hainan Base.', vol. 77, no. 4 (April 1951), p. 441.

'USSR – Baltic Strategy.', vol. 77, no. 4 (April 1951), p. 442.

'Canada.', vol. 77, no. 4 (April 1951), p. 443.

'Spain.', vol. 77, no. 4 (April 1951), p. 444.

'France.', vol. 77, no. 5 (May 1951), pp. 557–8.

'USSR – Submarine Reconnaissance.', vol. 76, no. 6 (June 1951), p. 669.

'1951 Subs.', vol. 77, no. 6 (June 1951), pp. 667–8.

'USSR – Baltic Build-up.', vol. 77, no. 8 (August 1951), p. 897–8.

'USSR – Defense Budget.', vol. 77, no. 8 (August 1951), p. 898.

'Great Britain – Carrier Completion.', vol. 77, no. 9 (September 1951), p. 1236.

'Modernization Program.', vol. 77, no. 11 (November 1951), p. 1236.

'Egypt.', vol. 77, no. 11 (November 1951), p. 1242.

'Israel.', vol. 77, no. 11 (November 1951), p. 1244;

Professional Notes.', vol. 82, no. 8 (August 1956), pp. 898–900.

'The First Fifty Years of U.S. Submarines.', vol. 82, no. 11 (November 1956), pp. 121–25.

'Colombia Soon to Take Delivery of Two Modern Swedish-Built Destroyers.', vol. 84, no. 8 (August 1958), p. 140.

'Our New Landing Ships.', vol. 84, no. 11 (November 1958), pp. 127–8.

'British Carriers.', vol. 87, no. 2 (February 1961), pp. 148, 151.

'Guam Chosen as Home Site for Pacific Fleet Polaris Subs.', vol. 88, no. 12 (December 1962), p. 143.

'Britain Set to Build Four Polaris Subs.', vol. 89, no. 4 (April 1963), pp. 162–3.

'Royal Canadian 1962 Summary.', vol. 89, no. 4 (April 1963), pp. 163–5.

'British Select A-Sub Base.', vol. 89, no. 7 (July 1963), pp. 156, 158.

'Australia's New Navy.', vol. 89, no. 11 (November 1963), pp. 155–6.

'Portugal.', vol. 91, no. 1 (January 1965), p. 139.

'Fifth Polaris Submarine Cancelled.', vol. 91, no. 6 (Junew 1965), p. 168.

'Britain May Give Up Aden Base.', vol. 91, no. 10 (October 1965), p. 145.

'Keeping Watch Off Beira.', vol. 92, no. 8 (August 1966), p. 166.

'Britain's Second Assault Ship Sails.', vol. 93, no. 8 (August 1967), pp. 153–4.

'French Progress on a Nuclear Force.', vol. 93, no. 11 (November 1967), pp. 154–5.

'U.K. Defense Plans Announced.', vol. 94, no. 8 (August 1968), pp. 156–7.

'A Review of the Royal Navy's Future.', vol. 94, no. 8 (August 1968), pp. 156–7.

'India's Naval Role Takes Shape.', vol. 94, no. 8 (August 1968), p. 158.

'Navy Seeks Faster Submarine.', vol. 94, no. 10 (October 1968), p. 154.

'Indian Navy Gets New Look.', vol. 94, no. 11 (November 1968), p. 158.

'Soviet/UAR Aircraft Eye Sixth Fleet.', vol. 94, no. 12 (December 1968), p. 157.

'Dutch Cruiser Retired.', vol. 94, no. 12 (December 1968), p. 157.

'Carrier Capacity Seen Stretched.', vol. 95, no. 1 (January 1969), p. 146.

'Soviets More Aggressive on the Sea.', vol. 95, no. 1 (January 1969), p. 147.

'Egyptian KOMAR Fleet Growing.', vol. 95, no. 1 (January 1969), p. 159.

'French Navy to Modernize.', vol. 95, no. 10 (October 1969), p. 157.

'France Tests Submarine Missile.', vol. 95, no. 10 (October 1969), p. 158.

'Canadians Developing Frigates.', vol. 95, no. 10 (October 1969), p. 158.

'New Delhi Buying Soviet Warships.', vol. 95, no. 11 (November 1969), p. 158.

'Smaller Warships Sought by Greek Navy.', vol. 96, no. 2 (February 1970), p. 124.

'Soviet Admiral Boasts Greatest Naval Power.', vol. 96, no. 4 (April 1970), p. 133.

'Strength of Soviet Navy, Naval Air Force Discussed.', vol. 96, no. 6 (June 1970), pp. 129–30.

'British Polaris Submarines Have Nuclear Warheads.', vol. 96, no. 6 (June 1970), p. 130.

'France Launches Second Nuclear Submarine.', vol. 96, no. 6 (June 1970), p. 130.

'Greek Navy Orders Four FPBs from French Shipbuilder.', vol. 96, no. 6 (June 1970), p. 130.

'Norwegian Navy Gets First of Six Fast Patrol Boats.', vol. 96, no. 7 (October 1970), p. 103.

'South Africa to Get First of Three French Submarines.', vol. 96, no. 10 (October 1970), p. 103.

'Navy to Retire 19 Ships from the Seventh Fleet.', vol. 97, no. 1 (January 1971), p.

101.

'Navy Hopes for Expansion of Forces in Indian Ocean.', vol. 97, no. 2 (February 1971), p. 109.

'U.S. to Lend 16 Ships to Spanish Navy.', vol. 97, no. 4 (April 1971), p. 112.

'Navy Designing Smaller Ships with Higher Speed, Lower Cost.', vol. 97, no. 8 (August 1971), p. 109.

'Plans to Build Two Frigates Are Dropped by Pentagon.', vol. 97, no. 8 (August 1971), p. 109.

'Chief of Soviet Navy Boasts of Its Global Nuclear Might.', vol. 97, no. 10 (October 1971), p. 109.

'Building of Indian Ocean Base is Well Underway by US Navy.', vol. 97, no. 11 (November 1971), p. 109.

'HMS *Sheffield* Launched; First Type 42 Destroyer.', vol. 97, no. 12 (December 1971), p. 112.

'Soviet Fleet Admirals Praise Russian Navy Striking Force.', vol. 98, no. 1 (January 1972), p. 111.

'Soviet Y-class Submarines Patrol off U.S. East Coast.', vol. 98, no. 7 (July 1972), p. 126.

'French Navy Expanding Fleet with Carriers and Other Ships'., vol. 99, no. 2 (February 1973), p. 117.

'First New Amphibious Ships Launched at Mississippi Yard.', vol. 100, no. 2 (February 1974), pp. 116–17.

'Mystery of the Northland – Norwegian Fjords Bugged?', vol. 100, no. 7 (July 1974), p. 122.

'Navy to Trim Fleet Below 500.', vol. 101, no. 1 (January 1975), p. 107.

'Iran Builds Indian Ocean Navy to Guard Oil Shipping Route.', vol. 101, no. 1 (January 1975), p. 108.

'Iran Agrees to Buy Four More Warships.', vol. 101, no. 1 (January 1975), p. 108.

'The French Navy: New Raison d'être.', vol. 101, no. 3 (March 1975), pp. 32–42.

'Nanuchka Class Increases Soviet Offensive Capability.', vol. 101, no. 4 (April 1975), pp. 106–7.

'USS *Spruance* (DD-963).', vol. 102, no. 2 (February 1976), pp. 61–9.

'French Nuclear Policy Stresses Submarines.', vol. 102, no. 2 (February 1976), p. 109.

'CNO Tells Congress USN Still Number One – But Barely.', vol. 102, no. 4 (April 1976), p. 114.

'*Jane's* Moore Makes a Case for Fast Attack Craft.', vol. 102, no. 7 (July 1976), p. 106.

'Soviet Ocean Surveillance Effort Employs Two Types of Satellites.', vol. 102, no. 8 (August 1976), p. 106.

'"Mayday" for *Mayaguez*.', vol. 102, no. 11 (November 1976), pp. 93–111.

'USS *Virginia* (CGN-38).', vol. 103, no. 8 (August 1977), pp. 95–105.

'Diego Garcia: The Seabees at Work.', vol. 105, no. 8 (August 1979), pp. 53–61.

'Polaris Subs Will Leave Guam.', vol. 106, no. 6 (June 1980), p. 125.

'Upgrading the Royal Netherlands Navy.', vol. 110, no. 3 (March 1984), pp. 184–5.

'Operation Praying Mantis: Communications During the Operation.', vol. 115, no. 5 (May 1988), p. 57.

Journal of the Royal United Services Institute for Defence Studies

'International Situation.': vol. xci, no. 561 (February 1946), pp. 121–2; vol. xciv, no. 574 (May 1949), pp. 273–6; vol. xciv, no. 575 (August 1949), p. 460; vol. xcv, no. 578 (May 1950), p. 302; vol. xcv, no. 580 (November 1950), p. 612.

'New Missiles.', vol. xcii, no. 566 (May 1947), pp. 248–55.

'Western Union Naval Exercises, 1949.', vol. xciv, no. 575 (August 1949), pp. 430–3.

'British Commonwealth Naval Operations during the Korean War – Part II', vol. xcvi, no. 584 (November 1951), pp. 609–16; 'Part III', vol. xcvii, no. 586 (May 1952), pp. 241–8; 'Part IV', vol. xcviii, no 589 (February 1953), pp. 106–15; 'Part V', vol. xcviii, no. 590 (May 1953), pp. 278–81; 'Part VI', vol xcviii, no. 592 (November 1953), pp. 606–8; 'Part VII', vol xcix, no. 593 (February 1954), pp. 102–9.

'Editor's Notes.': vol. cxiii, no. 651 (August 1968), pp. 189–90; vol. cxiv, no. 653 (March 1969), pp. 1–2.

'Navy Notes.': vol. xcii, no. 565 (February 1947), pp. 140–1; vol. xcii, no. 566 (May

1947), pp. 293–6; vol. xcii, no. 568 (November 1947), pp. 613–14; vol. xciii, no. 569 (February 1948), pp. 150–1; vol. xciii, no. 570 (May 1948), pp. 309–15; vol. xciii, no. 571 (August 1948), pp. 482–4; vol. xciii, no. 572 (November 1948), pp. 660–4; vol. xciv, no. 573 (February 1949), pp. 122–33; vol. xciv, no. 574 (May 1949), pp. 297–302; vol. xciv, no. 575 (August 1949), pp. 470–81; vol. xciv, no. 576 (November 1949), pp. 665–71; vol. xcv, no. 577 (February 1950), pp. 140–4; vol. xcv, no. 578 (May 1950), pp. 322–9; vol. xcv, no. 579 (August 1950), pp. 516–21; vol. xcv, no. 580 (November 1950), pp. 632–8; vol. xcvi, no. 581 (February 1951), pp. 169–75; vol. xcvi, no. 582 (May 1951), pp. 327–33; vol. xcvi, no. 583 (August 1951), pp. 506–12; vol. xcvi, no. 584 (November 1951), pp. 655–60; vol. xcvii, no. 585 (February 1952), pp. 120–3; vol. xcvii, no. 586 (May 1952), pp. 279–82; vol. xcvii, no. 587 (August 1952), pp. 459–62; vol. xcvii, no. 588 (November 1952), pp. 614–15; vol. xcviii, no. 589 (February 1953), pp. 141–4; vol. xcviii, no. 590 (May 1953), pp. 307– 10; vol. xcviii, no. 591 (August 1953), pp. 478–83; vol. xcviii, no. 592 (November 1953), pp. 636–9; vol. xcix, no. 593 (February 1954), pp. 138–42; vol. xcix, no. 594 (May 1954), pp. 297–301; vol. xcix, no. 595 (August 1954), pp. 470–3; vol. xcix, no. 596 (November 1954), pp. 619–23; vol. c, no. 597 (February 1955), pp. 133–7; vol. c, no. 598 (May 1955), pp. 309–13; vol. c, no. 599 (August 1955), pp. 497–84; vol. c, no. 600 (November 1955), pp. 636–9; vol. ci, no. 601 (February 1956), pp. 131–6; vol. ci, no. 602 (May 1956), p. 286; vol. ciii, no. 609 (February 1958), pp. 125–6; vol. ciii, no. 610 (May 1958), pp. 274, 276; vol. ciii, no. 611 (August 1958), pp. 427–31; vol. ciii, no. 612 (November 1958), pp. 583–5; vol. civ, no. 613 (February 1959), pp. 110–11, 113–14; vol. civ, no. 614 (May 1959), pp. 251, 253–5; vol. civ, no. 616 (November 1959), pp. 514, 516–18; vol. cv, no. 617 (February 1960), pp. 124, 126; vol. cv, no. 618 (May 1960), pp. 292–4; vol. cv, no. 619 (August 1960), pp. 427–9; vol. cv, no. 620 (November 1960), pp. 575–7.

Jane's Defence Weekly

'Who Takes the Blame for Severomorsk?', vol. 2, no. 1 (14 July 1984), p. 4.

'Frunze and Kirov Compared.', vol. 3, no. 11 (16 March 1985), pp. 445–7.

'Kiev Refit Gives Insight into Soviet Naval Air Developments.', vol. 4, no. 7 (17 August 1985), pp. 308–9.

'Japan Demonstrates Its Maritime Capabilities.', vol. 4, no. 6 (24 August 1985), p. 349.

'Kiev After Refit.', vol. 4, no. 8 (24 August 1985), pp. 352–3.

'Heavy Casualties in China-Vietnam Clash.', vol. 4, no. 14 (5 October 1985), p. 71.

'Shallow Water ASW: Sweden's Problems.', vol. 5, no. 2 (18 January 1986), p. 66.

'New Soviet Carrier Challenge to US Navy.', vol. 5, no. 3 (25 January 1986), p. 87.

'More Launches of "Akula" and "Sierra." ', vol. 5, no. 13 (5 April 1986), p. 596.

'Countdown to Operation El Dorado Canyon.', vol. 5, no. 16 (26 April 1986), p. 736.

'UK-Based F-111Fs the Best for Strike.', vol. 5, no. 16 (26 April 1986), p. 737.

'Libyan SAM Missiles Hit Civilian Areas, Says USA.', vol. 5, no. 16 (26 April 1986), p. 737.

'"Measured" Soviet Reaction to Crisis.', vol. 5, no. 16 (26 April 1986), p. 739.

'Libyan Scud B Attack on Lampedusa Island.', vol. 5, no. 16 (26 April 1986), p. 739.

'Effect on Alliance Cooperation.', vol. 5, no. 16 (26 April 1986), p. 740.

'Basis for UK's Decision over Use of Air Bases.', vol. 5, no. 16 (26 April 1986), p. 740.

'Capability of Soviet Spy Satellites.', vol. 5, no. 17 (3 May 1986), p. 815.

'Two New Warship Types for PLA Navy.', vol. 6, no. 4 (2 August 1986), p. 146.

'Greece Protests to Turkey over Shots.', vol. 6, no. 12 (27 September 1986), p. 655.

'Soviet SSBN Sinks After Explosion off US Coast.', vol. 6, no. 14 (11 October 1986), p. 759.

'Record-Breaking Trial for China's "Xia".', vol. 7, no. 2 (17 January 1987), p. 54.

'Soviet "Akula" Submarine in Close-up.', vol. 7, no. 7 (21 February 1987), pp. 256–7.

'Cam Ranh Bay: USA Shows Evidence.', vol. 7, no. 7 (21 February 1987), p. 269.

'First Views of "Mike" Attack Submarine.', vol. 7, no. 11 (21 March 1987), pp. 468–9.

'Stark Design Questioned After Iraqi Attack.', vol. 7, no. 21 (30 May 1987), p. 1040.

'Stark Locked onto Mirage Seconds Before Impact.', vol. 7, no. 25 (13 June 1987), pp. 1164–5.

'China's Drastic Cut in Defence Budget.', vol. 8, no. 9 (5 September 1987), p. 412.

'Aboard Santa Maria: Spain's Newest Frigate.', (12 September 1987), pp. 537, 539, 541.

'Naval Line-up in the Persian Gulf.', vol. 8, no. 12 (26 September 1987), pp. 671–3.

'Submarine Incursions into Swedish Waters Continue.', vol. 8, no. 17 (31 October 1987), p. 979.

'Soviet Space: December Launches Bring 1987 Total to 95.', vol. 9, no. 4 (30 January 1988), p. 184.

'India's SSGN Identified.', vol. 9, no. 5 (6 February 1988), p. 199.

'Indian Navy Greets First Nuclear-Powered Submarine.', vol. 9, no. 6 (13 February 1988), p. 241.

'Taiwan's First Submarine in 15 Years.', vol. 8, no. 6 (13 February 1988), p. 245.

'Defending New Zealand After ANZUS.', vol. 9, no. 6 (13 February 1988), pp. 263–5.

'Japan Completes Sea Trials of the Destroyer Asagiri.', vol. 9, no. 7 (20 February 1988), p. 326.

'Webb Resigns as US Navy Secretary after Clash over 600 Ships.', vol. 9, no. 10 (5 March 1988), p. 382.

'South African Defence Budget Rises by 22.6%.', vol. 9, no. 12 (26 March 1988), p. 567.

'Major Modernization for Pakistani Navy.', vol. 9, no. 14 (9 April 1988), p. 673.

'New Move in Danish Row with NATO.', vol. 9, no. 17 (30 April 1988), p. 819.

'India Accuses Pakistan Over Arms.', vol. 9, no. 17 (30 April 1988), p. 831.

'Aircraft Carrier Contracts Awarded.', vol. 9, no. 20 (21 May 1988), p. 1007.

'Soviets to Expand Tartus Base.', vol. 9, no. 20 (21 May 1988), p. 1035.

'Denmark "Indifferent" to NATO Defense, Says Taft.', vol. 10, no. 3 (30 July 1988), p. 156.

'Analysis of Changes to Baku.', vol. 10, no. 4 (6 August 1988), p. 225.

'Turks Launch Frigate, Name SSK.', vol. 10, no. 5 (13 August 1988), p. 251.

'Chinese Navy Shows Its Defects.', vol. 9, no. 30 (20 August 1988), p. 295.

'Carrier Tbilisi: STOL or V/STOL?', vol. 9, no. 9 (27 August 1988), p. 388.

'Pentagon Tells Japan: Limit Arms Build-up', vol. 8, no. 33 (10 September 1988), p. 516.

'Dutch Central Front Force Gets Priority.', vol. 8, no. 35 (24 September 1988), p. 688.

'Exclusive: First Picture of "Oscar II".', vol. 9, no. 13 (24 September 1988), p. 733.

'"Delta I" and "Charlie I" in View.', vol. 9, no. 14 (1 October 1988), p. 821.

'UK Rounds Up Arms Deal with Malaysia.', vol. 10, no. 14 (8 October 1988), p. 845.

'Three Bid to Replace Fearless and Intrepid.', vol. 10, no. 14 (8 October 1988), p. 853.

'First Picture of Baku's Layout.', vol. 10, no. 14 (8 October 1988), p. 893.

'Taft Hits Out over Burden Sharing.', vol. 10, no. 15 (15 October 1988), p. 908.

'Sweden Needs 3% Higher Defence Budget.', vol. 10, no. 16 (22 October 1988), p. 985.

'Cam Ranh Bay "Is Not A Soviet Base".', vol. 10, no. 17 (29 October 1988), p. 1044.

'Pacific Backfire Sightings Increase.', vol. 10, no. 17 (29 October 1988), p. 1082.

'New Defensive Stance for Naval Deployment.', vol. 10, no. 17 (29 October 1988), p. 1084.

'Liberals Put Freeze on Danish Budget.', vol. 10, no. 18 (5 November 1988), p. 1120.

'Taiwan Confirms Frigate Plans, But Numbers Drop to Eight.', vol. 10, no. 20 (19 November 1988), p. 1252.

'Blow-by-Blow Account of US Libyan Air Conflict.', vol. 11, no. 2 (14 January 1989), p. 36.

'Growing Interest in Asian Sea Areas.', vol. 11, no. 2 (14 January 1989), p. 851.

'Closeup on Baku's Defences.', vol. 11, no. 3 (21 January 1989), pp. 74–5.

'UK Reveals Next Generation Nuclear-Powered Submarine.', vol. 11, no. 5 (4 February 1989), p. 170.

'Baku View Analysed.', vol. 11, no. 7 (18 February 1989), p. 279.

'Denmark Agrees Zero Growth Defence Budget.', vol. 11, no. 11 (18 March 1989), p. 428.

'*Krivak* Class Replacement in Progress.', vol. 11, no. 11 (18 March 1989), p. 428.

'Soviet Analyst Details 40-Ship Pacific Fleet Cuts to Congress.', vol. 11, no. 12 (25 March 1989), p. 496.

'42 Die as "Mike" Submarine Sinks.', vol. 11, no. 15 (15 April 1989), p. 629.

'Greek Protest Over US Frigates for Turkey.', vol. 11, no. 15 (15 April 1989), p. 632.

'Soviets Count Cost of "Mike" Loss.', vol. 11, no. 16 (22 April 1989), p. 705.

'Swedish Missile Corvette *Göteborg* Launched.', vol. 11, no. 16 (29 April 1989), p. 729.

'Carrier Work Begins.', vol. 11, no. 16 (29 April 1989), p. 737.

'47 Die in *Iowa* Gun Turret Explosion, Inquiry Begins.', vol. 11, no. 17 (29 April 1989), p. 724.

'All "Golf IIs" to Leave Baltic by Next Year.', vol. 11, no. 19 (13 May 1989), p. 174.

'Test Failure Forces SLBM Delay.', vol. 11, no. 19 (13 May 1989), p. 851.

'Canada Reconsidering SSKs After SSN Cancellation.', vol. 11, no. 20 (20 May 1989), p. 907.

'Chinese Scepticism over Soviet Cuts.', vol. 11, no. 21 (27 May 1989), p. 980.

'Last Van Speijk Frigate Sold to Indonesia.', vol. 11, no. 21 (27 May 1989), p. 987.

'No CIWS for RN's Latest Type 23s.', vol. 11, no. 23 (10 June 1989), p. 1137.

'Turkey Steps Up Naval Force with Latest *Köln* Frigate.', vol. 11, no. 24 (17 June 1989), p. 1219.

'Pakistan Buys Weapons for Ex-US Frigates.', vol. 11, no. 24 (17 June 1989), p. 1223.

'Riviere Replacement Set for 1991 Delivery Date.', vol. 11, no. 26 (1 July 1989), p. 1371.

'Growth in Strength of Soviet Pacific Fleet.', vol. 12, no. 1 (8 July 1989), pp. 34–5.

'"SSN Cuts for RN."', vol. 12 no. 2 (15 July 1989), p. 59.

'West Germany Faces Major Cutback.', vol. 12, no 2 (15 July 1989), p. 74.

'Allies Must Take Bigger Share of Burden.', vol. 12, no. 2 (15 July 1989), p. 78.

'*Tbilisi* to Carry Only 10 Aircraft?', vol. 12, no. 2 (15 July 1989), p. 86.

'Japanese Defence Budget to Rise by 6.35% Next Year.', vol. 12, no. 3 (22 July 1989), p. 105.

'Japan Urged to Take Greater Share of Costs.', vol. 12, no. 6 (12 August 1989), p. 236.

'*Iowa* Fires Salvo from Two Turrets.', vol. 12, no. 7 (19 August 1989), p. 286.

'UK Confirms Type 23s to Sail Without SSCS.', vol. 12, no. 8 (26 August 1989), p. 332.

'M Class Frigate "Vulnerable".', vol. 12, no. 12 (23 September 1989), p. 555.

'RN: Dip in SSN Numbers Ahead.', vol. 12, no. 12 (23 September 1989), p. 557.

'Soviet Navy More Capable Despite Losing 20 Ships.', vol. 12, no. 14 (7 October 1989), p. 683.

'Egyptian Navy to Buy ex-RN Submarines.', vol. 12, no. 14 (7 October 1989), p. 701.

'UK Pulls Out of NFR 90 over Timetable.', vol. 12, no. 14 (7 October 1989), p. 726.

'NFR 90: The Pains of Collaboration.', vol. 12, no. 15 (14 October 1989), p. 783.

'Second "Charlie I" set for Indian Navy.', vol. 12, no. 17 (28 October 1989), p. 893.

'First Picture of *Tbilisi*', vol. 12, no. 18 (4 November 1989), p. 949.

'Golf Cuts Highlight Renewed Push for Naval Reductions.', vol. 12, no. 22 (2 December 1989), p. 1233.

'*Tbilisi* STOL Tests Successful.', vol. 12, no. 23 (9 December 1989), p. 1261.

'*Tbilisi* CTOL Tests.', vol. 12, no. 24 (16 December 1989), p. 1317.

'Three More Type 23 Frigates Ordered.', vol. 13, no. 1 (6 January 1990), p. 11.

'Third M Class Frigate Launched.', vol.

13, no. 1 (6 January 1990), p. 15.

'The Bear in the East.', vol. 13, no. 1 (6 January 1990), p. 23.

Aviation Week and Space Technology. 'USSR: Missiles.', vol. xcviii, no. 12 (19 March 1973), p. 121.

Bulletin d'Information de la Marine Française: 'French Submarine Fleet.' 3 January 1957; 'Steam Catapult in French Carriers.' 3 January 1957; 'Atomic Submarine Launched.' 5–12 November 1957; 'Launching of the Carrier *Clemenceau*.' 17–24 December 1957.

Congressional Quarterly. 'The Middle East.', 7th edn, Washington, 1987.

Deutsche Soldaten Zeitung. 'Soviet Base in Albania.' March 1957.

Douglas Air View News. 'New Guided Missile Now in Service.' 16 April 1956.

Evening Star Washington. 'Talos Soon to Join Land and Sea Missile Arsenal.' 7 March 1956.

La Revue Maritime: 'The "De Grasse" Commissioned.' November 1956; 'Italy: Additions to the Fleet.' July 1957.

Marine Journal. 'New Destroyers Use Aluminium Parts.' May 1956.

Marinens Pressdetalj. 'Sweden's Sea and Coastal Defence.' Stockholm, July 1956.

New York Times. '"Nautilus" Sets Many Marks.' 9 August 1958.

The Times London: 'Future of Five British Battleships. London, 30 January 1956; 'Fast Frigates for Royal Navy.' 13 March 1956.

Voyenizdat. 'Whence the Threat to Peace?' Moscow, 1982.

US Government Papers

US National Military Establishment. *First Report of the Secretary of Defense, 1948.* Washington, DC: GPO, 1948.

Department of the Navy. Annual Report of the Secretary of the Navy for Fiscal Years 1946, 1947, 1948, 1969, 1970. Washington, DC.

CNO Report: A Report by Admiral James O. Holloway, III, US Navy, Chief of Naval Operations, on the Posture of the US Navy, April 1977. Washington, DC: 1976.

CNO Report: The Fiscal Year 1980 Military Posture and Fiscal Year 1980 Budget of the United States Navy. Washington, DC: 1979.

Fiscal Year Report to Congress: 1984, 1985, 1986, 1987, 1988, 1989, 1990.

Statement of Admiral James O. Holloway, III, US Navy, Chief of Naval Operations, Before the Subcommittee on Defense, Committee on Appropriations, United States House of Representatives, 20 July 1976. Washington, DC: 1979.

Understanding Soviet Naval Developments, 4th edn. Washington, DC: GPO, 1981.

Department of Defense

Annual Report for Fiscal Year, Including the Reports of the Secretary of Defense, Secretary of the Army, Secretary of the Navy, and Secretary of the Air Force. Washington, DC: GPO, Fiscal years 1962, 1963, 1964, 1965, 1966, 1967.

Annual Report Fiscal Year 1979, Harold Brown, Secretary of Defense, 2 February 1978. Washington, DC: Department of Defense, 1978.

Annual Report of the Secretary of Defense and the Annual Reports of the Secretary of the Army, Secretary of the Navy, and Secretary of the Air Force, Washington, DC: GPO, 1958–59, 1959–60, 1960–61.

Report of the Secretary of Defense Donald H. Rumsfeld to the Congress on the Fiscal Year 1978 Budget, FY 1979 Authorization Request, and FY 1978–1982 Defense Programs, January 17, 1977. Washington, DC: 1977.

Report of the Secretary of Defense Harold Brown to the Congress on the Fiscal Year 1980 Budget, FY 1981 Authorization Request, and FY 1980–1984 Defense Programs, January 25, 1979. Washington, DC: 1979.

Second Report of the Secretary of Defense and the Annual Reports of the Secretary of the Army, Secretary of the Navy, and Secretary of the Air Force for the Fiscal Year 1949. Washington, DC: GPO, 1950.

Report of the Secretary of Defense James R. Schlesinger to the Congress on the Fiscal Year 1975 Defense Budget and FY 1975–1979 Defense Program, March 4, 1974. Washington, DC: 1974.

Report of the Secretary of Defense James R. Schlesinger to the Congress on the Fiscal Year 1976 and Transition Budgets, Fiscal Year 1977 Authorization Request and Fiscal Year 1976–1980 Defense Programs, February 5, 1975. Washington, DC: 1975.

Semiannual Report of the Secretary of Defense and Semiannual Reports of the Secretary of the Army, Secretary of the Navy, and Secretary of the Air Force. Washington, DC: GPO. *1950, 1951, 1952, 1953, 1954, 1955, 1956, 1957, 1958.*

Soviet Military Power. Washington, DC: GPO. 1st edn. 1981; 2nd edn. 1983; 3rd edn. 1984; 4th edn. 1985; 5th edn. 1986; 6th edn. 1987.

Soviet Military Power: An Assessment of the Threat. Washington, DC: GPO, 1988.

Soviet Military Power: Prospects for Change, 1989. Washington, DC: GPO, 1989.

Statement of Secretary of Defense Robert S. McNamara Before the Senate Subcommittee of the Department of Defense Appropriations on the Fiscal Year 1967–71 Defense Program and the 1967 Defense Budget. Washington, DC: 1966.

Statement of Secretary of Defense Elliot L. Richardson Before the House Armed Services Committee on the Fiscal Year 1974 Defense Budget and FY 1974–78 Program, Tuesday, April 10, 1973. Washington, DC: 1973.

Secretary of Defense Donald H. Rumsfeld. *Annual Defense Department Report, FY 1977.* Washington, DC: 1976.

Department of the Army

US Army Intelligence Threat and Analysis Center, US Army Intelligence Agency, *The Soviet Strategic Debate: Striving for Reasonable Sufficiency* (Washington, DC: US Army Intelligence Threat and Analysis Center, 1988).

Organization of the Joint Chiefs of Staff

United States Military Posture for 1981. Washington, DC: 1980.

United States Military Posture for 1982. Washington, DC: 1981.

United States Military Posture for 1983. Washington, DC: 1982.

United States Military Posture for 1985. Washington, DC: 1984.

United States Military Posture for 1986. Washington, DC: 1985.

United States Military Posture for 1987. Washington, DC: 1986.

United States Military Posture for 1989. Washington, DC: 1988.

Index